FINANCIAL MANAGEMENT IN MUSEUMS

Financial Management in Museums considers sustainable and innovative solutions to current museum financial challenges by analyzing the many changes and pressures affecting the museum field.

Presenting diverse perspectives from a range of authors around the world, the book shares and compares different funding models and methods of museum financial management. Arguing that museums need to be more effective in obtaining and managing financial resources, the volume also demonstrates how innovative and sustainable financial management strategies and structures can allow museums to respond to societal pressures and issues in a more effective way. It also demonstrates that museums must allocate resources responsibly to fulfill their goals of justice, equity, inclusion, and accessibility. The theoretical and practical contributions within the volume cover a comprehensive range of topics, including foundational concepts, revenue, expenses, budgeting, financial leadership, strategic planning, mission-based investment strategies and alternative revenue strategies.

Financial Management in Museums focuses on the unique financial needs and structures of museums, while also considering important lessons from adjacent sectors. It will be essential reading for students and academics engaged in the study of museums, arts and cultural management, and business. The book will also be useful to museum professionals working around the world.

Dr. Yuha Jung is a professor and the director of graduate studies of Arts Administration at the University of Kentucky, USA.

Dr. Rachel Shane is the department chair and a professor of Arts Administration at the University of Kentucky, USA.

Jaleesa Renee Wells is an artist, entrepreneur, and transdisciplinary scholar. She is an assistant professor of Arts Administration at the University of Kentucky, USA.

FINANCIAL MANAGEMENT IN MUSEUMS

Theory, Practice, and Context

Edited by Yuha Jung, Rachel Shane, and Jaleesa Renee Wells

Routledge
Taylor & Francis Group
LONDON AND NEW YORK

Designed cover image: © Julie Toy / Getty Images

First published 2025
by Routledge
4 Park Square, Milton Park, Abingdon, Oxon OX14 4RN

and by Routledge
605 Third Avenue, New York, NY 10158

Routledge is an imprint of the Taylor & Francis Group, an informa business

British Library Cataloguing-in-Publication Data
A catalogue record for this book is available from the British Library

ISBN: 978-1-032-31093-0 (hbk)
ISBN: 978-1-032-31091-6 (pbk)
ISBN: 978-1-003-30800-3 (ebk)

DOI: 10.4324/9781003308003

Typeset in Times New Roman
by MPS Limited, Dehradun

CONTENTS

FIGURES

TABLES

CONTRIBUTORS

Rebekah Beaulieu, PhD, is the Louise Taft Semple President & CEO of the Taft Museum of Art in Cincinnati, Ohio. She holds an MA in art history and museum studies from the University of Wisconsin-Milwaukee and an MA in arts administration from Columbia University, and earned her PhD in American and New England studies at Boston University. She previously served as director of the Florence Griswold Museum in Old Lyme, Connecticut, and as associate director of the Bowdoin College Museum of Art in Brunswick, Maine. Rebekah is the author of *Financial Fundamentals for Historic House Museums* (2017) and *Endowment Essentials for Museums* (2022). Her research interests include financial sustainability in museums, impact investing, and leadership models for the 21st century.

Tiffany Bourgeois returns to the Department of Arts Administration, Education and Policy as an assistant professor of arts management. Bourgeois earned both her PhD in arts administration, education and policy and master's degree in arts policy and administration at Ohio State. Her scholarly work is grounded in cultural policy, cultural diplomacy, soft power, and mega-events. Bourgeois' most recent publications can be found in *Place Branding and Public Diplomacy*, *Visual Inquiry: Learning and Teaching*, and *American Journal of Arts Management*.

Chris Burgess has taught in the arts administration field for over 18 years with particular focus on Arts Financial Management and Cultural Policy. He is the current director of the Arts Management Program at the College of Charleston (SC) and has also worked with many types of arts organizations in a variety of capacities. He is a former Barnett Fellow at The Ohio State University and his recent academic research projects consist of publications across various cultural policy topics, including deaccessioning, creative sector interrelationships, and arts financial management.

C. Lorenzo Evans III, MBA, a visionary finance executive and lecturer focuses on increasing financial literacy and management competencies in business and academia. His transformative work has impacted organizations like Westfield Corporation, Smithsonian Institution, and the University of Maryland. Recognized as a "Top Innovator" by *Modern Luxury* magazine, Evans is the founder of CLE Business Services, a consulting firm dedicated to innovation through education and customized business solutions.

Hannah Grannemann is an assistant professor and director of the Arts Administration Program at the University of North Carolina at Greensboro (UNCG). Her publications are as follows: *Journal of International Council on Small Business, Cultural Management: Science and Education, Arts Professional* (UK). She authored chapters in *Business Issues in the Arts* (Routledge) and *Cases on Arts Entrepreneurship* (Elgar). She received public scholarship: Row X (blog) on ArtsJournal.com. She completed BFA in theatre from New York University/Tisch School of the Arts, MFA/MBA in theater management from Yale School of Drama/Yale School of Management.

Natalia Grincheva is a program leader in arts management at LASALLE, University of Arts Singapore, and an Honorary Senior Research Fellow in the Digital Studio at the University of Melbourne. She is an internationally recognized expert on innovative forms and global trends in contemporary museology, digital diplomacy, and international cultural relations. She is the author of three monographs *Geopolitics of Digital Heritage* (Cambridge University Press, 2024), *Museum Diplomacy in the Digital Age* (Routledge, 2020), and *Global Trends in Museum Diplomacy* (Routledge, 2019).

Wen Guo is an assistant professor and MA director of Arts Administration in the Department of Art Education at Florida State University. She received her doctoral degree in cultural policy and arts administration from Ohio State University. She studies various topics in arts administration and cultural policy, including arts policy networks, entrepreneurship in the arts, and arts in community engagement. She served as a panel reviewer for the arts research grant of the National Endowment for the Arts. She currently serves as an editorial board member of the *American Journal of Arts Management* and a board member of the International Conference of Social Theory,

Politics, and the Arts. Her scholarly articles are published in *Review of Policy Research*; *Cultural Trends*; *Entrepreneurship Education and Pedagogy*; *Journal of Arts Management, Law, and Society*; *Studies in Art Education*; *Artivate: A Journal of Entrepreneurship in the Arts*; *American Journal of Arts Management*; and more.

Kaitlyn Hardiman is the founder and CEO of Oklahoma Arts Management Solutions, a research-oriented consulting firm that works with arts organizations to develop fundraising strategies and program evaluation tools. She is an adjunct professor of graduate-level arts administration and nonprofit coursework for Oklahoma City University and Ohio University. Currently pursuing a PhD in arts administration at the University of Kentucky, her research focuses on the civic engagement of arts organizations and the formulation of community-based fundraising strategies.

Leigh Nanney Hersey, PhD, is an associate professor and MPA coordinator at the University of Louisiana Monroe. She earned her doctorate in public administration from Arizona State University. Additionally, she has more than 12 years of experience working with nonprofit organizations, including serving as the membership coordinator for the Scottsdale Museum of Contemporary Art. Her research focuses on public assets, including the arts. She is the vice president of the Downtown Arts Alliance.

Daniel Hummel is an assistant professor of public administration and political science at the University of Louisiana Monroe. He received his PhD in public administration with a focus on budgeting and finance from Florida Atlantic University in 2013. He also received his MPA with a focus on public management from the University of Nebraska at Omaha. Dr. Hummel teaches public budgeting and finance, state and local government, American urban politics and intergovernmental relations. His research is focused on local government and nonprofit budgeting and finance with a specific interest in legacy cities. He has published in *Local Economy*; *Public Policy and Administration*; *Journal of Public Budgeting, Accounting and Financial Management*; *Public Budgeting & Finance*; and *Administration & Society*.

Yuha Jung is a professor and the director of graduate studies of Arts Administration at the University of Kentucky. Her research is focused on systems theory and cultural diversity in arts and culture organizations. Her work is interdisciplinary, including museum studies, arts management, historic preservation, and the law. She has published various peer-reviewed articles, co-edited a book, *Systems Thinking in Museums: Theory and Practice*, and completed a monograph in 2022, *Transforming Museum*

Management: Evidence-Based Change through Open Systems Theory. She is a lead editor for *The Oxford Handbook of Arts and Cultural Management* (2024). She holds an MA in museum studies, an MPA, a PhD in art education, and a JD (Juris Doctor).

Frances Liddell is a post-doctoral researcher on the DECaDE research center, Design Informatics, University of Edinburgh. She holds a PhD in museum practice from the University of Manchester and an MA in arts management and BA (Hons) in art history. Her research critically examines emerging technologies such as web3 as a tool to develop new ownership and participatory models in the cultural sector. She has previously been consultant lecturer at Sotheby's Institute of Art, London, where she set up the MA elective in blockchains and NFTs, and an associate research fellow at Arts & Antiquities Blockchain Consortium, New York.

Hristina Mikić is an associate professor at Metropolitan University, Faculty of Management in Belgrade. She holds a doctoral degree from the University of Belgrade's Faculty of Economics. With an extensive academic and professional journey, she specializes in the dynamic fields of creative economy, cultural economics, and creative industries. Her dedicated work centers around promoting economic fairness, enhancing economic well-being in cultural and creative sectors, and fostering sustainable development within the creative economy. She has contributed significantly to the global landscape through her roles at eminent organizations like the UNESCO Institute for Statistics, World Bank, Council of Europe, UNDP, British Council, and European Commission. Her versatile career spans research, education, and consultancy work. Since 2018, Dr. Mikić has been at the Head of Research and Development at the Institute for Creative Entrepreneurship and Innovation, steering initiatives that resonate with the essence of creative economy. In the dynamic field of creative economy, Dr. Mikić has successfully managed over 20 innovative projects, which explored areas such as sensory heritage, economic sustainability, and finance in culture.

Robin Nelson is an assistant professor at MacEwan University on Treaty Six Territory. Their research considers subnational museum and cultural policy, focusing on nonprofit and municipal community museums. They have also studied the significance of service organizations to the cultural sector and the role of heritage commemoration policy.

Geuntae Park is an associate professor and acting assistant dean of School of Culture and Creativity at BNU-HKBU United International College in Zhuhai, China. Before joining UIC, he was a curator for architecture at the

National Museum of Modern and Contemporary Art, Korea, and associate professor at School of Art and Design at Guangdong University of Technology in Guangzhou. As a cultural resource planner and manager, his research interests include museum planning and management, exhibition development, cultural space, creative industries, and culture and urban strategy.

Marek Prokůpek is an assistant professor in arts management at KEDGE Business School in France, where he is also a member of Creative Industries & Culture Research Center. His research interests lie primarily in the areas of museum fundraising and philanthropy and its ethical challenges, art market and innovative business models of arts and cultural organizations.

Rachel Shane is the department chair and a professor of arts administration at the University of Kentucky. She oversees the department's three degree programs, the BA, MA, and PhD in arts administration as well as several undergraduate and graduate certificate programs and continuing education offerings. She also teaches a variety of courses in the programs. Outside of University of Kentucky, Dr. Shane is the editor-in-chief of the *Journal of Arts Management, Law and Society*; the past president of the Social Theory, Politics, and the Arts; and was a former board member for the Association of Arts Administration Educators.

Rosie Siemer is the founder and CEO of FIVESEED and the author of *Museum Membership Innovation: Unlocking Ideas for Audience Engagement and Sustainable Revenue*. She also co-authored a comprehensive resource for membership managers titled *Membership Marketing in the Digital Age*. Rosie is the principal researcher of the Member Motivations Study™, co-founder of the Membership Innovation group at Museums as Progress, and a board member of the Denver Police Museum. Her research interests center around consumer behavior and include experimental and behavioral economics, museum pricing, and how social identity, social influence, values, attitudes, and judgments shape purchase decisions in membership.

Yingchong Wang is a Mellon Postdoctoral Researcher in the School of Data Science at the University of Virginia. She received her PhD in arts administration, education, and policy from the Ohio State University. She earned a master's degree in arts management from Carnegie Mellon University and a BA in English from Tsinghua University in Beijing. Her research focuses on cultural heritage, city branding, creative placemaking, and digital application in cultural institutions.

Jaleesa Renee Wells, is an artist, entrepreneur, and transdisciplinary scholar. She is an assistant professor of arts administration at the University of Kentucky. Her research investigates the hybrid intersections between culture, society, and enterprise, with a focus on creative social entrepreneurship and innovation; Black women's creative economic consciousness; and work, art, and gender in the academy. Dr. Wells is the co-founder of the Women's Perspectives in Arts Administration symposium. Learn more about Dr. Wells: drjaleesawells.com.

1

INTRODUCTION TO CONTEMPORARY MUSEUM FINANCIAL MANAGEMENT

Yuha Jung, Rachel Shane, and Jaleesa Renee Wells

Introduction

This book serves as an invaluable resource for individuals and institutions operating within the realm of museum financial management. It addresses a significant gap in the existing resources, offering a comprehensive exploration of the financial strategies and challenges faced by museums in the present day. In an era of shrinking funding and changing audiences—compounded by the lingering impact of the COVID-19 pandemic—more than ever museums need to run efficiently and purposefully. As such, museums are becoming more strategic, innovative, and sustainable to address the changing needs of their audiences and broader communities. Sound financial management is essential for their success in remaining relevant and competitive now and in the future. The book's distinctiveness lies in its focus on not only financial management but also recognizing the impact of critical integration of societal pressures and issues into museum financial management practices. It recognizes that museums play a unique role within the broader nonprofit sector, and their financial management requires tailored strategies and insights.

What Is Different about Museums?

This book generally adopts a museum definition by the International Council of Museums, "a museum is a not-for-profit, permanent institution in the service of society that researches, collects, conserves, interprets and exhibits tangible and intangible heritage. Open to the public, accessible and inclusive, museums foster diversity and sustainability. They operate and communicate ethically, professionally and with the participation of communities, offering

DOI: 10.4324/9781003308003-1

varied experiences for education, enjoyment, reflection and knowledge sharing." Based on this, some national and public galleries fall under this definition, excluding commercial galleries whose main purpose is to make profit by selling artistic and historical items. Museums are distinct among arts and cultural organizations. For example, they, as nonprofit organizations, have a unique funding structure of relying more on unearned or contributed revenue rather than earned revenue. Most museums have collections that are valuable, yet they are not evaluated as assets in their book (i.e., the value of museum collection is not included in the balance sheet for museums following Financial Accounting Standards Board guidelines [DePauw 2022]). Because of the lack of earned revenue opportunities compared to performing arts organizations that sell tickets to time-bound events and shows, museums have been more innovative in venturing into alternative earned revenue strategies, such as gift shops, restaurants, and rental services. While they cannot treat their collections as liquid assets, deaccession practices (i.e., officially removing or selling an item from museum collections) are common and acceptable as long as it is done in a specific, ethical manner. However, discussions on these different strategies and comprehensive understanding on museum funding and financial management are difficult to come by in both academic and practical settings. Because chapters include technical terms of financial management, the book includes a separate glossary, which is found in the front of the book.

Why This Book?

Based on our combined years of experience of teaching financial management for arts and cultural organizations, the editors realized that there is a need for substantial financial management books that can be used for teaching for arts and cultural organization financial management in general and museums specifically. While general nonprofit financial management books are helpful, there needs to be more nuanced, contextual, and focused supplemental teaching materials that help students understand museum financial management and strategies in depth. Additionally, if a practitioner or board member for a museum wants to know more about certain aspects of financial management, such as admission pricing models, corporate sponsorship, or socially responsible investment strategies, there is no collection of essays that can provide all of these in one place. For example, resources for financial management on the American Alliance of Museums (AAM) website are limited compared to other areas of museum management such as education and collections management. Most existing books are either for a very small subsection of museums (e.g., historic house museums), outdated, or not based on sound theory or research. Fortunately, along with some recent publications (Alexander 2023; Beaulieu 2022) on these topics, our edited volume fills this gap by covering comprehensive topics in museum financial management across many different areas, including environmental trends of the creative economy and social accountability; revenue, expenses, budgeting; strategic planning, ethics, and sustainability; innovative museum funding and financial strategies; and financial strategies to external influences and technological innovation. Thus, it emphasizes this important subject and function of museum operation, one that is arguably most important for survival of any business whether it is nonprofit or for-profit.

Diverse Authorship, Relevance, and Target Audience

The authors of the chapters are from around the globe and have different approaches to their topics, whether theoretical, empirical, or practical. Most chapters are based on secondary sources or direct professional experience, though some authors utilized primary research, such as document analysis, case studies, or interviews of professionals.

The varied backgrounds of the contributing authors included in this book mean the principles, practices, and theories could be applied to museums regardless of type. However, this also is a limitation of the book that it cannot be applicable to all museums in the world. While the editors of this book are most familiar with practices in North American museums, we strived to recruit authors from different parts of the world to offer multiple perspectives in funding models and financial management strategies from their region or country. Contributing authors are located and/or work in institutions from the United States, United Kingdom, Canada, China, Singapore, France, and Serbia. As we followed both open call and invitation models to recruit authors, the inclusion of countries is limited to who responded to our call for proposals and who was available when we invited them. We regret not being able to include any examples from Africa, South America, and Australia. Some authors are academics while others are practitioners whose responsibilities (e.g., director, financial manager, fundraiser) and focus of engagement (e.g., art museum, history museum, science museum) provide a spectrum of experience and expertise. Additionally, they were encouraged to write more generally for the concepts to apply to many different types of museums.

The intended audiences of our book are the following: (1) faculty who teach in museum studies, museum management, arts management, and cultural management; (2) advanced museum students (upper-level undergraduate students and graduate students) in the aforementioned fields, and (3) museum professionals and board members who work closely in areas of funding and financial management. Although not a primary audience, emerging museum scholars interested in financial management could find this book useful as well.

Museums' Vulnerability to Social and Economic Change

This book not only intends to address sound financial management practices but also how to respond to societal and economic pressures and issues in an effort to evolve with the changing needs and interests of the external environment through innovative financial management strategies and structures. Museums are especially vulnerable to external economic changes and societal pressures due to their unique funding model. By relying heavily on contributed income sources (e.g., major individual and corporate donors and private and public grants), museums face a higher risk of losing source of funding. Museums reportedly have more than 60% of their total income coming from contributed sources, including private and government sources (Sotheby's Institute 2018).

According to the AAM-commissioned survey of US museum board leadership, on average 35% of total operating budget came from charitable giving, 35% from earned revenue, 19% from public funding (local, state, and federal governments), and 11% from investment income (BoardSource 2017). Many European and Asian national or regional governments heavily support the general operations of their museums, which is different from the US private nonprofit model. However, while different nations fund their museums in different ways, some issues remain the same. Regardless of funding structure, a shrinking traditional donor base with fewer families giving to charities (IUPUI 2021) and reduced public funding for museums worldwide (UNESCO 2021), museums need to be more effective and efficient in obtaining and managing their financial resources. In times of economic crisis, people, companies, and governments often cut charitable contributions first when facing difficult budgetary decisions. For museums that are funded solely or mostly by public funds, government funding cuts in times of crises directly affect museum survival (Adams 2023). Yet, nonprofit and public museums have a legal and ethical obligation to fulfill their public mission of service to wider audiences (Jung, forthcoming), which puts them in a very difficult situation. Therefore, museums need to adopt well-grounded funding models and financial management strategies to meet their legal, ethical, and societal obligations to acquire, manage, and allocate their financial resources to advance their public mission (AAM n.d.).

Overview of Parts and Chapters

This book includes 22 chapters of in-depth discussions of various aspects of museum financial management. This current chapter (Chapter 1) is an introduction to the book, including its purpose, target audiences, characteristics, and overview and structure of the book, parts, and chapters. The rest of the chapters are categorized into five parts: (1) Economic and Social Contexts of Museums; (2) Financial Planning Standards; (3) Museum Finance

Strategies and Sustainability; (4) Innovative Museum Funding Practices; and (5) External Influences and Technological Innovations.

Part 1: Economic and Social Contexts of Museums

The first section includes two chapters that lay out the current economic and social climate as well as the trends in museum financial management.

Chapter 2, "Museum Funding: Moving up the Creative Economy Scale" by Natalia Grincheva, examines how museums are evolving into dynamic actors in the creative economy by adopting innovative funding strategies, such as leveraging their collections, integrating into urban tourism economies, and franchising their brands. It demonstrates how museums are becoming more economically self-sustaining and, in some cases, converging with for-profit businesses, creating hybrid forms of museum corporations.

Chapter 3, "Social Accounting for Museum Progress" by Jaleesa Renee Wells, addresses domains related to social accounting for museum progress, including the role of museums in society, the value of the museum entity, the museum's labor force, and its relationship with the community. It emphasizes social accounting as a practical tool for measuring and comprehending museum progress.

Part 2: Financial Planning Standards

The four chapters in Part 2 focus on topics related to revenue, expenses, and budgeting. These chapters offer insights into budgeting, evaluations of marketing strategies, pricing models, and the debate on free museum admission, fostering reflection on these approaches and their impact.

Chapter 4, "Museum Revenues, Expenses, and Budgeting" by Hristina Mikich, explores the budgeting process and expense planning in museums, aiming to provide insights into various budgeting methods, expenditure types, and models. It covers various topics, including an explanation of budgeting rules, an analysis of different budgeting methods, and discussions on expense principles, classifications, and the relationship between revenue and expenses.

Chapter 5, "Measuring Earned Revenue Performance of Museum Marketing" by Hannah Grannemann, presents an evaluation of museums' marketing activities that are not only measured in earned revenue generation but also in fulfilling the public mission of museums. Grannemann introduces examples of short- and long-term earned revenue metrics as well as common pitfalls and misconceptions of marketing evaluation.

In Chapter 6, "Pricing for Admission and Other Programs," Rosie Siemer discusses how museums can adopt sound pricing strategies for their admission and programs based on data-driven methodologies and models. This chapter explores diverse methods and data-driven approaches for evaluating museum pricing strategies, focusing on measuring perceived value, willingness to pay, customer segmentation, and price elasticity's impact on revenue. It discusses various pricing models and research methodologies, offering insights into balancing pricing strategies with diversity, equity, accessibility, and inclusion while maximizing revenue in museums facing resource constraints and growing competition.

Finally, Chapter 7, "Free Admission and Accessibility in Museums" by Hannah Grannemann, focuses on the ongoing debate surrounding free museum admission, exploring arguments based on moral and ethical principles, as well as those rooted in research and the balance between revenue generation, public perception, and stakeholder preferences. It summarizes various rationales and factors considered by museum leaders, presents research on the diversity impact, and concludes by encouraging readers to reflect on the approaches and research related to free admission.

Part 3: Museum Finance Strategies and Sustainability

These chapters discuss various challenges of financial planning, the significance of financial controls, legal and ethical considerations in funding, and the assessment of financial conditions for sustainable planning.

Chapter 8, "Financial Function in Museums and Business Planning" by Hristina Mikich, primarily focuses on the financial aspects of business planning in museums and aims to enhance understanding of financial planning and analysis tools applicable to various museum and business planning scenarios. Its various sections cover discussions on the financial function in museums, international business planning methodologies, financial planning principles, the preparation of financial plans and projections, and various financial analysis approaches and tools.

In Chapter 9, "Financial Considerations in Strategic Planning," Kaitlyn Hardiman highlights that while strategic planning is expected to enhance an organization's revenue, it can also limit adaptability when dealing with changing environments, thereby potentially hindering financial goals. A document analysis of 15 arts and cultural museums' strategic plans reveals a lack of financial consideration for significant programmatic and staffing goals and a lack of "what if" scenarios for societal trends. The chapter aims to enhance financial management's role in strategic planning by introducing a scenario planning framework consisting of four elements: scenario generation, probability/preference analysis, action plan organization, and response analysis.

Chapter 10, "Museums and Control Systems" by Rebekah Beaulieu, emphasizes the growing importance of financial controls in museums for achieving financial stability and discusses the need for control systems to support internal communication, transparency, and compliance. The chapter aims to define and describe various control systems, highlighting their significance in protecting assets, inter-departmental coordination, and sustainable practices, while providing recommendations for ensuring institutional viability with real-world examples.

Chapter 11, "Legal and Ethical Considerations" by Marek Prokůpek, states that museums operate within a complex legal environment influenced by various laws and policies, including tax incentives for donors to encourage private contributions. Some countries have special tax schemes for museums to promote entrepreneurial spirit. However, this has led to debates and ethical considerations about museums accepting money from potentially unethical sources. This chapter discusses these issues and highlights the development of new codes of ethics by museum associations to address cooperation with individuals and companies.

Finally, Chapter 12, "Museum Finances: Accounting for Capacity and Sustainability" by Daniel Hummel and Leigh Hersey, emphasizes assessing the financial condition of museums as a means to guide informed financial planning, aiming for sustainability and financial capacity in achieving their goals. This chapter provides specific examples and calculations of financial indicators and ratios that could be used for museum practitioners.

Part 4: Innovative Museum Funding Practices

This section explores diverse financial strategies in museums, showcasing how nonprofit and public organizations generate revenue through innovative solutions. It discusses how museums globally have embraced entrepreneurial approaches for financial stability amid challenges like reduced funding and the impact of the COVID-19 pandemic. Case studies, like Super Bowl 50, illustrate unique one-time but high-impact funding opportunities. This part also covers impact investing and corporate sponsorships, thereby showcasing financial support and challenges in museum-business collaborations, which reflect broader adaptations to contemporary art trends.

In Chapter 13, "Nonprofit Does Not Mean 'No Profit': An Overview of Smithsonian Enterprises (Formerly Smithsonian Business Ventures)," C. Lorenzo Evans III discusses the Smithsonian Enterprises as an example of how a nonprofit or public organization effectively generates unrestricted revenue through profit-driven business solutions, exploring its structure, operations, partnerships, financial management, and contributions to the Smithsonian Institution's mission.

Chapter 14, "Alternative Financing and Funding Structures and Strategies" by Marek Prokůpek, addresses the challenges global museums have faced in recent years like reduced public funding, competition, economic crises, and the COVID-19 pandemic, leading them to become more entrepreneurial in seeking financial stability and sustainability. Large museums in major cities have explored various strategies, including capitalizing on their assets through crowdfunding and blockchain technologies, redefining funding structures, and necessitating new business skills for museum professionals.

Chapter 15, "Unique, One-Time, or Temporary Funding Opportunities: Mega-Event Legacy Activities as Funding Opportunities for Museums" by Tiffany Bourgeois, presents a case study of Super Bowl 50 as a unique revenue strategy for museums, utilizing mega-event legacy theory to analyze how museums, such as the Children's Discovery Museum of San Jose, California Indian Museum and Cultural Center, Habitot Children's Museum, and the Asian Art Museum received grants from the 50 Fund, the legacy fund of the San Francisco Bay Area Super Bowl 50 Host Committee. By exploring the funding structure of the Super Bowl event and its impact on these museums, the study offers insights on how museum administrators can prepare and benefit from such funding opportunities in future Super Bowl or similar events.

In Chapter 16, "Mission-Based, Socially Driven Investment Strategies," Rebekah Beaulieu explores the history and forms of impact investing in the museum field, offering examples and resources to help organizations incorporate impact investing into their policies, highlighting how museums have used endowments to support local economies and communities. This chapter emphasizes a growing understanding of impact investing, where museums invest in socially and environmentally conscious funds, which can further their mission and role as cultural and economic drivers.

Lastly, Chapter 17, "Pros and Cons of Corporate Sponsorship at the National Museum of Modern and Contemporary Art in Korea (MMCA)" by Geuntae Park, focuses on the topic of corporate sponsorship at the MMCA. The exploration illuminates the advantages and challenges stemming from the collaboration between the MMCA and various companies via corporate sponsorship. While financial support is a significant advantage, the chapter also highlights the challenges that impact the traditional museum structure and the role of curators in exhibition development. The collaboration reflects MMCA's efforts to adapt to contemporary art trends and maintain its position as a leading art institution in Korea.

Part 5: External Influences and Technological Innovations

Part 5, the final section, discusses diverse financial strategies in relation to external influences and technological innovations. It explores the evolution of deaccessioning policy in the United States through specific case studies while other chapters focus on securing funding through policy attachment, the impact of non-fungible tokens (NFTs) on museum financial governance, achieving financial equity in co-produced exhibitions using NFTs and smart contracts, and balancing innovation and financial stability in museums through a three-stage evaluation framework for technology investments.

Chapter 18, "Understanding the Financial Impact of Deaccessioning" by Rachel Shane and Chris Burgess, discusses deaccessioning, a standard practice in museums worldwide to remove objects from their collections, which is usually uncontroversial and essential for maintaining a relevant collection. However, three specific case studies have brought about significant changes in deaccessioning policy and financial treatment for museums in the United States, and this research analyzes these cases to understand the evolution of US deaccessioning fiscal policy and the external pressures that drove these changes.

In Chapter 19, "Funding through Policy Attachment: An Examination of Funding for the Dawson City Museum," Robin Nelson examines how the museum utilized policy attachment—establishing links between their initiatives and various funding or policy programs to secure the necessary support for their operations—to secure funding and expand its activities, aligning with various funding initiatives. This approach allowed the museum to grow, but as core museum funding increased and experienced labor became less available, it faced limitations, leading to a shift in its focus toward essential work. It illustrates nuanced understanding of policy attachment as well as exploring the dynamics of funding, personnel, and policy alignment in the context of museum development and expansion.

Chapter 20, "Contextualizing the Potential of NFTs in Financial Governance of Art Museums" by Wen Guo, explores the growing involvement of leading art institutions with NFTs. NFT refers to a unique unit of data registered on a blockchain, and this chapter particularly focuses on the impact of NFTs on the financial governance of museum management. The analysis places the NFT discussions at the crossroads of existing research on museum funding strategies, digital transformation, technology adoption, and financial governance.

Chapter 21, "The Distributed Museum: Using Smart Contracts and NFTs to Find Financial Equity in Co-Produced Exhibitions" by Frances Liddell, discusses the challenge of fairly compensating participants in museum community engagement work and suggests using NFT ticketing, live minting, and smart donation boxes as potential tools to recognize and remunerate their labor. These proposals are based on the concept of the "Distributed Museum," which envisions the museum as a space where value circulates within and beyond the institution, fostering care, reciprocation, and accountability through NFTs and smart contracts in collaborative exhibitions.

Finally, in Chapter 22, "Accounting for Digital Assets in Museums: A Brief Discussion on Why, What, and How," Ying Chong Wang asserts that museums aim to enhance visitor experiences through technology innovation but often face financial constraints. To strike a balance between innovation and financial stability, this chapter discusses the importance of considering costs and benefits, suggesting a three-stage evaluation framework that integrates stakeholder perspectives and the quality of visitor experiences to assess the impact of technology investments beyond traditional accounting methods.

Conclusion

The chapters within this book collectively provide a comprehensive exploration of financial aspects crucial to museums, encompassing budgeting, revenue generation, expense management, legal and ethical considerations, innovative funding strategies, and the impact and influence of external factors. This holistic view underscores the pivotal role financial management plays in the sustainability and growth of museums. Serving as a crucial pedagogical tool and guide, the book addresses a significant gap in existing resources by offering tailored insights for effective financial management in the unique context of museums. It thoroughly examines contemporary financial strategies and challenges, emphasizing the integration of societal pressures and technological innovations, making it an indispensable resource for individuals and institutions operating within the realm of museum financial management.

With these innovative strategies, thoughtful guidelines, and insightful suggestions in addressing various challenges, this book can be a valuable text for teaching financial management for museums or similar cultural organizations, where students can be exposed to nuanced and complex financial responsibilities of museums. These students are current and future museum workers who can help museums to be more financially innovative and sustainable places. Current museum professionals and board members involved in financial management of their museums directly apply some of the strategies or reflect on their practice in relation to topics and strategies discussed in this book.

References

AAM (American Alliance of Museums). n.d. "Financial Stability Standards." Ethics, Standards, and Professional Practices. Accessed December 8, 2023. https://www.aam-us.org/programs/ethics-standards-and-professional-practices/financial-stability-standards/.

Adams, Geraldine Kendall. 2023. "Museums at Risk as Local Authority Funding Crisis Intensifies." *Museums Journal*. September 19, 2023. https://www.museumsassociation.org/museums-journal/news/2023/09/museums-at-risk-as-local-authority-funding-crisis-intensifies.

Alexander, Brian. 2023. *Museum Finance: Issues, Challenges, and Successes*. Lanham, MD: Rowman and Littlefield.

Beaulieu, Rebekah. 2022. *Endowment Essentials for Museums*. American Association of State and Local History book series. Lanham, MD: Rowman and Littlefield.

BoardSource. 2017. *Museum Board Leadership 2017: A National Report*. Washington, DC: BoardSource. https://www.aam-us.org/wp-content/uploads/2018/01/eyizzp-download-the-report.pdf.

DePauw, Karen. 2022. "Are Collections an Asset?" *Collections Advisor, Indiana Historical Society*, 130 (August). https://indianahistory.org/wp-content/uploads/2022.08-Are-Collections-an-Asset.pdf.

International Council of Museums. "Museum Definition." Accessed January 15, 2024. https://icom.museum/en/resources/standards-guidelines/museum-definition/.

IUPUI (Indiana University Lilly Family School of Philanthropy). 2021. *The Giving Environment: Understanding Pre-Pandemic Trends in Charitable Giving*. Indianapolis: IUPUI. https://scholarworks.iupui.edu/server/api/core/bitstreams/f5f188c8-285e-4ddd-ab10-6da930d82c6f/content.

Jung, Y. (forthcoming). "Do 'Elitist' Art Museums Deserve Tax-Exemption?: Toward an Affirmative Action Plan from Critical Race and Systems Theories Perspectives." *Houston Business and Tax Law Review*.

Sotheby's Institute. 2018. "The Business Model of the Nonprofit Museum." Sotheby's Institute of Art, January 8, 2018. https://www.sothebysinstitute.com/news-and-events/news/the-business-model-of-the-nonprofit-museum.

UNESCO. 2021. *Museums Around the World in the Face of COVID-19*. CLT/CCE/2021/RP/1. Paris: UNESCO. https://unesdoc.unesco.org/ark:/48223/pf0000376729_eng.

PART 1

Economic and Social Contexts of Museums

2

MUSEUM FUNDING

Moving up the Creative Economy Scale

Natalia Grincheva

Introduction

This chapter opens with a lengthy but useful quote from McClellan's (2008) foundational book that traced significant transformations of museums in the past centuries "from Boullée to Bilbao":

> Perhaps no development in the arts museum of the last half century has been more dramatic or controversial than the increase in commercialism, by which I mean the expansion of museum shops, the rise of the blockbuster exhibition and corporate sponsorship, and the influx of marketing and fund-raising personnel. A time traveler from the 1950s would surely be astonished to discover that it is now possible in our museums to eat (and eat well), shop, see a film, hear a concert, mingle at "singles night," and attend a corporate function or wedding reception without seeing a single work of art, or to globe-trot from one museum to another and experience a seemingly unending round of blockbuster exhibitions, each accompanied by wide-spread advertising, a dazzling array of more or less art related products for sale, and bundled package deals from airlines and hotels. (193)

These "dramatic" transformation of contemporary museums in recent decades are significant developments (McClellan 2008). They affect not only the financial management of museums, but more importantly, change their role and place in our society. While a lot has been written about various components that constitute a new financial model of museums from shops and restaurants to blockbuster exhibitions to collections deaccessioning, this

DOI: 10.4324/9781003308003-3

chapter aims to consolidate this scholarship, not for the purposes of accusing museums of controversial financial experiments but to reflect on these activities. In fact, these activities help museums sustain themselves in the context of post-industrial economies, while turning them into key actors in the creative economy.

In recent decades, various national governments have steadily reduced funding for cultural institutions, including museums. Due to financial challenges, including global economic crises with COVID-19 pandemic as the most recent one, poor development of some economies, and shifts in priorities toward support of more urgent causes, many governments have consistently been cutting funding to museums (Zimmer and Toepler 1999; Craik 2007; Lin 2010; Lawley 2015; Rex 2019). This economic transformation has resulted in new financial management norms, expectations, and culture leading to the adoption of the "market economy" model (Vivant 2011). As a result, museums increasingly restructure their financial operations as "their survival in the national and especially international context depends on their ability to compete, locally, nationally, and globally, for sponsorship and audiences" (Fraser 2006, 150). Contemporary museums are increasingly sensitive and responsive to contemporary audiences' demands, new management trends, and financial models of operation in the conditions of global liberalization. Specifically, there are several important museum management developments that constitute the key components of the "market economy" model employed by museums. They include (1) monetizing museum collections' assets, (2) commercial practices of museums that integrate them into a tourism economy, and (3) even franchising, as a culmination of museum corporatization processes.

This chapter tracks the transformation of museums from publicly funded cultural institutions to independent players in the creative sector by exploring each of the three components of the "market economy" model.

The first section demonstrates how museum collections could be employed as economic resources that generate high profits. The following part illustrates the integration of commercial practices of museums into urban creative and tourism economies which bring visitors to the door and ensure sustainable self-earned income. Finally, the chapter explores museum franchising as a financial strategy for museums to monetize their cultural assets, such as their brand value. It is important to note that historically the larger, more established, and recognized museums with more resources and more corporate and government connections and support have been the most active first adopters and innovators of novel financial management trends and strategies. No doubts, that such giants as the Guggenheim, for instance, that pioneered the franchise movement in 1997, or the Russia's State Hermitage Museum, that launched the Europe's first virtual NFT exhibition in 2021, have more leverage power, resources, and expertise to take a risk and jump into the bandwagon of experimentation with emerging technologies and new opportunities. This explains the main focus of the chapter on case studies and examples that in their majority illustrate the financial innovations of the first adopters among larger museums. However, the chapter also demonstrates that big operational budgets, globally recognized brand names and unique famed collections are not necessarily the prerequisites to successfully employ a wide range of new funding models. Smaller institutions could tremendously benefit from new financial opportunities in the post-industrial global economy if they are courageous enough to experiment and move beyond the public funding operational model.

Activating Collections as Dynamic Economic Assets

First and foremost, museums are repositories of cultural heritage that can include artifacts, collections, and objects as well as facilities, such as heritage sites, historical buildings, and exhibition spaces. However, gone are the times when these important museum resources have been sustained only at public or private expense. Instead, in the age of post-industrial economies, museums' rich collections can generate significant economic activity helping museums to sustain their expensive operations and offer a resource for creative cultural and media reproduction. As McNichol (2005) argued, museums, by their nature, are creative centers, exactly because their collections generate value beyond social or cultural. With the adoption of the "market economy" model, museum collections have acquired new meanings shifting from "a form of cultural patrimony or as specific and irreplaceable embodiments of cultural knowledge" to economic "capital, as stocks or assets whose value is one of pure exchange and thus only truly realized when they are put in circulation" (Krauss 1990, 5).

Collections management practices include two important activities: collection deaccessioning, which refers to legally removing objects from the collection, including objects' selling or trading (Feldstein 2009); and collection leveraging, or "moving it into the credit sector, or the circulation of capital" as loans or exchanges to other museums in the form of objects that can be efficiently entered into global circulation (Krauss 1990, 15). The start of such a gestalt shift of monetizing collections is usually associated with the Guggenheim Museum example, dating back to 1989. To overcome numerous financial problems experienced at that time, the museum sold paintings by Chagall, Kandinsky, and Modigliani, bringing $47 million into the museum budget, and saving it from deficiency (Kimmelman 1999, 53). More recent examples include the New York Albright-Knox Art Gallery's deal to sell off over 200 antiquities at auction in 2007 or the Orange County Museum's deaccessioning of 8 out of 20 California plein-air paintings to a private Laguna Beach collector in 2009, to name just a few cases from the US context, where deaccessioning of museum collections is legalized (Dickenson 2018). Even though the practice is not against the law, deaccessioning has always been controversial especially when it is done in search of quick cash to save operational budgets in times of hardship. For example, in 2014, when the Delaware Art Museum decided to sell a part of its collection to make a dent in its $19.8 million debt, the Association of Art Museum Directors sanctioned the museum for "treating works from its collections as disposable assets" (Blakemore 2015).

Despite the controversy, though, museums across countries and continents now sell objects from their collections in pursuit of economic sustainability. "With government subsidies to public institutions being cut back, museums in countries like Britain, the Netherlands and Germany need the income from art sales to close budget gaps, make repairs or finance expansions" (Carvajal 2015). As for circulating or renting collections, in 1991 the Museum of Fine Arts in Boston signed an agreement with new Japanese museums planned for the city of Nagoya to share its extensive collections to develop both long-term and temporary exhibitions (Heilbrun 2010). "France also was inspired by the export of cultural heritage and began renting its national collections": in 2006 the Louvre loaned works from its collections, for a three-year period in exchange for 13 million euros, to the High Museum of Art in Atlanta, Georgia (Fabelová 2010, 55). Opened in 2017, new Louvre Abu Dhabi on the Saadiyat Island, for example, features iconic pieces from over 30 museums in France, a 747 million dollars art loan deal between the French and Abu Dhabi governments (Grincheva 2019a).

Even though deals of such a scale are quite rare in the world of museums, employing the cultural assets of museum collections and monetizing their circulation in wider economies is a practice that museums of different sizes could employ. There is a growing "enhanced market for the products of artists and craftspeople and for antiques and artworks" around museums' heritage collections which become invaluable resources for co-productions and the creation of new design products and services (Keene 2006, 163). For example, among large museums, a significant portion of the Louvre's activity involves the co-publication of written works or the co-production of audiovisual materials relating to its cultural assets, in collaboration with publishing houses or production companies. More than a decade ago, this impact reached up to around two million euros a year for the publication of written works and co-production of films (Greffe 2011). Likewise, the Museum of Modern Art (MoMA) in New York has also produced products inspired by its rich collections. In fact, since 1938, MoMA held exhibitions about mass product design in collaboration with a leading mid-west American department store, Marshall Fields (Riley and Eigen 1994). With its on-site and online design stores, MoMA established a vast international consumer base with high revenues flowing back to the museum to sustain its expensive ongoing programming (Pantalony 2013).

Among smaller museums, Derby Museums in the United Kingdom, who "attracts customers, partners and income through a clear and compelling offer centred around creativity, innovation and making" can provide a convincing illustration of a working business model based on sharing collection assets through effective co-productions (Robinson and Practice 2015). Transforming in 2012 from the public organization Museums Service of Derby City Council into a limited company and independent charitable trust, Derby Museums, put a stress on innovation centered in the new "Value Proposition and finding new uses for Key Resources" (Robinson and Practice 2015). Museums brought together its audiences, collections, and corporate partners through Project Labs as human-centered design spaces for co-creation of new sustainable programs, displays, and spaces in the city through public participation (DM 2016). The museum developed a more compelling use of its collection, based on a relatively simple financial model with the rapidly growing proportion from retail and commercial activity. It diversified its income streams and drove partnerships with major regionally based international companies such as Rolls Royce and Toyota, who invested "in 3D printers, CNC machines, laser cutters and other usable technology for the public to use in workshops" (Robinson and Practice 2015). As a result, in May 2021, the trust opened a new Museum of Making in Derby that, as the Executive Director Tony Butler (2021) proudly shared, not only "tells the story of our industrial and creative past, but it is also a hub for modern makers through the facilities and support on offer."

Another appealing alternative in generating revenue based on collections' circulation has become "print-on-demand" service, pioneered by the National Gallery in London (Simal 2005). In 2003, it collaborated with Hewlett Packard to develop a kiosk for visitors to order a reproduction of any painting from the museum's permanent collection (Simal 2005). Five years later, the V&A in London and MoMA in New York reported significant revenues from its print-on-demand services (Smith 2009). The ubiquity of Internet and smartphone devices as well as innovations in the print-on-demand technologies have pushed collection monetization even further. For example, in 2018, the State Museum of Contemporary Art (SMCA) in Thessaloniki, Greece, successfully tried its mobile print-on-demand solution, the Infinite Museum Store (IMS), that allowed visitors to order reproductions of museum artifacts using their mobile phones either from home or while traversing the exhibition halls and picking items they enjoyed the most (Valeonti et al. 2019).

However, after the COVID-19 pandemic crises, even this innovation seems outdated with NFT, nonfungible tokens of the digital objects, taking the stage of museum collections monetization, "with sales estimated in the tens of billions" (Reyburn 2022). This digital technology, that not only authenticates digital artwork but makes it unique, has quickly gained traction among museums around the world (Agustinoy and Ramirez 2021). The British Museum, for instance, entered an exclusive five-year partnership with the Ethereum-based NFT platform LaCollection through which it has made several sales with prices ranging from $500 to $40,000 (Reyburn 2022). In April 2021, the Rijksmuseum in Amsterdam participated in the NFT auction, where it sold an NFT of its famous Rembrandt painting "The Night Watch" for $540,000. The State Hermitage Museum, in St. Petersburg, Russia, held an auction of NFT replicas of five of its best-known paintings that raised $444,000 (Reyburn 2022). While experimentation with NFTs might seem controversial in the context of the Open Access digitization agenda of museums unfolding in the past decade, it seems like an appealing funding strategy that could bring some quick cash without putting museums of different size, "from the British Museum to the Universal Hip Hop Museum" (Deakin 2022), under the stress of collections deaccessioning. Among less globally known museums engaged in NFT auctions and raising funds through their digital collections include the Academy Museum, the Universal Hip Hop Museum in the Bronx, the National Art Museum of Ukraine, the Charles H. Wright Museum of African American History, or Whitworth Art Gallery in Manchester, which raised £30,000 ($40,300) through NFT sales (Cuseum 2021).

In fact, the NFT business economy and fastly growing decentralized autonomous organizations (DAOs), which are built on blockchain technologies, offer new models for small and emerging artistic collectives and museums to exist and even thrive. For example, Cyber Baat is a DAO, featuring works of artists from Senegal, Nigeria, Zimbabwe, Rwanda, and the African diaspora internationally. It was created by the collective of artists in Africa to empower members, foster collaborations and preserve African culture. Existing solely virtually this new museums space as the Co-Founder, Kenza Zouari (2023) revealed during her public lecture in Singapore, was empowered by the digital technologies' affordances that allowed the collective in a short time to put together existing resources and collections to empower African contemporary artists to go internationally to overcome the lack of funding, institutional support and exposure in the global arts circles. NFT Asia is another example of a new museum model emerging in the digital realm that employs blockchain technology to support contemporary artists and feature their work globally. Founded by a team of artists working across the traditional and digital art worlds, NFT Asia (2023) is an "open and inclusive community, centred on uplifting Asian and Asia-based artists" by sharing resources and establishing international connections. Since founding in March 2021, it brought together 3,000 artists in Asia and participated in major international events, including 2022 Art Dubai, visited by 30,000 attendees, NamesteyNFT in Bangalore, India, which saw over 10,000 visitors, as well as NFT NYC 2022, that attracted over 15,000 people (NFT Asia

2023). These examples are evidence that innovative technologies could offer affordable platforms and new opportunities for different size organizations to navigate the digital economic landscape by creating new value around their cultural heritage resources and collections to generate income.

Integrating into the Tourism Economy

McLaughlin (1997) pointed out that a contemporary museum is a result of the "convergence of museums, the heritage industry, and tourism, profit-making and pleasure-giving." This convergence is grounded in expanding museum activities and services to attract visitors and tourists generating self-earned revenue. First, these activities include opening museum shops, which encourages cultural consumption and consumer logic. "International political economy enables large art museums to become international bazaars that sell ersatz art as neckties, scarves, jewelry, mugs, dinnerware, and vases" (Sylvester 2009, 2). For instance, in 2003, the Metropolitan Museum of Art earned $39 million from its house-managed retail operations: "its rug department alone seems a cross between a smart Fifth Avenue shop and a market in Dubai" (Sylvester 2009, 2). Second, museums expand their commercial offerings and transform into multiple-use cultural centers that attract consumers by providing unique spatial experiences as well as a wide range of interactive activities (Rectanus 2002, 172).

An important component of an attractive museum venue is the very design of the space and the presence of a "signature" architecture (Conn 2010, 230). "Whereas museums have always been identified with their collections, the new museum is identified with its architecture" (Newhouse 2006, 260). The Guggenheim Museum building in New York, designed by Frank Lloyd Wright, for instance, has become "an architectural icon that has inspired countless visitors" and even received the status of a UNESCO World Heritage Site (Guggenheim 2020). While the Guggenheim rotunda is a classic example, many world-recognized institutions have invested in ambitious architectural projects, which aim to attract audiences through appealing designs. They include the glass pyramid at the Louvre, the Sainsbury Wing of the National Gallery in London, or the addition to the Royal Ontario Museum in Toronto. The Museum of Modern Art invested $650 million for its expansion, "having taken over and demolished the entire Dorset Hotel on West 54th Street" (Loughery 2001, 632). Some other examples include the Boiler House Yard extension of the Victoria & Albert Museum in London or the Tate Gallery's Bankside project (Chong 2007). Among more recent ones are the Japanese National Art Centre's seven enormous column-less exhibition halls by Tokyo Architect, Kisho Kurokawa, opened in 2007, Louvre Abu Dhabi's gigantic steel dome, designed by Jean Nouvel and inaugurated in 2017, or opened in 2021 gigantic M+ in Hong Kong by Herzog & de

Meuron Swiss architects. All these cases provide convincing examples of the growing "starchitecture" trend employed by museums to ensure sustainable visitorship over time.

More importantly, museum architecture reconceived "the relationship between institution and public, locating itself on the cutting edge of where the museum meets commerce" (Conn 2010, 229). Museums are understood by contemporary visitors as urban spaces where they can enjoy walking, interacting with each other and spending their leisure time (Conn 2010). For example, many visitors of the Pompidou Centre in Paris "simply come to view the city from the top of the building and depart without setting foot in a gallery" (Kramer 1991). Varieties and configurations of spaces allow museums to organize more interactive activities: "theatres, galleries, cafeteria[s], courts and elegant fountains all attract energetic and admiring visitors" pleasantly surprising their visitors, encouraging them "to esteem, cherish, sit and relax" (Awoniyi 2001, 303).

Indeed, extracurricular activities like movies, live music, cultural events, and after-work cocktails in day-to-day programming of museums ensure a constant and regular flow and circulation of visitors and increase income (Conn 2010). For example, Paris's Louvre Pyramid, a large glass pyramid in the main courtyard, not only serves as the main entrance to the museum, but it also opens the way to the underground shopping gallery, which includes boutiques and fast-food restaurants that constantly attract the public (Kramer 1991). As architect Pei noted regarding the commercial entities he integrated in the new design of the Louvre, rental revenue generated from those commercial enterprises covered the costs of building the museum's underground garage (Awoniyi 2001, 305). Reflecting on the benefits of these cultural economics, former French Minister of Culture Jack Lang stressed, "museums must offer cinemas, auditoriums, pleasant restaurants, rest areas, bookstores, boutiques, and gardens. Simply put, the museum must be receptive to the spirit and flesh of human beings" (Davis 1990, 7). However, observing the transformations happening with museums under the financial pressures of the global economic environment, James Wood, the director of the Art Institute of Chicago, argued that it led museums to shift from "nourishment to gratification, from teaching and expertise to entertainment and celebrity, from memory to manipulation, from conservation to consumption" (Wood 2004, 126).

Indeed, the boundaries between entertainment industries, theme parks and museums continue to blur, attracting public capital and transforming museums into profitable businesses (Rentschler and Gilmore 2002; Mejón et al. 2004). In the past decade, some museums have become dependent on retail-based income generation strategies. For instance, in the United Kingdom, over 70% of museums rely primarily on commercial revenues. Mary Rose Museum in Portsmouth, for example, generates 90% of its annual income exclusively from visitors, including membership dues, tickets sales, and retail operations (Larkin and Burtenshaw 2021). Andy Warhol once remarked, “All department stores will become museums and all museums will become department stores” (Gomez 2002, 43). In the 21st century, this prophecy has become a reality in the economic context of contemporary China, where direct government incentives facilitated rapid development of the museum industry, primarily as a commercial enterprise (Gaskin 2014).

From only 45 museums in the 1950s, many of which were destroyed during the Cultural Revolution, China established over 1,000 museums in the 2000s (Hsu 2014). China’s museum world has grown even larger with almost 5,772 museums that exist now (Statista 2023). At the cost of hundreds of millions of dollars, these museums, funded by the new generation of Chinese billionaires, not only emulate but significantly exceed the “economic model” of museum success. The majority are designed by famous architects, ensuring high visibility in the urban context, and inviting larger visitation by locals and tourists. Moreover, these newly developed museums in China usually form part of larger commercial complexes that combine a variety of restaurants, shopping malls, and even hotels. A good example is the Himalayas Center in Shanghai, developed by Zendai Group and designed by renowned Japanese architect Arata Isozaki. The Center houses the Zendai Museum, the Himalayas Theatre, and a huge shopping mall with a number of restaurants and coffee shops, as well as the Jumeriah Hotel (Grincheva 2019b).

These corporate trends in museum development have been strongly encouraged by government policies and regulations which stipulate that museums could legally carry out business activities without violating their nonprofit status and without departing from their mission. These policies aim to ensure that museums adapt to the needs of the cultural and leisure economy and to integrate them into the cultural tourism industry (SACH 2011). Museums are encouraged “to raise funds through multiple channels to promote their own development” (The State Council 2015). Furthermore, the Ministry of Education set new roles for contemporary museums in China to become “cultural carriers” of creative industries and key landmarks in “tourist routes across the country” (Yan 2017). While this model served well to many museums around the world to tap on the tourism economies opportunities, sustained national lockdowns during the COVID-19 pandemic in 2020–21 vividly demonstrated the weakness of the funding model.

Due to the economic crisis caused by onsite closures during the pandemic, institutional resources suffered a considerable loss of income reaching in certain cases up to 80% (NEMO 2020). The American Alliance of Museums, for instance, estimated that museums in the United States have been losing $33 million per day during the first wave of COVID-19 in 2020 (AAM 2020). According to the Network of European Museum Organisations’ Survey, conducted in April 2020 and covering respondents from 48 countries, three out of five museums reported losing an average of €20,300 ($22,000) a week due to closure and travel restrictions (NEMO 2020). Indeed, the coronavirus crisis has intensified the financial instabilities of museums, questioning the sustainability of the tourism-oriented economy (Burini 2020). However, to survive in the new conditions, many museums quickly transferred their retail-based operation to the online world, pushing for more integrated e-commerce services. Many museums across countries experimented by producing culturally themed products for online sails and even embarked on digital platforms to launch fundraising campaigns to "build monetisable digital communities" (Larkin and Burtenshaw 2021). For example, the Tank Museum in Bovington, United Kingdom, enjoys a large Patreon fellowship of around 1,000 members who pay monthly fees up to $250, generating for the museum almost $10,000 each month (Patreon 2021).

Beyond the Western hemisphere, for instance, Chinese museums were quick to embark on their extensive online market channels, like Tmall, to sell their goods to multimillion audiences even before the pandemic started. The Tmall platform connects museums to 700 million users daily (Li 2020). "More and more young consumers show great enthusiasm for cultural products," director of Tmall Marketing Department, Chen Bingchao, explained, "more than 100 million people born in the 1990s are actively searching, browsing and buying" cultural products, co-designed with famous global brands (Li 2020). The Palace Museum in Beijing features over 12,000 cultural and creative products and the total turnover of its online operations reached 1.5 billion yuan, which is approximately $218 million (Bianji 2019). To tap on these opportunities, many major museums outside China, like the Hermitage Museum, the British Museum, or the Metropolitan Museum among the global giants quickly joined the platform in recent years to connect to a vast market of Chinese netizens.

As the first overseas museum to open an online store on Tmall, the British Museum, for instance, reported an increase of 2.5 times in its annual sales. All products were sold out within two weeks of opening its Tmall flagship store (GT 2020). According to the 2021–22 annual report alone, the British Museum's trading income topped £6.2 million ($7.9 million) (BM 2022). One reason for such a popularity of the online sales success is, of course, the brand value of the museum which is globally recognized for its collections of around eight million objects "bringing together under one roof the cultures of the world, spanning continents and oceans" (BM 2023). The next section expands the propositions that the brand value of the museum could undergo pretty sophisticated monetizing operations going far beyond creative products design and sales.

Monetizing Museum Brands

In the growing conditions of post-industrial economies, museums have developed business strategies allowing them to monetize their brand value via franchising. For example, the Guggenheim Museum not only offers a compelling case of urban "starchietcture," ensuring its annual admission charges revenue to exceed $22 million (Guggenheim 2020), it also pioneered museum franchising. Museum franchising is "the culmination of global changes in the management of museums," leading to a more entrepreneurial style of operations within the professional museum community (Wu 2002; Werner 2005). In the business world, franchising is known as a method of organization that combines large and small businesses into a single administrative unit. It is a contract-based practice of granting the right to use the company brand name and utilize a well-developed business model in different places to distribute goods or sell services in new markets (Dicke 1992). The franchise model was effectively adopted by some contemporary art museums which have started to build branches in different countries. These franchises are owned by local authorities, but they use the museum name and operate under a single management model, which in most cases centralizes curatorial control of collections and the circulation of exhibitions within the museum chain (Fabelová 2010; Vivant 2011).

Museum franchising has proven to be an economically effective model of strategic development and management of institutional resources, cultural programming, and fundraising (Wu 2002; Fabelová 2010; Vivant 2011). Indeed, relying on the support of local stakeholders, museum branches in different countries significantly strengthen global fundraising by attracting new powerful patrons and investment opportunities from across borders (Grincheva 2017). More and more, museums around the world are adopting a franchising model to establish new branches across countries and continents. In addition to such famous cases as Hermitage Amsterdam (2004), Louvre Abu Dhabi (2017), and Centre Pompidou Shanghai (2019), there is also Science Gallery International, that stands out from this list of globally recognized museum giants with wealthy cultural resources as a new type of institution that puts a stress on public engagement and collaborative exhibitions rather than permanent collections. It opened in 2008 in Dublin at Trinity College "to pioneer creative collisions between art and science" by operating through a long-term partnership with academic institutions and corporate supporters (SGI 2023a).

In only a few years, the Science Gallery has rapidly grown into a global network. At the moment it has branches in Dublin, London, Melbourne, Bengaluru, Rotterdam, Atlanta, Berlin, and Monterrey and boasts of engaging 9,500 artists and scientists across borders, bringing each year around 400 university researchers together to develop 300 programs to benefit the Network (SGI 2023a). Not only does the Global Science Gallery Network successfully emulate the Guggenheim franchise idea but, more importantly, it also demonstrates that in an era of increasing globalization, a new generation of museums, either big or small, actively employs global expansion models of operations. These practices allow them to reach wider audiences across borders and draw on artistic creativity, cultural resources and financial support across multiple local communities in different countries. For example, the Science Gallery reports that its franchise network is a powerful platform that not only generates new income through enhanced corporate, philanthropic and government relationships but allows branches in different geo-locations to benefit from "new earned income streams, broadening scope of commercial activities" (SGI 2023b).

Illustrating further the franchise museum commercialization and corporatization idea, it is important to discuss the example of K11 Art Mall, opened in Hong Kong in 2008 by Chinese billionaire Adrian Cheng. It is the first hybrid institution in the world, converging the world of museums and corporations by employing an art-commerce business franchise model (Grincheva 2019b). K11 brands itself as an "art playground, where culture, entertainment, shopping and living revolve around art" (K11 2023). Integrating contemporary art into luxury retail spaces, K11 taps into young consumers' expectations in China to enjoy more sophisticated and stimulating cultural experiences, not just shopping opportunities. Art in K11 shopping malls is not strictly confined to dedicated museum or gallery spaces. Instead, it is distributed across all floors of a mall, integrated into interior and exterior design, and placed for sale along with other consumer goods. K11 brings together multiple art events and interactives, top-floor gardens, multicultural community hubs, and large-scale urban design projects. These offerings aim to expand trivial shopping into educational and cultural experiences, bridging the worlds of contemporary arts and commerce.

As a retail-based museum franchise, K11 generates large audiences in its branches that are rapidly growing in different cities across China. In the last decade, satellites were established in Hong Kong (2008 and 2020), Wuhan (2010), Shanghai (2013), Shenyang (2016), Hankou (2017), Guangzhou (2018), Tianjin (2019), and a new branch is opening in Beijing soon (K11 2023). The central location of K11 malls in each city works in combination with signature architecture buildings that "revitalise and awaken a surrounding urban community" (Ying 2014). At K11, mega-popular transnational luxury brands, such as Dolce & Gabbana and Burberry, coexist with expensive fashionable restaurants as well as contemporary art sculptures, installations, and experimental exhibitions. Not only does K11 employ the economics model of the museum to its full extent, but it also expands it further, reinforcing the "art-commodity dialectic" of the neo-liberal age. Indeed, K11 Malls attract a large number of customers, exceeding one million per month in the biggest branches located in Hong Kong and Shanghai. As a result, K11 Art Malls branches bring high profits maintaining a growth rate of annual sales at 20%, which allows the corporation to use its own profits to support contemporary art in China and globally. For example, K11 established its own not-for-profit Art Foundation to sponsor Chinese artists' presence at the most prestigious international arts events, including Venice Biennale or Art Basel. The Foundation also fully funds multimillion dollar international artists residencies and collaborations with leading museums around the world, such as the Serpentine Galleries in London, Centre Pompidou in France or MoMA PS1 in New York (Grincheva 2019b). This ability to sponsor one's own ambitious artistic projects and international programs makes K11 a completely autonomous player in the global cultural field neither subjected to government dependencies nor influenced by other national or transnational corporate actors.

However, whether this successful art commerce model has a future across other museums in China and beyond is questionable. Since the opening of K11 Art Mall in 2009, the concept of a retail-based museum has been emulated numerous times in the country, but in all cases unsuccessfully. In many Chinese museums, the focus on "hardware (architecture, space utilization, customer services) rather than software (art exhibitions)" keeps attendance growth low (Chen and Yong 2016). Adrian Cheng explained: "They don't see our hard work behind the scenes on art curation and exhibition management, our core philosophy and a genuine dedication to contemporary arts is not easily transferable as a pure business model" (Chen and Yong 2016). The key differences between the museum and other spaces, according to Cheng, are its educational function and brand recognition (Grincheva 2019b). These are things one cannot achieve by focusing only on the business component and maximizing economic potential.

Conclusion

The example of K11 discussed in the last section of the chapter is no doubt an extreme of what a museum could become in the pursuit of sustainable economics. According to the most recently adopted definition by the International Council of Museums, a museum remains to exist as "a not-for-profit, permanent institution in the service of society" (ICOM 2022). While museums in their majority remain loyal to their public nature, this chapter demonstrated that they are dynamically moving on the scale of development from passive organisms dependent on government or public funding to active institutions that can generate their own income, without breaking their commitments to "research, collect, conserve, interpret and exhibit tangible and intangible heritage" (ICOM 2022). From a mere monetization of museum cultural assets either through designing cultural products for sale or auctioning NFTs, museums have progressed to employ purely commercial business models, like franchising, that bring them to the forefront of the global expansion. While this transformation of museums into more active and independent economic actors is inevitable, it is important to remember that museums are enormous resources of cultural creativity and human memory that fuel and inspire the progress of humanity. In order to fulfill their main missions, museums can employ a new "market economy" model to sustain their expensive operations and engage with wider communities. When this model is used as a tool for cultural support and not as a means to an end in pursuit of higher profits, museums can remain loyal to their original mission of preserving and sharing cultural heritage with their communities for "education, enjoyment, reflection and knowledge sharing" (ICOM 2022).

References

Agustinoy, Albert and Pablo Ramirez. 2021. "How NFTs will change museums and art in general." Cuatrecasas. https://bit.ly/3nVDQDy

American Alliance of Museums (AAM). 2020. *National Survey of COVID-19 impact on United States Museums*. Accessed April 7, 2023. https://bit.ly/4180lnb

Awoniyi, Stephen. 2001. "The Contemporary Museum and Leisure: Recreation as a Museum Function." *Museum Management and Curatorship* 19 (3): 297–308. 10.1080/09647770100601903

Bianji, Hongyu. 2019. Palace Museum's Cultural and Creative Products Net 1.5 Billion Yuan in 2017. Accessed April 7, 2023. https://bit.ly/40PEOA7

Blakemore, Erin. 2015. Cash-Strapped Museums Are Selling Their Art. Smithsonian Magazine, April 6.

British Museum (BM). 2022. Report and Accounts for the Year Ended 21 March 2022. Accessed April 7, 2023. https://bit.ly/3Mn10No

British Museum (BM). 2023. About us. Accessed April 7, 2023. https://www.britishmuseum.org/about-us

Burini, Federica. 2020. *Tourism Facing a Pandemic: From Crisis to Recovery*. Accessed April 7, 2023. https://bit.ly/3ZWEAWI

Buttler, Tony. 2021. "Brand New Museum of Making in Derby Opens for the First Time | Derby Museums." Derby Museums. Accessed June 26, 2023. https://www.derbymuseums.org/news/brand-new-museum-of-making-in-derby-opens-for-the-first-time

Carvajal, Doreen. 2015. Needing Money, Some Museums Selling Their Art. *The New York Times*, April 4.

Chen, Xuehui and Yuan Yong. 2016. K11: Art and Business Combination: Interview with Adrian Cheng. *Economic Daily*, 8.

Chong, D. 2007. "Why Critical Writers on the Arts and Management Matter." *Studies in Cultures, Organizations, and Societies* 6 (1): 225–41. 10.1080/10245280008523548

Conn, Steven. 2010. *Do Museums Still Need Objects*? Philadelphia: University of Pennsylvania Press.

Craik, Jennifer. 2007. *Re-Visioning Arts and Cultural Policy: Current Impasses and Future Directions*. Canberra: Anu E Press.

Cuseum. 2021. "How 21 Museums & Cultural Organizations Engaged with NFTs in 2021." Accessed June 26, 2023. https://cuseum.com/blog/2021/11/16/how-21-museums-amp-cultural-organizations-engaged-with-nfts-in-2021

Davis, Douglas. 1990. *The Museum Transformed: Design and Culture in the Post-Pompidou Age*. New York: Abbeville.

Deakin, Tim. 2022. "Museums and NFTs: What's the Opportunity, Who's Doing It Best and Why Question Marks Remain." *MuseumNext*. July 19, 2022. https://www.museumnext.com/article/museums-and-nfts/
Derby Museums (DB). 2016. Human-Centred Design & Co-production Handbook. Accessed June 26, 2023. https://southeastmuseums.org/wp-content/uploads/PDF/DM_HCD_Toolkit_V4_for_website.pdf
Dicke, Thomas. 1992. *Franchising in America: The Development of a Business Method, 1840–1980*. UNC Press Books.
Dickenson, Wendy. 2018. The Deaccession Dilemma: Themes in the American Debate about Art Museum Deaccessions. *Theory and Practice*. Accessed April 7, 2023. https://bit.ly/3MkrJKE
Fabelová, Karolína. 2010. "Museums for Sale: The Louvre and Guggenheim in Abu Dhabi New Presence." *The Prague Journal of Central European Affairs* 12 (2): 53–8.
Feldstein, Martin. 2009. *The Economics of Art Museums*. Chicago: University of Chicago Press.
Fraser, Andrea. 2006. "Isn't This a Wonderful Place? (A Tour of a Tour of the Guggenheim Bilbao)." In *Museum Frictions*, edited by Ivan Karp and Corinne Kratz, 135–60. Durham, NC: Duke University Press.
Gaskin, Sam. 2014. China's Aggressive Museum Growth Brings Architectural Wonders. *CNN*. April 30. Accessed April 7, 2023. https://cnn.it/2EgpvtF
Global Times (GT). 2020. Chinese Netizens Support Russia's State Hermitage Museum Opening Chinese Online Store. Accessed April 7, 2023. https://bit.ly/3MoTstK
Gomez, Edward. 2002. "If Art Is a Commodity, Shopping Can Be an Art." *The New York Times*, December 8: 43.
Greffe, Xavier. 2011. "The Economic Impact of the Louvre." *The Journal of Arts Management, Law, and Society* 41 (2): 121–37. 10.1080/10632921.2011.573323
Grincheva, Natalia. 2017. "Sustainable Fundraising in the 21st Century: Behind the Scenes of the Global Guggenheim Success." In *Systems Thinking in Museums: Theory and Practice*, edited by Yuha Nancy Jung and Love, 181–90. Lanham, Mariland: Rowman & Littlefield.
Grincheva, Natalia. 2019a. "Glocal Diplomacy of Louvre Abu Dhabi: Museum Diplomacy on the Cross-Roads of Local, National and Global Ambitions." *Museum Management and Curatorship* 35 (1): 89–105. 10.1080/09647775.2019.1683883
Grincheva, Natalia. 2019b. *Global Trends in Museum Diplomacy*. London: Routledge.
Guggenheim. 2020. The Solomon R. Guggenheim Foundation Financial Statements December 31, 2020 and 2019. Accessed April 7, 2023. https://bit.ly/3Uj81AR
Heilbrun, James. 2010. "Managing a Museum's Collection." *The Journal of Arts Management, Law, and Society* 23 (1): 69–76. 10.1080/10632921.1993.9944426
Hsu, Claire. 2014. What Does China's Art Boom Tell Us About Its Society? World Economic Forum. https://www.weforum.org/agenda/2014/01/chinas-art-boom-tell-us-society/
International Council of Museums (ICOM). 2022. Museum Definition. Accessed April 7, 2023. https://bit.ly/3ZNcJYD
K11. 2023. About. Accessed April 7, 2023. https://www.k11.com/corp/brand-story/#about-k11
Keene, Suzanne. 2006. *Fragments of the World: Uses of Museum Collections*. London: Routledge.
Kimmelman, Michael. 1999. "The Globe-Straddler of the Art World: The Guggenheim's Thomas Krens." *Museum International* 51 (1): 51–5.
Kramer, Hilton. 1991. "Has Success Spoiled the Art Museum?" *The New Criterion*. Accessed April 7, 2023. https://bit.ly/437tOQ9

Krauss, Rosalind. 1990. *The Cultural Logic of the Late Capitalist Museum.* Massachusetts: The MIT Press. 10.2307/778666
Larkin, Jamie and Paul Burtenshaw. 2021. *Museums and New Business Models.* Accessed April 7, 2023. https://bit.ly/3nPNhVg
Lawley, Ian. 2015. "Local Authority Museums and the Modernizing Government Agenda in England." *Museum and Society* 1 (2): 75–86.
Li, Qiong. 2020. *World's Major Museums Target Chinese Consumers through Tmall.* CGTN. Accessed April 7, 2023. https://bit.ly/3mdcmsK
Lin, Wen-Ling. 2010. "To Subsidize or Not? Reflections and Debates on the Issue of Museum Subsidy." *Museology Quarterly* 24 (3): 47–61.
Loughery, John. 2001. "The Future of Museums: The Guggenheim, MoMA, and the Tate Modern." *The Hudson Review* 53 (4): 631–8.
McClellan, Andrew. 2008. *The Art Museum from Boullée to Bilbao.* Berkeley, Calif.: University of California Press.
McLaughlin, D. 1997. "Is the Development and Touring of the Blockbuster Exhibition in Australian Museum and Science Centers a Long-Term Strategy?" In *National Museums Australia Conference.* National Museums Association, ASTEN.
McNichol, Theresa. 2005. "Creative Marketing Strategies in Small Museums: Up Close and Innovative." *International Journal of Nonprofit and Voluntary Sector Marketing* 10 (4): 239–47. 10.1002/nvsm.28
Mejón, Jaume, Eduard Fransi, and Ann Thorsson Johansson. 2004. "Marketing Management in Cultural Organizations: A Case Study of Catalan Museums." *International Journal of Arts Management Law and Society* 6 (2): 11–22.
Network of European Museum Organization (NEMO). 2020. *Survey on the Impact of the COVID-19 Situation on Museums in Europe Final Report.* Accessed April 7, 2023. https://bit.ly/4049Rah
Newhouse, Victoria. 2006. *Towards a New Museum.* New York: Monacelli Press.
NFT Asia. 2023. NFT Asia. Accessed June 26, 2023. https://nftasiaofficial.com/
Pantalony, Rina Elster. 2013. *Managing Intellectual Property for Museums Guide.* Geneva: Wipo.
Patreon. 2021. The Tank Museum. Accessed April 7, 2023. https://www.patreon.com/tankmuseum
Rectanus, Mark. 2002. *Culture Incorporated: Museums, Artists and Corporate Sponsorship.* Minneapolis: University of Minnesota.
Rentschler, Ruth and Audrey Gilmore. 2002. "Museums: Discovering Services Marketing." *International Journal of Arts Management* 5 (1): 62–72.
Rex, Bethany. 2019. "Which Museums to Fund? Examining Local Government Decision-Making in Austerity." Local Government Studies, June 1–20. 10.1080/03003930.2019.1619554
Reyburn, Scott. 2022. "Museums Are Cashing in on NFTs." *The New York Times,* March 25. Accessed April 7, 2023. https://nyti.ms/413VYdv
Riley, Terrence and Edward Eigen. 1994. "Between the Museum and the Marketplace: Selling Good Design." In *The Museum of Modern Art at Mid-Century at Home and Abroad,* edited by John Thames Szarkowski, 150–80. New York: Hudson Press.
Robinson, Mark. 2015. *Derby Museums Business Model Case Study.* London: Arts Council England. Accessed June 26, 2023. https://www.culturehive.co.uk/wp-content/uploads/2016/02/Derby-Museums-Business-Model-Case-Study.pdf
Science Gallery International (SGI). 2023a. About The Network. Accessed April 7, 2023. https://sciencegallery.org/about-network
Science Gallery International (SGI). 2023b. Network Benefits. Accessed April 7, 2023. https://sciencegallery.org/benefits

Simal, J. 2005. "On-Demand Printing Transforming Museum Visitors Experience." *International Conference on Digital Production Printing and Industrial Applications*. Amsterdam: The Society for Imaging Science and Technology, 141–2.

Smith, Claudia, J. Brock Smith and Eleanor Shaw. 2017. "Embracing Digital Networks: Entrepreneurs' Social Capital Online." *Journal of Business Venturing* 32 (1): 18–34. 10.1016/j.jbusvent.2016.10.003

Smith, K.K. 2009. "V&A Images: Image licensing at a cultural heritage institution." *Ithaka Case Studies in Sustainability*. New York: Ithaka.

State Administration of Cultural Heritage (SACH). 2011. Ministry of Long-Term Development Plan for the Career of the Museum (2011–2020). Accessed April 7, 2023. https://bit.ly/3ZIOHhH

Statista. 2023. Number of Museums in China 2011–2021. Accessed April 7, 2023. https://bit.ly/419SLZc

Sylvester, Christine. 2009. *Art/Museums: International Relations Where We Least Expect It*. London: Paradigm.

The State Council. The People's Republic of China. 2015. State Council Order. No. 659. Museum regulations. Accessed April 7, 2023. https://bit.ly/2BVCheM

Valeonti, Foteini, Melissa Terras and Andrew Hudson-Smith. 2019. "Examining Mobile Print-on-Demand as an Alternative to Image Licensing for Monetising Digitisation to Promote OpenGLAM." *Museums and the Web* 23 (1): 1–18.

Vivant, Elsa. 2011. "Who Brands Whom? The Role of Local Authorities in the Branching of Art Museums." *Town Planning Review* 82 (1): 99–115.

Werner, Paul. 2005. *Museum Inc: Inside the Global Art World*. Chicago, Ill: Prickly Paradigm Press.

Wood, James. 2004. "The Authorities of the American Art Museum." In *Who's Muse: Art Museums and the Public Trust*, edited by James Cuno. Princeton and Oxford: Princeton University Press.

Wu, Chin-Tao. 2002. *Privatising Culture: Corporate Art Intervention since the 1980s*. London: Verso.

Yan, Huang. 2017. "Exploring the Development of Museums from the Current National Cultural Tourism Policy." *Art Education* 16 (1): 149–52.

Ying, Lin. 2014. K11: The Idea Is Reflected in Every Detail. China Advertising, 8. Accessed April 7, 2023. https://bit.ly/2E52Yil

Zimmer, Annette and Stefan Toepler. 1999. "The Subsidized Muse: Government and the Arts in Western Europe and the United States." *Journal of Cultural Economics* 23 (1): 33–49.

Zouari, Kenza. 2023. "Decentralised Autonomous Organisations (DAOs) and Art." Accessed June 26, 2023. https://sg.eduprofile.net/events/170323

3

SOCIAL ACCOUNTING FOR MUSEUM PROGRESS

Jaleesa Renee Wells

Assistant Professor of Arts Administration, University of Kentucky, Lexington, KY, United States

Introduction

In museums, as across the creative and cultural sector, there has been a growing desire for social progress and change. Museums serve as symbols of culture in society. In today's contemporary society, museums have been tasked with engaging their communities in more interconnected ways than standard diversity, equity, and inclusion (DEI) initiatives, especially those that lead to the tokenization and exploitation of people both within and outside of the museum walls. Museums are being held to task to measure their progress against a backdrop of significant civil change in today's society. This chapter explores academic, media, and industry literature surrounding museums and their intersections with sociocultural progress, by asking: what are the social issues impacting the ability and effectiveness of museums to account for the soft assets and liabilities of social progress? Moreover, how should museums measure their accountabilities within social progress, utilizing social accounting as a practice-led tool to promote museum progress? Broadly, social accounting is an organizational practice that measures the social impact of an organization, by expanding accounting and accountability practices and behaviors beyond the conventional accounting and monetary foci present in financial management. In order to understand what needs to be accounted for, it's important to consider what are the social issues that are affected, or even caused, by current museum intersections within society.

Study Design

After attending the 2022 symposium "On Black Museum Anthropology: An ABA & CMA Conversation" co-hosted by the Association of Black

DOI: 10.4324/9781003308003-4

Anthropologist and the Council for Museum Anthropology and listening to the panel discussion about how museums can contribute to necessary social change, four domains of inquiry for this chapter were formed: (1) the role of museums in society, (2) value of the museum entity, (3) the labor force within museums, and (4) the museum within its communities. From these domains, a narrative review of academic literature was employed to frame the main research questions of this chapter, utilizing the domains as keywords to search Web of Science databases for academic literature pertaining to museums and social accounting. Dominant discussions in broader museum studies and social progress heavily focused on museum education efforts were delineated, though literature involving educators within museums as part of the labor force was included. Additionally, the literature related to museums and financial management was searched and resulted in zero publications that intersect museums, social progress, and financial management. The remainder of the literature involved broad themes focused on racial, gender, and disability disparities both within and outside of a museum; surprisingly there were very little studies conducted on the intersection of socioeconomic disparities and museums beyond museum outreach and education. The narrative literature review served as a useful method for exploring the broad discourse surrounding the research questions of this study, particularly illuminating the social issues that impact museum progress, as well could be expanded to include literature in media and industry, which this study embraced.

Sociocultural Role of Museums

Museums are much more than the sum of their parts. They play a significant role in the preservation, knowledge, and understanding of the past, present, and future of a given society of people and their cultures. According to the International Council of Museums (ICOM), the definition of a museum is

> a not-for-profit, permanent institution in the service of society that researches, collects, conserves, interprets and exhibits tangible and intangible heritage. Open to the public, accessible and inclusive, museums foster diversity and sustainability. They operate and communicate ethically, professionally and with the participation of communities, offering varied experiences for education, enjoyment, reflection and knowledge sharing. ("Museum Definition - International Council of Museums" 2022)

The ICOM conducted a series of consultations to arrive at this definition, but does this definition account for the ways in which museums take on a sociocultural role in society? Brown and Mairesse (2018) further explored the definitional role of museums through their social roles stating:

> … throughout the world the social role of museums is gaining agency, and recent years have seen—in Latin America especially—the development of new, experimental museums that challenge the canon and prompt us to ask whether we can still insist on the museum being a permanent "institution" rather than a more inclusive kind of organisation … (2018, 526–7)

The ICOM's definition already embraces notions of a socially led museum, one that is "in service of society," but, as Brown and Mairesse outline, doesn't necessarily move beyond a classical perspective steeped in the administration of the museum, rather than its "social utility" and wider impact (530). Ultimately the museum as an institution needing administrative direction and as a contributor to sociocultural progress and impact is multifaceted and "by taking a longer view of museum purposes and values, reaching back to the nineteenth century and taking stock of the pivotal museological moments not least in the 1970s, the social trends of today can be more clearly understood" (535).

Coffee (2008) expands this notion of the role of museums to its formative role in relation to cultural inclusion and exclusion stating that how museums engage in the inclusion-exclusion dichotomy of its sociocultural network is part of an evolving and ongoing discourse surrounding museums (261). Museums are useful places and spaces that "document social relationships represented in languages, music and song, agriculture, architecture, contests of skill, visual art, religions, dramaturgy, educational systems, scientific disciplines, and the many other practices that symbolize those relationships … Museum use is also a cultural practice" (262–3). As such, museums create *enabling conditions* that symbolize activities unique to humans and the human condition (263). This also attributes the sociocultural role of *enculturation and socialization* to museums where cultural transference can occur and the social construction of cultural exchange evolves (264). However, "inclusivity and exclusivity are neither abstract nor absolute qualities" of museums; Coffee argues that it is in the ways people use, interact, and engage with museums that create privileges and social stratification in society (271).

Furthermore, there have been studies conducted on the role of the museum as a place for shared access to diverse narratives portrayed through artworks and cultural artifacts (Topaz et al. 2019; Aspegren 2021). In diversifying the collections of museums the focus is on a paradigm shift from "the aesthetic to the political" (Aspegren 2021, 68), where artworks such as feminist works should be less interested in feminist acceptability than with its ability to usher in progress and social change. And yet there is still a lingering question about how to measure the acceptability of diversity among a museum, its collections, and exhibition practices such that identifiability, geography, and a focus on time periods can contribute to the growth or suppression of a diverse museum (Topaz et al. 2019).

Regardless of useability, there is still a strong discourse surrounding the *legacy of prejudice* many museums face today. As Lynch and Alberti (2010) state, "museums have been complicit in the construction of physical and cultural hierarchies that underpin racist thought from the Enlightenment until well into the twentieth century, in marked contrast to the inclusionary role that many now seek to fulfill" (13). They posit that "radical trust in the museum" should be a foundation of any museums accountability efforts to create and enact museum progress, asking "[i]s it enough to face up to prejudice and its legacies in museum practice as we seek to do now, or to host open and seemingly self-critical debates on museums and racism as we did then?" (29).

Social and Public Value of Museums

Where the sociocultural role of museums centers around the museum in society, it's equally important to consider the social and public value of the museums as organizational entities, including and beyond the value of its assets. Internally and organizationally, Janes (2010) posits the notion of a mindful museum, one where the contemporary business model moves away from consumption, entertainment, and ancillary knowledge sharing and toward a heightened sense of social, environmental, and economic stewardship (325). Janes asks, "[a]re museums mindful of what is going on in the world around them?" (ibid.). This is a useful question to consider when exploring the ways that museums hold themselves accountable for social progress and the accountability tools they may use to promote internal museum progress. As discussed in the previous section, the museum as an entity is not only a place of sociocultural construction, but also is subjected to the evolution of the human condition and humanity's sociocultural needs. What is happening around them is just as important as what is happening within them. Janes posits that the "meaning and value of enhanced mindfulness have yet to be tapped by the museum community at large, and its potential might well be limitless" (336), particularly at the various levels of leadership and within the museum workforce in toto.

Furthermore, the museum as a contributor to society and culture has been subject to "successive iteration of public sector reform [that] have progressively required museums to prove that they are worthy of public support" (Scott 2006, 45). How does this impact museum perspectives from professionals and the public alike (ibid.)? Social value and social capital have continued to impact organizations and institutions within a broad public sector, especially at the macro-institutional level of society that is concerned with the well-being of communities (ibid.). The efficiency and effectiveness of the use of public funding, for example, is bedrock by a larger focus on social policy than economic contribution; "in part, this shift in emphasis reflects the growing pressure on governments to deal with the impact of rapid social change" (47). Accordingly, Scott concludes that the public value of the museum is in the *intangible* resources it offers for public use (70).

As an entity, museums are contending with their internal shift toward mindfulness at every aspect of their organizational functionalities and in conjunction with a global external governance and funding shift toward social impact through the measurement of social value. Social value, in the organizational sense, tends "to focus on the connections that we make through social networks and social capital, as well as through the social benefits or disadvantages of communities" (Wells 2016, 5). As such, Janes (2010) offers a look at the ideal, yet unrecognized museum; where a rethinking of "the role of museums as social institutions will require no less than a reinvented museum—a mindful organization that incorporates the best of enduring museum values and business methodology, with a sense of social responsibility" (325).

Labor in Museum Institutions

Within the museum as an entity are the people who drive the entity forward: leaders, workers, and everyone in between. In recent years there have been examinations of not only the actions of museum leaders but the representative makeup of the leaders, employees, and other workers that contribute to museum progress (Kenney 2021; Pogrebin 2022). Reports have shown that museums are still led by people who present as predominantly white, cis-male, able-bodied, neurotypical, middle-aged, and bourgeois and/or upper class, where "93% of museum directors are white, as are 92.6% of board chairs and 89.3% of board members" (McCambridge 2017). The leadership progression pipeline in museums continues to narrow in favor of this group of people, despite the realizations that the wider museum workforce is made up of a range of marginalized and minoritized people whose careers are relatively precarious. The pipeline, as further discussed in the literature, doesn't begin at the point of hire, but at the point of knowing: knowing the museum careers are accessible and welcoming to those outside of the dominant identity lexicon. While there have been significant strides in changing the labor landscape for museum work, such as more utilization of labor unions (Irish 2023), a lot of work remains to be done to achieve accountable museum progress. As more funders provide access to funding that is geared toward culturally specific groups of people and the preservation of their heritages, the majority of public funding is geared toward the growth of programs and projects within and around a museum, with very few funding opportunities focused on the professional and career development of people who work within the museum. This issue of a diverse workforce is further complicated as more interest in preserving the legacy of marginalized and minoritized cultures and communities brings into question not just what is collected, preserved, and shared, but *who* is doing the collecting, preserving, and sharing. Whitaker (2021) argues that a reframing of museums in terms of their people is necessary and warranted in the continuing climate for social progress,

> The history of collecting objects and placing them in near-sacred buildings of structural or symbolic civic import may seem to be the point but actually those institutions depend even more so on the people who make up the workforce and the audience. Those people may appear interchangeable or expendable, but to center their stories is to pave a pathway toward a more stable and exciting future for art museums in the United States. (254)

In order to move beyond the status quo in museums, from the objects it houses to a place people can call their professional *home*. Home, as a concept, is a complex notion for marginalized and minoritized people who have been kept from owning homes, forced to change their home locations, or experienced institutional violence within and around their homes (Wells 2022, 254). Cultural institutions must contend with the legacies of oppression that have been propagated by formal infrastructures of traditional institutional structures (ibid.). Adjoiningly, the issue of *who* bears the question of *where and how* should the collecting, preserving, and sharing occur. For Whitaker, "[t]his focus on people raises the importance of socioeconomic and racial inclusion in the workforce as a linchpin of sustainability …" (2021, 254) and positions pay equity is the "lever that can most catalyze change in the larger arts ecosystem" (255).

Haupt et al. (2022) also argue that the internal workforce is a litmus for museum progress through diversity, equity, access, and inclusion (DEAI). Where most DEAI initiatives focus on the external impact on audiences and communities, there is a mindshift that needs to also focus on measuring DEAI change within the organizational life-cycle and culture. Importantly, though, "there is no overall museum sector strategy for workforce diversity, which is a cause for concern if real change is to be made in the future, especially in the context of the current economic climate with increased competition for funding" (Davies and Shaw 2013, 190). Arguably, there's a lack of "strategic leadership" to accompany the necessary changes and measurement of changes set to happen within the museum organization (ibid.), and "[t]here is a real fear that without energetic and strategic leadership to promote and implement actions such as those identified by [the project findings], there will in fact be little practical action and the diversity of the workforce might get worse" (191).

Community Involvement of the Museum Institution

Considering the role, value, and labor force of museums, these institutions and organizations are widely created for the purpose of providing a public service to their communities, and more widely to society at large. Going beyond evaluative practices of museum outreach and engagement, museums are also measured by their culturally representative qualities and broad social impact. As such there has been a growth in the establishment and recognition of culturally embedded museums and their ability to engage in a social reciprocity with their communities. In essence, some museums have become subjects of their environments, contributing to credibility, legitimacy, and legacies of marginalized and minoritized communities, such as smaller museums organizations centered on, embedded within, and geographically located in their culturally specific communities. This phenomenon is in stark contrast to *mainstream* public museums still struggling to acknowledge their colonial roots through lackluster temporary programming that feels like an afterthought to the communities they wish to reach.

Morrissey and Dirk (2020) discuss that

> [m]useums have long been criticized for practices that have privileged, ignored, or misrepresented many identities. Encouraged by field-wide priorities and pressures, most museums are attempting to be more inclusive in their practices and diverse in the voices and perspectives they reflect in their collections, exhibits, programs, and leadership. (555)

However, addressing criticism in discourse and actioning museum progress can be increasingly complex and costly. Museum progress is "promising and yet problematic, with sparks of innovation pushing against stubborn traditions … [yet], studies still endorsed museums as institutions with the unique capacity and the profound responsibility to shape and influence a more equitable society" (567).

One such study is by Kinsley (2016) who addresses the issue that museums have traditionally equated inclusion with "ensuring and increasing public access to their activities and services that are believed to constitute a public good" (475). Kinsey, however, argues that inclusion in museums is a matter of "social justice" and a centering on justice is what will bring about internal change in the museum workforce and beyond (ibid.). This justice that Kinsey discusses is meant to move beyond redistributive and affirmative justice, and toward a radical transformation (487), such as one that systemically reframes the purpose and actions of a museum within its communities. Similarly, Ünsal (2019) argues that museums as entities and subjects should serve as

> [S]paces of representation and keepers of cultural memory, museums produce knowledge about societies based on artifacts and stories collected, and share this through museological methods, [that] [t]he foremost contribution of the museum to society is this capacity of knowledge production and dissemination based on tangible and intangible cultural heritage. (605)

Essentially, museums serve as *contact zones* that allow for and/or create opportunities for transformation and decolonization of cultural knowledge to occur, and it is the charge of the museum community, stakeholders, and workforce to contribute to and lead social progress (606).

Further studies contribute to this holistic view of museum progress and argue that a key part of progress is embracing accessibility in addition to efforts toward more inclusion and diversity (Ang 2005). Embracing a multifaceted approach to progress also encourages the "assertion of an ever-widening range of groups making their presence felt on the cultural landscape, and claiming the right to express their different cultural identities and allegiances" (2005, 305). The continued emergence of multiculturalism and interculturalism is a unique predicament for museums that have tended toward institutional bureaucracy rather than organizational democracy. As such, "social and cultural pressures are bringing about changes in exhibition practice which affect a gradual repositioning of art, opening it up to a more diverse range of experiences and relationships" (319).

As an example of community involvement through museum progress, Jennings (2015) discusses museum activism surrounding Michael Brown, an unarmed Black teenager who was shot and killed by a white police officer in 2014 in Ferguson, MO. Jennings argues, after tracking museums use of #museumsrespondtoFerguson, that the role of museums in the wider social discourse was not just a narrative about the events that transpired in Ferguson, but also about the lack of inclusion across cultural spaces. Jennings advocates that

> [m]useums—whose foundations penetrate the soil in our cities, towns, and rural areas, whose buildings occupy civic space, whose boards and directors are influential and respected citizens, whose members and visitors make up our communities—cannot stand to the side and let this sad national story repeat endlessly. (104)

Social Accounting as a Tool for Museum Progress

The above sections addressed the first question positioned in this chapter and highlighted four domains involving social issues that have impacted the ability and effectiveness of museums to account for their progress. This section addresses the second question: how should museums measure their accountabilities within social progress, utilizing social accounting as a practice-led tool to promote museum progress? As defined earlier in the chapter, social accounting is an organizational practice that measures the social impact (as well as environmental) of an organization, by expanding accounting and accountability practices and behaviors beyond the conventional accounting and monetary foci present in financial management. It "explores how accounts of the social, the environmental and the (putatively) sustainable are articulated, resisted, employed, and proposed … and should be taken to embrace social, environmental, ethical, responsibility and sustainability accounting, accountability, reporting, auditing, investment, and costing and management" (Gray 2010, 12). The utilization and practice of social accounting can impact financial and economic bottom lines, but also the social and public performance of an organization (Nikolaou 2010, 562). At its most basic understanding,

> All social accounting (regardless of its actual title) relates to the presentation of information about organizational activity. The resulting account (whatever the form it takes) is presented to someone—even if it is only the organization itself … The social account, as with any other account, presupposes some defined accounting entity (there has to be something about which to account), although, as we shall see, the relationship is reflexive. Equally, there is an implication of complexity and size in the relationship between the accounting entity and those to whom the account is presented. (Gray et al. 1997, 330)

And, "there are both political and social issues embedded in the social accounting" (328), meaning that an organization's stakeholders (leaders, investors, funders, workers, communities, etc.) have their own political and/or social agency and agendas implied and applied to the outcomes of an organization's social impact. As such, the focus of social accounting is, by its own use, accountability, where "[a]ccountability is conceived of as relating to the rights to information of a participatory democratic society" (329).

Only recently has social accountability been applied to and modeled within the museum landscape (San-Jose et al. 2022). Utilizing *social value* as a foundation, social accounting for museums can be differentiated between market value, the financial data transformed from quantified added and created social values, and non-market value, involving a stakeholder analysis approach to understanding intrinsic and extrinsic social values (9–10). In San-Jose, Garcia-Merino, and Retolaza's study stakeholders were outlined across of range of groups including: the local community, friends of the museum, artistic community, the network of professional organizations and institutions (including those in the tourism sector), visitors to the museum, the general media, private sponsors, public administrators, suppliers, and employees (11). Furthermore they outlined the value indicators of the stakeholder groups, such as: education and pedagogy, training and professionalism, development and promotion of critical thinking and awareness, generation of knowledge and dissemination of culture, generation of quality content and programming, use of space, reinforcement of identity, social cohesion, visibility, prestige, culture, research, preservation of heritage and memory, promotion of professional networks, and a boost and opportunity for professional development (12–15). These value indicators align with many of the discussions and the wider discourse presented from the literature in previous sections, that the museum is a site for people to have shared experiences that better their understanding of themselves in society. And as such, museums are spaces for cultural reflexivity to occur and to be experienced by a range of stakeholders. So, how do museums measure these values against their own progress actions and systems, when the above summary of San-Jose, Garcia-Merino, and Retolaza's study results provides an indication that the use of social accounting as a tool for museum progress positions the museum as an intrinsic value within society rather than an instrumental asset (16)?

In exploring and creating value indicators, social accounting can be utilized to measure the sociocultural role, social and public value, labor force, and community involvement of, in, and around museums. It would be useful to understand which stakeholders are more prevalent in each of these domains. For example, managers and leaders in museums would have a significant stake in the development of a healthy, robust, and engaged museum workforce. An indicator for them to consider would be the value of the museum as a progressive workplace and *professional home* for workers to invest their time, energy, and resources into and vice versa. With a people-centered approach, managers and leaders would approach their employees and other museum workers as stakeholders with significant social investment potential. Furthermore, "if managers promote internal measurement systems within their organisations, [this] allows [them] to know in greater detail the activities they carry out, in many cases routinely, and that can be improved or redefined based on their assessment by their stakeholders" (17).

Lessons from social accounting in the museum environment are not specific to managerial practices. Understanding the internal and external influences that impact, or even disrupt, museums is key to understanding how a societal appetite for civil progress would be measured against the structures and systems of a museum. Leading to understanding a "triple bottom line" of the value of a museum has a sociocultural role model (Wells 2016), where cultural value, social value, and economic value become intertwined with the purpose and identity of a museum, and museums at large. Faculty and researchers could utilize this approach as a way to incorporate social accounting as a praxis—theory and practice—for learning about the roles and values of museums. Similarly, students may find that social accounting and its umbrella (corporate social responsibility) are useful sites for building knowledge around the impact of museums on professionalism and career development. By considering their own stake in museum progress, students should consider the implications of stale leadership models that permeate the exploitation and degradation of museum innovation and progress brought about by a diverse labor force. Ultimately, key stakeholders who are affected by and also implement museum progress are those on the ground: the current and future museum professionals and leaders. Investigating the intersections between social progress and financial management in the museum is paramount to museum progress; and, as such, an interpretive approach is warranted. It is not the purpose of social accounting to be applied to financial management, but, instead, to be utilized reciprocally and in conjunction with financial management as part of wider strategic decision-making and operations. What occurs financially within a museum impacts the people in and around it, and what occurs socially within and around museums impacts its financial health and effectiveness. Thus, the question arises: what is the role of finance in museum progress and what is the value of museum progress in building a financially sustainable and socially impactful cultural institution? Embedding people within a social accounting framework that is specific to a particular museum's context is a place to start. Considering the embeddedness of people at each juncture of strategic decision making allows for measurement and accounting of social progress throughout the museum.

Concluding Insights

This chapter explored the state of museum progress from four distinct domains: sociocultural role, social and public value, labor force, and community involvement of, in, and around museums. Through a narrative review of extant academic literature, this chapter explored two main questions: what are the social issues impacting the ability and effectiveness of museums to account for the soft assets and liabilities of social progress; and how should museums measure their accountabilities within social progress, utilizing social accounting as a practice-led tool to promote museum progress?

A limitation but also an area of opportunity is the reliance on past literature to discuss and outline an evolving issue surrounding museums, as well as the creative and cultural sector overall. In essence, this chapter highlighted that museums want to remain relevant and that people find museums to be intrinsic contributors to cultural relevance. This chapter thus serves as a call for more research studies (whether conceptual or empirical) to explore and investigate the necessities of measuring progress and wider societal impact of museums.

References

Ang, Ien. 2005. "The Predicament of Diversity: Multiculturalism in Practice at the Art Museum." *Ethnicities* 5 (3): 305–20. 10.1177/1468796805054957

Aspegren, Astrid. 2021. "Representation of Women in Art Museums: How Can We Improve Gender Balance in Exhibition Practice?" *European Journal of Cultural Management & Policy* 11 (1): 56–70.

Brown, Karen and François Mairesse. 2018. "The Definition of the Museum through Its Social Role." *Curator: The Museum Journal* 61 (4): 525–39. 10.1111/cura.12276

Coffee, Kevin. 2008. "Cultural Inclusion, Exclusion and the Formative Roles of Museums." *Museum Management and Curatorship* 23 (3): 261–79. 10.1080/09647770802234078

Davies, Maurice and Lucy Shaw. 2013. "Diversifying the Museum Workforce: The Diversify Scheme and Its Impact on Participants' Careers." *Museum Management and Curatorship* 28 (2): 172–92. 10.1080/09647775.2013.776799

Gray, Rob. 2010. "A Re-Evaluation of Social, Environmental and Sustainability Accounting: An Exploration of an Emerging Trans-Disciplinary Field?" *Sustainability Accounting, Management and Policy Journal* 1 (1): 11–32. 10.1108/20408021011059205

Gray, Rob, Colin Dey, Dave Owen, Richard Evans, and Simon Zadek. 1997. "Struggling with the Praxis of Social Accounting: Stakeholders, Accountability, Audits and Procedures." *Accounting, Auditing & Accountability Journal* 10 (3): 325–64. 10.1108/09513579710178106.

Haupt, Gretchen, Marjorie Bequette, Megan Goeke, and Choua Her. 2022. "'… Yet, It Is Still Very White': Structural and Cultural Impediments to DEAI Change in Science Museums." *Museum Management and Curatorship* 37 (2): 196–213. 10.1080/09647775.2022.2052161

Irish, Anni. 2023. "Changing Institutional Culture from the Inside Out: Why More and More US Museum Workers Are Forming Unions." The Art Newspaper. May 18, 2023. https://www.theartnewspaper.com/2023/05/18/changing-institutional-culture-from-the-inside-out-why-more-and-more-us-museum-workers-are-forming-unions

Janes, Robert R. 2010. "The Mindful Museum." *Curator: The Museum Journal* 53 (3): 325–38. 10.1111/j.2151-6952.2010.00032.x

Jennings, Gretchen. 2015. "The #museumsrespondtoFerguson Initiative, a Necessary Conversation." *Museums & Social Issues* 10 (2): 97–105. 10.1179/1559689315Z.00000000036

Kenney, Nancy. 2021. "Exclusive Survey: What Progress Have US Museums Made on Diversity, after a Year of Racial Reckoning?" The Art Newspaper. May 25, 2021. https://www.theartnewspaper.com/2021/05/25/exclusive-survey-what-progress-have-us-museums-made-on-diversity-after-a-year-of-racial-reckoning

Kinsley, Rose Paquet. 2016. "Inclusion in Museums: A Matter of Social Justice." *Museum Management and Curatorship* 31 (5): 474–90. 10.1080/09647775.2016.1211960

Lynch, Bernadette T. and Samuel J.M.M. Alberti. 2010. "Legacies of Prejudice: Racism, Co-Production and Radical Trust in the Museum." *Museum Management and Curatorship* 25 (1): 13–35. 10.1080/09647770903529061

McCambridge, Ruth. 2017. "Museums So White: Survey Reveals Deep Lack of Diversity." *Nonprofit Quarterly*. May 9, 2017. https://nonprofitquarterly.org/museum-boards-directors-whitest-getting-whiter

Morrissey, Kris and Grayson Dirk. 2020. "Identity & Museum Practice: Promises, Practices, and a Broken Pipeline." *Curator: The Museum Journal* 63 (4): 555–70. 10.1111/cura.12396

Museum Definition - International Council of Museums. 2022. International Council of Museums. https://icom.museum/en/resources/standards-guidelines/museum-definition/

Nikolaou, Ioannis E. and Konstantinos I. Evangelinos. 2010. "Classifying Current Social Responsibility Accounting Methods for Assisting a Dialogue between Business and Society." *Social Responsibility Journal* 6 (4): 562–79. 10.1108/17471111011083446

Pogrebin, Robin. 2022. "Museums Change Their Approach to Showing White Male Artists: In the Wake of the Black Lives Matter Movement, Business-as-Usual Gets a Rethink." *The New York Times*. April 27, 2022. https://www.nytimes.com/2022/04/27/arts/design/museums-white-male-artists.html

San-Jose, Leire, Jose Domingo Garcia-Merino, and Jose Luis Retolaza. 2022. "Social Value in the Orange Economy: Social Accounting Applied to Museums." *Museum Management and Curatorship*. 10.1080/09647775.2021.2023901

Scott, Carol (2006). Museums: Impact and value. *Cultural Trends*, 15, 45–7510.1080/09548960600615947.

Topaz, Chad M., Bernhard Klingenberg, Daniel Turek, Brianna Heggeseth, Pamela E. Harris, Julie C. Blackwood, C. Ondine Chavoya, Steven Nelson, and Kevin M. Murphy. 2019. "Diversity of Artists in Major U.S. Museums." *PLoS ONE* 14 (3): 1–15. 10.1371/journal.pone.0212852

Ünsal, Deniz. 2019. "Positioning Museums Politically for Social Justice." *Museum Management and Curatorship* 34 (6): 595–607. 10.1080/09647775.2019.1675983

Wells, Jaleesa Renee. 2016. "Entrepreneurial Axiology: Hybrid Values in Creative Social Enterprise." (Peer Reviewed Paper Presentation). 39th Annual Conference of the Institute for Small Business and Entrepreneurship, Paris, France. October 26–28, 2016.

Wells, Jaleesa Renee. 2022. "Black Representation in British Cultural Policy." In *Arts Management & Cultural Policy across the African Diaspora*, 253–73. Cham: Springer International Publishing. 10.1007/978-3-030-85810-0_16

Whitaker, Amy. 2021. "Reconsidering People as the Institution: Empathy, Pay Equity, and Deaccessioning as Key Leadership Strategies in Art Museums." *Curator: The Museum Journal* 64 (2): 253–68. 10.1111/cura.12420

PART 2

Financial Planning Standards

4

MUSEUM REVENUES, EXPENSES, AND BUDGETING

Hristina Mikich

Associate Professor, Faculty of Management, University Metropolitan, Belgrade, Serbia

Budgeting Processes in Museums

The budgeting process is a set of methods, techniques, and activities for planning and execution of expenditures and revenues in museums. The result of this process is a budget. A budget is the translation of a museum's goals and strategies into the accounting planning framework. The Chartered Investment and Management Accountant defines a budget as a "quantitative expression of a plan for a defined period of time" (CIMA 2005, 5). Thus, a museum budget is a document in the form review of all the museum's expenses and revenues that will occur in a certain period. This chapter explores the analysis of the budgeting process and expense planning in museums. It will also explain budgeting rules and procedures in museums and pay attention to the type of institution(s) responsible for their operations (e.g., government, private, foundation, association, etc.). Additionally, the chapter presents various budgeting methods employed within museums, along with the diverse types of budgets. It explains the guiding principles of budgeting expenses, in accordance with both the Generally Accepted Accounting Principles (GAAP) and the International Financial Reporting Standards (IFRS). This clarification outlines how different museum expenditures are handled based on the specific accounting standard applied. At the end, the chapter will discuss classification and categories of expenses and their purpose as well as revenues and expenses as two crucial aspects of budgeting.

Origin of the word "budget" comes from the Latin term "bulga" meaning a leather bag, a wallet for carrying money and various necessities (Lewis and Short 1879). Flesher and Flesher (1979) state that the modern meaning of the word budget emerged during the time of troubadours in medieval France. It

DOI: 10.4324/9781003308003-6

was used to describe members of troubadour companies who collected money and kept it in a leather bag—*bougette* (Fr.). Until the beginning of the 20th century, budgeting was related to the state and the term was mainly used to describe government spending and public revenue generation. Later, budgeting appears as a topic in business economics and management disciplines. In the business sphere, budgeting had its renaissance during the first half of the 20th century when James O. McKinsey, one of the founders of accounting education in the United States, published "Budgetary Control" (Flesher and Flesher 1979, 1985). In Europe, after World War II, social and economic changes affected economic structures in such a way that they became consolidated, large industrial systems were created, and various financial disciplines became more specialized.

Cultural organizations were also part of this trend. At first, until the 1970s, a budget was used as a tool for the control of spending in cultural organizations. In museums, this approach was based on the assumption that they, like all other cultural institutions, have patrons—the state, private philanthropists, and corporations, which provide them funding and other resources. In such circumstances, museum management aimed to reconcile the expenses with the available income. This process of bureaucratization of financing was a characteristic of the cultural sector at the time. Its main feature was a large national cultural institution that administers (mostly) state finances and allocates them to various cultural programs. In European countries of the former Eastern Bloc,[1] budgeting was based on five-year plans for the development of the economy and social activities.[2] The process was centralized and planned at the level of the state and its vision of how cultural needs should be fulfilled. In turn, museums did not have much freedom and independence in deciding about their programs and managing costs and income.

Further development of budgeting resulted from the economization of culture where more emphasis was placed on marketing and opening of the cultural sector to tourism. The synergy between museums and tourism was driven by economic arguments—culture provides various attractions that can encourage tourist travel while tourism generates revenues needed to support culture (Richards 2016, 32). Thus, budgeting became a complex discipline, expected to enable the efficiency of a museum's operations. The increasingly complex environment, with more diversified sources of financing that need to be harmonized according to financial maturity, dynamics of activities and programs, is now turning the discipline of budgeting into a real "art" of expenditure and income management.

Budgeting is the process of creating a budget. It is an integral part of strategic management and systematic thinking in museums. Involving all museum sectors and departments, it comprises the collection of all relevant data and its analysis in order to make the most effective budget plan. Budgeting in museums requires the management, curators, and other staff to be able to adapt to the changing business conditions by revising costs and reprogramming some activities. Cooperation between different museum departments, curators, and other museum specialists is very important in the process of budget preparation. They should all provide inputs on the planned museum activities, resources needed to realize them, and related costs. All that information will be consolidated by the financial department.

The main difference between the terms "budgeting" and "budget" is that the former represents the planning process while the latter denotes the result of that process. However, the significance of the process itself and its result depend on the type of museum. There are museums where a budget is considered a strategic tool that enables financial sustainability and development of program activities while in others it is a document of a formal nature, simply verifying the distribution of certain financial resources. Budgeting has three basic functions: to be a means of communication with internal and external stakeholders; to help the process of planning and achieving the organization's strategic goals; and to serve as an evaluation tool (Franklin et al. 2019).

In literature and practice, the term "budget process" is used in a broader and narrower sense. In its broader sense, it includes two phases: budget preparation/planning and budget execution. In a narrower sense, it mainly refers to the preparation (planning) of the budget. Budget planning includes all activities that precede the formal adoption of the budget by the board of directors or other governing body. It is the process of collecting data on the budget execution in the previous year, programs planned for this year, and financial projections. The museum's staff in different departments is responsible for estimating preliminary expenditures. In some museums, the first estimates are usually based on the cost of past exhibitions and discrete elements specific to the concrete project (Smithsonian Institution 2002). In private museums, the initial assumptions for financial projections are conditioned with the results achieved in the past and expectations from the external environment—sponsors, private donors, commercial income, international funds, and the changes in costs and prices on the market. In public museums (financed by different levels of government), these projections are based on the fiscal memorandum, and the budget calendar. Museums can use different methods to improve the level of accuracy of cost estimation, including regression analysis, to create predictive models for their project's costs (Smithsonian Institution 2002), or impact statements to guide the budget planning process during, for example, a recession (Korn 2017). How detailed a budget will depend on the complexity of a museum (national, regional, local, complex, artistic, natural history, technical, etc.) and its programs. Therefore, apart from the budget as a strategic tool for managing costs and revenues, museums can also have an expenditure plan, which is the list of systematized costs and expenditures, or a revenue plan, which is the list of systematized museum revenues to be achieved in the future. All of these, in different ways, are elements of the budgeting process.

The following steps in the budgetary process will be focused on making detailed estimates of costs and producing more precise budgets. Budget execution includes activities that allocate planned or available funds to expenditures and costs. It begins after the administrative body, which is usually the board of directors, approves the financial plan for the current year. That is a formal act of approving the budget after which its spending is considered purposeful and in accordance with the legal regulations, the mission, and the work plan of the museum.

It is a very common case in museums that program or project budgets are developed within the so-called budget (analytical) spreadsheets. That is a kind of additional financial documentation, which allows the financial team (or office) to standardize the budgets of different museum departments, and consolidate them into a single budget framework. Budget analytical spreadsheets consolidate budget planning with execution. They contain approved appropriations, executed expenditures, and the difference between the planned and realized costs and revenues. In this way, they enable the curator or the head of a museum department to monitor the flow of costs and react in case of deviations from what was planned and expected, or to better manage exhibition planning and budgeting of programs.

Budget execution is a similar procedure in non-profit and state museums. Namely, its main feature is that any budgeted and appropriated cost is considered a designated, regular expenditure. If a difference between the planned (estimated costs of products and services that need to be acquired) and executed budget (actual costs or the amount of money actually paid to acquire products or services) occurs, or it is necessary to reallocate costs from one budget item to another,[3] the approval of the board of directors or another management body is sometimes required. Usually, appropriations in the budget can be changed up to 5–10% of their value without prior approval, while bigger changes require written, explicated approval from the board of directors or the founder. The application of this rule enables monitoring of how well museums use relevant data to forecast their costs and revenues, and how effective their budgeting techniques are.

Types of Budgeting Methods in Museums: Advantages and Disadvantages

Budgeting methods are different approaches used to make a budget. Five basic budgeting methods are the following: traditional institutional budgeting, incremental budgeting, zero-based budgeting, activity-based budgeting, and gender-based budgeting. Note that example budgets included in this chapter are not meant to be realistic in their numbers. Rather, they are created to demonstrate the concepts of budget methods and types.

Traditional Institutional Budgeting

In traditional institutional budgeting, costs are budgeted according to the data from the previous year (see Table 4.1). This method starts from the assumption that costs from the previous period are standard costs that should be used during planning. In the process of planning, this approach tries to answer the question—where do the costs come from? Application of this approach is possible in a stable environment. Traditional institutional budgeting is easy to implement but its main shortcoming is the lack of flexibility due to which the museum team loses motivation to think developmentally. In this way, the budget is most often planned by the higher levels of museum management and passed on to the lower ones. For this reason, many authors call it "centralized bureaucracy" (Rothberg 2011), indicating that it suppresses creativity and innovation in organizations (Bourmistrov and Kaarboe 2013). Aiming to reduce costs, traditional institutional budgeting can encourage dysfunctional

TABLE 4.1 An example of a museum budget prepared with traditional institutional budgeting approach

Item	*Amount in the previous year (base for projection)*	*Estimated in the current year*	*Actual*
Sales revenues	1,000	1,000	1,000
Revenues from donations	1,000	1,000	1,000
Revenues from cooperation with the business sector	1,000	1,000	1,000
Revenue from international foundations and developmental grants			
Other revenues	1,000	1,000	1,000
TOTAL	**4,000**	**4,000**	**4,000**
Salaries and fees (costs relating to permanently employed personnel, fees, and service contracts)	1,000	500	1,000
Administrative costs	1,000	1,000	1,000
Care collection costs			
Museum exhibitions			
Other museum program costs			
Overhead	1,000	500	1,000
Equipment and building costs			
TOTAL	3,000	2,000	3,000
Total balance	**1,000**	**2,000**	**1,000**

behavior in the organization and strengthen vertical organizational control (Neely et al. 2003). Another drawback of such a top-down budgeting process is that all stakeholders below the top do not have the opportunity to participate (CIMA 2005).

Incremental Budgeting

This approach to budgeting appeared during the 1950s and 1960s when Lindblom, Wildavsky, and others defined the theory of budgetary incrementalism (Berry 1990). Primarily, the term was used to describe methods of budgeting public funds and planning state budgets. Incremental budgeting starts from the idea that fixed or variable increases in budget items should be added to the average costs from the previous year (see Table 4.2). Such increases are gradual and small (LeLoup 2002; Andreson and Harbridge

TABLE 4.2 An example of a museum budget prepared with incremental budgeting approach

Item	*Previous year*	*Current year*	*Average (starting base for the planning cost/revenue in the next year)*
Number of units	10	10	10
Sales revenues	1,000	1,100	1,050
Revenues from donations	1,000	1,100	1,050
Revenues from cooperation with the business sector	1,000	1,100	1,050
Revenue from international foundations and developmental grants	1,000	1,000	1,000
Other revenues	0	100	50
TOTAL	**4,000**	**4,300**	**4,150**
Revenue per activity unit (total revenue / number of exhibitions, programs)	**400**	**430**	**415**
Salaries and fees (costs relating to permanently employed personnel, fees, and service contracts)	2,000	1,500	1,750
Administrative costs	100	110	100
Program costs	2,000	2,100	2,050
Overhead	500	500	500
Equipment and building costs	0	0	0
TOTAL	**4,150**	**4,210**	**4,400**
Cost per activity units (total expenses / number of exhibitions, programs)	**415**	**421**	**440**

2010). Weights for budget correction can be different in absolute and relative sizes. In the simplest case, the inflation rate is used for the correction of the costs. In other cases, for example, the average costs realized in the previous year (such as costs for employees, acquisition of a new collection, etc.) can be used for weighing future costs. Certain studies have shown that annual average increases range from 5% to 10% (LeLoup 2002), but this proportion cannot be accepted as a general rule to call a certain gradual increase "incremental" (Andreson and Harbridge 2010). As can be seen in the following example (Table 4.2), in the column "previous year" we used data on costs and revenues for the previous year, and in the next column "current year" those costs and revenues are increased by the inflation rate (10%). The last column "average" shows the average costs and revenues for these two budgeted years, and the data from it will be the basis for budgeting costs and revenues in the following year.

Zero-Based Budgeting

Zero-based budgeting starts from the current year in which costs and revenues are budgeted and treats that year as a starting point (zero base) for cost planning (see Table 4.3). This approach to budgeting appeared at the end of the 1960s in the company Texas Instruments (Grasso 1997). In its essence, arguments about spending resources on specific activities and programs are (re)considered every year. Such a system begins by determining groups of activities/programs by sectors/programs, followed by determining their priorities, assessing their costs and effects, and allocating funds in the budget based on the established priorities. The process has a strategic character because every year it identifies those program activities needed by the organization and therefore represents the best relationship between costs and benefits (Innes 2004; Antić and Novićević 2011). The main advantage of this budgeting method is that it is flexible and allows adjustments both on the sides of costs and available income (Drury 2018). Furthermore, it encourages motivation among employees and managers and helps to identify and remove inefficiencies in the implementation of certain activities (Kaplan and Cooper 1998). As can be seen in the following example (Table 4.3), the column "estimated" shows data on revenues and costs that we estimate for current year, and the column "actual" shows data on revenues and costs incurred in the current year. "Estimated" value will be used as a "zero base" during the year. The last column "Differences" shows us the difference in certain budgetary appropriations and how much funds from one budget item can be diverted to cover the costs of other items.

Activity-Based Budgeting

Activity-based budgeting starts from the assumption that costs are associated with the activities that generate their occurrence. CIMA defines this method

TABLE 4.3 An example of a museum budget prepared with zero-based budgeting approach

Item	*Estimated*	*Actual*	*Differences*
Sales revenues	**1,500**	**1,000**	**500**
Admissions	500	300	200
Trading revenue	100	50	50
Fees for workshops	0	0	0
Capital grants	0	0	0
Investment income	200	100	100
Membership schemes	300	200	100
Conservation services	400	300	100
Training revenue	0	0	0
Revenues from donations	**1,000**	**500**	**500**
Individual donations			
Legal entities donations			
Revenues from cooperation with the business sector			
Corporate donations			
Sponsorship			
Business cooperation and services			
Revenue from international foundations and developmental grants			
Grants			
Donations			
Other contributions			
I Total Income during the period	**2,500**	**1,500**	**1,000**
Administrative costs			
Payroll expenditure	1,000	500	500
Renting cost for buildings			
Renting cost for equipment			
Conservation of artifacts	1,000	1,000	0
Interest payment			
Advertising and public relations			
Supplies			
Care collection costs			
Museum exhibitions	500	0	500
Other program costs			
Current repairs/maintenance			
Security costs			
Printing costs			
Taxes and licenses			
Accounting and legal services			
Insurance			
Travel			
Utilities			
Fees for services			
Subscriptions, member fees			
II Total Expenses during the period	**2,500**	**1,500**	**1,000**
Total balance during the period	**0**	**0**	**0**

TABLE 4.4 An example of a museum budget prepared with activity-based budgeting approach

Item	*Museum activity 1*	*Museum activity 2*	*Total*
Number of activities	10	10	20
Sales revenues	1,000	1,000	2,000
Revenues from donations	1,000	1,000	2,000
Revenues from cooperation with the business sector			
Revenue from international foundations and developmental grants			
TOTAL	**2,000**	**2,000**	**4,000**
Revenue per activity/unit	**200**	**200**	**400**
Salaries and fees (costs relating to permanently employed personnel, fees, and service contracts)	500	500	1,000
Museum exhibition costs	500	500	1,000
Museum collection care costs			
Overhead			
Equipment and building costs			
TOTAL	**1,000**	**1,000**	**2,000**
Cost per activity units	**100**	**100**	**200**

as "budgeting on an activity framework and utilizing cost driver data in the budget setting and variance feedback processes" (CIMA 2005, 3). In this budgeting method, the scope of the program or activity is determined first, and only then the costs that are necessary for their execution (see Table 4.4). The budgeting process itself should provide an answer to the question—which activities generate costs? Unlike previous approaches, this one is much more oriented toward the external environment (Turney 2000)—toward the audience and visitors of the museum. This budgeting technique is most useful to those museums which apply a design thinking approach and aim to understand the needs and aspirations of visitors in order to respond to them (see Nasta and Pirolo 2021). Activity-based budgeting is based on "bottom-up budgeting approach where all budget holders have the opportunity to participate in setting their own budgets" (CIMA 2005, 6). It also enables greater participation and links the costs of museum programs to their results. It is not a rare case that some cultural institutions practice the creation of participatory budgets whereby the audience is invited to vote for programs/activities that will become part of an institution's annual work plan and budget.

Gender-Based Budgeting

Following the increased importance of gender equality that marked the beginning of the 21st century, the so-called gender-based budgeting method,

TABLE 4.5 An example of a museum budget prepared with gender-based budgeting approach

Item	*Projected*	*Actual*	*Allocated by gender*	
			*Female**	*Male**
Sales revenues	1,000	1,000	10	0
Revenues from donations				
Revenues from cooperation with the business sector				
Revenue from international foundations and developmental grants				
Other revenues	1,000	1,000	10	0
TOTAL	**2,000**	**2,000**	**20**	**0**
Salaries and fees (costs relating to permanently employed personnel, fees, and service contracts)	1,000	1,000	50	50
Administrative costs				
Care collection costs				
Museum exhibitions	1,000	1,000	80	20
Other museum program costs				
Overhead				
Equipment and building costs				
TOTAL	**2,000**	**2,000**	**130**	**70**

Note
* Per female/male visitor.

also known as gender-responsive budgeting (GRB), has emerged over the last decade (OECD 2023). The United Nations' 2030 Agenda for Sustainable Development and its goals related to achieving greater gender equality are contributing to the growing popularity of this method. According to GRB, expenditure should be budgeted so that it accounts for different needs from the aspect of gender (see Table 4.5). The goal is to respond to the specific demands of women, men, and their gender-diverse groups (Rownes et al. 2017a). The first step is the assessment of gender needs (*gender need assessment*) based on which budgetary needs become identified and recognized through a participatory process. In countries of the European Union[4] and those that are OECD's members, gender budgeting can be a mandatory requirement of public cultural policies (Mikić 2022) while in some other countries, e.g., Australia it is combined with performance budgeting[5] (Rownes et al. 2017a). In museums, this approach is mainly focused on costs in the budget. It is a useful tool for providing data on how the funds are spent according to the gender component (e.g., costs of museum programs per female/male visitor, museum budget spent on female/male staff …).

Type of Budgets in Museums

Line-Item Museum Budget vs. Program-Based Museum Budget

Line-item budgets and program-based budgets differ in how expenses are grouped and presented in them. Line-item budget is based on the economic classification of costs that groups costs according to their economic character (e.g., salary costs, procurement of goods and services, costs of legal services, transport costs, rental costs, etc.). Such a budget enables tracking of spending according to the budget positions used in accounting and is used mainly for the preparation of final financial statements. Its basic purpose is the control of budget spending.

The program-based budget connects objectives and results with the expenditure of funds. In the museum's program-based budget, activities can be grouped into programs (following the museum's medium-term plans) and project activities and projects (following the museum's short-term plans).[6] Grouping museum activities in this way makes it possible to monitor the performance of various museum departments and their programs. Program-based budgeting is often mandatory in state-funded museums as a part of improving the overall effectiveness of public budgets (Rownes 2017b). The reasons behind this type of budgeting are establishment of accountability, greater transparency of the spending of funds, and gain of an insight into the efficiency of spending and its effects (OECD 2018).

Static Budget vs. Flexible Budget

The difference between static and flexible budget is whether or not the level of income fluctuates during the observed period. In a static budget, cost projections are planned at only one level of income. In that case, a museum plans its annual expenses according to the expected annual income and that forecast remains unchanged in the following year even when the facts (actual costs and income) are different from what was planned. In a flexible budget, expenses are planned at different levels of income. In that case, the costs are usually planned according to more than one income scenario—optimistic one (the highest potential annual income that the museum could have), pessimistic one (the lowest potential annual income) and those in-between. As a result, the museum's management can assess how a museum would function in relation to pessimistic and optimistic forecasts of the inflow of funds. Generally, flexible budget is made at the end of the accounting year while a static budget is made before the accounting year begins (Franklin et al. 2019).

Master, Operating, and Capital Budgets

Regarding the time frame and strategic directions, there are usually three types of a budget: master budget, operating budget, and capital budget. Master budget of a museum shows the entire structure of expenditures and revenues of all organizational units over a period of 3–5 years (see Table 4.6), cash flow (planned outflows and inflows of cash), and financial plan (long-term financial projections and strategy).

Operating budget of a museum contains current expenditures and revenues that will be realized during one fiscal year (see Table 4.7).

Capital budget refers to the planned costs of acquiring property, museum collections/artifacts, equipment, investment in intangible assets (copyrights, software, licenses, etc.) and instruments (i.e., all those assets with a lifetime longer than one year), as well as their investment costs (see Table 4.8).

TABLE 4.6 An example of master budget in a museum

Item	*Total Year 1*	*Total Year 2*
Sales	10,000	10,000
Revenues from donations		
Revenues from cooperation with the business sector		
Revenue from international foundations and developmental grants	800	1,000
Other revenues		
TOTAL	**10,800**	**11,000**
Labor costs	**10,000**	**10,000**
Production costs		
Program costs		
Overhead costs		
Administrative costs		
Equipment and building costs		
TOTAL	**10,000**	**10,000**
Cash inflows	**10,800**	**11,000**
Cash outflows	**10,000**	**10,000**
=Net increase (decrease) in cash flow	**800**	**1,000**

TABLE 4.7 An example of operating budget in a museum

Item	*Total Year 1*		
	Projected	*Actual*	*Remaining*
Sales revenue	10,000	8,000	2,000
Revenues from donations			
Revenues from cooperation with the business sector			
Revenue from international foundations and developmental grants	1,000	0	1,000
Other revenues			
TOTAL	**11,000**	**8,000**	**3,000**
Administrative costs	8,000	5,000	3,000
Renting cost for buildings			
Payroll expenses			
Renting cost for equipment			

(Continued)

TABLE 4.7 (Continued)

Item	*Total Year 1*		
	Projected	*Actual*	*Remaining*
Conservation of artifacts	2,000	1,000	1,000
Interest payment			
Exhibition costs			
Advertising and public relations			
Supplies			
Current repairs/maintenance			
Security costs			
Printing costs			
Taxes and licenses			
Accounting and legal services			
Insurance			
Travel			
Utilities			
Fees for services			
Subscriptions, membership fees			
TOTAL	**10,000**	**6,000**	**4,000**
Cash inflows	**11,000**	**8,000**	
Cash outflows	**10,000**	**6,000**	
=Net increase (decrease) in cash flow	**1,000**	**2,000**	

TABLE 4.8 An example of capital budget in a museum

Item	*Cash inflows*	*Cash outflows*	*Net cash flows*
Investment Year 1	**1,000**	**500**	**500**
Repairs			
Investment in museum collections			
Construction	1,000	500	500
Investment in equipment			
Conservation-restauration works			
Investment in intangible assets			
Investment Year 2	**1,000**	**800**	**200**
Repairs			
Investment in museum collections			
Construction	1,000	800	200
Investment in equipment			
Investment in intangible assets			
Conservation-restauration works			
Investment Year 3			
Repairs			
Investment in equipment			
Drafting project			
Investment in museum collections			
Construction			
Conservation-restauration works			
Investment in intangible assets			

Installations for complex exhibitions and various other constructions that will become an integral part of a museum (e.g., in natural history museums) will also be budgeted in the capital budget (Guthe 1957, 24). From country to country, depending on accounting regulations, capital expenditures are related to acquiring property and equipment of different value. In some countries, equipment that has an acquisition cost of less than $1,000 US and life expectancy of less than one year will not be part of the capital budget (US). In some other countries, (non)capital expenditure is determined by comparing its value with average monthly gross earnings.[7]

Principles of Budgeting Expenses

This part of the chapter will explain the principles of budgeting expenses concerning the Generally Accepted Accounting Principles (GAAP) and the International Financial Reporting Standards (IFRS), clarifying how different museum expenses are treated depending on the standard applied.

At the international level, there are financial reporting standards that enable financial transparency and make financial data comparable. Each serves as a tool for the harmonization of accounting regulations between different countries. The two most known standards are GAAP and IFRS. They regulate the valuation and recognition of certain elements of financing in different organizations.

Generally Accepted Accounting Principles

Developed by the Financial Standards Accounting Board (FSAB) and the Governmental Accounting Standards Board (GASB), Generally Accepted Accounting Principles (GAAP) are most often applied in the financial reporting of companies in the United States but can be applied by other entities as well. GAAP system is based on ten rules (GAAP 2020; FASB) shown in Table 4.9.

The presented rules must be respected (even when they are not binding) especially if the projects are financed with funds or grants of the federal government. This requirement is standardized in the post-award reporting system where the Federal Financial Report (SF-425) must be filled out. This report is used by the recipients of US federal grants for reporting on their grant's financial progress. The system of federal financial reporting includes GAAP's concepts and principles through: budgetary integrity (government funds should be used in accordance with the appropriations defined by laws/regulation/grant letter), operating performance (budget report should assist users in evaluating the costs and the results of a funded project; performance measurement information is adequately presented; transactions are consistent with the purpose of project/program), stewardship (report should assist users in the evaluation of impact of the project/program), system and control

TABLE 4.9 GAAP rules

Rules	*Description*
Principle of regularity	Implies that the organization applies GAAP in its accounting system.
Principle of consistency	Implies that budgeted and disclosed data must be consistent and that accounting records must be clear and comparable in each reporting period.
Principle of sincerity	Implies that financing is presented accurately and correctly.
Principle of permanence	Implies that accounting practices are consistent throughout different reporting periods.
Principle of non-compensation	Implies that all financial aspects are presented fully and that there are no reservations in their disclosure.
Principle of prudence	Implies that all accounting entries must be timely and realistic.
Principle of continuity	Implies that the classifications used in accounting should be continuous and consistent.
Principle of periodicity	Implies that accounting periods are consistent.
Principle of materiality	Implies that assets are valued according to the costs of their acquisition and that information in all financial reports are true.
Principle of utmost good faith	Implies that persons involved in accounting should act with the highest honesty.

(federal financial report should assist users in accounting control and financial management; transactions are recorded with federal accounting standards; assets are properly used).[8]

International Financial Reporting Standards

The International Financial Reporting Standards (IFRS) became international at the beginning of the 1970s when the national associations of accountants formed the International Accounting Standards Committee (IASC). There are about 40 international standards and some of them affect the valuation of costs, their recognition, and disclosure during budgeting and compiling financial reports. The budgeting process is governed by four basic IFRS principles (2022): clarity, relevance, reliability, and comparability which is presented and described in Table 4.10.

Both systems of financial standards are based on the same logic—transparency and a fair presentation of the financial condition. However, their natures differ. GAAP can be considered a soft regulation in the financial field. Its rules are not as binding as those integrated into laws on financial accounting. IFRS can be considered a part of hard financial regulation because the application of its standards is enabled mostly through the laws and by-laws related to financial accounting. In museums, both systems of standards are enabling the correct evaluation of costs and revenues, the presentation of the budget in a credible manner, and the presentation of the financial condition in a transparent way. That is why it is necessary to understand them when creating a budget. Key differences between GAAP and IFRS are presented in Table 4.11.

TABLE 4.10 IFRS main principles

Principle	*Description*
Clarity	Implies that financial and other reports must be clear and understandable to users. Reports should provide a realistic picture of a project or organization. Income and expenses should be presented through specific, clearly explained categories.
Relevance	Implies that budget items must be relevant. For example, revenues and expenses of small value/amount should not be shown individually but within a larger expense category. Each financial report should present the main financial issues of an organization or a project while irrelevant details should not be given the same importance or should be left out.
Reliability	Implies that the values used should be those used during budgeting or financial planning. Here, when valuing revenues and expenses, two additional principles are applied. Revenues are budgeted in their lower value (e.g., if we requested a grant from the Ministry of Culture in the value of 10,000 EUR, but we know that the Ministry usually grants 50% of the requested amount, we will plan that the revenue from the Ministry of Culture will be 5,000 EUR). The opposite rule applies when budgeting expenses—they should always be overestimated, i.e., budgeted at a slightly higher value.
Comparability	Implies that budgeting must be reliable. All financial projections must be based on recorded evidence (i.e., invoices, suppliers' offers, and reports on prices on the market).

TABLE 4.11 Differences between IFRS and GAAP (concept, expenditure, revenues)

	GAAP	*IFRS*
Basic orientation	The system of standards is based on rules	The system of standards is based on principles
Number of principles/ rules	10 general rules of financial reporting	4 general principles for valuation and recognition in financial reports
Application	Instructions, manuals, opinions, and protocols of a relevant association of accountants	40 standards prescribe how certain balance sheet items should be valued, recognized and disclosed
Obligatory character	The rules are voluntary and not legally binding except when legal entities are listed on stock exchange	The standards are accepted and used by a large number of countries, so they may become legally binding
Valorization of inventory costs	(3 methods) First-in, First-out (FIFO) or Last-in, First-out (LIFO) and "net asset value"	(2 methods) First-in, First-out (FIFO) and Weighted Average Cost
Research and Development expenditures	Costs are valued at the time of their occurrence	Costs can span over several years

Classification, Categories, and Types of Expenses in Museums

The subject matter of this section will be discussion concerning the classification and categories of expenses and their purpose.

Classification of costs is an "arrangement of elements of cost into logical groups with respect to their nature, function or use in the business of the entity" (CIMA 2005, 11). The classification of costs and expenses in museums depends on various factors but first of all the criteria we use to classify them. Typical criteria for museum costs classification are the following:

- *Economic classification* of costs shows their economic character and nature (e.g., salary costs, program costs, costs of legal services, administrative costs, etc.).
- *Organizational (functional) classification* of costs is made according to the place of occurrence or a broad division of functions such as administrative department, library, security service, legal service, collections, etc.
- Concerning *the size and time frame* of expenditures: current costs (costs of lower value that are spent in one calendar year), and capital costs (costs of greater value which arise over several years or in phases).
- Concerning *the sources of income* from which they are financed (e.g., costs financed from own sources, costs financed from commercial income, costs financed from designated donations, costs financed from sponsorship, etc.).

It is also important to consider how museums categorize costs and expenses in their coding system in accounting—a list of accounts used in business books based on which booking records are made. Generally, coding system in accounting follows the economic nature of costs and there are three main groups of costs:

- *Material (productive) costs*—all costs associated with the museum's services, programs, and activities.
- *Labor costs*—all costs associated with investing in the intellectual capital of a museum. Those costs include salary expenses (amount paid to employees, social and pension contributions) as well as expenses of staff training and education.
- *Business (non-productive) expenses*—all expenses necessary to run a museum as an organization. They include rent, utilities, communication, office supplies, small-scale repairs, office expenses, taxes, bank charges, and legal expenses.

Depending on the project or program, these costs will be grouped into different categories to make it easier to follow their structure. In practice, some funders limit their giving for administrative costs of certain projects. In that case, during budgeting, such costs should be shown in one group. In some other cases, there are recommendations or custom rules on how to group costs. For example, the American Association of Museums in its guide for small museums and their business operations suggests the following classification of expenses (Guthe 1957):

- *Administrative expenses* (office supplies, telephone and telegraph charges, postage, travel, and membership costs)
- *Building, grounds and equipment maintenance* (insurance, supplies, repairs)
- *Collection care* (insurance and supplies)
- *Exhibits* (construction supplies, insurance, rental fees and transportation charges for exhibitions on loan)
- *Activities* (lectures, concerts, social events, membership programs, catering costs)

Standardized classifications of costs can also appear within the framework of certain donor programs. Very often, international organizations and foundations, by way of their guidelines and application procedures, prescribe cost budgeting methods. These methods have two dimensions: the first structures costs and the way they are planned, and the second limits the amounts that can be planned for certain budget items (e.g., per diems per day, travel costs, maximum consultant costs per day/engagement, administrative costs). Some examples of typical cost groupings in organizations that safeguard cultural heritage and are financed by international donations are (Mikić 2014):

- *Salaries and fees* (costs relating to permanently employed personnel, fees, service contracts, etc.)
- *Program costs* (costs relating to the realization of program activity, as well as those of the promotion of the program, such as brochures, flyers, promotional prints, website, representative photos, conservation of movable goods, etc.)
- *Overhead* (lease, electricity bill, utilities, heating, etc.)
- *Investment costs* (most commonly include construction works, project documentation, infrastructural investments, works on conservation, etc.)
- *Equipment cost* (equipment for performance of activities upon the completion of rehabilitation)

Revenues and Expenses as Two Crucial Aspects of Budgeting

This section of the chapter will examine revenue and expenses as two crucial aspects of budgeting.

Budgeting is a strategic tool that allows museums to monitor and manage their development. Budgeting of revenues and expenses is a critical aspect of this process because museums often operate in conditions where there are not enough funds for the full achievement of their goals. Budgeting, therefore, becomes the main strategic tool for the management of a museum's development and setting its priorities. However, budgeting also shows the museum's policies that are responsive to various circumstances in which the museum operates. Depending on their approach to budgeting and planning of revenues and expenditures, museums can be classified into three models: those with a defensive budgeting policy, those that are proactive in this area, and those with an integrative budgeting policy (Mikić 2017).

Defensive budgetary policy is often based on static budget and depends on a single source of funding. These museums will keep the same revenue structure despite the rise in costs. In such circumstances, museums will rather cancel programs if there are not enough funds for their realization than try to attract new or additional financial resources in order to realize planned program activities. Typical budgetary features of those museums are traditional institutional budgeting and a strong hierarchical structure.

Proactive budgetary policy has the characteristics of a market-oriented and dynamic policy. Such museums are very active in the development of financial resources and/or react to various budget constraints with the optimization of costs. The structure of expenditure and revenue in these museums changes every year. Museums that implement this budgetary policy are interested in reducing their dependence on a single source of financing. They are very active in attracting and increasing different revenue streams (by level of alternative financial resources as well as by number of financiers) or in reducing, optimizing and/or reorganizing the structure of their expenditures.

Integrative budgetary policy means a balanced approach to budgeting. Museums that implement such a policy have clear financial rules for financing programs and their costing. For example, there may be a rule that every dollar from donors must be covered with one dollar from the market income; or that the program's administrative costs cannot exceed 10% of its total cost. In other words, museums with integrative budgetary policy are setting up their budgeting and financing rules to prevent different departments from performing inefficiently. The basis of this budgetary policy is the rule of rational behavior and achieving "the best value for money"—the best combination of costs, program quality, and sustainability that meets the needs of visitors.

Conclusion

Budgeting is an integral part of the process of strategic management and systematic thinking in museums. Our contemporary environment is one of changes and museums must respond with a proactive approach to budgeting and planning of their costs and revenues. It is worth noting that the strategies for achieving financial sustainability in museums 20 years ago were mainly focused on the control of spending and incremental budgeting. Today, museums are required to manage their development through budgeting. In itself, this is not an easy task. The environment in which museums operate is turbulent and the conditions during program implementation may be different from those that existed at the time of budgeting. Budgeting in museums requires management and curators to be able to adapt to the changing business conditions by revising costs and reprogramming some activities. The energy crisis and the increase in general prices of goods and services show that budgeting processes must be agile, responsive to changes, and that budgeting methods must be flexible to allow for an ever-growing diversity of options.

Notes

1 The Eastern Bloc existed during the Cold War (1947–91) as the coalition of communist states and the major opposition to the capitalist Western Bloc. Under the political power of the Soviet Union, several countries in Europe—East Germany, Poland, Czechoslovakia, Hungary, Romania, Bulgaria, Albania (and Yugoslavia until 1948)—belonged to the Eastern Block. Following the ideology of Marxism–Leninism, these countries rejected the characteristics of market economies and their development, including cultural, was fully centralized and managed by the Communist Party. Such an administrative-command system developed its own type of investment planning, financing, and management of the economy, cultural activities, education, and healthcare system.

2 For more, see Mikić (2020).

3 When planned and actual costs are not balanced (e.g., when the planned cost of a budget item is greater than the actual cost, or when some costs were not incurred and therefore fewer funds are needed), it is necessary to optimize the budget by reallocating budgeted funds from one item to another.

4 In 2018, the European Commission suggested that all European Union funds (Cohesion Fund, European Maritime and Fisheries Fund, Internal Security Fund, etc.) and funded projects should apply gender-based budgeting method. For more, see Proposal for a REGULATION OF THE EUROPEAN PARLIAMENT AND OF THE COUNCIL laying down common provisions on the European funds COM/2018/375 final—2018/0196 (COD).

5 Performance budgeting is a budgeting technique that connects the goals of financed activities with the results of their realization. It is result-oriented budgeting. For example, the cost of a certain museum program (budget item) should result in 100 new museum visitors (objective of the program) aged 15–19 (performance indicator).

6 Medium-term plans outline the museum's direction for several years ahead, setting goals that usually take three to five years to complete. Short-term plans, often called action plans, are those covering one year or less (half a year, a month or similar).

7 For example, equipment of small value, up to three average monthly gross earnings, is balanced as an operating cost of the period. *Opinion of the Ministry of Finance of the Republic of Serbia No.* 430-07-55/2005-04 *from October 30, 2005*, Ministry of Finance of the Republic of Serbia, Belgrade.

8 For more details, see FASAB (2017) Federal Financial Reporting https://fasab.gov/wp-content/uploads/2017/09/handbook_sffac_8.pdf (Accessed: 22.08.2022).

References

Andreson, S. and L. Harbridge. 2010. "Incrementalism in Appropriations: Small Aggregation, Big Changes." *Public Administration Review* 70 (3): 464–74.

Antić, Lj. and B. Novićević. 2011. "Budžetiranje na nultoj osnovi i budžetiranje zasnovano na aktivnostima kao alternativni sistemi računovodstvenog planiranja." *Ekonomske teme* XLIX (3): 379–96.

Berry, W. 1990. "The Confusing Case of Budgetary Incrementalism: Too Many Meanings for a Single Concept." *The Journal of Politics* 52 (1): 167–96.

Bourmistrov, A. and K. Kaarbøe. 2013. "The Planning-Regime Concept and Its Application to Three Examples of Organizational Budgeting." In *Managing in Dynamic Business Environments—between Control and Autonomy*, edited by K. Kaarbøe, P. Gooderham, and H. Nørreklit. Cheltenham: Edward Elgar.

CIMA. 2005. *CIMA Official Terminology 2005*. Oxford: CIMA Publishing.

Drury, C. 2018. *Management and Cost Accounting*. Andover: Cengage Learning.

European Commission. 2018. Proposal for a REGULATION OF THE EUROPEAN PARLIAMENT AND OF THE COUNCIL laying down common provisions on the European funds COM/2018/375 final—2018/0196 (COD).

FASAB. 2017. Federal Financial Reporting. https://fasab.gov/wp-content/uploads/2017/09/handbook_sffac_8.pdf (Accessed: 22.08.2022).

Financial Accounting Standard Board. unk. FASB Accounting Standards Codification. https://asc.fasb.org/ IRS. (Accessed: 1.11.2022).

Flesher, D. L. and T. Flesher. 1979. Short History of Budgeting. Woman C.P.A.: Vol. 41: Iss. 1, Article 4. Available at: https://egrove.olemiss.edu/wcpa/vol41/iss1/4 (Accessed: 1.10.2022).

Flesher, T. and D. Flesher. 1985. "James O. McKinsey." *The Accounting Historians Journal* 12 (2): 117–28.

Franklin, M., P. Graybeal, and D. Cooper. 2019. *Principles of Accounting*, Volume 2. Managerial Accounting. OpenStax, Rice University.

General Accepted Accounting Principles (GAAP). 2020. https://www.ojp.gov/sites/g/files/xyckuh241/files/media/document/GAAP_Guide_Sheet_508.pdf (Accessed: 1.11.2022).

Grasso, L. 1997. "Is It Time to Revisit Zero-Base Budgeting?" *Journal of Cost Management* 11 (2): 22–9.

Guthe, C. 1957. *A Guide to the Management of Small Museums*. The American Association of Museums.

Innes, J. 2004. *Handbook of Management Accounting*. Oxford: CIMA Publishing.

International Financial Reporting Standards. 2022. https://www.ifrs.org/supporting-implementation/supporting-materials-by-ifrs-standards/ (Accessed: 1.11.2022).

Kaplan, R. and R. Cooper. 1998. *Cost and Effect: Using Integrated Cost Systems to Drive Profitability and Performance*. Boston: Harvard Business School Press.

Korn, R. 2017. Intentional Practice. A Way of Thinking, A Way of Working. In Jung, Y. and Roswon, L. A. (eds). *System Thinking in Museums: Theory and Practice*. London: Rowman & Littlefield. 49–58.

LeLoup, L. 2002. "Budget Theory for a New Century." In *Budget Theory in the Public Sector*, edited by A. Kahn and B. Hildreth. London: Quorum Books.

Lewis, Ch. and T. Short. 1879. *A Latin Dictionary*. Oxford: Clarendon Press. Available at: http://www.perseus.tufts.edu/hopper/text?doc=Perseus:text:1999.04.0059:entry=bulga (Accessed: 1.10.2022).

McKinsey, J. O. 1922. *Budgetary Control*. New York: The Ronald Press Company.

Mikić, H. 2014. *Biznis plan za rehabilitaciju kulturnih dobara*. Beograd: Republički zavod za zaštitu spomenika kulture.

Mikić, H. 2017. *Handbook for Basics of Financial Analysis in Cultural Sector (teaching material)*. Belgrade: University of Arts, UNESCO Chair for cultural management and intercultural mediations in Balkans.

Mikić, H. 2020. "Gender (In)Equality in the Creative Industries: Insights from Serbia." In *Global Perspectives on Women's Leadership and Gender (In)Equality*, edited by D. Kurochkin, E. Shabliy, and G. Y. A. Ayee, 93–115. Basingstoke: Palgrave Macmillan.
Mikić, H. 2022. "Economic Instruments and Measures of Cultural Policy and Fair Practice: Case of Female Artists and Creative Entrepreneurs in Serbia." In *Gender Equity: Global Policies and Perspectives on Advancing Social Justice*, edited by E. Shabliy, K. Engerman, and D. Kurochkin, 39–57. London: Rowman & Littlefield.
Nasta, L. and L. Pirolo. 2021. "A Design Thinking Approach for Museum Institutions." In *Creativity: A Force to Innovation*, edited by J. Pooja. London: IntechOpen.
Neely, A., M. Bourne, and C. Adams. 2003. "Better Budgeting or Beyond Budgeting?" *Measuring Business Excellence* 7 (3): 22–8.
OECD. 2018. *OECD Best Practices for Performance Budgeting*. GOV/PGC/SBO(2018) 7. Geneva: OECD.
OECD. 2023. *Gender Budgeting in OECD Countries 2023*. Paris: OECD Publishing.
Richards, G. 2016. "The Challenge of Creative Tourism." *Ethnologies* 38 (1–2): 31–45.
Rothberg, A. 2011. Traditional Budgeting vs. Beyond Budgeting. https://www.cfoedge.com/blog/financial-planning/traditional-budgeting-vs-beyond-budgeting-three-core-differences/ (Accessed: 1.11.2022).
Rownes, R. et al. 2017a. *Gender Budgeting in OECD countries*. Geneva: OECD.
Rownes, R. et al. 2017b. *Budgeting and Performance in the European Union: A Review by the OECD in the Context of EU Budget Focused on Results*. Geneva: OECD.
Rubin, I. 1990. "Budget Theory and Budget Practice: How Good the Fit?" *Public Administration Review* 50 (2): 179–89.
Smithsonian Institution. 2002. *The Cost and Funding of Exhibitions*. Washington: Office of Policy and Analysis.
Turney, P. 2000. "The State of 21st Century Cost Management." *Journal of Cost Management* (5): 45–7.

5

MEASURING EARNED REVENUE PERFORMANCE OF MUSEUM MARKETING

Hannah Grannemann

Introduction

Imagine you are the president, chief executive officer, director of marketing, member of the board's finance or marketing committees, or equivalent position at a museum. How can a museum's marketing efforts be evaluated from a financial standpoint? Measuring marketing effectiveness can be a controversial activity at a nonprofit museum—or at least a delicate topic because the marketing function in a museum is asked to balance two goals.

On the one hand, a primary goal of the marketing department is to bring in revenue to the museum. Specifically, the marketing department is responsible for earned revenue, or revenue generated by the activities of the museum. Admission is the most prominent of the revenue streams that marketing is responsible for. The department may also be responsible for marketing educational services and community-facing events. Marketing is not responsible for contributed income, but typically collaborates closely with the fundraising department on its efforts that reach a broader public, especially in designing digital and print materials for fundraising and media relations.

On the other hand, the marketing department is responsible for bringing in the public to the museum, which is a mission function (Mclean 1997). As nonprofit organizations founded to serve public rather than private interests, a museum likely has an implicit or explicit mandate to serve as wide and diverse a public as possible. Metrics that only measure a marketing department by the revenue it brings in (or net revenue after marketing expenses) do not capture the full scope of the marketing department's goals.

Knowing the functions and purposes of a department on this fundamental level of revenue or cost is an essential place to begin when evaluating the

DOI: 10.4324/9781003308003-7

financial performance of that department. In this chapter, I will discuss how to select appropriate measurements for evaluating the financial performance of museum marketing functions, offer specific measurements for evaluating short and long-term performance of a marketing function, and discuss various other considerations for ensuring that measurements are considered in the right context for museums.

Choosing Measurements

A car dashboard is where a driver gets vital information: speed, RPMs, check engine lights, and overheating signals. What should be on the dashboard for a museum marketing department? Any financial measurement needs to be useful and connected to the mission, strategy, and current circumstances of the museum. It is possible to measure many aspects of marketing, but not all measurements are useful. Here are some questions to ask when considering metrics and measurements for the museum marketing function that will better ensure that data collection and analysis is focused and useful.

How will the information and data be gathered? Operationally, a museum needs a way to collect and organize data, a method by which decisions are made, a method for planning, and a method for adjusting plans. Kotler et al. (2008) recommend a system that "may vary in sophistication" based on the abilities and needs of the museum, but should have four elements: internal reporting, market research, methods for differentiating external influences on results from results produced by the museum's marketing efforts, and models and other ways of analyzing data.

How will this information be used? Will it help make decisions? Who will be using it? What is their level of familiarity with understanding metrics related to museum financials? For example, is it a metric needed for reporting to funders or that our board wants to track?

How long will this information be used? Is this a measurement the museum wants to commit to tracking for the foreseeable future, or just this one time? If the former, what systems are in place to gather the information accurately and sustainably?

Is this a "key performance indicator" or a more minor data point? Not all information is equally important or will be used in the same way.

Looking at the entirety of the metrics, **is there an over- or under-emphasis on a certain goal**? For example, it would be easy for financial metrics to over-emphasize efficiency, but impact of the mission is the ultimate goal of the organization. Stepping back and reviewing the entire set of metrics is an important check point to ensuring they are supporting the mission.

Approaches to Marketing Measurements

Here is a simple but powerful framework for financial (or any kind of data) analysis. When analyzing numbers, consider the numbers from three different angles: absolute, scale, and trends. Analyzing financial data in these three ways goes a long way to painting a complete picture of a data set and the results can serve different purposes.

Absolute: These measurements are usually expressed in numbers and denominations of money. Absolute numbers are important because they describe the most tangible resources and performance. For example, when deciding on a staffing budget for a specific year, projections for absolute numbers for admissions revenue will matter more than Scale or Trends measurements because it will be one part of the total available revenue to pay staff.

Scale: These measurements are usually expressed with relational numbers, such as percentages and ratios. Context is important for scale numbers. For example, a museum exhibition reaches 3,000 visitors. For a museum that typically attracts 1 million visitors each year, 3,000 visitors is a small turnout. But for a museum that typically has 25,000 visitors in a year, 3,000 visitors for one exhibition is highly significant. Same number, different scale.

Trends: Trends track change over time. For example, one year of declining rates of visitation to exhibitions from a museum collection might not cause alarm but beginning in the second year and certainly into the third year of decline, the staff and board would begin to be concerned, even if the number of visitors might be relatively small in terms of absolute numbers or even scale.

Museums may periodically undertake a deeper analysis of their marketing effectiveness in **a marketing audit**, a systematic and comprehensive analysis (Kotler et al. 2008). A deeper examination of marketing analytics may happen during a strategic planning process as well.

Some Additional Considerations

Beware Averages

Averages are a measurement that could be considered in the absolute or scale category and can be useful to look at how they trend over time. For example, average paid admission price can be a useful measure to compare between exhibitions or over time. But be careful of relying too heavily on averages. Averages can betray the amount of change that's occurring. For example, if three exhibitions have attendance of 30,000, 100,000, and 200,000, the average is 110,000 visitors. Hidden in the average is that the range of attendance was quite big. The average attendance measurement does not "tell the story" of the visitation rates of the museum across those three exhibitions.

Bias toward Trackable Measurements

A challenge in marketing is being able to attribute results to actions taken by the organization. Knowing which tactics are working is difficult. Did someone attend because they saw an advertisement on a news website they were visiting, or because they drive past a billboard on their way to work every day, or because they saw an ad on Instagram? Or did they visit because they were reached with all three of those tactics, plus a friend invited them? It can be hard to tell—and it is often unknowable.

The purchasing path is a useful concept for understanding the journey of a visitor from before they attend to the time of their visit (see Figure 5.1). Visitors progress through a process of becoming aware of the museum as being interesting or useful to them, they research the options for attending or participating (even so briefly just to look up location, hours, and admission prices), they consider alternative options for their needs and interests, they decide to attend, and follow through on attending.

Tactics that support awareness, the beginning of the purchasing path, are often expensive—and untrackable. These are tactics that are considered **brand marketing**. Their purpose is to increase awareness of the museum. Tactics that are at the end of the purchasing path are often less expensive—and trackable. These are tactics like digital display advertising, search ads, and social media advertising. These are called **direct marketing**. When set up properly with tracking, the digital advertising can be measured to some extent because when a visitor clicks on an ad then makes a purchase, the fact that they navigated from the ad to purchasing can be known by the museum. There are even ways that it can be tracked from when a person interacted with an ad to purchasing on another day. In a more analog form, effectiveness of ads or promotions can be tracked when a purchasing code is offered for a benefit (usually a discount), allowing the museum to know where the visitor saw the ad.

Therefore, in the desire to be able to demonstrate the effectiveness of marketing and use scarce marketing dollars wisely, cultural organizations

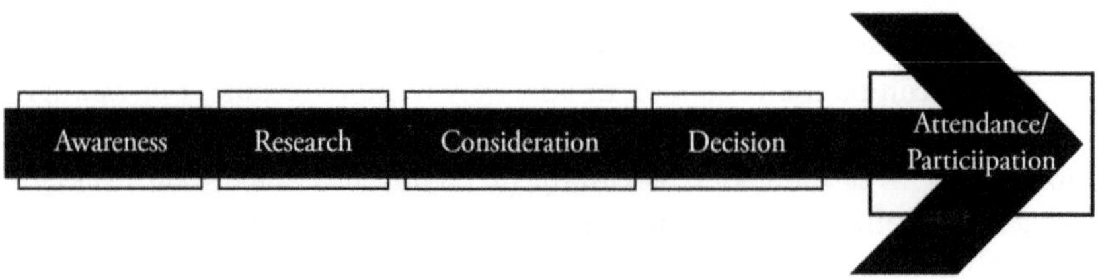

FIGURE 5.1 Diagram of a visitor's purchasing path.

often over emphasize direct marketing techniques because it is possible to directly track sales to marketing efforts. However, this bias leads to less effective marketing overall because the persuasive techniques of direct marketing are most effective when the potential visitors are already familiar with the organization through brand marketing (Rhine and Pension 2022).

Another weakness negatively impacting the accuracy of marketing measurements is **data collection**. As with deciding on marketing measurements, deciding which data to collect, then collecting it consistently and accurately is challenging. Not doing this well can result in missing, incomplete, or inaccurate data. For example, it is common that many visitors "walk up" to the museum without any kind of prior reservation. At the visitor services desk, visitors who are not members pay their admission fee and walk in. Even though a museum has a customer relationship management (CRM) system that is a database for collecting information about customers, their spending, and donations to the museum, this entrance process system allows thousands of people to enter the museum without giving any kind of information that would allow the museum to know anything about them and, more importantly, be able to get in touch with them for marketing purposes so they might be inspired or enticed to visit again. Some museums ask visitors for their ZIP code as a compromise between being able to process many transactions quickly and get visitors into the museum faster and capturing data that could tell the museum where the visitor is coming from. Worse (from a data collection standpoint) are museums with free admission where visitors do not have to stop at the entrance.

Why is this a problem? Because the marketing cost of acquiring a new visitor is higher than the cost of inspiring or enticing a person who has previously visited to return for another visit. Therefore, this data collection gap increases overall marketing costs and inefficiency because the museum does not have the data needed (name, contact information, purchase history) to use effective and efficient marketing tactics like email marketing, direct mail, and digital ad retargeting. I recently visited an art museum in my home state of North Carolina for the first time. I paid my admission fee with a credit card and entered the museum. No one asked me for my name, mailing address, email address, or even a ZIP code. They have no idea who I am. The museum has no way to reach me directly with its marketing efforts. It is dependent on me taking actions to stay aware of its exhibitions and events and only my own whims of when I might return; the museum has no ability to influence my decision making directly.

Challenges of a Changing Product

A challenge of museums and other art forms in measuring marketing impact is that the product itself changes. A business that sells the same products year after year can have more confidence in attributing reasons for changes in sales, whether the change is due to the company's actions, external circumstances, or a change of some kind in the consumer. Museums are offering different exhibitions every few months, and each one is different, sometimes drastically different. Was it the marketing tactic or the attractiveness of the exhibition that brought a customer in? It can be difficult to tell. A museum marketing department cannot be entirely held responsible for attendance and revenue goals. Engaging exhibitions and programming are the main factors in the interest of the public. Even the best marketing relies on potential visitors having interest in the offerings.

Efficiency

Using financial resources efficiently is important for any business, but it carries extra importance for nonprofits because using resources efficiently is an important component of trust among the public and donors (Burt 2014). However, focusing too much on efficiency can have deleterious impacts on marketing. A bigger risk than inefficiency is under-resourcing marketing, which we will discuss later in the chapter.

One negative impact is related to the above discussion on the bias toward measurable marketing. Though branding marketing impacts the effectiveness of direct marketing, branding marketing is less measurable and can appear less efficient. Another reason to avoid overvaluing efficiency in museum marketing is that museums are mission-oriented organizations, not businesses with a financial model built on low costs. Spending on marketing above what is correspondingly earned in revenue is needed to fulfill that mission, especially in reaching visitors with lower incomes and less education who report price as a barrier to arts participation and yet are still interested in the arts (Blume-Kouhout et al. 2015; Olivares and Piatak 2022). Finally, using measurements such as marketing efficiency can also trigger short-term thinking. A common measurement of a museum's effectiveness with its marketing is its marketing efficiency.

Generally, having a high marketing efficiency is seen as desirable. Spending less to get more is seen as efficient and a marker of a skilled staff. However, if there is too much focus on efficiency, a disincentive for experimentation to try new marketing tactics or a reluctance to spend money to develop a new group of visitors through sustained marketing efforts that do not "pay off" in the short term can easily creep into the culture of the museum. This short-term focus hurts the organization in the long run, and the museum can be caught on its heels when marketing efforts lose their effectiveness, but the organization's staff has not built up knowledge of different tactics through experimentation.

Measurements of Earned Revenue

To illustrate how measurements can be used to evaluate marketing, I will describe examples of a few metrics that examine the relationship of attendance and revenue through an evolution from short-term time horizon to long-term, using the framework of absolute, scale, and trends metrics. I am using only the word "exhibition" in this table, though these metrics can also be used for other projects, events, or initiatives that take place within one fiscal year.

Short-Term Performance Measurements

Short-term performance is generally defined as financial performance within the fiscal year. This time period is likely the measurement that museum directors, department heads, directors of finance, and board members will pay most attention to day-to-day. That is where the "rubber meets the road" because this annual performance is the primary financial data reported to funders and goes on documents like the informational tax return Form 990s that are used in the United States. Short-term performance on specific exhibitions, programs, or initiatives will be important, as will overall results for the year. Here are some examples of key metrics for short-term performance (see Table 5.1).

Long-Term Performance Measurements

The financial performance of the marketing function of a museum can be measured for the long term, where "long term" refers to a period longer than

TABLE 5.1 Metrics that measure short-term marketing performance

Name of metric	*Type of metric*	*Formula/method*	*Interpretation*
Attendees in each price point	Absolute	Count the number of attendees in each price type for each exhibition. Visualizations like histograms and pie charts can be helpful for interpretation	Shows use rates of different price points which can inform future pricing decisions and impact of marketing to specific groups.[1]
Percentage of discounted admissions	Scale	Revenue from discounted admissions ÷ Total revenue from the exhibition	Shows relative impact of discounted tickets on the revenue of an exhibition.
Average income per visitor for exhibitions in a year	Trend	Calculate for each exhibition: (Admissions revenue + ancillary revenue) ÷ Number of visitors	Show the relative per capita revenue for each exhibition to the total earned revenue for a year.

one fiscal year. The focus of analyzing marketing performance over long time periods is on trends. At least three years of data is best when looking at trends to have more confidence that a trend is a trend and not an anomaly. Here are ways to analyze the three short-term metrics described above in a long-term context. Therefore, we will look at measurements of absolute and scale, but as trends across years:

Distribution of price points (Absolute metric)
Formula/method: Count the number of attendees using each price type in each year of analysis.

Trend interpretation: Represent in a table, adding year-to-year percentage of change or change across the entire time period. Including easy-to-read graphics such as up or down arrows to indicate increases or decreases is helpful, as are visualizations that denote time such as line graphs. To facilitate analysis and decision making, carefully consider how many price points to analyze since too much data can be overwhelming; perhaps only the top five price points need deep scrutiny.

Percentage of discounted admissions (Scale metric)
Formula/method: Calculate the percentage of discounted admissions for each year as described above in short-term measurements. In addition, combine data across the years to be analyzed to get a larger set of data to consider: (Number of discounted admissions in Year 1 + Year 2 + Year 3) ÷ (Total admissions in Year 1 + Year 2 + Year 3) x 100% = Three-year percentage of discounted admissions.

Trend interpretation: Understanding the percentage of visitors that use discounts can inform decisions about revenue goals, price points, and reliance on admission income for budgeting and planning purposes. Analyze the trend over multiple years and in the analysis period, as illustrated in Table 5.2. A trend of increasing or decreasing numbers of visitors using discounts is not positive or negative on its own; interpreting the data must be done in the broader context of the museum's goals (see Table 5.2).

Average income per visitor (Trend metric)
Formula/method: Calculate the average amount that a visitor paid for admissions in each year of analysis as described in the short-term measurements above. Repeat for the average amount of ancillary spending such as parking, food, and gift shop purchases.

TABLE 5.2 Sample calculation of trend in discount ticket usage

Percentage of discounted admissions				
Year 1	*Year 2*	*Year 3*	*3-year total discount admissions*	*Trend*
45%	52%	56%	51%	Increasing ↑

TABLE 5.3 Sample calculation of trend in visitor spending

	Year 1	*Year 2*	*Year 3*	*3-year trend*
Average paid admissions purchase	\$14.63	\$16.24	\$18.05	Increasing ↑
Average ancillary spending per visit	\$7.02	\$6.55	\$6.05	Decreasing ↓
Total average spending per visitor	\$21.65	\$22.79	\$24.10	Increasing ↑

Trend interpretation: Examining visitor spending in a way that illustrates separate trends in admissions and ancillary spending offers a comprehensive picture of the revenue impact of the average visitor. It can also reveal a relationship or correlation between these two revenue streams (see Table 5.3).

In this example, ancillary spending decreases as average admissions increases. If the museum increased prices in Year 2 and 3, they might investigate further to see if the increase in admissions price had a dampening effect on ancillary spending by visitors.

Lifetime Value of a Visitor

A tool for measuring long-term performance of marketing is the lifetime value of a visitor. Lifetime value is a projection of the net revenue that a visitor is expected to bring to an organization or a business over the total time expected that they will continue to be connected to the museum (Ryals 2012). The purpose of this calculation is to understand concretely the net revenue different types of visitors bring to the museum. Marketing staff can then make decisions about marketing spending on different segments of current and potential visitors. For example, here are two different scenarios for customers (see Table 5.4).

Visitor #1 Lifetime value calculation:

2 visits × \$20 × 10 years = \$400 revenue
\$20 acquisition cost + \$3 retention cost × 9 years = \$47 expenses
Lifetime value = \$400 − \$47 = \$353

TABLE 5.4 Examples of visitor lifetime value

	# Years anticipated visitation	*Admission paid per year*	*Contributed revenue*	*Acquisition cost (marketing expense)*	*Retention cost (marketing expense after first year)*
Visitor #1	10	2 visits × \$20 per visit	\$0	\$20	\$3
Visitor #2	5	2 visits × \$20 in the first year only	\$100 membership in years 2–5	\$20, plus \$3 membership acquisition cost	\$3

Visitor #2 Lifetime value calculation

(2 visits × \$20) + (\$100 × 4 years) = \$440
(\$20 + 3) acquisition costs + (\$3 retention cost × 4 years) = \$35 expenses
Lifetime value = \$440 − \$35 = \$405

The data used for these calculations come from actual revenue of a typical visitor from a segment. A segment is a group of visitors with a distinctive buying behavior pattern. Relevant data needed is the typical length of time that a visitor will be engaged with the museum, the spending of a typical visitor in the segment, and the expenses that can be directly attributed to attracting a person for that segment. In this example, Visitor #1 is a steady visitor who comes to the museum twice a year and pays the admission fee. Visitor #2 is a visitor who upgrades to a membership after coming twice and seeing the value in having a membership that gives unlimited access.

With this information, marketing staff can make informed decisions about which segments to pursue and how much to spend on marketing to that segment. The net revenue that a visitor brings to the museum is not the only value that a visitor brings. Even if a visitor lifetime value calculation results in a low or even negative number, each individual visitor matters and should be valued as such.

Customizing

Museums operating in different circumstances will have different emphases for their measurements. For museums that rely more on one-time visitors, such as tourists, then measuring spending per visit will be an important consideration because they are unlikely to return. A museum that caters more to locals will be more likely to emphasize conversion from single admission to memberships and donors because that will deepen the visitor's relationship with the organization, maximize lifetime value, and less measurable benefits like spreading awareness.

Reluctance to Spend Money on Marketing

A general reluctance for nonprofits to spend money on infrastructure and revenue generation can undercut their ability to be effective in delivering on their mission (Gregory and Howard 2009). Many stakeholders such as donors hold deep-seated beliefs that nonprofits should spend as little money as possible on anything that is considered "overhead" and not directly related to delivering the mission (Gneezy et al. 2014; Garven et al. 2016). In the case of museums, collections, exhibitions, and other public programming would be seen as mission critical activities. Marketing is seen as an "overhead" expense, even though marketing activity drives attendance to museums to fulfill the public-oriented portion of their mission. Under-resourcing marketing efforts has several specific negative impacts on the ability of a museum to further its mission.

A reluctance to spend money on marketing often results in neglecting to develop new segments of visitors. This leaves the museum vulnerable when another group's attendance rate or spending begins to decline. Further, it results in a museum that does not meet its potential in its reach across its community. A museum that serves only a small portion of its community risks losing its credibility as a museum serving the general public (Levitt 2015; Simon 2016). Both of these situations were common in the post-COVID lockdown period when museum attendance by formerly frequent museum visitors changed and fewer attended (American Alliance of Museums 2023). Also, beginning in 2020, museums were under increased pressure to ensure that museums were welcoming and relevant to all racial groups to make meaningful progress on being relevant to increasingly diverse communities (Frost 2021; Olivares and Piatak 2022; Chevalier et al. 2023). Facing these circumstances, many museums wished that they had spent more time and money on developing a more diverse visitor base for their museum, as cultivating new visitors is often a lengthy process of learning, experimentation, and trust-building.

A desire for efficiency drives this avoidance of spending on cultivating new visitors. Costs will be higher to attract less likely groups, as discussed above. The effort may not be "efficient," but it is still money well spent because serving a broad community is part of the museum's mission and because new visitors will replace the revenue and attendance volume of visitors that stop attending. Under-resourcing marketing can lead to a self-fulfilling defeat. For example, if a museum plans an exhibit and anticipates a small audience and a correspondingly small, targeted marketing budget, they can play right into their low expectations and miss out on reaching visitors that might have been interested.

Conclusion

Financial management of nonprofit organizations often focuses on mitigating risk and ensuring accountability. The financial performance of the marketing function for a museum is different. The marketing function at a museum is at the center of the mission and the financial performance of the institution. This dual purpose can be overlooked if marketing is seen as separate from—or worse, antithetical to—the mission and purpose of the museum. Museums typically have three prongs to their mission: collection/preservation, education, and public access. The professional staff, boards, and volunteers at museums take their responsibility to all parts of the mission seriously: to be an institution with a mandate for a broader public engagement with the objects held by the museum and the related ways that those objects have meaning in contemporary society. This means that marketing is an essential function and part of the education and public engagement process.

Looking at the marketing function in a museum through a financial lens is a valuable exercise and is an important part of the responsibility of the stewards of the organization. However, maximum efficiency of spending to increase revenue is not the leading goal of marketing. The goal of marketing is to meet the earned revenue needs of a museum at the same time it meets its community impact goals.

Note

1 Many price points are related to a visitor's identity and can indicate how many people came with that identity. For example, students, senior citizens, local residents/non-residents, individuals with low income. By analyzing marketing spending and revenue of each of these price points, a museum could better understand their costs related to reaching those groups.

References

American Alliance of Museums. 2023. "National Snapshot of United States Museums 2023." American Alliance of Museums. https://www.aam-us.org/wp-content/uploads/2023/06/SnapshotReport_v3.pdf.

Blume-Kouhout, Margaret E., Sarah R. Leonard, Jennifer Novak-Leonard, and National Endowment for the Arts. 2015. "When Going Gets Tough: Barriers and Motivations Affecting Arts Attendance." 59. NEA Research Report. Washington, DC: National Endowment for the Arts. https://www.arts.gov/sites/default/files/when-going-gets-tough-revised2.pdf.

Burt, Christopher D. B. 2014. "Improving Charity Efficiency and Accountability in Order to Develop a Foundation to Build Transactional Trust." In *Managing the Public's Trust in Non-Profit Organizations,* edited by Christopher D. B. Burt, 25–31. SpringerBriefs in Psychology. New York, NY: Springer. 10.1007/978-1-4939-0560-7_3.

Chevalier, Juline A., Gretchen M. Jennings, and Sara A. Phalen. 2023. "Nothing Can Be Changed Until It Is Faced: Museum Solidarity Statements as Reflections of Understanding Systemic Racism." *Curator: The Museum Journal* 66 (2): 257–75. 10.1111/cura.12544.

Frost, Stuart. 2021. "Pandemic, Protests and Building Back: 20 Months at the British Museum." *Museum International* 73 (3–4): 70–83. 10.1080/13500775.2021.2016277.

Garven, Sarah A., Mary Ann Hofmann, and Dwayne N. McSwain. 2016. "Playing the Numbers Game." *Nonprofit Management and Leadership* 26 (4): 401–16. 10.1002/nml.21201.

Gneezy, Uri, Elizabeth A. Keenan, and Ayelet Gneezy. 2014. "Avoiding Overhead Aversion in Charity." *Science* 346 (6209): 632–5. 10.1126/science.1253932.

Gregory, Ann Goggins and Don Howard. 2009. "The Nonprofit Starvation Cycle." *Stanford Social Innovation Review*, Fall 2009.

Kotler, Neil G., Philip Kotler, and Wendy I. Kotler. 2008. *Museum Marketing and Strategy: Designing Missions, Building Audiences, Generating Revenue and Resources.* 2nd ed. San Francisco: Jossey-Bass. http://catdir.loc.gov/catdir/enhancements/fy0829/2008014814-t.html.

Levitt, Peggy. 2015. "Museums Must Attract Diverse Visitors or Risk Irrelevance." *The Atlantic*, November 9, 2015.

Mclean, Fiona. 1997. *Marketing the Museum*. London: Taylor & Francis Group. 10.4324/9780203033661.

Olivares, Alexandra and Jaclyn Piatak. 2022. "Exhibiting Inclusion: An Examination of Race, Ethnicity, and Museum Participation." *VOLUNTAS: International Journal of Voluntary and Nonprofit Organizations* 33 (1): 121–33. 10.1007/s11266-021-00322-0.

Rhine, Anthony and Jay Pension. 2022. *How to Market the Arts: A Practical Approach for the 21st Century*. 1 online resource (viii, 269 pages): illustrations vols. New York, NY: Oxford University Press. 10.1093/oso/9780197556078.001.0001.

Ryals, Lynette. 2012. "Customer Lifetime Value." In *Managing Customers Profitably*, 83–102. Chichester, England: John Wiley & Sons, Ltd. 10.1002/9781119208846.ch5.

Simon, Nina. 2016. *The Art of Relevance*. Santa Cruz, CA: Museum 2.0.

6

PRICING FOR ADMISSION AND OTHER PROGRAMS

Rosie Siemer

Museums have a fundamental role in connecting us to the cultural, artistic, historical, natural, and scientific heritage of humanity and our world. In recent years, myriad external forces have compelled museums to reassess how their pricing strategy supports their institution's mission, values, and objectives. As museums compete for share of wallet against a growing range of leisure and educational options, they must reevaluate their approach to pricing to demonstrate value and develop more holistic revenue strategies.

Examining several models and data-driven methodologies for evaluating the central aspects of pricing strategy, this chapter provides insight into various approaches in strategic pricing and revenue optimization, including measuring perceived value, assessing willingness to pay (WTP), utilizing customer segmentation strategies, and the effect of price elasticity on sales and revenue.

Approaches to Price Setting

Price is a critical determinant of profitability and accessibility. Effective pricing requires a thoughtful approach, yet pricing strategies in museums are often hastily devised, arbitrarily implemented, or worse, entirely unmanaged. When developing a pricing strategy, museums must consider cost, competition, perceived value, and customer segmentation. Four primary methods for price setting include the following:

- **Cost-Plus Pricing** calculates all costs, fixed and variable, incurred in producing the product or service and adds a percentage surcharge to arrive at the price. The simplicity of cost-plus pricing makes it a popular

DOI: 10.4324/9781003308003-8

approach (Dholakia 2018). However, cost-plus pricing is entirely inward focused, ignoring both WTP and the competitive market. Furthermore, costs are often subjective, inaccurate, and difficult to quantify. As these challenges lead to suboptimal pricing, costs alone should not determine prices.

- **Market-Based (or Competition) Pricing** is an approach employed by many museums in which the price for various products is determined based on a review of competitors' prices. The primary drawback to this method is that it does not allow a museum to capitalize on the differential perceptions that audiences may hold comparative to other cultural, leisure, and educational options within its market. This can lead to an undervaluing of a museum's offering and risks leaving money on the table (Schindler 2012, 29). Further, pricing admission drastically higher or lower than the museum's competitors within its market may have a negative impact on attendance or admissions revenue.
- **Value-Based Pricing** uses customers' perceived value as the key driver of price setting. While this method is superior to cost-plus and market-based pricing, few organizations have adopted it (Liozu et al. 2015, 412). The risk in applying a value-based pricing approach is that there can be a significant difference between perceived value and what customers are actually willing to pay.
- **Dynamic (or Variable) Pricing** utilizes algorithms, software, and a defined set of variables to determine optimal prices and adjust pricing on a near real-time basis (Byrnes 2022, 403). Dynamic pricing can serve many objectives, including increasing revenue, producing volume, managing capacity, and improving accessibility (Merritt 2020). As dynamic pricing becomes more commonplace in museums, there needs to be greater discourse about the impact of such methods to ensure that pricing is fair and equitable for all. Implementing effective dynamic pricing in museums requires more than a strategy that simply maximizes revenue at the expense of other objectives such as accessibility and customer loyalty.

In almost every case, a blend of cost-plus, market-based, and value-based methods is ideal. This approach ensures that costs, competition, and customer value are all part of the price setting equation. Likewise, dynamic pricing delivers the best target range of prices when implemented with a combination of the other three methods.

Museum Pricing Models

The business model of a typical museum includes admissions, programs, special exhibitions, and membership, among other revenue sources. Operating independently and working together, the pricing models of these functions must be aligned to optimize revenue operations.

While the majority of the world's museums are funded by governments, universities, or other public institutions, the number of private and independent nonprofit museums is growing rapidly (Lord 2012). Often, museums that do not charge an admission fee receive significant public funding or have large endowments. For example, museums funded directly by the UK government offer free admission (Museums Association n.d.). Similarly, the majority of museums in China have a mandated free admission policy (Zhang and Courty 2021). Most university and local authority museums globally also operate with free admission. In contrast, most museums in the United States largely depend on grants, private donations, and earned income to fund their operations (Sotheby's Institute of Art n.d.). Therefore, a museum's governance structure and funding mix are critical factors in its autonomy to set prices as well as how the organization defines its revenue strategy.

Admissions

Admission fees in museums are the subject of much debate. While there is valid concern that paid admission may reduce public grants, private donations, or income from other revenue areas, the fear that admission fees will make museums less accessible is unfounded (Maddison 2004, 89). First, studies have concluded that demand for museums is price inelastic (Luksetich 1997, 1553). Second, data shows that free admission museums generally attract visitors with a similar household income as paid admission museums (Dilenschneider 2019b). Thus, other barriers such as lack of time, transportation, or general disinterest are far more important factors than admission price in the decision to visit a museum (Kirchberg 1998, 1).

While both free and paid admission models have advantages and disadvantages, the decision to charge for admission is not a singular choice between a rigid compulsory fee or no fee at all. There are a variety of pricing models that lie between these two extremes. Consider pay-as-you-wish (PAYW), a consumer elective pricing model in which visitors can choose to pay any price they want, including zero. In this way, a PAYW model attempts to capture WTP for admission through the form of donations (O'Hagan 1995, 33). Research shows that in a PAYW model, people often pay for admission that they could have for free (Jung et al. 2014, 414). Consequently, a PAYW model is likely to provide at least some revenue in the form of a donation when implemented in an otherwise free admission setting.

Another pricing model found in museums is bundling. Broadly defined, bundling is the practice of marketing two or more distinct products in a single package for a special price. For example, a museum may offer a set of experiences (such as a film and/or special exhibition) bundled with admission for a discounted price. As a pricing model, bundling has been shown to decrease price sensitivity and increase the likelihood of purchase (Soman and Gourville 2001, 30). Additionally, bundling can drive higher average spend as well as higher scores for metrics such as value for cost and overall satisfaction (Dilenschneider 2022). Nevertheless, bundling admission with other experiences may negatively impact membership sales as visitors may be more likely to select the bundle package over the option of membership. Therefore, the decision to bundle or not must be weighed with the museum's membership goals.

There is no standard formula for how much a museum should charge for admission. In practice, museums should aim to maximize revenue from visitors who have a higher WTP which can help subsidize targeted access programs (Dilenschneider 2015). Further, as admission price models directly affect other revenue areas, museum leaders must evaluate how a specific pricing strategy will impact sales goals for programs, special exhibitions, and membership at their institution.

Programs

Mission-aligned programs can generate revenue, increase repeat visitation, promote deeper engagement, and provide opportunities to attract new members (Alvarez 2010, 267). Thus, museums must seek ways to "bridge the gap between mission and revenue in programming, building upon one to support the other" (Hughes 2010, 279).

Many of the same pricing models discussed for admissions can be applied to both in-person and virtual programs. In addition, museums should consider establishing pricing tiers for different types of programs based on objectives and costs. For example, a program with low costs may be offered for free to attract a broad audience while a lecture series or evening event with higher costs may carry a moderate to sizeable ticket price. This approach allows for more effective management of a portfolio of programs, each with its own objectives and pricing strategy.

Special Exhibitions

When pricing special, or temporary, exhibitions, some museums employ an upcharge model by charging an additional fee for entry. Special exhibitions can help increase per capita spend, drive attendance from new audiences, and boost membership sales when free or discounted tickets are included as a member benefit. Nevertheless, special exhibitions can be a double-edged sword resulting in a boom-bust cycle for visitation and membership as well as lowering visitors' perceived value for cost (Dilenschneider 2017). Therefore, museums must carefully consider how ticketed special exhibitions fit into their overall revenue and engagement strategy.

Membership

Membership programs, or friends' schemes, are an important revenue source for museums (Dilenschneider 2019a). By offering a package of transactional benefits such as free admission, guest passes, and exclusive discounts for a special price, membership is another example of bundling. However, membership is unique in that it also creates an opportunity for philanthropic- and identity-related outcomes such as contributing to mission impact and creating a sense of belonging (Dilenschneider 2016).

Depending on the museum's goals, the *breakeven point* may be an important consideration when setting membership prices. Tied to admission fees, the breakeven point is the price at which the average number of member visits covers the cost of membership. This calculation is performed to ensure that membership makes economic sense and can be marketed as a "good value for the money." At free admission museums, the primary benefit of access is eliminated. Thus, the value proposition of membership must be adjusted at free admission museums to focus on other benefits and/or retooled to emphasize the mission and identity features of membership.

The pricing model applied to membership can have significant implications not only for revenue, but also for participation. Consider the following membership models:

- **Traditional** includes several levels of membership in which the price increases along with the quantity and value of the benefits offered at each level.
- **Basic and Premium** offers two tiers of membership benefits at two different prices—one lower and one higher. In a basic and premium membership model, the premium tier offers additional or more valuable benefits than are offered at the basic tier.
- **Free** aims to democratize the traditional membership model by removing the cost associated with becoming a member. In recent years, museums have experimented with the concept of free membership with varying degrees of success (Siemer 2020, 23–5, 187–92).
- **Subscription-Based** enables members to pay a specified amount automatically each month. By breaking the annual cost of membership into smaller monthly payments, this structure can make joining more affordable (Siemer and Lewis 2021). In some cases, a monthly subscription model may be combined with an autorenewal program thereby establishing an evergreen giving structure.
- **Annual Pass** attracts visitors who join for purely economic reasons by removing most of the other benefits of membership besides free admission. In 2019, the Art Gallery of Ontario introduced the *AGO Annual Pass*

which offers a full year of unlimited admission and access to all special exhibitions for $35CAD, just $10CAD more than a single general admission ticket (Sandals 2019).

It should be noted that these five membership models are not mutually exclusive. For example, an annual pass may be offered to complement a traditional membership model. Similarly, a traditional membership model may provide a free level and/or an option to pay monthly. There are also variations on these models such as seasonal membership and build-your-own membership. Further, innovative technologies and digital platforms such as crowdfunding and non-fungible tokens are creating opportunities for museums to engage with audiences in new and unique ways. As there is no one-size-fits-all approach to membership, each organization must weigh the advantages and disadvantages of a particular strategy within the context of its own circumstances and objectives.

Price Discrimination

The practice of strategic discounting, or what economists call price discrimination, allows museums to implement targeted access programs by charging different prices to different groups of customers (Rushton 2020, 441–5). Examples of price discrimination include the following:

- Philadelphia Museum of Art offering (1) free admission for members, (2) PAYW admission on the first Sunday of each month, (3) free admission for visitors who meet certain income eligibility requirements, (4) free summer admission for active-duty military personnel, (5) free admission for youth under 18, (6) reduced admission prices for people over 65, and (7) reduced admission prices for students (Philadelphia Museum of Art n.d.).
- Singapore Art Museum offering reduced admission prices for Singaporeans (Singapore Art Museum n.d.).
- Tel Aviv Museum of Art offering reduced admission prices for disabled visitors (Tel Aviv Museum of Art n.d.).
- Los Angeles County Museum of Art offering free admission after 3 p.m. Monday through Friday for residents of Los Angeles County (Los Angeles County Museum of Art n.d.).
- Louvre Abu Dhabi offering a discounted membership for 18- to 25-year-olds (Louvre Abu Dhabi n.d.).

By targeting discounts to specific groups, museums can maximize revenue from those who have both the capacity and willingness to pay full price. Thus, price discrimination is a more effective pricing strategy than lowering prices for everyone. As part of a holistic pricing strategy, strategic discounting is an important lever for increasing access, engaging diverse audiences, and encouraging participation from priority customer segments.

Pricing Research Methodologies and Forecasting

Novel research and access to more and better data are dramatically improving how museums develop their pricing strategies. There are a variety of research methods that can be leveraged to obtain critical insights and reduce uncertainty in price setting, including:

- **Gabor-Granger Method** is a straightforward survey-based technique for measuring price sensitivity which involves asking people about their intention to buy a product at a given price (Rao 2023, 84–7). The price is then lowered or increased until reaching a level at which the potential customer would no longer buy the product. A key output of the Gabor-Granger method is a demand curve which displays customers' WTP at different prices—the steeper the demand curve, the more price-sensitive customers are in relation to the tested product. The Gabor-Granger method is somewhat limiting, however, as customers may under or overstate their purchase intent or the price they are willing to pay.
- **Van Westendorp's Price Sensitivity Meter** is a survey method that measures customers' price sensitivity and reveals a range of prices deemed psychologically acceptable to the market (Rao 2023, 87–90). By ranking and plotting respondents' answers to four price questions as cumulative distributions, this method identifies three key intersection points that provide valuable insight into the range of acceptable prices: (1) the point at which, if the price were any lower, customers would think the product is too cheap; (2) the point at which, if the price were any higher, customers would think the price is too expensive; and (3) the optimal price for the product.
- **Conjoint Analysis** is a survey-based method famed for its ability to predict consumer behavior. The fundamental premise of conjoint analysis is that any product can be described as a profile of attributes and price (Eggers et al. 2022, 781–819). An ideal method for optimizing a museum's membership offering, choice-based conjoint analysis simulates real-world decision making by asking respondents to choose between different product packages. This forced choice comparison measures how customers value different attributes, or features, of a product. This information can be used to determine which benefits should be included in a membership offering, and at what price, to drive sales and revenue. The key outcomes of conjoint analysis include the price elasticity of demand, customer segments, the relative value of membership benefits, and the revenue

maximization price. If revenue maximization is not a priority or goal for the membership program, this information can still be useful. For example, understanding demand relative to price can help identify a price that will encourage the greatest uptake of membership.

To aid in forecasting, the results from such pricing research are modeled to predict how pricing decisions will influence consumer behavior, revenues, and profits. As museums become more data-driven in their pricing strategy, analysis into the behavioral, attitudinal, and demographic profiles of their current and potential audiences can inform pricing decisions and demand models. For example, transactional data contained within the museum's customer relationship management (CRM) and ticketing systems can reveal patterns and trends in behavior such as visitors WTP for special exhibitions. Similarly, attitudinal and demographic research can allow for improved customer segmentation, including the development of personas which can be leveraged to implement targeted pricing strategies. Coupled with one or more pricing research methods, data from behavioral, attitudinal, and demographic research can enhance a museum's understanding of the implications of its pricing decisions.

Conclusion

Price is a powerful lever that museum leaders can pull to create balance and harmony within their institution's revenue mix. As a museum's pricing strategy can serve many objectives—signaling quality, increasing attendance, managing capacity, maximizing revenue, improving accessibility, growing membership—effective pricing requires alignment of each of the museum's revenue functions to ensure they are working together to achieve the organization's long-term goals. Therefore, it is necessary to examine how pricing decisions are made and the implications of such decisions. Critically, museums must get better at evaluating and implementing the methods and models that will have the greatest positive impact on sales, revenue, and participation. To build more sustainable organizations, museum leaders must invest in comprehensive research and analysis to guide pricing decisions. With a clearly articulated goal and the right blend of validated data to inform and execute on their strategy, museums can optimize pricing to fulfill their mission, values, and objectives.

Case Study: National Museum of Women in the Arts

Founded in 1981, the National Museum of Women in the Arts (NMWA) is the first museum in the world solely dedicated to championing women through the arts. Located in Washington, DC, the Museum closed for major renovations in 2021 with a vision to restore, revitalize, and reimagine its historic building. Recognizing the momentous opportunity of the Museum's grand reopening in 2023, the NMWA team realized that they needed answers to five critical questions to inform their planning:

1 How can the Museum attract a more diverse visitor and member base?
2 Are admissions, programs, digital content, and membership priced to maximize revenue and achieve the Museum's long-term goals?
3 Who are the Museum's best customers, and do they have different needs, motivations, or price sensitivity compared to other audiences?
4 Which benefits *actually* affect the decision to join or renew a membership?
5 How does pricing for admission, programs, and membership impact the decision to become a member?

With these questions in mind, the Museum invested in a comprehensive planning process involving multiple phases of assessment and research, including:

- Behavioral analyses to identify patterns and trends among current audiences.
- Audience research with current and past visitors, members, and donors.
- Market research with potential audiences, including the Washington, DC, market and a nationally representative sample.
- Demand modeling and revenue forecasting.

With an objective to develop a holistic pricing strategy and optimize the Museum's membership program, a mix of quantitative and qualitative research methodologies were employed. Researchers analyzed transactional data to develop a 360-degree view of NMWA's current audiences. Next, a combination of survey-based research methods was used to measure the price sensitivity of current and potential visitors and assess willingness to pay (WTP) for admission and programs. To understand the goals, needs, and motivations of the Museum's current and potential audiences, several target personas were developed. Finally, in-depth interviews and conjoint analysis were leveraged to inform a new membership structure, benefits, and pricing strategy.

Behavioral Analyses

Behavioral analyses were conducted utilizing data from NMWA's customer relationship management and ticketing systems, and a demographic append was performed to investigate how geography, gender, age, household income, net worth, race and ethnicity, education, and household composition affected

WTP. Through this process, NMWA learned that members are incredibly loyal, with more than half having been members for 20 years or more. This longevity in tenure was reflected in the average age of a member, with more than 80% representing the Baby Boomer or Silent Generation.

Another key finding was that fewer than 30% of members lived in the Washington, DC, metro area, indicating a significant opportunity to engage members outside of the Museum's local market. Coupled with findings from subsequent phases of research, this insight highlighted the specific benefits that would appeal to a geographically dispersed membership. Analysis also revealed trends in visitation by time of year, day of week, and time of day which helped to inform decisions regarding operating hours upon reopening, including the revenue and cost implications of free days, evening hours, and opening earlier.

Audience and Market Research

By assessing the attitudes, perceptions, motivations, and barriers of current and potential audiences, three distinct personas were identified that encompass NMWA's target audiences:

1 **Engaged Progressive Feminists** are especially motivated to become a member to be recognized as a supporter and have a strong interest in raising awareness of the mission by conspicuously displaying their support on social media, their car, and clothing.
2 **Traditional Feminist Advocates** are motivated to become a member to find ways to get involved with a cause they are passionate about and want to become more knowledgeable about the focus area of the organization.
3 **Young and Working** hold the dual family-focused identities of being supporters of arts and culture and being career-focused.

Data showed that NMWA was already doing a good job of attracting *Engaged Progressive Feminists* and *Traditional Feminist Advocates*; however, the *Young and Working* persona represented a significant development opportunity for the Museum.

These findings illuminated the importance of conspicuous affiliation for members and provided the Museum with actionable profiles that could be leveraged for marketing purposes. In addition, data indicated that each of the three personas would consider joining for access to digital content alone—a key insight which informed the new membership structure.

Admission and Program Pricing

Using Van Westendorp's Price Sensitivity Meter, researchers found that the optimal admission price was nearly double what the Museum was charging

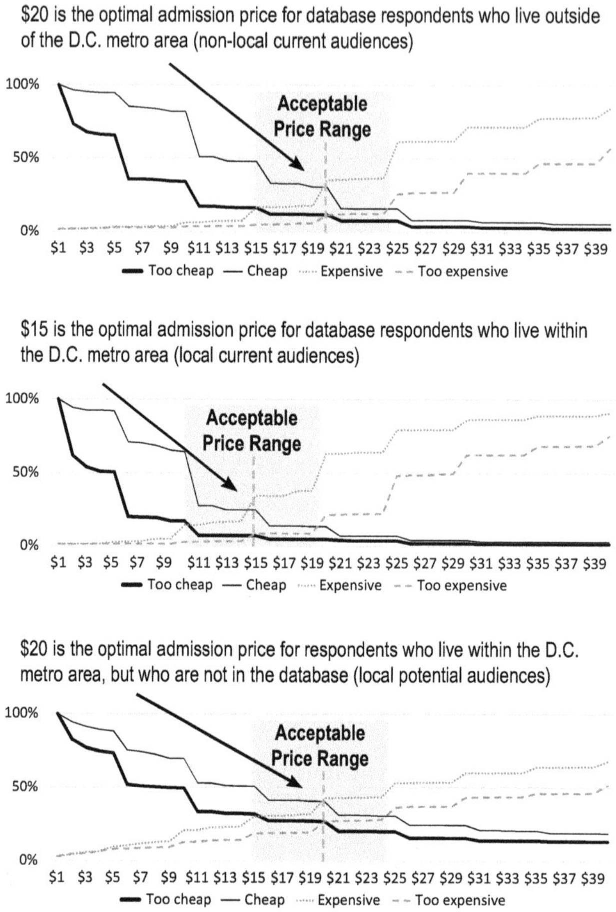

FIGURE 6.1 Optimal admission price by customer segment.

before closing for renovations. Further, findings indicated that there was a higher WTP for admission from both non-local database respondents (US $20) as well as potential visitors from within the Washington, DC, metro area (US$20) compared to local audiences within the Museum's database (US$15) (Figure 6.1). This data suggested that local current audiences were more price sensitive likely due to the effect of anchoring from exposure to the Museum's previous admission price. These findings ultimately informed NMWA's decision to increase admission prices upon reopening.

Utilizing the Gabor-Granger technique, researchers confirmed that WTP for programs among current and potential audiences is quite inelastic. Notably, data indicated that NMWA's three target personas had a higher WTP for programs leading to several key strategic insights:

- NMWA could set higher prices for its public programs without significantly losing demand.
- A higher price point for programs would reinforce the value proposition of membership if free or discounted programs were offered as a membership benefit.
- The additional revenue earned from higher-priced programs could help underwrite free programs and expand the Museum's educational outreach efforts.
- A tiered approach to program pricing would help NMWA balance revenue, capacity management, and accessibility goals.

Conjoint Analysis for Membership

To determine which benefits were most appealing to current and potential audiences, choice-based conjoint analysis was used to test several possible membership packages and prices. The benefits tested included guest passes, access to public programs, virtual events, recognition (such as inclusion in the Museum's magazine), and reciprocal admission to other museums. Different levels for each of the benefits were tested along with price. For example, the difference among offering no guest passes, two guest passes, four guest passes, or six guest passes with a membership at various price points. Benefits were randomized for each package combination and for each person. The appeal of each benefit could then be quantified into utility scores and preference shares based on each respondent's most preferred features and levels.

Data revealed important information about the price elasticity of demand. Respondents showed some elasticity when it came to membership pricing indicating that an increase in price could result in a significant decline in the number of members whereas a decrease in price could greatly increase the number of members. Perhaps the most persuasive finding, data indicated a strong difference in benefit preferences by geographic location. People who live in the Washington, DC, metro area perceived guest passes and access to public programs as the most important benefits while those outside of the local market valued virtual events much more highly than any of the other tested benefits.

Importantly, researchers identified three distinct segments for membership: (1) a price sensitive segment within the Museum's database, (2) a non-price sensitive segment within the Museum's database, and (3) a DC market segment representing prospective members living within the Washington, DC, metro area who are not known to the Museum. Analysis highlighted a different price for each segment at which revenue would be maximized: US $75 for the price sensitive segment, US$200 for the non-price sensitive segment, and US$95 for the DC market segment (Figure 6.2). Considering that NMWA's current entry-level membership price is US$50, this customer

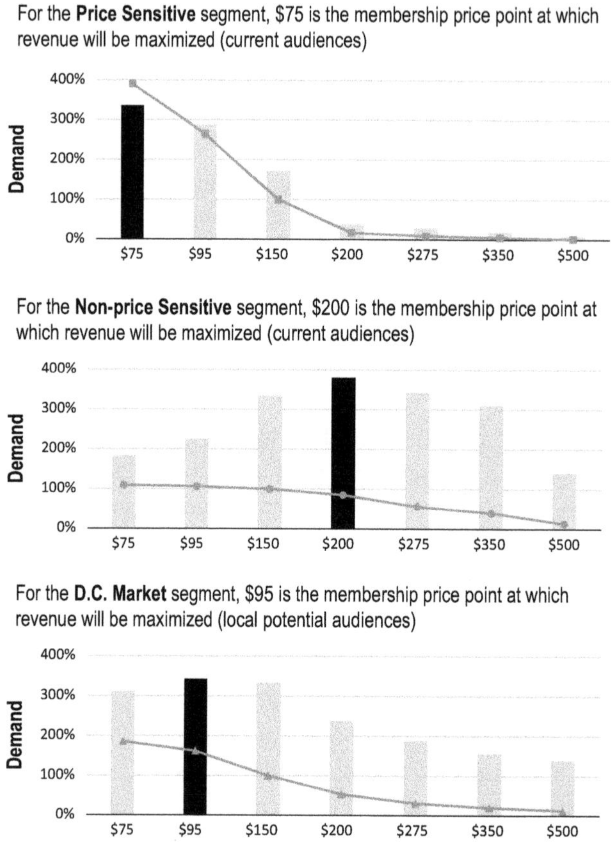

FIGURE 6.2 Revenue maximization price by customer segment (demand is indexed against NMWA's current mid-level membership price of US$150).

segmentation suggested that there was indeed some headroom to increase membership prices by focusing marketing efforts on acquiring new members from within the Washington, DC, metro area and upgrading non-price sensitive audiences into higher levels of membership.

Building a Sustainable Future

NMWA's investment in research and the leadership team's thoughtful approach to planning has enabled the Museum to become a more data-informed organization. The findings from the pricing research have added value to each department and empowered NMWA to find harmony and balance within its revenue strategy. Armed with objective data, pricing decisions can now be made with confidence and full visibility into the associated risks and opportunities. Moreover, NMWA now has a new language for describing how strategic pricing supports the Museum's bottom line and audience development objectives. With a commitment to diversity, equity, accessibility, and inclusion and a solid foundation for building a sustainable future, NMWA is well-positioned to invite new audiences into the Museum and chart a path for growth.

To establish an effective pricing strategy, museum leaders must first articulate their objectives. As price can impact numerous aspects of a museum's operations, including attendance, revenue, accessibility, and membership growth, effective pricing requires a broad and comprehensive approach. Importantly, price optimization at museums must consider mission, revenue needs, market factors, costs, and customer segmentation. As the business model of a typical museum includes several, often competing, revenue sources, the pricing models of each museum function must be aligned to implement a customized, holistic pricing strategy. Various research methods can be applied to aid museum leaders in making data-informed pricing decisions. By measuring perceived value, assessing willingness to pay, and understanding the effect of price elasticity on sales and revenue, museums can build more responsive and sustainable organizations.

References

Alvarez, Sarah E. 2010. "Putting Art to Work: Revenue-Generating Museum Education Programs for the Twenty-First Century." *The Journal of Museum Education* 35 (3): 267–77.

Byrnes, William J. 2022. *Management and the Arts*, 6th ed. New York: Routledge.

Dholakia, Utpal M. 2018. "When Cost-Plus Pricing Is a Good Idea." *Harvard Business Review*. Accessed January 30, 2023. https://hbr.org/2018/07/when-cost-plus-pricing-is-a-good-idea.

Dilenschneider, Colleen. 2015. "Admission Pricing Is Not an Affordable Access Program." *Know Your Own Bone*. Accessed January 30, 2023. https://www.colleendilen.com/2015/09/16/admission-pricing-is-not-an-affordable-access-program-fast-fact-video/.

Dilenschneider, Colleen. 2016. "Mission Motivated vs. Transaction Motivated Members: What Your Cultural Organization Needs to Know (DATA)." *Know Your Own Bone*. Accessed January 30, 2023. https://www.colleendilen.com/2016/07/06/mission-motivated-vs-transaction-motivated-members-what-your-cultural-organization-needs-to-know-data/.

Dilenschneider, Colleen. 2017. "Special Exhibits vs. Permanent Collections (DATA)." *Know Your Own Bone*. Accessed January 30, 2023. https://www.colleendilen.com/2017/05/17/special-exhibits-vs-permanent-collections-data/.

Dilenschneider, Colleen. 2019a. "Crunching the Numbers – Just How Valuable Are Your Members? (DATA)." *Know Your Own Bone*. Accessed January 30, 2023. https://www.colleendilen.com/2019/04/09/crunching-the-numbers-just-how-valuable-are-your-members-data/.

Dilenschneider, Colleen. 2019b. "Let's Talk Freely about Free Admission – Does It Really Impact Who Visits? (DATA)." *Know Your Own Bone*. Accessed January 30, 2023. https://www.colleendilen.com/2019/08/14/lets-talk-freely-about-free-admission-does-it-really-impact-who-visits-data/.

Dilenschneider, Colleen. 2022. "To Price Bundle or Unbundle Ticketed Experiences? Here's the Research (DATA)." *Know Your Own Bone*. Accessed January 30, 2023. https://www.colleendilen.com/2022/09/28/to-price-bundle-or-unbundle-ticketed-experiences-heres-the-research-data/.

Eggers, Felix, Henrik Sattler, Thorsten Teichert, and Franziska Völckner. 2022. "Choice-Based Conjoint Analysis." In *Handbook of Market Research*, edited by Christian Homburg et al., 781–819. Switzerland AG: Springer. 10.1007/978-3-319-57413-4_23.

Hughes, Margaret W. 2010. "Bridging the Divide." *Journal of Museum Education* 35(3): 279–88. 10.1080/10598650.2010.11510675.

Jung, Minah H., Leif D. Nelson, Ayelet Gneezy, and Uri Gneezy. 2014. "Paying More When Paying for Others." *Journal of Personality and Social Psychology* 107 (3): 414–31. 10.1037/a0037345.

Kirchberg, Volker. 1998. "Entrance Fees as a Subjective Barrier to Visiting Museums." *Journal of Cultural Economics* 22 (1): 1–13. 10.1023/a:1007452808105.

Liozu, Stephan, Dick Boland, Andreas Hinterbuber, and Sheri Perelli. 2015. "Mindful Pricing: Transforming Organizations through Value Based Pricing." *Developments in Marketing Science: Proceedings of the Academy of Marketing Science*, 412–21. 10.1007/978-3-319-10912-1_137.

Lord, Barry, ed. 2012. *Manual of Museum Planning: Sustainable Space, Facilities, and Operations*. Lanham: AltaMira Press. Kindle Edition.

Los Angeles County Museum of Art. n.d. "Tickets." Accessed January 30, 2023. https://www.lacma.org/tickets.

Louvre Abu Dhabi. n.d. "Louvre Abu Dhabi Membership for Young Adults." Accessed January 30, 2023. https://www.louvreabudhabi.ae/en/join-and-support/membership-for-young-adults.

Luksetich, William A. and Mark D. Partridge. 1997. "Demand Functions for Museum Services." *Applied Economics* 29 (12): 1553–9. 10.1080/00036849700000031.

Maddison, David. 2004. "Causality and Museum Subsidies." *Journal of Cultural Economics* 28 (2), 89–108. 10.1023/B:JCEC.0000019515.96628.f5.

Merritt, Elizabeth. 2020. "Museum Pricing for Affordability and Profit." *American Alliance of Museums Center for the Future of Museums Blog*. Accessed January 30, 2023. https://www.aam-us.org/2020/01/20/variable-pricing/.

Museums Association. n.d. "FAQs: About Museums." Accessed January 30, 2023. https://www.museumsassociation.org/about/faqs/#are-all-museums-in-the-uk-free.

O'Hagan, John W. 1995. "National Museums: To Charge or Not to Charge." *Journal of Cultural Economics* 19 (1): 33–47. https://www.jstor.org/stable/41810531.

Philadelphia Museum of Art. n.d. "Admission." Accessed January 30, 2023. https://philamuseum.org/visit/admission.

Rao, Vithala R. 2023. *Advanced Introduction to Pricing Strategy and Analytics*. Cheltenham: Edward Elgar Publishing Limited.

Rushton, Michael. 2020. "Pricing the Arts." In *Handbook of Cultural Economics*, 3rd ed., edited by Ruth Towse and Trilce Navarrete Hernández, 441–5. Cheltenham: Edward Elgar Publishing.

Sandals, Leah. 2019. "Art Gallery of Ontario Launches $35 Annual Pass." *Canadian Art*. Accessed January 30, 2023. https://canadianart.ca/news/art-gallery-of-ontario-launches-35-annual-pass/.

Schindler, Robert M. 2012. *Pricing Strategies: A Marketing Approach*. Los Angeles: SAGE Publications, Inc.

Siemer, Rosie. 2020. *Museum Membership Innovation: Unlocking Ideas for Audience Engagement and Sustainable Revenue*. Lanham: Rowman & Littlefield.

Siemer, Rosie, and John Lewis. 2021. "Monthly Subscriptions Make Membership Easy to Say Yes To." *American Alliance of Museums Center for the Future of*

Museums Blog. Accessed January 30, 2023. https://www.aam-us.org/2021/02/24/monthly-subscriptions-make-membership-easy-to-say-yes-to/.
Singapore Art Museum. n.d. "Plan Your Visit." Accessed January 30, 2023. https://www.singaporeartmuseum.sg/visit#admission.
Soman, Dilip, and John T. Gourville. 2001. "Transaction Decoupling: How Price Bundling Affects the Decision to Consume." *Journal of Marketing Research* 38 (1): 30–44. 10.1509/jmkr.38.1.30.18828.
Sotheby's Institute of Art. n.d. "The Business Model of the Nonprofit Museum." Accessed January 30, 2023. https://www.sothebysinstitute.com/news-and-events/news/the-business-model-of-the-nonprofit-museum.
Tel Aviv Museum of Art. n.d. "Accessibility." Accessed January 30, 2023. https://www.tamuseum.org.il/en/visit/accessibility/.
Zhang, Fenghua and Pascal Courty. 2021. "The China Museum Visit Boom: Government or Demand Driven?" *Journal of Cultural Economics* 46. 10.1007/s10824-021-09410-x.

7

FREE ADMISSION AND ACCESSIBILITY IN MUSEUMS

Hannah Grannemann

Introduction

> I think making a museum free is a start. The hard part is everything else.
>
> —Juliette Bianco, Anne and Ben Cone Memorial Endowed Director, Weatherspoon Art Museum, University of North Carolina Greensboro (Bianco 2022)

What do we know about free museum admission and its impact on museum accessibility? Accessibility is a significant concern and focus of efforts in many countries where museum visitation rates are much higher for more affluent and more educated people. In the United States and Britain, people of European descent also participate at much higher rates than people of non-European heritage (Falk and Dierking 2016; National Endowment for the Arts 2019; Martin 2002). While increasing accessibility was not always something that all leaders of museums wanted (Cortell Vandersypen 2012), being perceived as open and accessible to the public is now necessary to be seen as a legitimate nonprofit organization (Rentschler et al. 2007).

O'Hagan and Duffy distinguish two distinct measurements of accessibility: first, as the rate of participation by the population the museum serves and second, the distribution of that participation across society using measures such as participation by people of different geographic, racial/ethnic, or socio-economic groups. This approach distinguishes between the "equality of opportunity" and the "equality of outcome," where offering access ("opportunity") is not enough; the goal must be to reach an outcome that shows that participation rates are as high as possible across all groups in a society (O'Hagan and Duffy 1993). Offering free admission may increase the equality

DOI: 10.4324/9781003308003-9

of opportunity, but evidence does not support that free admission alone increases equality of outcome.

Approaches to Free Admission Decisions

There are several ways of thinking about this issue of free admission and accessibility.

Access Is a Moral Obligation

One way of thinking about it is as a moral, ethical, or philosophical issue. Many feel people quite strongly that free admission is a moral imperative of museums and perceive admission fee decisions as ethical decisions. Sir Neil Cossons, director of the Science Museum in London, called admission fees "evil" (Dickenson 1993).

There are several rationales for this view. One rationale is that the objects in collections or, in the case of a kunsthalle, in their care for display, are examples of the creativity and ingenuity of humanity or the wonders of the natural world and should therefore be made available for the education and inspiration of as many people as possible. Charging admission, therefore, is perceived as counter to one of the fundamental reasons that museums exist: to provide access to educational or inspirational objects (Bailey et al. 1997; Rentschler et al. 2007).

Elaine Heumann Gurian's perspective is that charging admission fees undercuts a museum's claim to be fulfilling its responsibility in collecting:

> Museums cannot argue that they hold the patrimony of all if only some can afford to see it … And they cannot argue that they are a resource for those impelled to learn something if the learner must first determine if they can afford to learn. There is a fundamental disconnect between the mission statements we write and the act of imposing an entry fee. (Gurian 2006)

Public Funding Requires Public Access

Another rationale for free admission is that museums that are supported primarily by public sources, whether directly through government-directed funds, indirectly by the tax incentives offered by governments to individuals when they make donations (either monetary or of tangible objects or land), or both, should offer free admission because the public is "paying for it." The Smithsonian Institution articulates this reasoning as, "National collections belong to the citizens and should be available to them without charge. Charging admission contradicts the notion of inclusion" (Office of Policy and Analysis, Smithsonian Institution 2008).

A phrase used by free admission advocates are that museums are a "public good." In the economics field, a public good is a commodity or service that is made available to all people in a certain area (a "catchment") regardless of their individual payment toward providing the good. Another defining aspect of a public good is that its use by one person doesn't preclude the use by another person (Rutherford 2012). Since people's willingness and ability to pay for public goods varies (O'Hagan and Duffy 1993), taxation is the typical means of paying for public goods (Rutherford 2012). Some advocates of free admission who use the term "public good" may not be using it with the specific economic definition in mind; they may use the term as a means of arguing that everyone has a right to access museums and their objects.

Price as Part of Value

The decision to attend a museum is a complex cost-benefit analysis by the visitor. The price of admission to a museum can be conceptualized as one factor in the entire attendance decision. Falk and Dierking describe the decision to visit a museum as "a negotiation, a consideration between the relative costs, such as the investment of time and money, and the benefits, such as value and importance attached to the activity" (Falk and Dierking 2016, 42).

Value is a useful concept to consider when thinking about the effectiveness of free admission on increasing accessibility. Falk and Dierking highlight "value" as the net total of all these considerations and tradeoffs of the museum visitor—financial, social, psychological, etc.—and price of admission is but one element (Falk and Dierking 2016). Bitgood focuses on the tradeoffs that result in value for the museum visitor: "While benefits such as satisfying curiosity, enjoyment, and fun are an important part of what motivates attention, these benefits are offset by the costs in terms of time, effort, and money" (Bitgood 2013, 66). The presence or absence of price doesn't necessarily mean that everyone will visit a museum.

Individual Museum Decisions

The final approach to consider is that of the individual museum on a case-by-case basis, according to their specific circumstances. A museum has many options for how it measures its impact and success: number of visitors, revenue (earned and contributed), reputation for quality, reputation for openness, etc. Management of museums will set admission fee policies according to their goals. Executives and other senior staff, board members, funders, politicians, and civil servants, all influence the decisions. Different museums will make different choices about admission fees, balancing their philosophical ideas about the mission and purpose of museums, and their museum in particular, with the financial, functional, and political realities they face.

These approaches to considering free admissions decisions are not mutually exclusive, of course. A museum could offer free admission but recognize that it is only one part of the visitor's decision, for example. It is also possible that the preferred policy is not enacted; a museum leader may wish that they could offer free admission, but they think the financial realities don't make it possible. Nina Simon, director of the Santa Cruz Museum of Art and History, wrote "The philosophical rationale is simple: if we are really a community institution, an institution for and with the public, we should be free. The financial rationale is a bit more complex ..." (Simon 2015).

Variations of Pricing Policies

Decisions around admission fees are not binary—free or not; there are many ways to offer free admission to visitors and many forms of offering free admission to a museum are practiced around the world. Described here are several of the most common ways of offering free admission to show the range of free admission policies in practice.

The broadest approach is to offer free admission to everyone, all the time. Government-run and university museums are the most common type of museums that practice universal free admission. The rationale at these institutions aligns most closely with the "public good" approach described above because a significant part of their facilities and operating costs are provided through public funds, though it also meets the moral/ethical reasoning for free admission.

Another common approach used by independent nonprofit museums and government-run museums alike is to offer free admission to standing exhibitions, usually the exhibitions that feature the museum's collection, but charge for admission to special exhibitions. This approach is rationalized under the public good and moral/ethical reasons and is seen as an acceptable compromise by some free admission advocates such as Maxwell Anderson (M. L. Anderson 2007).

A narrower approach to admission policy is to offer free admission as part of a "differential pricing" (Rushton 2015) policy. Differential pricing, also called variable pricing or price discrimination, simply means that a different price is charged for the same product, service, or experience. Examples of differential pricing using free museum admission include:

- Free admission to certain visitors based on factors such as age, financial status, where they live, or whether or not they are in school.
- Free admission on certain days or at certain times, on a regular or irregular basis.

Operational Considerations of Free Admission

Decision makers, which may be museum staff or staff and board members working together, have many considerations when setting admission fees. These decision makers are charged with being stewards and caretakers of the museum in the present and for the future and balance many factors and stakeholder interests. Let's consider some of the major factors that go into creating or revising a free admission policy.

Revenue

Victoria Dickenson mused about the irony of museums having valuable collections and buildings, but struggling for operating funds as they pursue their mission of accessibility as best they can. She writes that museums are "asset-rich but very often revenue-poor, and raising revenues is neither simple nor straightforward" (Dickenson 1993, 224). As stewards of the museum, decision makers are responsible for its short- and long-term financial and operational sustainability. Sir Neil Cossons, despite his feelings about evil admissions fees, said

> We have to balance the needs of the museum in terms of the quality of what it represents and the needs of the visitor … it is irresponsible to have a museum which is providing its service at no cost to the customer at the point of consumption but which is deteriorating rapidly in quality. (quoted in Bailey et al. 1997, 361)

Offering free admission means purposely holding back on generating revenue for the museum, thereby reducing available funding for a museum's ability to care for its collection, one of the primary purposes of a museum, or limiting funds needed to operate and deliver on its mission through its programming because there is less money available for needs such as staffing, facility maintenance, and program delivery—or to be more accessible by opening the museum at alternative times. As a rebuttal to these arguments, advocates of free admission cite opportunities to achieve the same financial result through means other than charging admissions fees, such as museum stores, restaurants, and space rentals. Free admission is often offered to donors as a benefit of donating to a museum, so is generally counted as contributed rather than earned revenue (Rosett 1992; Cilella and Cilella 2011).

Public Perception

Public support of museums is important for driving attendance rates, donations, public funding, and favorable relationships with community stakeholders. Offering free admission can position a museum favorably as a positive force in the community and justifying their tax-exempt, charitable status that's essential to their business model (Frey and Meier 2006). On the other hand, charging admission can be seen as increasing pressure, in a good way, to have exhibitions, facilities, and amenities that are attractive enough to interest visitors in paying for the museum visit (O'Hagan and Duffy 1993).

Increased Costs

Offering free admission creates a financial bind. Removing admission fees hampers the ability of the museum to pay for the upkeep and operation of the facilities to deal with increased crowds that may result from dropping admission fees (Office of Policy and Analysis, Smithsonian Institution 2008).

Impact on Other Revenue Sources

Admission fee decisions, especially to start charging when there isn't currently a fee, is not a decision without ripple effects. It could negatively impact the level of public or private funding (O'Hagan and Duffy 1993; Bailey and Falconer 1998; Johnson and Thomas 1998; Frey and Meier 2006). On the other hand, entrepreneurially minded donors might like to support museums that are maximizing their earned income and therefore more robustly demonstrating that, if they need more money, it truly does need to come from donations.

Political or External Forces

In some cases, charging an admission fee might be out of the control of the museum leadership; they might be legally or quasi-legally required to offer free admission due to the terms of public funding or terms by which public facilities are being used (Bailey and Falconer 1998).

What the Research Says

Research and industry studies have evaluated the effectiveness of free admission on increasing the number of visitors to museums, primarily using methods of economics research and market research. Analyzing the impact of price or free admission on museum visitation is difficult and the measures available are imperfect (O'Hagan and Duffy 1993; Steiner 1997; R. G. W. Anderson 1998). Even so, let's discuss the evidence that we have.

Results of Removing Admission Fees

Countries that removed admission price from their national museums show that attendance increases significantly after admission fees are removed. Australia and Sweden experienced double the visitor volume after dropping their admission fees (Office of Policy and Analysis, Smithsonian Institution 2008). Visits to nationally funded museums in Britain had nearly doubled by the fourth year following the removal of admissions charged as compared to the final year admission was charged (Cowell 2007). Museum visits in China grew nearly four-fold in the first 8 years after admission fees were removed from most government-run museums in 2008 (Zhang and Courty 2022).

Barriers to Visitation

Visitors report that price is a barrier to museum attendance, both in countries with low admission fees such as Germany (Kirchberg 1998) and higher admission fees such as the United States (Blume-Kouhout et al. 2015). In the United States, "costs too much" is the third most often cited barrier by who want to attend an arts event but don't (Office of Policy and Analysis, Smithsonian Institution 2007; Blume-Kouhout et al. 2015). The entire cost of a cultural visit including travel, parking, food, etc. is also a concern of visitors and potential visitors (Martin 2002; Falk and Dierking 2016).

Kirchberg, Frey, and Meier find that price is not much of a consideration for middle or higher income visitors, but that price sensitivity increases as income decreases (Kirchberg 1998; Frey and Meier 2006). This research supports the claim that admission fees do prevent some people from attending museums. However, offering free admission doesn't inspire universal attendance. In Britain after fees were removed in 2001, 74% of the people that knew that admission charges had been removed said they didn't change their visitation rate at all (Martin 2002).

Other Factors Drive Visitation More than Price

While price is a consideration of visitors when deciding whether or not to attend a museum and a barrier for some, it is not the primary barrier. Kirchberg's found that cultural preferences and lifestyle, even more than socioeconomic status, was the main driver of demand (Kirchberg 1998), just like the British and US studies showed (Martin 2002; Blume-Kouhout et al. 2015). An analysis of the increase in visitation to Chinese museums after admission fees were removed in 2008 showed that an increase in quality and size of museums was a bigger driver of the attendance increase than removing the fee (Zhang and Courty 2022).

As the discussion earlier about applying the concept of value shows, admissions fees, the exhibitions, and the services offered intertwine to create the total experience of the visitor. Museums in China that improved and expanded their facilities experienced longer lasting visitation increases after removing admissions fees than museums that did not invest in their facilities (Qin 2008; Zhang and Courty 2022). A study of a ten-year period after introducing admissions charges to the Long Room at Trinity College in Dublin (which holds the Book of Kells, one of the most important pieces of Irish cultural heritage) during the time of year when tourists visit most showed that the introduction and steady increase of admissions fees was accompanied by increased attendance. This was the same period where renovations and improvements to services were also undertaken (O'Hagan and Duffy 1993).

Absolute but Not Relative Impact on Diversity

One of the main hopes of offering free admission to museums is that it will increase attendance of people with lower incomes and increase the racial/ethnic diversity of museum visitors. Unfortunately, the results of national studies show that free admission does not meaningfully change the rates of attendance of these groups. Individual museums might see different results.

In Britain, when admission charges were removed in 2001, there was an increase in museum visitation overall, but the mix of social classes visiting did not change (Martin 2002). Visits by lower income visitors increased by fewer than a million visits in the first three years of the change to free admission by nationally funded museums in Britain and BME (a term for "Black and minority ethnic" people) attendance increased by just under 700,000 visits in the first five years after admissions fees were removed, even though total visits increased by over 6 million (Cowell 2007). In absolute terms, more people with lower incomes and more non-White visitors attended after the removal of admission fees, which can be counted as a success. But in relative terms, the percentages of different income and racial/ethnic groups did not change. The biggest group of people who increased their rate of attendance in Britain after admission fees were removed in 2001 were people with a college degree (Martin 2002). In the United States, Dilenschneider's research shows a similar result of the ineffectiveness of free admission on audience diversity (Dilenschneider 2019, 2022).

Some researchers speak bluntly when discussing the impact of low or free admission.

> It is a myth … to suggest that zero admission charges bring about an even distribution in attendance across income classes, as all available evidence … suggests that museum attendance is predominately taken by the higher-income groups. The reasons for the high non-attendance among the lower-income groups have to be found somewhere other than the cost of entry. (O'Hagan and Duffy 1993, 144)

No studies in the intervening 30 years since O'Hagan and Duffy's report have proven that free admission attracts a highly diverse audience.

Economic Analysis

Economists who have analyzed the pros and cons of free admission, taking factors such as visitation rates, uses of available funds, and the institutional structures driving incentives of various stakeholders, conclude against offering free admission broadly.

Rushton argues that charging a daily admission fee and offering a membership rate is "grounded in efficiency," with overall efficiency of resources always being the economist's measure of success. He writes "any member willing to cover their marginal cost [the cost of one additional visitor] to the museum is welcome" because museum visitors by and large are willing to pay to attend and free admission has not been proven to be effective in increasing visitation from groups of people who have not heretofore attended (as described above). Therefore, in not charging an admission fee, a museum gives up revenue they could earn to work toward their mission goals, including attracting a diverse group of visitors, and cover the cost of offering free admission to those who truly need it (Rushton 2017). With purposeful approaches, economists argue, a higher level of equitable participation can be reached by charging admission fees than without admission fees due to the revenue that would be generated that can be directed toward increasing participation more broadly and dismiss claims of indifference of museums with admission fees toward issues of equity a "red herring" (Bailey and Falconer 1998).

Countering an argument by some museum leaders that lost revenue from offering free admission could be replaced, Steiner found that a free admission day did not make up for the lost revenue from admissions through other income streams (Steiner 1997), though any specific museum might have a different result.

Zhang and Courty's econometric model using Chinese attendance and museum expenditure data after free admission was introduced shows that offering free admission would indeed maximize visitation rates, but at the sacrifice of some quality of the museum or its visitor experience, when considering tradeoffs between revenue from admissions and expenses of facilities and size of museums (Zhang and Courty 2022).

Overall, museum visitors are not price sensitive, which means that visitation rates would not be significantly negatively impacted by increases in admission fees, while increasing the revenue they earn that could be used by the museum (Johnson and Thomas 1998; Rushton 2017). On the other hand, averages can be deceptive. Johnson and Thomas (1998) concur with Kirchberg (1998) that price sensitivity is higher for people with lower incomes (Johnson and Thomas 1998), which would support differential pricing according to income levels.

Use of Public Funds

With the results that free admission doesn't meaningfully change the mix of visitors, the public funds spent on museums and the foregone tax revenue provided through tax exemption of private donations serve disproportionately as a subsidy to higher income individuals as the most frequent visitors to museums (Bailey and Falconer 1998). Frey and Meier describe an argument for even heavily publicly funded museums charging a fee: the "public good" is delivered through the positive externalities (aka overall community benefit) such as the education it provides, spending in the community etc., therefore the direct beneficiaries (visitors) should pay an admission fee, even though they are already paying taxes to support the museum (with some free options for those who can't afford any admission fee) (Frey and Meier 2006).

Relationship of Value and Price

Marketing and consumer behavior research shows that people perceive a connection between the quality of products, services, and experiences and their price (Monroe 2012). By offering museum visits for free, museums risk devaluing museums in the eyes of the public. "[N]o price is a price" (Rentschler et al. 2007), after all. Charging admissions fees is one way to signal the value of the museum, its objects, its staff and volunteers, and its place in society (Cortell Vandersypen 2012) and if it's offered for free, the public might see it as having an equally low value. But a high price causes a different problem. A high price can "perpetuate the idea that museums are for the 'elite,' particularly with noncustomers" (Rentschler et al. 2007, 168).

The only person whose perception of price that matters is the potential visitor. If they feel the price is too high, or if the museum's offering is insufficient interest to them, they will not attend, even with free admission. Kirchberg notes that the admission fee for German museums was just a few Deutschemarks yet, in his interpretation, it still created a "perceived" or "imagined" barrier in his respondents (Kirchberg 1998). It didn't matter that the museum leaders (or Kirchberg) thought their price was accessible to all, some potential visitors thought it was too high.

Conclusion

Does offering free admission increase accessibility to museums? The answer from the examples of countries who have switched to free admission for their government-run museums is yes, in the sense of "equality of opportunity." But not in the sense of "equality of outcome" (O'Hagan and Duffy 1993) as is shown from the many analyses described in this chapter.

Economic studies and market research showing the ineffectiveness of free admission on audience diversity will not persuade someone who feels a moral obligation to offer museum attendance free to all, so it may not be worth an argument between those two sides. Taking all this information in, recognizing the revenue generated by admission fees, the perception of value that comes with paying for a museum visit, and the need to diversify the museum audience, how should we analyze a specific museum's free admission practices to understand the role that free admission plays in the organization's mission and financial objectives? Here are some factors to consider.

What Exactly Are the Museum's Practices?

Free admission practices are often not an all-or-nothing approach. For example, museums might offer free admission only to exhibitions of objects from the collection and charge for special exhibitions, or offer free admission only on certain days or times, or offer free admission only to certain groups of people. Understanding the museum's practice specifically is the place to start when analyzing policies and practices.

Is the Museum Required to Offer Free Admission?

Often museums that are government institutions or located on university campuses are required to offer free admission, or it may be a condition set by a donor.

To What Extent Does the Museum Currently Depend on Admission Revenue?

Unless the museum is entirely and always free to its visitors, it collects some admission revenue. Looking at financial records, such as the museum's IRS 990 form (the informational tax return required for nonprofit organizations in the United States) or annual reports can give a sense of the importance of admission income to the organization's financial health.

What Does the Museum Charge When It Does Charge Admission Fees?

A museum's pricing practices can give a peek into the minds of the museum's leadership, their strategy for the organization, and their view of its role in the community, visitors, and potential visitors. This information is best understood not on its own, but in the context of other local cultural and entertainment options and in relation to the admission fees of other museums in the same country. But beware of making conclusions without sufficient information. Just because a museum charges a high admission fee doesn't mean it seeks to cater only to wealthier people. Nor does offering free admission mean that the museum has a universally magnanimous or egalitarian world view.

How Does the Museum Measure Success?

There are many ways that a museum, or any arts organization, can consider itself successful. Measurements could include the number of annual visitors, its reputation among its peer institutions, whether or not it is viewed favorably by the public, whether or not it receives positive critical reviews of its exhibitions, the amount of donations it receives, and many more. For museums that receive significant public funding, it is likely that the museum's reputation amongst the public officials that fund the museum is the most important. Understanding the museum's free admission practices is only possible in the context of how it is measuring its own success.

What Is the Museum's History and Reputation with Accessibility?

A museum's current practices are situated in the continuum of time. What were its practices of admission fees in the past? What was the impact of those policies? Aside from the museum's own views of its approach, what do the various stakeholder groups think of their pricing approach?

Museum visitors may be more sophisticated about these issues than museum staffers might at first assume. When asked, a broad cross-section of the public is willing to pay a low rate to attend a museum (O'Hagan and Duffy 1993; Bailey and Falconer 1998). A survey in major Chinese cities after admission fees were removed showed that 27% responded negatively to free admission and some respondents told researchers that at least some museums should charge a fee in order to limit crowds and offer a nice environment for visiting (Qin 2008), demonstrating that the public has an appreciation that money beyond public funding is needed to run and maintain a museum.

The debate over the merits of free admission will never be "solved," and the same approach will not fit every museum, nor does it need to. but it's worth the effort to continue to find ways to achieve as near universal participation in the museum experience as possible so everyone can take in the wonders of our world.

References

Anderson, Maxwell L. 2007. "Prescriptions for Art Museums in the Decade Ahead." *Curator: The Museum Journal* 50 (1): 9–17. 10.1111/j.2151-6952.2007.tb00245.x

Anderson, R. G. W. 1998. "Is Charging Economic?" *Journal of Cultural Economics* 22 (2): 179–87.

Bailey, Stephen and Peter Falconer. 1998. "Charging for Admission to Museums and Galleries: A Framework for Analysing the Impact on Access." *Journal of Cultural Economics* 22 (2): 167–77. 10.1023/a:1007506019008

Bailey, Stephen, Peter Falconer, Malcolm Foley, Gayle McPherson, and Margaret Graham. 1997. "Charging for Admission to Museums and Galleries: Arguments and Evidence." *Museum Management and Curatorship* 16 (4): 355–69. 10.1080/0964 7779700301604

Bianco, Juliette. 2022. Interview with Juliette Bianco, Anne and Ben Cone Memorial Endowed Director, Weatherspoon Art Museum, University of North Carolina Greensboro Interview by Hannah Grannemann.

Bitgood, Stephen. 2013. *Attention and Value: Keys to Understanding Museum Visitors.* Walnut Creek, UNITED STATES: Taylor & Francis Group. http://ebookcentral.proquest.com/lib/uncg/detail.action?docID=1187037

Blume-Kouhout, Margaret E., Sarah R. Leonard, Jennifer Novak-Leonard, and National Endowment for the Arts. 2015. "When Going Gets Tough: Barriers and Motivations Affecting Arts Attendance." 59. NEA Research Report. Washington, DC: National Endowment for the Arts. https://www.arts.gov/sites/default/files/when-going-gets-tough-revised2.pdf

Cilella, Salvatore G. and Salvatore G. Cilella Jr. 2011. *Fundraising for Small Museums: In Good Times and Bad.* Blue Ridge Summit, UNITED STATES: Rowman & Littlefield Unlimited Model. http://ebookcentral.proquest.com/lib/uncg/detail.action?docID=675426

Cortell Vandersypen, Sarah. 2012. "A Genealogy: Tracing the Origins of Museum Admission Charges." *The Journal of Arts Management, Law, and Society* 42 (4): 176–88. 10.1080/10632921.2012.746764

Cowell, Ben. 2007. "Measuring the Impact of Free Admission." *Cultural Trends* 16 (3): 203–24. 10.1080/09548960701479375

Dickenson, Victoria. 1993. "The Economics of Museum Admission Charges." *Curator: The Museum Journal* 36 (3): 220–34. 10.1111/j.2151-6952.1993.tb00795.x

Dilenschneider, Colleen. 2019. "Let's Talk Freely About Free Admission—Does It Really Impact Who Visits? (DATA)." *Know Your Own Bone* (blog). August 14, 2019. https://www.colleendilen.com/2019/08/14/lets-talk-freely-about-free-admission-does-it-really-impact-who-visits-data/

Dilenschneider, Colleen. 2022. "Does Free Admission Result in More Diverse Audiences? A Pandemic-Informed Update (DATA)." *Colleen Dilenschneider* (blog). November 9, 2022. https://www.colleendilen.com/2022/11/09/does-free-admission-result-in-more-diverse-audiences-a-pandemic-informed-update-data/

Falk, John H. and Lynn D. Dierking. 2016. *The Museum Experience Revisited.* London: Routledge. https://www.taylorfrancis.com/books/e/9781315417851

Frey, Bruno S. and Stephan Meier. 2006. "The Economics of Museums." In *Handbook of the Economics of Art and Culture*, edited by Victor A. Ginsburg and David Throsby, 1: 1017–47. Oxford, United Kingdom: Elsevier. 10.1016/S1574-0676(06)01029-5

Gurian, Elaine Heumann. [1937] 2006. *Civilizing the Museum: The Collected Writings of Elaine Heumann Gurian.* London: Routledge. http://catdir.loc.gov/catdir/toc/ecip0515/2005018536.html

Johnson, Peter and Barry Thomas. 1998. "The Economics of Museums: A Research Perspective." *Journal of Cultural Economics* 22 (2): 75–85.

Kirchberg, Volker. 1998. "Entrance Fees as a Subjective Barrier to Visiting Museums." *Journal of Cultural Economics* 22 (1): 1–13.

Martin, Andy. 2002. "The Impact of Free Entry to Museums." *Cultural Trends* 12 (47): 1–12. 10.1080/09548960209390329

Monroe, Kent B. 2012. "Price and Customers' Perceptions of Value." In *Visionary Pricing: Reflections and Advances in Honor of Dan Nimer*, edited by Gerald E. Smith, 19: 129–52. Advances in Business Marketing and Purchasing. Bingley, United Kingdom: Emerald Group Publishing Limited. 10.1108/S1069-0964(2012)0000019012

National Endowment for the Arts. 2019. "U.S. Patterns of Arts Participation: A Full Report from the 2017 Survey of Public Participation in the Arts."

Office of Policy and Analysis, Smithsonian Institution. 2007. "Going Free? Cooper-Hewitt National Design Museum and General Admission Fees." https://repository.si.edu/bitstream/handle/10088/22996/07.04.Admissions.Final.pdf?sequence=1&isAllowed=y

Office of Policy and Analysis, Smithsonian Institution. 2008. "The Smithsonian Institution and General Admission Fees." Smithsonian Institution.

O'Hagan, John W. and Christopher Duffy. 1993. "Access and Admission Charges to Museums: A Case Study." *Journal of the Statistical and Social Inquiry Society of Ireland* XXVII: 125.

Qin, Cai. 2008. "A Survey of Approaches on Access to Museums in China." *Museum International* 60 (1–2): 68–77. 10.1111/j.1468-0033.2008.00638.x

Rentschler, Ruth, Anne-Marie Hede, and Tabitha R. White. 2007. "Museum Pricing: Challenges to Theory Development and Practice." *International Journal of Nonprofit & Voluntary Sector Marketing* 12 (2): 163–73. 10.1002/nvsm.289

Rosett, Richard N. 1992. "Art Museums in the United States: A Financial Portrait." In *The Economics of Art Museums*. Chicago, IL: University of Chicago Press. http://ebookcentral.proquest.com/lib/uncg/detail.action?docID=432216

Rushton, Michael. 2015. *Strategic Pricing for the Arts*. London, United Kingdom: Routledge.

Rushton, Michael. 2017. "Should Public and Nonprofit Museums Have Free Admission? A Defence of the Membership Model." *Museum Management and Curatorship* 32 (3): 200–9. 10.1080/09647775.2016.1263969

Rutherford, Donald. 2012. *Routledge Dictionary of Economics*. London: Taylor & Francis Group. http://ebookcentral.proquest.com/lib/uncg/detail.action?docID=1244570

Simon, Nina. 2015. "Is There a Formula for Free Admission?" *Museum 2.0* (blog). January 14, 2015. http://museumtwo.blogspot.com/2015/01/is-there-formula-for-free-admission.html

Steiner, Faye. 1997. "Optimal Pricing of Museum Admission." *Journal of Cultural Economics* 21 (4): 307–33.

Zhang, Fenghua and Pascal Courty. 2022. "The China Museum Visit Boom: Government or Demand Driven?" *Journal of Cultural Economics* 46 (1): 135–63. 10.1007/s10824-021-09410-x

PART 3

Museum Finance Strategies and Sustainability

8

FINANCIAL FUNCTION IN MUSEUMS AND BUSINESS PLANNING

Hristina Mikich

Associate Professor, Faculty of Management, University Metropolitan, Belgrade, Serbia

Financial Function and Business Planning Process in Museums

The financial function in a museum includes activities that take place in the financial department. Its responsibilities are to govern the museum's finances, consolidate the budgeting process, make payments, control regular spending of funds, and manage the museum's finances. In a museum's work, the financial function has two important roles: one is to enable the creation of the financial policy that a museum will implement in the long term or in the current year, and the other is to support the business planning process. This chapter provides different arguments for better understanding of financial function in the process of business planning in museums, methodologies such as the World Bank, United Nations Conference on Trade and Development (UNCTAD), and the Council of Europe. We will explain approaches and tools that can be applied in different museums, institutions, and business planning situations. Discussion on analytical values of business plans for different stakeholders are also explained in this chapter. The process of preparation of a financial plan and financial projections in museums will be elaborate from the perspective of planning revenue forecast, payroll forecast expenditure, operating cost forecast, and investment forecast sheet. Readers will gain insight into basic financial reports and framework for projection of financial statements. Finally, it discusses different approaches and tools of financial analysis in the museum with special focus on break-event point, financial ratios, and sensitivity analysis, which are often used in museum practice.

Business planning includes the elaboration of a museum's strategic orientation and goals during the period of 3–5 years. The purpose of a business plan is to define the development of a museum or to secure the

DOI: 10.4324/9781003308003-11

museum's external financing. A business plan is a planning document that specifies a museum's future activities and assesses their feasibility (Ambrose and Runyard 1991; Lord and Markert 2007). A business plan can be created for an expansion and development of the museum activities, or of a new investment. A business plan is defined by three important features: it is a planning document; it refers to the future; and it assesses the financial feasibility of a certain project. It shows the financial road map of a museum and offers answers to the following questions: (1) where the museum is now? (2) where the museum is going? (3) how to reach the goals? (for more, see Ambrose and Runyard 1991).

In the Anglosphere, there is a very clear division between different museum's plans: strategic, business, and operative plan(s). Historically, management in culture has a longer tradition and is more developed, especially when it comes to business planning techniques and methods. In continental Europe, especially the Eastern (former socialist bloc), management in culture is a hybrid discipline (between culturology, sociology, and organization) and is insufficiently developed. Very often strategic and business plans of cultural institutions are considered the same thing, as well as that strategic and operational goals are mixed. Business planning (if it exists) is reduced to the creation of some formal document that has the character of a cultural institution's work plan, mostly in the form of a "wish list." Such plans are submitted to the founders of cultural institutions, who are deciding whether to adopt them or not, usually concerning the available budget funds. The analysis of such plans shows that there are no significant strategic reflections on the sustainable development of organizations (for more, see Rikalović and Mikić 2014). Even in cases where strategic and business planning is encouraged through external projects and external funding requirements (e.g., the European Capital of Culture in Novi Sad), museum management is poorly developed in practice, and a business plan is mostly a pro forma document. In that kind of cultural management, a business plan is a goal of a museum, not a tool that serves the sustainable management of a museum and its financial resources.

The process of creating a business plan includes several stages. The most common are team formation (involvement of experts in different professions, and distribution of tasks), data collection (statistical data, market analysis, trends), analysis and projection of economic indicators (estimates of market developments and changes), and drafting preliminary version of a business plan.

Types of Business Planning Methodology and the Role of Financial Function

Some of the most well-known methodologies for business planning are those developed by the World Bank and UNCTAD. Because of their long tradition, these methodologies are very popular in practice, especially in planning of investment projects. At the end of this section, the methodology of the Council of Europe, which was designed for the purposes of developing cultural heritage rehabilitation/museum projects, is presented. Apart from these methodologies, one can find a lot of guidelines on this topic, published by museum societies and art councils (e.g., Association of Independent Museums, Arts Council England, and others).

World Bank

The World Bank's[1] methodology for creating a business plan contains various instructions on how a business idea should be presented to investors. It was primarily developed for the purposes of evaluating business ideas that the World Bank finances through its operations, but it is often used by other international funds and foundations. It implies that a business idea should be presented through the following eight units (World Bank 2007):

- *A brief description of the project or business*—description of a business idea's constituent elements, especially goals of its realization.
- *A profile of its management and key personnel*—team that will implement a business idea, brief biographies, and business (project) functions of key people who will manage the implementation of a business idea; the management plan with the list of people and their qualifications that are needed for the realization of the business idea, as well as the way how those people will be engaged (selected and contracted for work).
- *The operational or production processes*—the way in which the idea will be realized (service provision, organization of production, etc.). This part also includes the shorter description of a technical solution—how the business idea will be implemented in a technical sense.
- *A list of tangible and intangible assets*—the list of tangible and intangible assets and the method of their acquisition.
- *The market analysis and strategy*—this part includes the market analysis and marketing strategy, how the pricing policy will be conducted, how the distribution channels will be managed, what are the promotion plans and strategy.
- *The financial plan and document*—this part includes the basic projections of financial figures, including the projected balance sheet, income statement, and cash flow.
- *References and supporting documents*—additional documents, permits, referential opinions about the business idea.
- *An executive summary*—summary of a business idea.

UNCTAD

This methodology was developed by the United Nations Conference on Trade and Development (UNCTAD) and is applied to their projects. It consists of the following elements (UNCTAD 2002; Oyewole 2018):

- *Executive summary*—a summary of the business idea and its goal.
- *Business vision*—vision, mission, values, and goals of the business venture, as well as the strategies that will lead to its realization.
- *Organization, ownership and management*—description of the organizational structure, the team that will manage the business idea and its key competencies.
- *Program plan*—describes the main program activities.
- *Market analysis*—provides an analysis of the business environment, main challenges, and competitors, as well as components of a strengths, weaknesses, opportunities, and threats (SWOT) analysis for a given business venture.
- *Financial statements and projections*—description of the basic principles for the financial projection, the main financial strategy, as well as the projected income statement, balance sheet, and cash flow; here, a ratio analysis is also provided, which will be used for the evaluation of realized business ideas.

Council of Europe

The Council of Europe's methodology was created within the "Ljubljanski Process II" project, which was implemented in the countries of Southeast Europe, from 2006 to 2014. One of its goals was to build the capacities of institutions for the protection of cultural heritage for better management of cultural heritage rehabilitation projects, open-air museums, and other museums (for more, see Rikalović and Mikić 2014; Bartlett et al. 2015). The methodology included an assessment of the feasibility of a project idea through the preparation of a preliminary technical assessment (PTA), feasibility study (FS), and business plan (BP). A business plan would be made only after the assessment of a business idea as feasible and sustainable. According to this methodology, a business plan contains the following parts (Mikić 2014):

- *Executive summary*—a brief overview of a business idea and the main qualities of a business plan. This part should be no longer than 2–3 pages, and it should be drafted at the end, after a preliminary version of a business plan is created. This summary should briefly outline each part of the business plan.
- *Background and history of the cultural monument/museum/collection*—this part should present the values and the significance of a cultural monument/

museum/collection. The purpose of this part is to give an insight into the monumental values museum project, and its importance.

- *Project description*—this part of the business plan should offer basic elements of an investment project and an appropriate future purpose and way of (re)using rehabilitated building/collection.
- *Market appraisal and assessment of the economic potential*—here elements of the economic valorization of a cultural asset should be considered.
- *Financial strategy*—the part that includes the strategy of financing projects and its economic benefits.
- *Financial projections*—the estimated revenues and expenditures of implementation projects.
- *Marketing and communication strategy*—describing how the visibility of cultural assets will be achieved through the strategy of communication and marketing.
- *Risk assessment*—here cultural assets risks should be assessed, and appropriate measures for mitigation or neutralization of potential risks should be stated.
- *Monitoring and evaluation*—the part that explains the procedures of evaluation and monitoring of a business plan's realization.

Business Financial Planning in Museums: Basic Characteristics and Principles

A business plan is intended for a large number of users. It includes project team members, state authorities, local self-governments, donors, investors, companies, international funds, etc. Since each of the aforementioned users has different expectations from a business plan, its contents need to be adapted to specific requirements and needs of the users. With this regard, it is common that those aspects that take into consideration information users are emphasized in business plans. Table 8.1 contains an overview of potential users of the business plan and aspects to which they pay most attention when making decisions on supporting a certain project.

Financial Plan and Financial Projections in Museums

As mentioned above, a business plan is future-oriented, so all financial items projected in it are planned figures. Financial projections are predictions of certain items based on historical data and evidence. The key questions on which the financial function in a museum should have answers are the following: What is the critical level of resources required to finance the museum/museum project? What is the risk of financing the project/investment? What is the museum's financing structure and what risks does it pose

TABLE 8.1 Informative values of business plan vs. different stakeholders

Traditional donors	Development dimension, wider benefits for the local community, effect of the project on the socio-economic development of the area, compliance with development policies and priorities at local, regional, or national level, project sustainability, relevance, and credibility of the applicant
Banks, credit institutions	Cash flows, stability, loan servicing, applicant's credibility, credit history of the project owner
EU funds	Development dimension, size of the target group of project beneficiaries, rational financial plan, co-financing from other sources, number of partners included in project realization and quality of the partnership, harmonization between project objectives, activities, and results, project sustainability, financial transparency
International organizations, multilateral donors	Developmental dimension, cost effectiveness, wider benefits for the local community, project sustainability
Social impact philanthropists	Development dimension, wider benefits for the local community, social impacts, financial sustainability
Sponsors	Size of the target group of project beneficiaries, project visibility and communication strategy, inclusion of state authorities in project realization or financing thereof, project exclusivity, number of other companies included in the project
Business partnership	Size of audience, project visibility, wider benefits for the local community

Source: Adapted from Mikić (2014), 20.

to the feasibility of the planned project? Museum's resources are allocated efficiently and if they are being employed in a way that will have maximum effects? (Pearce 1991, 42).

In museums, the most common mistakes made during the creation of a business plan and its financial projections are an overfull program plan and overemphasized information about program orientation of a museum, neglected information about a museum's market, unrealistic financial projections, and the omission of financial analysis and risk analysis.

The first step in financial planning is the explanation of financial assumptions and starting points for projections of financial figures. This part enables investors, donors, and other partners to see that projected figures (revenues and expenditures) are realistic. The assumptions and starting points for planning can be, for example, historical costs, inflation rate, expected revenue growth, expected increase in the volume of museum activities. When evaluating the quality of a museum's business plan, investors can apply different approaches. Most often, business ideas are analyzed and their credibility evaluated in terms of financial projections and the way how they are made. There are two key questions that financiers of business ideas in museums are asking: (1) Are the projections based on realistic assumptions and are they accompanied by appropriate explanations in the business plan? (2) Are the projections based on the principles of prudence and comparability? If not, is there a detailed explanation for such an exception?

Other steps of financial planning include the creation of financial tables that provide forecasts of the change in basic cost categories in the next 3–5 years:

1 *Costs of investments* (in museum equipment, building, procurement of collections, etc.)—this table provides an insight into the projected figures of investment costs. It will be used mostly by project managers in charge of investments in a museum, for the monitoring of an investment realization. The Table 8.2 will be further elaborated throughout the main project and updated in relation to the realization of an investment. Depending on the complexity of an investment, sometimes a separate investment project is created, and the figures projected in it are entered in Table 8.2.
2 *Operating costs of a museum*—the list of basic costs necessary for the operation of a museum and realization of its program plan (see Table 8.3). These are, for example, costs for rent, interest payments, advertising and public relations, supplies, repairs/maintenance, taxes and licenses, accounting and legal, insurance, travel, utilities, fees/dues/subscriptions, etc.
3 *Costs of salaries and management compensation*—key table of financial planning used in a museum by the Human Resources Department or the general management, in order to better organize the work of a museum. Each salary cost is planned in gross value, including taxes. Planned net salary is usually based on the historical salary cost for a specific position, and is increased by the planned salary increase or bonuses and awards. In this category, the costs of part-time and occasionally engaged specialists in a museum will be also planned (see Table 8.4).
4 *Revenues*—the spreadsheet with all sources of museum funding (see Table 8.5). Depending on the type of museum, these revenues can be grouped in different ways as self-generated income (e.g., admission, trading income, charitable giving, capital grants, investment income, membership schemes …) or market revenues (earned by a museum on the market), sales revenues (e.g., admissions, fees from workshops, training, conservation

TABLE 8.2 Example 1: Investment forecast sheet

Item	*Year 1*	*Year 2*	*Year 3*
Phase 1.			
Repairs			
Drafting project			
Construction			
Conservation-restauration works			
Phase 2.			
Construction			
Installations			
Main project			
Project for electric installation			
Phase 3.			
Interior furnishing			
Interior project			
Project management			
Investment auditing			
TOTAL			

TABLE 8.3 Example 2: Operating cost forecast

Item	*Year 1*	*Year 2*	*Year 3*
Administrative costs			
Renting cost for buildings			
Renting cost for equipment			
Conservation of artifacts			
Interest payment			
Advertising and public relations			
Supplies			
Current repairs/maintenance			
Security costs			
Printing costs			
Taxes and licenses			
Accounting and legal services			
Insurance			
Travel			
Utilities			
Fees for services			
Subscriptions, member fees			
TOTAL			

services), revenues from cooperation with the business sector (corporate donations and sponsorships), revenues from donations (from individuals and legal entities), revenues from international foundations and developmental funds (grants, donations).

TABLE 8.4 Example 3: Payroll forecast expenditure

Item	*Number of people*	*Year 1*			*Year 2*			*Year 3*		
		Net amount	*Payroll tax*	*Gross amount*	*Net amount*	*Payroll tax*	*Gross amount*	*Net amount*	*Payroll tax*	*Gross amount*
Full time										
Museum specialists										
Administrative staff										
Part time										
Museum specialists										
Administrative staff										
Contractors										
Museum specialists										
Administrative staff										
Management compensation and bonus										
Other personal expenses										
TOTAL										

TABLE 8.5 Example 4: Revenues forecast

Item	*Number of units*	*Price per unit*	*Year 1*	*Year 2*	*Year 3*
Sales revenues					
Admissions					
Trading revenue					
Fees for workshops					
Capital grants					
Investment income					
Membership schemes					
Conservation services					
Training revenue					
Revenues from donations					
Individual donations					
Legal entities donations					
Revenues from cooperation with the business sector					
Corporate donations					
Sponsorship					
Business cooperation and services					
Revenue from international foundations and developmental grants					
Grants					
Donations					
Other contributions					
TOTAL					

Table 8.2 gives examples of forecasts of all above-stated categories of costs and revenues.

Projections of Financial Statements: Income Statement, Balance Sheet and Cash Flow

Based on the projected expenditures and revenues, it is possible to create projections of financial statements. Financial statements include three basis statements: income statement, balance sheet, and cash flow. The income statement is a financial statement showing the result of a museum's business. It is a tabular presentation of revenues and expenses during one calendar year. The income statement is made in a way that shows the structure of the business result—does it come from business, financing, or extracurricular activities? A simple example of an income statement is shown in Table 8.6.

The balance sheet is a financial statement that shows the planned balance of assets and liabilities. It is made according to the principle of decreasing or increasing financial maturity. The decreasing financial maturity implies that the assets and liabilities that are the most difficult

TABLE 8.6 Example of hypothetical profit and loss statement

Item	*Fiscal year ... XXXX*	*Fiscal year ... XXXX*
Operating income and expenses		
Sales of goods/services		
Increase in inventories		
Decrease in inventories		
Other operating income		
Operating expenses		
Cost of goods/services		
Raw material costs		
Salaries and other personal expenses		
Other operating expenses—selling, general and administrative expenses		
Operating profit/loss		
Financial income—interest income		
Financial expenses—interest expenses		
Financial profit/loss		
Other income		
Other expenses		
Depreciation		
Taxes		
Total profit/loss		
Taxes on profit		
Net profit/loss		

to monetize should be shown first, and those that are easiest to convert into cash at the last. The principle of increasing financial maturity implies a reversed ordering of items. Assets and liabilities in the balance sheet must be in balance. A simple example of a hypothetical balance sheet is shown in Table 8.7.

The cash flow (Table 8.8) shows inflows and outflows based on expenses and revenues that will be realized in the period covered by the business plan.

TABLE 8.7 Example of balance sheet

Item	*Fiscal Year … XXXX*	*Fiscal Year … XXXX*
I. Long-term assets (1+3)		
1. Property, plants, and equipment		
2. Intangible assets (licenses, patents)		
3. Long-term financial investments (stocks, bonds)		
II. Current assets (1+4)		
1. Inventories (materials and goods)		
2. Short-term investment		
3. Cash and cash equivalents		
4. Accounts receivables		
TOTAL CURRENT ASSETS (I+II)		
III. Long-term liabilities (1+3)		
1. Long-term loans		
2. Long-term income and donations		
3. Long-term deferred expenses		
IV. Short-term liabilities (1+2)		
1. Short-term financial liabilities		
2. Operating liabilities		
TOTAL LIABILITIES (I+II+III+IV)		

TABLE 8.8 Example of cash flow

Item	*Fiscal year … XXXX*	*Fiscal year … XXXX*
I. Cash flows from operating activities		
1. Inflows from sales and prepayment (tickets, selling services, renting spaces, copyrights income …)		
2. Other inflows from operating activities (donations, grants …)		
II. Cash outflows from operating activities		
1. Trade payables and prepayments		
2. Salaries and other personal expenses		
3. Interests expenses		
4. Tax on profit		
5. Other outflows from operating activities		
=Net cash inflows from operating activities (I–II)		
=Net cash outflows from operating activities (I–II)		
Net increase (decrease) in cash flow		

It shows how changes in the balance sheet and the income statement affect a museum's liquidity. This table is often used and broken down into quarterly and monthly projections, in order to monitor the cash flow of a museum and plan the settlement of its expenses accordingly. Liquidity management is very important in museums today. Depending on it, a museum will fulfill its mission or not, and any disruption in the inflow and outflow of cash is reflected in a museum's policy. It should be noted that when museums cannot pay their obligations within the deadline, or within the next six months, then they become insolvent. Insolvency is the basic condition for a museum to start bankruptcy proceedings, and in the worst case, the process of its liquidation.

Financial Analysis in Museum Business Plan: Approaches and Basic Tools

Although there is a wide range of financial techniques and analyses, those that are most often used in museums are break-even point, financial ratios, and sensitivity analysis.

The Break-Even Point

The break-even point is a simple analysis of financial decision-making, which evaluates the profitability of current business operations, as well as the opportunities for further development. This method enjoys great popularity in cultural institutions, especially in museums, because it is easy to use. It enables museums to relatively easily estimate the costs of profitability, and allows the control of the cost-income-result relationship. The break-even point can be expressed in terms of value, quantity, and price. It shows the volume of activity in which the total revenue becomes equalized with the total expenditure.

The procedure for its calculation follows the following order. The first step is to divide all costs into fixed and variable categories. Then the parameters for the revenue projection are selected and the point at which they equalize is calculated.

The simplest way of classifying costs into fixed and variable is that variable costs are considered to be all those that change due to a change in the scope of museum programs, while fixed costs are considered to be all those that do not change due to such a change. In practice, the situations in which it is difficult to assess whether a cost is fixed or variable occur quite often. The following rule applies here—variable costs are all costs that are directly conditioned by a change in the volume of production (e.g., costs of materials, energy, fees, production services, etc.), while fixed costs are costs that do not change, regardless of whether the museum has one or ten programs.

TABLE 8.9 Different types of break-even point

Indicator	*Calculation*	*Analytical value*
Sales value break-even point	Value of fixed costs: contribution profit rate	Represents the volume of activities in which total expenditures and total revenues are equalized.
Capacity break-even point	Sales value break-even point: total revenue	Represents the degree of use of the planned capacity, at which the total revenues are equaled with the total expenses.
Unites break-even point	Capacity break-even point: volume of sales (amount)	Shows the physical volume at which the total costs are equaled with the total expenditures.
Break-even point in terms of price	Price: efficiency coefficient	Shows the price of the museum service/entrance ticket at which the total revenue equals the total expenditure.
Margin of safety	Business revenues: sales break-even point	Shows a decrease in activity in relation to the planned revenue without the risk of the museum entering the loss zone.

The main elements for planning revenues in museums are as follows: revenue from tickets, sponsors, donors, and founders. When a museum plans its revenue, a few rules should be kept in mind. Only revenues that can be realized with a high degree of certainty should be planned, reliable data should be used during planning and corrected in relation to price fluctuations. These corrections should be done in a restrictive manner, meaning that the lowest possible revenues should be planned.

After that, it is necessary to calculate all figures necessary for the calculation of break-even point, namely: contribution profit (difference between total revenue and variable costs), variable cost rate (quotient between the value of variable costs and the value of total revenue), contribution profit rate (quotient between the value of contribution profit and the value of total revenue), and efficiency coefficient (quotient of the total revenue and total expenditure). Based on this data, different types of break-even points can be calculated. The ways of their calculation and their analytical values are shown in Table 8.9.

The break-even point is a useful analysis for museums because changes in the museum's revenue, variable and fixed costs have an impact on its profitability. The break-even point analysis allows the monitoring of such changes and enables museums to quickly react to them and take corrective measures.

Financial Ratios

Financial ratios are used for the evaluation of financial and economic results of museum activities in a certain period. Ratio numbers can also be used to

TABLE 8.10 Financial ratios for museums

Ratio type	*Analytical value*	*Calculation*	*Optimal value*
Efficiency ratio	Indicates how efficiently resources are used and financial vitality	Revenue/costs	>1—a lower value of this indicator suggests that the financial vitality is interrupted. Along with this indicator, it is good to analyze the debt ratio. If its value is high, then it is a signal to change the financial policy
Debt ratio	Measure museum total depts. comparing to the value of its assets	Total debts/total assets	The value of this ratio depends on the type and size of a museum, as well as the way it is financed. The indicative value ranges from <1.2
Market income ratio	Measures market orientation of museum as well as trends in current financial policy	Market income/total income	>0.35 is strong market orientation of a museum; = 0.4 means mixed financial resources; and <0.35 indicates poor market orientation (domination of government resources)
Sales income ratio	Measures earnings power of museum	Sales income / total income	High sales income ratio indicates market penetration of a museum and management's effectiveness in the use of market potential. Lower ratio indicates that management is not effective in market penetration or that some of market potentials are not exploited
Cost per visitor	Indicate attractiveness and competitiveness of museum programs for the business sector	Running expenses + personal expenses/number of visitors	The general rule is to reduce the cost of a program per visitor, because that makes your program more attractive for sponsors and donors. This indicator is often used by sponsors while deciding which project to support
Sales income ratio per visitors	Measures efficiency of earning power of museum	Sales income / number of visitors	The movement of this ratio shows a museum's effort to diversify its revenue from sales

(Continued)

TABLE 8.10 (Continued)

Ratio type	*Analytical value*	*Calculation*	*Optimal value*
Subsidy ratio	Measures the percentage of subsidized income	Subsidies income/total income	While the goal of some museums is to be totally self-sufficient, the goal of another is simply to diversify its revenue base. The lower the percentage, the more fully independent a museum is in covering all its costs
Fundraising income ratio	Indicates cultural organization power for fundraising and cooperation with the business sector	Fundraising resources/total income	Higher level of this ratio indicates the amount of fundraising income generated by one unit of total income
Current Ratio	Measure museum ability to pay its obligations	Current assets/current liabilities	Higher value of this ratio shows better liquidity of a museum
Quick ratio	Measuring museum ability to pay its short-term obligations	Current assets—inventory—pre-paid expenses/current liabilities	Higher value of this ratio shows better short-term liquidity of a museum

Source: Adopted from Mikić (2017).

compare a museum's performance with the performance of other cultural organizations, or museums on average (taking into consideration all museums at the local, regional, or national level).

Ratios compare two or more positions from the financial statements (balance sheet, income statement, and cash flow statement). Variety of ratios can be used to help determine the current and future condition of a museum. The basic groups of ratios in museums are as follows: liquidity ratios (showing the liquidity of a museum, i.e., its ability to settle due obligations), efficiency ratios (showing the efficiency of resources use and financial vitality), and profitability ratios (showing the earning power of the museum).

Financial ratios present in Table 8.10 are used for the evaluation of financial and economic results of museum activities in a certain period. Ratio numbers can also be used to compare a museum's performance with the performance of other cultural organizations, or museums on average (taking into consideration all museums at the local, regional, or national level).

Ratios compare two or more positions from the financial statements (balance sheet, income statement, and cash flow statement). Variety of ratios can be used to help determine the current and future condition of a museum. The basic groups of ratios in museums are the following: liquidity ratios (showing the liquidity of a museum, i.e., its ability to settle due obligations), efficiency ratios (showing the efficiency of resources use and financial vitality), and profitability ratios (showing the earning power of the museum).

Sensitivity Analysis

The sensitivity analysis is used for the assessment of how sensitive an investment project is to changes of various parameters (e.g., revenues, costs). In this analysis, it is assumed that due to the length of the investment cycle, various changes in the environment occur. It is most often used in investment projects and capital budgeting. Changes within the following parameters are being tested in museums: volume of revenue, visits, and various costs. This analysis serves to predict possible investment scenarios (Franklin et al. 2019, 157) and is often combined with the break-even analysis.

Conclusion

The financial function in museums has an important role in business planning and creation of a business plan. It enables desires and plans to be aligned with resources. The financial function has two important roles: it is crucial in planning the financial part of a business plan, and then in its realization. In the process of business planning, the reliability, and financial viability of a business idea depend on the financial function. When business plan life begins, the financial function in museums will be responsible for monitoring and evaluation of the implementation of business idea. In each stage of its realization, a business plan is updated and corrected, and the role of the finance function in this process is to provide an answer to the question—how can we manage financial resources better and more efficiently? Such experience is important not only for a specific business idea that is being realized, but also as a model of work and business planning for some subsequent business ventures of a museum. The role of the financial function is particularly important if an investment is financed from external funds because they entail certain obligations of a museum. Delay in the payment of a loan installment has legal consequences. Therefore, a well-organized financial function in a museum can act preventively, preserving the financial health of a museum, but it can also correct the actions of certain museum's departments, if their current behavior will threaten the financial stability of an institution.

Note

1 In this chapter, we have presented methodology of World Bank because this organization finances investment projects in the field of cultural heritage and museums. Such projects mean capital investment in the construction of visitor centers, museum buildings, and projects that are increasing attractiveness of cultural heritage sites with, for example, new or renovated museum units. Examples of such projects can be browsed in the World Bank's database (https://projects.worldbank.org/en/projects-operations). Some other donors also prefer this methodology, asking from potential applicants to prepare their project proposals accordingly.

References

Ambrose, T. and S. Runyard. 1991. *Forward Planning: A Handbook of Business, Corporate and Development Planning for Museums and Galleries*. London: Routledge.

Bartlett, W., N. Branković, H. Mikić, N. Oruč, K. Scanlon, C. Whitehead, and B. Zečević, 2015. *Wider Benefits of Investment in the Cultural Heritage in South-East Europe*. Strasbourg: Council of Europe.

Council of Europe. 2014. *Ljubljana Process II: Rehabilitating Our Common Heritage—Business Planning and Fundraising Strategy*, AT (2014) 118. Strasbourg: Council of Europe.

Franklin, M., P. Graybeal, and D. Cooper. 2019. *Principles of Accounting, Volume 2: Managerial Accounting*. Houston: OpenStax, Rice University.

Lord, D. G. and K. Markert. 2007. *The Manual of Strategic Planning for Museums*. Lanhman: AltaMira Press.

Mikić, H. 2014. *Biznis plan za rehabilitaciju kulturnih dobara*. Beograd: Republički zavod za zaštitu spomenika kulture.

Mikić, H. 2017. *Handbook for Basics in Financial Analysis Financial Analysis in Cultural Sector (Teaching Material)*. Belgrade: University of Arts, UNESCO Chair for cultural management and intercultural mediations in Balkans.

Oyewole, B. 2018. *Business Plan Guidline for Small and Medium Scale Enterprises.* Geneva: UNCTAD.
Pearce, S. 1991. *Museum Economics and Community*. London: Athlone Press.
Rikalović, G. and H. Mikić. 2014. *Heritage for Development: New Vision and Perception for Cultural Heritage in SEE through Ljubljana Process*. Strasbourg: Council of Europe.
UNCTAD. 2002. *How to Prepare Your Business Plan.* New York: United Nations.
World Bank. 2007. *The Basics of a Business Plan for Development Professionals.* Washington: World Bank Group. http://documents.worldbank.org/curated/en/727411468315293008/The-basics-of-a-business-plan-for-development-professionals (Accessed: 1.11.2022).

9

FINANCIAL CONSIDERATIONS IN STRATEGIC PLANNING

Kaitlyn Hardiman

Introduction

Over the past several years, museums have had to adapt to countless unpredictable circumstances. Between navigating the unknowns of a worldwide pandemic, rising civil unrest, technological advancements, and changes in funding priorities from donors, foundations, and governmental entities alike, some museums have had to make sweeping organizational decisions to remain relevant within society. However, through an analysis of strategic plans conducted for this chapter, it has been found that museums seem to be making these pivotal decisions without fully articulating the fiscal implications, positive or negative, that those decisions will ultimately have on the organization. External shifts in economics, politics, and societal expectations can easily cause financial instability for museums if they do not proactively plan for unanticipated scenarios. This chapter aims to strengthen financial management influence within the strategic planning process by introducing and weaving together concepts from scenario planning to build a more holistic framework for accomplishing both missional and budgetary goals. While this planning process has been studied within other sectors, there is minimal evidence to show that museums have adopted scenario planning into their strategic processes (McKenzie, 2019).

Traditionally, organizations develop a strategic plan to guide their decision-making processes. Within the context of a nonprofit museum, a strategic plan is guided by the organization's mission, vision, and values, working to establish goals and objectives over 3–7 years. The intention behind the strategic plan is to build a framework for the organization that will prepare them in three ways: (1) to be more proactive; (2) to anticipate events; and (3) to avoid bad surprises

DOI: 10.4324/9781003308003-12

(Varbanova 2012). The original framework may seem to encourage organizational adaptability to contend with unanticipated future events like museums have faced over the past several years; however, both practitioners and scholars have posed the argument that the strategic plan does just the opposite, promoting inflexibility and constricting innovation (Spee and Jarzabkowski 2011; Arend et al. 2015). Despite philosophical opposition, developing a long-term strategy is critical to ensuring that the organization as a whole is working toward a shared vision and securing the resources necessary to achieve that vision. If the current approach to the strategic planning process is deemed ineffective due to rapidly changing social, political, and economic factors, how can the process be approached differently, allowing organizations to best prepare for the unknown and quickly adapt while achieving optimal fiscal success with intended outcomes?

Studying the Landscape

In order to adequately answer this question, there needs to be an understanding of how financial resources are considered within museums' current strategic planning processes. To achieve this, a study was conducted on nonprofit art and cultural museums' strategic plans to analyze the attention given to pending financial priorities. The study gathered and evaluated strategic plans published and posted online, representing 15 nonprofit arts and cultural museums across the United States and developed post-2021. Due to substantial differences in fiscal resource acquisition and management, museums operated by government or university institutions are not considered in this collection process. Additionally, strategic plans conducted before 2021 were not considered in the study since post-pandemic is being considered a "new normal," and the strategized elements may not be relevant to the emerging needs of museums today.

Each strategic plan was analyzed and coded for similar themes in priorities. Of the priorities listed in each plan, six key mutual themes emerged: collections/programming (93%), facilities (73%), resource expansion (73%), community engagement (60%), internal culture (46%), and audience engagement (33%).

The most prominently discussed theme, *collections/programming*, emphasized a critical desire to expand its collections and internal programming in a relevant way that reflects the priorities of the communities they serve. Much of the intended programming revolved around education initiatives such as establishing guided tours and hosting internal events for different community groups. The collection expansion would be the driving force behind the development of new programming, with intentional efforts placed on making collections more accessible to the public and working to ensure the collections portray accurate perspectives from different cultural groups involved. Additional prominent themes include:

- *Facilities*, the second most trending theme and equal to *expanding resources*, highlighted the intended goal of museums to expand or renovate current facilities to make room for more collections and human capacity.
- *Fiscal resources* were elements of the plan that outlined intentions of increasing the organization's financial assets.
- *Community engagement* themes address program development taken off museum property to occur in the surrounding communities. The suggested approaches to this work include offering new, free programming and expanding its reach with new and established community partners.
- *Internal culture* emphasizes the development and investment in the museum's staff. The presented goals include conducting an annual competitive pay analysis, and offering raises to employees with salaries below the market average. It was also identified here that museums are actively working toward offering competitive employee packages that include benefits such as paid professional development/education and increased vacation time.
- *Audience engagement* is intentional efforts created to increase the foot traffic of both new and returning visitors and develop a marketing and communications strategy to maintain a relationship with these visitors over time.

Considerations

Efforts to expand collections, increase facility capacity, offer free programming, and elevate staff benefits all represent excellent goals, and they are vital to the long-term growth and impact of a museum; however, each requires a substantial increase in financial assets. While 78% of studied museums consider the expansion of fiscal resources in their strategic plans, few offer meaningful explanations of the financial growth necessary in successfully achieving staff and programmatic goals. For example, one plan identified to "drive an increase in contributions to Annual Fund, Membership, and Corporate Partnership" without indicating the percentage increase needed to achieve its mass financial goals (Mattatuck Museum 2021). However, what happens if individual giving declines and related funds do not increase? How will the museum continue to operate with its current expenditures and meet new goals if revenue decreases?

In another instance, an organization identified specific government grant funding that would be written to support the capital expenditures of a new building but did not offer any alternative funding measures in case the grant fell through (Hudson River Museum 2021). Nevertheless, what happens if this grant funding is eliminated or awarded elsewhere? How will the museum fund its capital project if this grant is unavailable?

The American Alliance of Museums identifies that a strategic plan is "a mutually agreed upon vision of where the museum is going and what it wants to achieve … to ensure the vision meets the needs of its audiences and community and requires that a museum identify how it will obtain resources to fulfill that vision" (American Alliance of Museums, n.d.). A key element of this definition is the emphasis on how the organization will obtain resources to meet its goals. However, based on the analyzed strategic plans, museums are not fully considering the necessary expansion of fiscal resources in relation to its strategic goals. This approach will generally produce inflexible plans for resource-building that are not suitable to the world's ever-shifting economic climate. Alternatively, perhaps the reverse is true, that a perception of rigidity within strategic planning prevents leadership from looking at resource-building beyond projecting numbers and establishing conventional steps to meet those numbers without considering unpredictable factors in the environment (Turner 2011). Regardless, the result is the same: current strategic planning processes generally do not produce effective, flexible systems for expanding or stabilizing the organization's financial capacity, ultimately placing the organization's continued existence in the hands of an unstable world.

Based on the plans evaluated in the study, there is no question that museums are diligently working across the sector to re-establish themselves as vital cornerstones of their community. While there has been much intentionality in establishing relationships within the community and identifying ways to grow outreach initiatives, museum visitor rates have dropped 25–30% from pre-pandemic levels, predicted to stabilize around 85% of pre-pandemic levels for the foreseeable future, presenting a "new normal" to which museums must adapt (Farber 2023). To quote Phillip Sneed, president and CEO of the Arvada Center, "How many arts organizations might be able to survive if 85% becomes the new normal?" (Moore 2023).

This question articulates that finances, in particular, need to be considered highly within the strategic planning process. Museums are creating strategies around achieving a significant societal impact but are not considering the fiscal implications of achieving those outcomes to their fullest capacity. Continuing with this trend of linear thinking can result in the museum eventually ceasing to be a viable entity in a legal or economic sense due to its depleted finances. To reevaluate the strategic planning approach, museums can integrate principles from scenario planning. This shift can facilitate a more complex comprehension and flexible adaptation strategies toward achieving financial success.

Scenario Planning

Scenario planning analyzes the multiple pathways an organization might take in its future by evaluating emerging trends within its environment and "diminishes reliance on past performance to predict the future" (AEA Consulting 2020). This approach will allow organizations to anticipate and plan for future events rather than reactively make decisions, which would result in a loss of revenue, capacity, or mission alignment (Wernet and Austin 1991). While this planning process has been studied within other sectors, there is minimal evidence to show that museums have adopted scenario planning into their strategic processes (Filho et al. 2019). In response to this need, a framework for scenario planning is provided for museums to consider, which includes four elements: (1) scenario generation, (2) probability/preference analysis, (3) action plan organization, and (4) response analysis.

Scenario Generation

When preparing a scenario plan, a museum should begin with a process of *scenario generation.* This starts with an understanding of the emerging environment, and it then evaluates the arts ecology of the nation at large to "reveal the trends that are facing your industry and discuss implications for future strategies" (Kaiser 2019). These trends are identified by conducting a Strengths, Weaknesses, Opportunities, and Threats (SWOT) analysis. Museums can most optimally utilize the SWOT analysis as a tool for developing a holistic understanding of both internal and external factors that can influence the sustainability and impact of the organization, paying particular attention to both positive and negative impacts of financial resources (Varbanova 2012). The SWOT analysis identifies internal factors by assessing organizational strengths and weaknesses, while external factors are recognized by examining opportunities and threats.

Specific approaches to this type of analysis are accomplished in a multitude of ways. One recommended approach is to categorically structure the process, looking at broad but specific categories to have a more narrow focus on the specific ways that the organization might be impacted. For instance, AEA Consulting offers insights on six external-impact areas that should be considered when developing the scenario plan, particularly within the SWOT analysis, which includes observing trends in creative activity, society, technology, economy, environment, and politics (AEA Consulting 2020). Using this approach, museums can categorically compare themselves to their environment on each point separately to further delineate how their opportunities and threats currently set them up for success or failure in various anticipated scenarios. During this phase, the organization analyzes actual trends that have the potential to impact the organization, and it is these trends that will be used to build scenarios to which the organization will respond (Varbanova 2012). Figure 9.1 provides an example table with each of these external factors, a sub-respective influence that can impact the museum, current trends of how the influential factor is being affected by the external environment, and if the anticipated trend continues, whether or not it will be an opportunity or a threat to the museum.

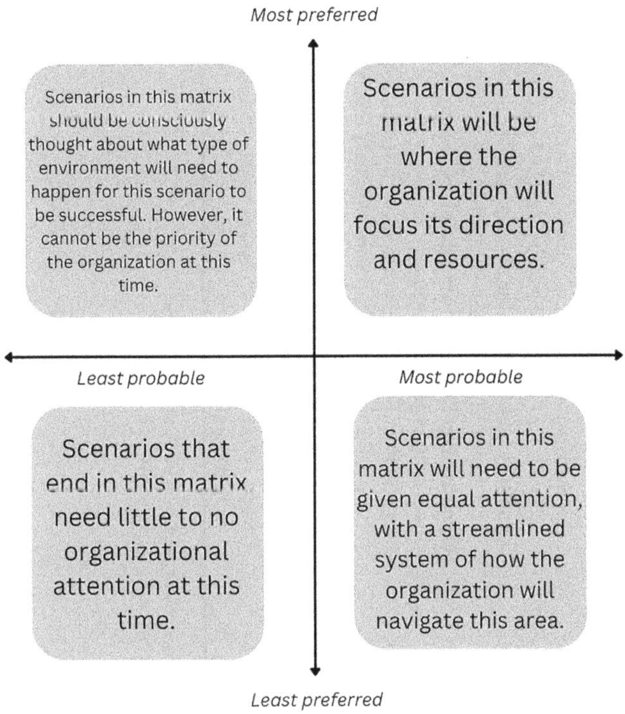

FIGURE 9.1 Probability-preference matrix.

Once the external factors are identified, and the opportunities and threats facing the organization have been considered, the next step is to begin hypothesizing different scenarios that can happen in an unpredictable environment through *scenario generation*. For museums to remain adaptive and proactive within their environments, they cannot assume that external and internal circumstances will remain static or neutral. If circumstances were so predictable, an organization might only need a single course of action for dealing with the future. However, because trends can dramatically shift without warning, it becomes necessary to account for as many potential scenarios as possible, even including situations that are considered undesirable or unlikely. Once the external factors are identified, and the opportunities and threats facing the organization have been considered, the next step is to begin hypothesizing different scenarios that can happen in an unpredictable environment through scenario generation.

An example of scenario generation is developed from concepts presented in Table 9.1, in this case, by further exploring the *creative activity* impact area. The identified trend in this area is that admission fees are expected to stabilize at around 85% of pre-pandemic levels. However, this is only one potential

TABLE 9.1 External factors facing museums

External factors	*Influence*	*Current trends impacting museums*	*Opportunity or threat*
Creative activity	Participation	Admission fees are expected to stabilize around 85% of pre-pandemic levels	**Threat:** Due to museums dependent on foot traffic to drive revenue
Society	Travel	Visitors are traveling 30 minutes or less to art destinations	**Threat:** Museum is not driving tourists to the city **Opportunity:** Get more involved with and reflective of local communities
Technology	Virtual access	Online and TV are the second preference to accessing arts and cultural events, with the first preference being in person	**Opportunity:** Utilize online platforms for virtual galleries, expanding its reach to beyond local audiences
Economy	Inflation	Individuals are financially worse off	**Threat:** A lack of expendable income for individuals can result in a decrease of earned revenues **Opportunity:** Provide more free classes and workshops to the public
Environment	Pandemic	COVID-19 continues to recede with minimal chances of spreading the virus.	**Opportunity:** Resume operations as normal, pre-pandemic without compromising staff and visitors
Political	Social values	Majority of younger audiences prefer to go to cultural events at venues who share their values	**Opportunity:** Align museums values with those of target audiences **Threat:** Making stances on social issues can result in pulled fiscal support

Notes: All data trends were taken from the Summer 2023 Cultural Audience Monitor researched by The Audience Agency. The table was influenced by AEA Consultanting's trend analysis but has been modified and expanded by the author.

scenario based on the current external trends. To exercise scenario generation, museums should consider other scenarios based on reasonably foreseeable variations in these trends. Examples of other scenarios that a museum may consider in the context of admission fees are:

Scenario 1: Paid admission **stabilizes at 85% of pre-pandemic** levels over the next three years.
Scenario 2: Paid admissions to museums **return to pre-pandemic levels** within the next three years.
Scenario 3: Paid admission **rapidly increases, significantly exceeding pre-pandemic levels** within the next three years.
Scenario 4: Paid admissions to museums **decline even further** from anticipated predictions.

Probability/Preference Analysis

After developing a list of emerging trends, the museum can then expand upon scenario implications to determine the primary focus of an eventual tactics plan. In this planning process, a matrix is developed to account for four categories of scenarios, as determined by cross-analysis of two factors: *probability* and *preferability* (McKenzie 2019). A scenario's probability and organizational preferability are not always congruent, and it is critical for an organization's success to understand that they may be unexpectedly subjected to scenarios that are highly probable but not preferred. When determining the probability level, the museum should consider how likely the scenario is to occur based on current environmental trends. To determine the level of preferability, there needs to be consideration of how the scenario will impact the museum and whether this impact will have a positive or negative effect on its mission and budgetary goals. These scenarios will then be ranked independently based on their probability or preferability. For example, consider a high-low ranking of the previously mentioned scenarios in admission levels.

Probability

1. **Scenario 1:** It is most probable that museums will maintain at 85% of pre-pandemic levels.
2. **Scenario 2:** It is somewhat probable that numbers will return to pre-pandemic levels.
3. **Scenario 4:** It is not very probable that numbers will decline below 85% of pre-pandemic levels.
4. **Scenario 3:** It is very improbable that numbers will exceed pre-pandemic levels.

Preferability

1 **Scenario 3:** It is highly preferable to exceed pre-pandemic levels.
2 **Scenario 2:** It is somewhat preferred to return to pre-pandemic levels.
3 **Scenario 1:** It is less preferred to maintain at 85% of pre-pandemic levels.
4 **Scenario 4:** It is highly non-preferable to decline below pre-pandemic levels.

After sorting scenarios along these parameters, museums can use the probability-preference matrix in Figure 9.1 to visualize their scenario planning priorities. The x-axis signifies *probability*, with the left side representing less probable scenarios and the right representing more probable scenarios. The y-axis measures organizational *preference*, where the top represents scenarios that are preferred, and the bottom represents scenarios that are not preferred. This matrix divides scenarios into four possible groups: preferred and likely, preferred but unlikely, not preferred but likely, and neither preferred nor likely.

This dual-axis ranking system plots scenarios onto a graph, with a continued example from above provided in Figure 9.2. One scenario was plotted into each of the four quadrants of the graph. The matrix can help develop a sense of strategic and tactical priorities. However, scenarios do not necessarily have to match up one-to-one like in the example. There could be only two or three hypothetical scenarios worth consideration. Perhaps there are eight potential scenarios that break down into an uneven distribution on the matrix, favoring the "preferred but improbable" quadrant. In any case, this remains an insightful tool that can help visualize potential organizational trajectories.

Developing the Action Plan

Next, scenarios are sorted according to their designations within the probability-preference matrix into action plans. This step aims to ensure that scenarios receive appropriate prioritization and attention within the planning process. For instance, if a particular scenario is highly preferred and highly likely, it should be ranked as a major priority so that the museum can develop a specific strategy to produce that scenario or capitalize on it when it does happen. On the other hand, if a scenario is neither preferred nor likely, it should receive minimal attention during the planning process. This frees up time and resources to anticipate needs for more likely contingencies and emergencies.

An *action plan model* for this is as follows:

1 General plan—focused on scenarios that are both likely and preferable
2 Best-case plan—includes scenarios that are NOT likely but preferable
3 Contingency plan—focused on scenarios that are likely but NOT preferable
4 Worst-case plan—includes scenarios that are NEITHER likely nor preferable

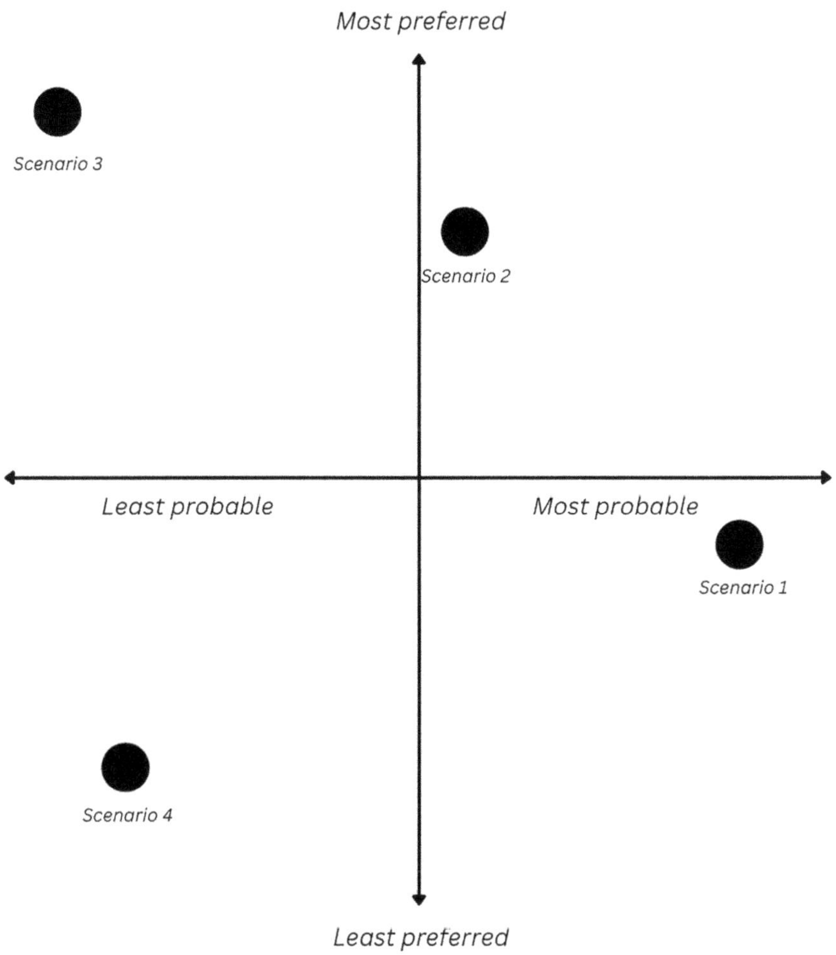

FIGURE 9.2 Hypothetical probability-preference matrix

In this arrangement, the *general plan* functions as a list of anticipated scenarios that are both desirable and likely for the museum. It will form the core of the scenario planning process, establishing realistic goals for the organization to pursue. This section will also be comparable with the traditional conception of a strategic plan since it will typically be concerned with navigating neutral or positive external circumstances. These scenarios and their respective action plans should be treated as the "standard operating procedure" for the organization and its leadership.

In the example matrix in Figure 9.2, scenario two is plotted as both preferable and probable. While the probability is less likely than scenario one, the scenario is still written as if it is reasonably possible, and the museum can work toward increasing the number of visitors to pre-pandemic levels. The museum should consider the *contingency plan,* which is discussed further later in this chapter, to ensure financial success when establishing financial projections. However, they should consider reaching and obtaining this scenario when setting programmatic goals and action plans by brainstorming tactics. Example tactics in this scenario might be to:

- Increase community outreach programs within the outskirts of primary attending communities to raise interest in attending the museum.
- Develop ticket purchasing incentives, such as a buy one get one or family package, to encourage larger groups to attend the museum while minimizing costs.
- Increase marketing with local partners in efforts to raise awareness of museum programs.
- Offer a free day at the museum for families, but partner with local vendors and organizations to sponsor booths to tap into new audience markets.

Next, the *best-case plan* can be thought of as an addendum to the *general plan.* This will include scenarios that are preferred but not likely. Examples may include positive but difficult-to-anticipate circumstances such as the passage of favorable legislation or the donation of an unexpected windfall. Developed tactics in this plan might be structured as "stretch-goals" or funding reallocations when compared with the more likely alternatives of the *general plan,* but they do not necessarily need to be related. This section might receive minimal attention when developing tactics due to the unlikely nature of the scenario occurring. However, should the scenario become more likely over time, the organization may consider planning an outline of potential tactics to pursue if the *best-case plan* is ranked higher in preferability than that listed in the *general plan.*

Scenario 3 is plotted as a highly preferable but rather improbable scenario, making this scenario part of the *best-case plan.* An organization may be tempted to set organizational goals and revenue projections around this idealization, but they will likely do more harm within the organization than good. For example, if the museum is dependent on admission revenue and projects that revenue will increase, surpassing pre-pandemic levels, and if they increase staff capacity to manage the influx of visitors, then not only will the organization be scrambling to make their budget at the end of the year, but it will also most likely have to let go of staff who had put their trust in the organization because the museum did not create financial projections around sustainable goals and probable scenarios.

The *contingency plan* is the negative counterpart to the *general plan.* Its scenarios are undesirable for the organization, but analysis determines they are likely or reasonably foreseeable. When scenarios are included in this section of the matrix, they represent a meaningful risk to the organization, and the organization should develop contingency plans to achieve two broad goals: (1) mitigate risk and (2) mitigate harm. In the latter case, even if all reasonable risk mitigation strategies have been implemented, what else can be done to reduce damage to the organization and its stakeholders in case something bad happens?

In the given matrix, scenario one is plotted as probable but not preferable and shows that this scenario is more likely to happen than scenario two. It is not preferable due to museums working diligently to return to full capacity pre-COVID and exceed those numbers. However, the current trends indicate that museum admissions will likely stabilize at 85% of capacity before 2020 (Moore 2023). While this is the most probable scenario, museums should be pushing to at least meet pre-pandemic levels within the next several years. Still, they can prepare for success by budgeting as if 85% of pre-pandemic admissions will be the new normal. Suppose museums budget for the revenue generated by 85% of admissions, but maintain budgetary expenses to account for the hypothetical costs of serving pre-pandemic admissions as a contingency measure. In that case, an influx of attendees will place the organization in a surplus for admission revenue, rather than setting a financial goal that reflects returning to normal, only to struggle with operations when those numbers are not achieved. Further, identifying fiscal means of maintaining pre-pandemic overhead could achieve the additional benefits of preventing lay-offs, maintaining greater operational capacity as a funnel for admission-growth initiatives, and instill confidence in funders that the museum is both in need of and capable of effectively utilizing continued or even increased support. However, even if it is not feasible to account for decreased admissions revenue without cutting back operational costs, preparing a plan for this contingency in advance will aid museum administration by preemptively analyzing potential cuts, their impacts on staff and programs, and their impacts on the museum's mission, vision, and values.

Finally, the *worst-case plan* is an addendum to the *contingency plan.* If a scenario is considered both highly undesirable and highly unlikely, it does not merit much thought during the planning process. However, as with the *best-case plan*, this does not mean it should not receive any thought. For instance, before the COVID-19 pandemic, there were not many strategic plans that included substantial contingency plans for a large-scale social shutdown and the ensuing economic fallout. Assigning a scenario to the worst-case section generally does not take precedence over the organization's higher-scored preferability and probability scenarios. However, the organization has acknowledged its possibility and considered some mitigating measures. Also, similar to the *best-case plan*, the organization should continually position itself as best it can to avoid scenarios in the *worst-case plan*, as long as this does not unreasonably hinder the *general plan* or conflict with more urgent concerns in the *contingency plan.*

In the given matrix example, scenario four is considered a *worst-vase plan.* If museums are confident that audiences will not continue to decrease below 85% of pre-pandemic levels, there still has to be thought given to this "what-if" scenario. There are several instances where this scenario could come to fruition, including inflation continuing to increase and leaving less room for disposable income, or another spike in the pandemic that forced museums to restrict the number of visitors, or worse, close their doors. While a museum should generally not focus much of its attention operating from a worst-case perspective, it should still consider a few risk-mitigation tactics as well as implementation tactics if the trend were to emerge that it can immediately implement if the worst-case were to occur in a manner that will not jeopardize its fiscal resources. Some example strategies might include:

- Positive risk mitigation tactics:
  - Consider working toward building a small endowment that will be used as a rainy day fund in the event that the museum has to close their doors to the public for a chunk of time. This endowment funding can be used to supplement overhead costs or salaries to keep internal operations afloat for the time being, without having to lay off staff.
- If the above is not achievable but the scenario becomes a reality, then the museum may have to consider:
  - Laying off staff, and identifying which staffing areas will need to be let go.
  - Pause or terminate programming that is absorbing funds.

While it is difficult to grapple with the worst-case scenarios, museums still need to have these hard conversations to determine how they effectively and proactively move forward in these scenarios.

Response Analysis

The last step for incorporating a *scenario plan* into a larger *strategic plan* is to develop realistic and practical responses to each scenario within the plan. As mentioned above, more significant consideration should be given to scenarios that are most likely or have a more significant impact, whether positive or negative (i.e., scenarios in the general and contingency plans). While deliberating over how an organization might respond to a future circumstance, it may be challenging to determine which responses will be the most appropriate or effective, especially in scenarios where the most feasible solutions present apparent drawbacks. This is why a scenario plan should include a tool for analyzing potential responses to determine which ones best fulfill the most organizational needs, which can be accomplished using a high, medium, or low (HML) scale.

The HML scale rates potential responses on a scale of 1–3, with 1 indicating ineffective impact and 3 indicating highly effective impact. However, the true strength of the HML scale is that it can simultaneously evaluate multiple organizational needs. This is particularly useful when an organization struggles to decide between responses that address competing needs. In these cases, the multiple metrics of HML can help determine either a response that is most holistic in addressing the scenario or one that best meets the most pressing demands of the scenario. Ideally, the best response will rank as a three on all metrics.

There are four metrics when utilizing this scale for strategic planning, which are return on investment, mission/vision/values (MVV) alignment, community impact, and organizational impact. Below is a brief description of how these metrics are evaluated in an HML scale:

Return on investment:

- High (3): Receives more income than what is spent.
- Medium (2): Breaks even between program and spending.
- Low (1): Costs more to produce than what is financially received.

Mission/vision/values alignment:

- High (3): Significantly aligns with intended MVV.
- Medium (2): Only moderately aligns.
- Low (1): Does not align with organizational purpose.

Community impact:

- High (3): Initiative will positively impact the target community, if not done there will be severe negative consequences in the community.
- Medium (2): Initiative will positively benefit the target community, but there will be limited consequences if not conducted.
- Low (1): Initiative will either produce no meaningful impact in the target community, or potentially alienate members of another community. Impact is negative or neutral.

Organizational workforce impact:

- High (3): Initiative will positively impact the work culture of the organization, if not done there will be negative consequences to the organization's culture.
- Medium (2): Initiative will positively benefit employee culture, but there will be limited consequences if not conducted.
- Low (1): Employee impact is neutral or consequential to/for staff.

An example of this framework is seen in Table 9.2. After conducting this analysis, the organization should choose its leading response(s) to each scenario and list them with their HML ratings for each category and any relevant notes on potential strengths or drawbacks. In Table 9.2, for example, the tactic to

TABLE 9.2 Scenario planning framework

Museum's general plan	Scenario: Paid admissions to museums return to pre-pandemic levels within the next three years.		
Tactic 1: Increase community outreach programs within the outskirts of primary attending communities to raise interest in attending the museum.			
Metric	*HML*	*Value*	*Notes*
Return on investment	M	2	Community outreach programs do not bring in revenue, but should raise community interest enough to increase admission to the museums. Between staff time to implement the program and the material costs, there is a chance that outreach loses money due to not seeing enough visitors as a result of the outreach program.
MVV alignment	H	3	The museum values accessibility and works to eliminate barriers to communities receiving the opportunity to participate. A community outreach program allows the museum to make connections with community members who have been unable to access the museum's internal programming.
Community impact	H	3	A community outreach program allows the museum to make connections with community members who have been unable to access the museum's internal programming.
Organizational workforce impact	L	1	This would expand the work responsibilities of an already stretched-thin staff. If this tactic is what the organization is depending on to increase visitors to the museum, it can easily lead to burn-out and lack of attention to higher priority areas.
	Total	9	

Tactic 2: Develop ticket purchasing incentives, such as a buy-one-get-one deal or a family package to encourage larger groups to attend the museum.			
Return on investment	H	3	Offering special rates on admission fees, whether one-off or routine, can attract more visitors to the space. With trends indicating that disposable income in families is decreasing, this will be a great option to attract families who might not come if tickets were full price.
MVV alignment	H	3	The museum believes in access for all community groups. It is part of the museum's values and vision to remove barriers for participation.
Community impact	H	3	Family or friend groups are able to experience the museum's offerings with a reduced financial burden.
Organizational impact	H	3	To retain current staff and expand team members, the museum must have an increase in museum visitors to make positions both financially sustainable and labor indispensable.
	Total	12	

develop ticket purchasing incentives scored higher than increasing community outreach events. Because of this, the museum should prioritize tactic two within the organization. While tactic one can still be considered and implemented, that should only be developed once tactic two has been carried out, and the organization has both the staff capacity and confidence in the financial inputs and outputs to be successful in its implementation. After developing this HML scale, the organization will have a complete picture of its scenario plan, including environmental and internal analyses, foreseeable scenarios categorized by probability and desirability, and potential responses ranked according to each scenario's needs.

Conclusion

Since its inception, the strategic plan has become a mainstay of organizational leadership, and institutions across all sectors frequently use it to reorient and refocus their goals. However, due to the constantly shifting trends in the environment, the traditional approach to the strategic planning process has left museums restricted in their abilities to proactively respond and adapt to these trends. In efforts to be more proactive in this planning process and consider more highly the financial assets required to achieve organizational goals, museums should turn to scenario planning within their strategic planning process. Through the implementation of the *SWOT analysis* to generate and predict future scenarios, the *preference-probability matrix* to visualize potential trajectories, the *action plan model* to analyze and establish scenario priorities, and the HML scale to analyze and establish response priorities, museums will be better equipped to plan and adjust their financial goals for future success and sustainability.

References

Allison, Michael and Jude Kaye. 2005. *Strategic Planning for Nonprofit Organizations: A Practical Guide and Workbook*. Newark: John Wiley & Sons.

Allison, Michael and Jude Kaye. 2015. *Strategic Planning for Nonprofit Organizations: A Practical Guide for Dynamic Times*. Newark: John Wiley & Sons.

American Alliance of Museums. n.d. "Strategic Institutional Plan." American Alliance of Museums. https://www.aam-us.org/programs/ethics-standards-and-professional-practices/strategic-institutional-plan/

Arend, Richard J., Y. Lisa Zhao, Michael Song, and Subin Im. 2015. "Strategic Planning as a Complex and Enabling Managerial Tool." *Strategic Management Journal* 38 (8): 1741–52. 10.1002/smj.2420.

Bryson, John M. 2018. *Strategic Planning for Public and Nonprofit Organizations: A Guide to Strengthening and Sustaining Organizational Achievement*. Newark: John Wiley & Sons.

Calafato, Kathryn. 2011. "Starting a Nonprofit Organization: The Business Side." In *The Arts Managament Handbook: New Directions for Students and Practitioners*, edited by Meg Brindle and Constance DeVereauz, 252–89. New York: Routledge.

Catlin-Legutko, Cinnamon. 2009. DIY Strategic Planning for Small Museums. *Technical Leaflet 242*. Nashville, TN: AASLH.

Farber, Jim. 2023. “The Wake-Up Call: Performing Arts Face the Post-Pandemic World.” San Francisco Classical Voice. https://www.sfcv.org/articles/feature/wake-call-performing-arts-face-post-pandemic-world.
Fathi, Mohammad Reza, Mohammad Hasan Maleki, Seyed Mohammad Sobhani, and Can Deniz Koksal. 2020. “Future Study of Operations Research Based on Scenario Planning and Soft Systems Methodology.” *Foresight* 22 (2): 223–49.
Gilman, Amy. 2015. “Institutionalizing Innovation at the Toledo Museum of Art.” In *Fundraising and Strategic Planning: Innovative Approaches for Museums*, edited by Juilee Decker, 103–10. Lanham, MD: Rowman & Littlefield Publishers.
Godet, Michel. 2000. “The Art of Scenarios and Strategic Planning.” *Technological Forecasting and Social Change* 65 (1): 3–22. 10.1016/s0040-1625(99)00120-1.
Kachaner, Nicholas, Kermit King, and Sam Stewart. “Four Best Practices for Strategic Planning.” *Strategy & Leadership* 44 (4): 26–31. 10.1108/SL-06-2016-0046.
Hudson River Museum. 2021. “*Strategic Plan 2021–2023*.” Hudson River Museum. April 2021. https://www.hrm.org/wp-content/uploads/2021/04/Publication-2021-Strategic-Plan.pdf
Kaiser, Michael. 2019. *Strategic Planning in the Arts: A Practical Guide*. Waltham, MA: Brandeis University Press.
Martinet, Alain-Charles. 2010. “Strategic Planning, Strategic Management, Strategic Foresight: The Seminal Work of H. Igor Ansoff.” *Technical Forecasting and Social Change* 77 (9) (November): 1485–7. 10.1016/j.techfore.2010.06.024.
Mattatuck Museum. 2021. “*Strategic Plan: Strengthening Our Community*.” Mattatuck Museum. September 2021. https://www.mattmuseum.org/wp-content/uploads/2021/09/Strategic-Plan_2022-2026.pdf
McKenzie, Bridget. 2019. “The Possible Museum: Anticipating Future Scenarios.” In *Addressing the Challenge in Communicating Climate Change across Various Audiences*, edited by W.L. Filho et al., 443–56. Cham: Springer.
Moore, John. 2023. “Attendance Data Dive: Local Performing Arts Groups May Never Fully Recover.” Denver Gazette. Accessed January 11, 2023. https://denvergazette.com/arts-entertainment/attendance-data-dive-local-performing-arts-groups-may-never-fully-recover/article_4aaa224a-b707-11ed-ae6b-0bc4a01299e1.html.
“Navigating Uncertain Times: A Scenario Planning Toolkit for the Arts & Culture.” AEA Consulting. October 2020. https://aeaconsulting.com/uploads/1100011/160337214998/AEA-Wallace_ScenarioPlanning_Overview_202010_FINAL.pdf.
Rosewall, Ellen. 2014. *Arts Management: Uniting Arts and Audiences in the 21st Century*. New York: Oxford Press.
Spee, Paul E. and Paula Jarzabkowski. 2011. “Strategic Planning as Communicative Process.” *Organization Studies* 32 (9): 1149–1316. https://doi-org.ezproxy.uky.edu/10.1177/0170840611411387open_in_new
Taft, Marilyn. 2008. “Leadership in the Arts: An Inside View.” Bloomington, Indiana: Authorhouse.
Turner, Geoff. 2011. *Effective Financial Management: The Cornerstone for Success*. New York: Business Expert Press.
Varbanova, Lidia. 2012. *Strategic Management in the Arts*. London: Taylor and Francis Group.
Wallace, Sue-Ann. 1998. *Strategic Planning Manuel*. Australia: Museums Australia, Inc.
Wernet, Stephen P. and David M. Austin. 1991. “Decision Making Style and Leadership Patterns in Nonprofit Human Service Organizations.” *Administration in Social Work* 15 (3): 1–17. 10.1300/J147v15n03_01.

10

MUSEUMS AND CONTROL SYSTEMS

Rebekah Beaulieu

The years 2020 to 2023 were a turning point for museums. The global COVID-19 pandemic warranted novel measures such as social distancing, institutional closures, and a new reliance on virtual programming and exhibitions access. Museums were forced to adapt operational and financial models nearly overnight, and the term "financial sustainability" was no longer an abstract concept, but a tangible objective realized only through collaboration with local and federal funders to secure emergency relief funds, innovative business modeling, and consistent attention to financial exercises, such as scenario planning and cash flow projections.

Professionals and academics in the museum field soon observed that those organizations with diversified income streams not overly reliant on earned revenue weathered the storm far better than those without the ability to absorb operating losses. Furthermore, museums with strong control measures were able to make use of institutional resources and processes to enact a swift response while still maintaining observance of best practices. This chapter introduces the concept of financial controls and the ways in which control systems can be activated to ensure institutional stability, internal communication, and external transparency.

What Are Controls?

The term "controls" is familiar to many in financial and legal positions, yet less common among the museum profession in general. We typically use the word "controls" to refer to "policies regarding the protection of the organization from fraud and error" (Granger 2013, 12). Controls are mainly a financial concern but are also embedded in a variety of functions across a museum

DOI: 10.4324/9781003308003-13

institution, such as legal and governance issues, labor laws and volunteer protections, and collections stewardship. Controls are intended to provide objective and compliant structures to all operations, financial resource, and personnel management, including museum staff, trustees, volunteers, and even visitors.

Internal Control Systems

We can consider controls as parameters for asset and people management in three broad categories: internal controls, management controls, and fiduciary oversight and governance. Internal controls are those that are enacted on a regular basis to create regularized structures for specific roles and tasks. In human resources, for example, the creation of consistent job description elements (education and experience requirements, accountability structure, responsibilities, and priorities) would be considered a control, as would an orientation process and a performance review structure. In finance, internal controls are essential to minimize risk exposure, particularly to individual administration and preferential treatment of financial processes. This is why, for example, we require multiple signatures on checks above a certain amount, which can often include documentation of approval from the director or chief executive officer, as well as the treasurer or other board representative. We refer to the need for multiple individuals to participate in financial tasks as a segregation of duties, in which no single individual holds responsibility for all duties related to revenue and/or expense processing and approval. We typically divide segregation of duties according to the following:

- *Authorization*: Formal recognition of revenue and expense activities should be shared among multiple individuals. This includes any spending on behalf of the organization or processing of earned revenue, contributed income, or institutional fund transfers. Authorization will typically take place at the department level and then again within the finance department. Within the finance department, any transaction will be documented and approved by at least one additional individual. For those many organizations without staff resources to segregate duties internally, board members can be enlisted to serve documentation and/or approval needs.
- *Supervision of funds*: The supervision of institutional funds is typically shared between a governing body, who may make decisions on behalf of the organization, regarding investments, fund transfers, and spending policies. Within the staff, the finance department must have a segregation between those requesting fund transfers and withdrawals versus those approving such activity. As with the authorization needs of the organization above, board members can support the supervision of funds in order to fully segregate duties.

- *Record keeping*: All transactions that an institution undertakes must be documented. Transactions, for clarity, are all exchanges of assets in return for goods or services, as well as assets received for which no return is anticipated. This definition includes the four general types of transactions (sales, purchases, receipts, payments) as they relate to income, such as sales generated from admissions, memberships, or donations received, as well as to expenses, like payments on behalf of the museum to its vendors, acquisitions of artwork or other collections, or employee compensation. Every exchange of assets is a transaction and in order to best track transactions accurately. Abundant and accessible records are a necessity in financial management, and policies regarding digital and hardcopy record retention critical to structuring access.
- *Reconciliation*: Referring to the comparison of data between two data sets to verify the information is accurate, reconciliation typically refers to the financial data held within the organization as compared to that held by an external source, such as in bank statements. Additional controls encourage interdepartmental reconciliations: for instance, an exhibition budget that accurately reflects the spending activity documented in the finance department.

Management Control Systems

Management controls, on the other hand, are those which account for the consistent documentation and presentation of financial data in the form of statement templates. In nonprofit organizations, the financial report typically consists of the following:

- *Balance sheet*: The balance sheet summarizes the organization's assets, liabilities, and net assets at a specific point in time.
- *Income statement*: Also known as the statement of activities (and in for-profit accounting, the profit and loss statement), the activity shows all financial activity of the organization over a specific period of time.
- *Cash flow statement*: Cash flow statements show the movement of cash in and out of an organization, and typically include the movement of cash as a result of operating activities, investing activities, and financing activities.[1]

Unlike internal controls which function mainly at the employee level, the management control is designed to provide a consistent system of data for review by the governing body. The above statements are typically shared at least quarterly with a finance and/or executive committee of the board, followed by dissemination to the entire board of trustees. Such controls are designed to provide the opportunity for re-orientation if the organization is off course financially and may warrant additional forecasting exercises, such as scenario planning, forecasting, or cash flow projections.

Management Controls and Fraud Mitigation

Management controls are also designed to reduce exposure to fraud, which is all too common in museums and can take via a variety of methods.[2] Tampering with billing payments, checks or account access, skimming fractional amounts from accounts, creating fake or embellished expense reimbursement requests, the use of fraudulent data in the creation of financial statements, and non-cash theft of collections, inventory or equipment are all fraud tactics.

It is important to keep in mind that fraud can take place in institutions of all sizes and locations and can be propagated by anyone with relevant knowledge and access, and even by the organizations themselves. Fraud in museums is an unfortunately common occurrence and has taken place in the smallest regional history museums as well as the largest and most well-known institutions in the world. Here are only a few examples:

- In 1990, the Los Angeles County Museum of Natural History faced an audit dispute with the National Science Foundation. When the museum's record of employee time was insufficient for grant reporting purposes, employees were encouraged to recreate timecards to record time spent on a grant-funded project months after they were originally submitted (Parachini 1990).
- The American Association for State and Local History, the national membership association for historic sites in the United States, was a victim of embezzlement by its finance manager, employed for over 20 years by the organization (Van Balgooy 2017).
- A former bookkeeper at the Tucson Museum of Art in Arizona was convicted of stealing almost $1 million over a period of five years (Office of the Arizona Attorney General 2009).
- In 2010, a former CFO of the Fruitlands Museum in Harvard, Massachusetts, pled guilty to stealing $1.3 million over six years (Trachtenberg 2010).
- In 2023, an employee of the Art Institute of Chicago in Illinois in charge of payroll was accused of embezzling more than $2 million (United States v. Maurello 2023).

The cases of embezzlement evidence certain similarities, such as a lack of segregation of duties and/or enforcement of such policies, and often trust placed in a longtime employee. As Max Van Balgooy (2017) points out in his article for *History News*—a journal published by AASLH, the victim of a fraud case itself—40% of fraud cases are identified by a tip, not through careful controls. This data points out both the need for documented whistleblower policies[3] and, moreover, institution-wide dedication to controls (Van Balgooy 2017, 21).

Almost as important as the control systems themselves are "control cues," the messages museum leadership members such as the director and trustees send about the safeguarding of assets and commitment to transparency (McLaughlin 2002, 191–2). Such cues include the repeated verbal and written references to control systems in place, such as in board meetings, staff meetings, and in orientations for volunteers. The centrality of consistent communication is key, and prioritization of dialogue within and among departments of the museum, as well as between staff and board, imperative. Communication of such priorities is not limited to verbal discussion or written policy and can also take the place of physical measures to ensure protection of physical and financial assets. Password protections, keyed access to facilities, strictly enforced security procedures, and even references to insurance coverage that predicates criminal activity is punishable by law can all function as control cues.

Fiduciary Oversight and Controls

The third platform for control systems is that of fiduciary oversight by the governing body, in which trustees and members of board committees act in accordance with governance principles for museum officials. Such principles outline the impetus for ethical conduct and include language related to conflicts of interest, good faith efforts to protect and not obstruct best practices, and necessary and relevant business and personal disclosures. The three duties to which trustees commit as members of a governing body are as follows:

- *Duty of care*: Each trustee will exercise the level of care that any individual would do in dealing with his own property and following all measures of prudence.
- *Duty of loyalty*: Each trustee commits to participation in organizational leadership with a goal to benefit the organization and not the individual.
- *Duty of obedience*: Each trustee must show obedience to the institution's founding documents, mission, and charitable purpose.

Additional principles are outlined regarding fiduciary oversight, asset management, and investments. In the United States, the Employee Retirement Security Act (ERISA) was established in 1974 to outline responsibilities related to institution fund oversight. They include the following:

- *Duty to diversify*: Funds should be diversified in order to minimize the risk of high losses.
- *Duty to incur only reasonable costs*: Fund management fees must be aligned with market rates and activities that incur costs are to be exercised with prudence.

- *Duty to monitor*: Trustees are responsible for holding regular and consistent meetings, and to document such meeting proceedings and the status of investments.
- *Duty to avoid prohibited transactions*: Funds cannot be invested imprudently, in illegal activities, or in businesses that directly or indirectly benefit committee members (Demmert 2019, 16).

The fiduciary responsibility with which all trustees are charged consistently dictate rules against personal gain, formally known as private inurement, and in enforcement of the business judgment rule: trustees are not expected to hold expert knowledge in all aspects of museum operations, but to act "in good faith and in good care" (Kuruvilla 2016, 221). Such tenets should be documented in all resources that reflect the trustee code of conduct and ultimately set the foundation for controls, such as but not limited to:

- Bylaws, which outline the terms of board service and responsibilities
- Disclosure statements, such as conflict of interest forms
- Articles of incorporations, such as an organizational charter, or other founding document
- If relevant, a memorandum of understanding (MOU) if the museum is a subsidiary of a parent organization, such as a municipality or university
- Mission and policy statements, such as the collections policy, code of conduct, and statement of values
- Committee charters

The above documents should systematize the elements of control for which trustees are responsible and to which they are subject, and should be included in orientation protocols and printed materials for all trustees.

Inter-Departmental Controls and Risk Mitigation Strategies

As we consider controls, we must take a comprehensive view toward ways in which we can reduce liability and risk as they relate to standards and best practices in the museum field and in nonprofit administration. Field-wide resources available through organizations such as the American Alliance of Museums, the Association of Art Museum Directors, and the International Council of Museums offer resources to determine compliant practices in areas of governance, financial stability, and operations. In the management of tangible and intangible assets—including but not limited to financial assets—we prioritize protections against fraud, as well as devaluation of property, misallocation of funds, misuse or destruction of property, and even inequitable compensation models.

In addition to financial considerations, protections of tangible property are of concern to museums. Certain standards are particular to museums in the management of collections and applicable to museums in the Americas, Europe, and elsewhere. Such protections can be subject to changes in federal priorities but can affect funding and the ability to travel objects internationally. International cultural property legislations include a number of policies that have been inaugurated in recent decades through a number of summits, such as the Convention for the Protection of Underwater Cultural Heritage, The Hague Convention for the Protection of Cultural Property in the Event of Armed Conflict, the UNIDRIOT Convention on Stolen or Illegally Exported Cultural Objects, and the UNESCO Convention for the Protection of World Cultural and National Heritage and the Convention of the Means of Prohibiting and Preventing the Illicit Import, Export, and Transfer of Ownership of Cultural Property. Such meetings have had far-reaching implications in a global code of ethics and control systems for the protection of cultural property, resulting in standard-bearers including the establishment of the Cultural Property Advisory Committee, the International Register of Cultural Property under Special Protection, Recommendations for the Protection of Movable Cultural Property, and the Cultural Property Implementation Act.[4] Laws, regulations, and best practices shift from country to country. In the United States, museums are subject to the Native American Graves Protection and Repatriation Act of 1990 (NAGPRA), which provides a process for federal agencies and museums to repatriate objects, particularly the transfer of objects and artifacts from museum collections to lineal descendants and indigenous affiliations.

Collections care and financial controls intersect in the protection of collections from capitalization. In 2017, a white paper drafted by the American Alliance of Museums and the American Association for State and Local History served as the final word on object deaccessions, stating that use of proceeds raised through deaccessions should fund direct care of the collection and/or new acquisitions, but should not be used to support general operations (American Alliance of Museums 2019). The policy was revised in 2019 to fully align with Federal Accounting Standards Board (FASB) language and later supported by the Association of Art Museum Directors.

The capitalization of collections refers to the monetary valuation of collections, which includes listing as an asset category on the institutional balance sheet and leaving collections vulnerable to potential sale. The regulation against the capitalization of collections is not only a standard in the field but is formally supported by FASB and disclosed in the notes to the annual audit of financial statements. While it can be a challenge for trustees of a museum to comprehend why the most valuable holdings of an organization are not monetized, it must be communicated that as stewards of their collections, museums are charged with holding collections for their charitable and educational purposes (American Alliance of Museums, n.d.). This commitment to collections protections is a new development in the 21st century, whereas previously the market valuation and even sale of collections were frowned upon, but allowable (White 1996).[5]

Issues with valuation of objects collections extend beyond the balance sheet. Collections controls limit risk exposure not only in financial matters, but in the best practices employed in collections departments. Fastidious record keeping regarding provenance and authenticity is of paramount importance to museum professionals, especially in recognition that any object displayed in or purchased by a museum increases in value by association. Undermining the process, either intentionally or through mismanagement, can have devastating consequences for a museum: take the case of the Orlando Museum of Art, which hosted a 2022 exhibition of works by then 20th century American artist Jean Michel Basquiat. After the exhibition had opened, however, works were discovered to be fraudulent and initiated the dismissal or resignation of multiple trustees, the museum director and other senior staff, incited a global maelstrom about museums and the public trust, and warranted a formal review of the accreditation status by the American Alliance of Museums (Sokol 2022).

Systematic Controls

As argued in this chapter, controls are an indispensable and comprehensive tool to ensure compliant and transparent processes in museums. Yet they are only as effective as the organization allows them to be through systematic activation. In terms of internal systems, financial processes should be executed according to a schedule that is most appropriate to the organizational scale: one example would be to process and record transactions weekly, including both payables and receivables, to reconcile budgets on a monthly basis, and to create quarterly financial reports for the trustees. A schedule of regular and consistent review encourages a rhythm of data review, creating a pace by which the staff and board contribute specific roles of data processing, compilation, and analysis. Such consistency furthers informed preparation of the annual financial statements and budget, and for productive interim reporting.

One financial exercise that creates a reference for activity is the activation and monitoring of data through budgets for operating and non-operating activities. The operating budget can be the best method by which to manage data for regular institutional functions through the documentation of departmental work, facilities and property needs, and staff compensation tracking. Informed by historical institutional data, as well as responses to market fluctuations, cost estimates, and vendor proposals if relevant, the operating budget provides insight into needs and capacity. The same methodology applies to the creation of non-operating and special project budgets, often implemented to documented term projects such as institutional planning, capital projects, or other initiatives. All budgets serve as records of project or operational priorities, income expectations and fundraising goals, and are especially beneficial when updated and monitored regularly. With regular oversight, the budget tool can inform museum leadership regarding the need to shift expectations and implement effective planning and prioritization. Additionally, the budget can be a crucial tool for forecasting and expense/income projections, as well as to evidence data amalgamated in the creation of the annual report.

The creation of the annual report is a critical control system in and of itself, for it follows external financial standards and is compiled by an external firm, meaning that the report process should be a neutral analysis of financial health and the internal controls themselves. The creation of the audited financial statements, consisting of a statement of financial activity, a statement of financial position, a statement of cash flows, and a statement of functional expenses is expected of museums in the United States that gross income above a threshold determined by the Internal Revenue Service. In addition to the four statements, the annual report also consists of a completed IRS Form 990, the Return of Organization Exempt from Income Tax, required of almost all nonprofit organizations in the United States.[6] Together, these documents provide detail regarding organizational business dealings and asset management, including foreign transaction filings, demonstrate financial stability and risk exposure, and record any changes to financial systems due to leadership transitions and/or special projects.

The annual report is the essential tool to support the nonprofit museum's commitment to its mandate of public trust and transparency, designed to evidence ethical and compliant management. The financial statements and 990 filing are available for public review in print and digital forms. As nonprofit organizations are not subject to certain taxes, they must share data with the public to show the dedication to their charitable purpose and to best practices.[7] Together, the components of the annual report are the form by which the organization proves its reliance on contributed income, stewardship of its property and financial assets, and even records the compensation of its highest-earning employees. In the case that the report documents activity in violation of generally accepted accounting principles (GAAP) or management of investments in opposition to the Uniform Prudent Management of Institutional Funds Act (UPMIFA), the organization may face consequences ranging from ineligibility for certain funding opportunities to donor disengagement to investigation; in the United States, the state attorney general can file to revoke an organization's tax exemption (Lichtblau 2015, 160–1).

Along with the creation of a schedule of processing that informs a strong and comprehensive annual reporting process, the documentation of such functions should be recorded in a strong financial management handbook. The handbook should serve as the primary resource for board and staff members, outlining procedures related to topics such as mission relevance, financial allocations, performance measures, approvals systems, financial controls, procurement, governance framework, and internal and external audit expectations.[8] The articulation of board and staff duties in a financial management handbook, also referred to as a fiscal operations policy manual can include documentation of a variety of processes as relevant to the organization; in addition to those detailed above, Cinnamon Catlin-Legutko and Stacy Klingler further specify the inclusion of indemnification language, record retention and destruction policies, account management and reconciliation measures, capital depreciation calculations, credit card issuance and use policy, conflict of interest, and whistleblower policies (Granger 2013, 17–18). Documentation of such activities are often a focus of external audits and should be revised and made current on at least an annual basis.

Communications and Control Systems

Communications remain a priority and function well as part of an integrated systems approach, in which departmental needs are unified with a focus on shared vision and accountability. Systems of communications should be well understood, transparent, and regularly reviewed. The segregation of duties, for instance, should be reviewed and potentially revised on an annual basis; likewise, interdepartmental needs and priorities must be regularly discussed. The budget process can be an effective tool to determine institutional priorities, as well as financial opportunities and limitations. The integrated systems approach encourages dialogue about decisions with financial implications, such as the potential deaccessions of a work that earns income to be restricted to collections care and/or purchases, or the security team that identifies a platform that should be updated to minimize risk and thus prevent increased liability costs, such as insurance premiums.

Reiterating the point of fiduciary responsibility that befalls trustees, the maintenance and revision of governing policies, committee charters, and financial policies is vital. On at least an annual basis, the governing body should ensure that such resources are easily accessible and regularly referenced, and that any updates are disseminated to the board as a whole. Processes ranging from new trustee orientation to the preparation of the annual audit are essential to ensure trustees are informed and acting in the governance role, and serve to prepare the organization to function according to a cohesive value structure should there be the need to face unusual institutional conditions, such as the launch of a capital project, or external conditions, such as a state-mandated closure.[9]

Recommendations for Sustainable Practices

As we can see, the regularization of internal and management control systems is vital to ensure consistent and informed accounting, financial management, and fiduciary oversight. Creating systems that dictate expectations of accountability, communication, and documentation requires the investment of staff and board to commit to hold themselves accountable to federal financial standards and field-wide expectations on a global scale. To summarize, this chapter recommends:

- Internal controls that invite inter-departmental communication and highlight segregation of duties, process orientation, and control cues.
- Management controls that warrant board-staff dialogue, align with mandates regarding governance and financial prudence, and reduce risk exposure.
- And external controls, including the annual audit process, designed to show a commitment to financial and professional practices as well as the public trust.

This chapter elucidates controls systems, their various forms, and responsible parties. We can observe that the creation of controls is only one piece of the puzzle; even more important is the correspondence of such systems with daily financial data management, internal financial reporting models, and external formal reporting. Engagement with control systems can even help us answer questions such as: How is the organization activating its mission through compliant measures? Is the museum responsibly managing its assets with financial prudence? Is the museum employing operational models that demonstrate a commitment to long-term viability and minimizing exposure to risk, including fraud? The establishment and regularization of control systems and communication are critical to financial management and informed fiduciary oversight.

Notes

1 Operating activities are those that occur as part of regular business, investing activities include the sale or purchase of long-term assets (such as equipment or property), and financing activities typically refer to loans.

2 For additional information on museum fraud and embezzlement, see Max Van Balgooy (2017) "Embezzlement: Is It Our Dirty Little Secret?"

3 Whistleblower policies encourage staff and volunteers to disclose credible information regarding illegal practices or policy violations on behalf of the organization without retaliation, according to the National Council of Nonprofits. While whistleblowers are federally protected by law, there are numerous examples of retaliation, such as layoffs or demotion of whistleblowers. Internal whistleblower policies detail methods for whistleblowers to come forward with information and commit the organization to their protection.

4 For additional information on these organizations and policies, see Marilyn E. Phelan's *Museum Law: A Guide for Officers, Directors, and Counsel* (2014).
5 Though museums are strongly discouraged from valuing objects for financial purposes, museum staff is charged with keeping current insurance valuations in cases of theft, loss, or damage.
6 Though classified as charitable organizations, houses of religious worship are not required to complete financial statements for public dissemination (however, many elect to do so as a commitment to transparency).
7 For a robust discussion of the concept of the public trust in the United States and Great Britain, see Katherine Groninger, "An Introduction to Museum Accountability."
8 A thorough and surprisingly relevant example of a financial handbook can be found in the British Museum's 2016–2020 Management Agreement.
9 For more information about integrated systems, see Susan Mann's "The Application of Systems Thinking to Museum Sustainability" (2017).

References

American Alliance of Museums. 2019. "Direct Care of Collections." https://www.aam-us.org/wp-content/uploads/2018/01/Direct-Care-of-Collections_March-2019.pdf

American Alliance of Museums. n.d. "Capitalization of Collections." Accessed April 1, 2023. https://www.aam-us.org/programs/resource-library/financial-stability-resources/capitalization-of-collections/

British Museum. *British Museum Management Agreement 2016–2020*. https://www.britishmuseum.org/sites/default/files/2019-10/British-Museum-management-2016-2020.pdf

Demmert, James E. 2019. *The Sustainable Endowment: 10 Principles to Make Your Foundation or Nonprofit Last for Decades*. Ontario, CA: New Insights Press.

Granger, Brenda. 2013. "The Good, the Best, and the IRS: Museum Financial Management Solutions and Recommendations." In *Small Museum Toolkit: Financial Resource Development and Management*, edited by Stacy Klingler and Cinnamon Catlin-Legutko, 1–26. Lanham, MD: Altamira Press.

Groninger, Katherine. 2016. "An Introduction to Museum Accountability." *The Museum Scholar* 1 (1): 1–15. https://articles.themuseumscholar.org/2016/08/02/vol1no1groninger-2/

Kuruvilla, Heather Hope. 2016. *A Legal Dictionary for Museums*. Lanham, MD: Rowman & Littlefield.

Lichtblau, Anita. 2015. "Endowments and Restricted Gifts: Accessible or Hands Off?" In *The Legal Guide for Museum Professionals*, edited by Julia Courtney, 160–1. Lanham, MD: Rowman & Littlefield.

Mann, Susan. 2017. "The Application of Systems Thinking to Museum Sustainability." In *Systems Thinking in Museums: Theory and Practice*, edited by Yuha Jung and Ann Rowson Love, 171–80. Latham, MD: Rowman & Littlefield.

McLaughlin, Thomas. 2002. *Streetsmart Financial Basics for Nonprofit Managers*. New York: John Wiley & Sons.

Office of the Arizona Attorney General. 2009. "Tucson Museum Bookkeeper Given 5 Year Term for Embezzling Nearly $1 Million." Press release, September 3, 2009, https://www.azag.gov/press-release/tucson-museum-bookkeeper-given-5-year-term-embezzling-nearly-1-million

Parachini, Allan. 1990. "Museum Dispute Focuses on Re-Created Time Cards: Audit: A Science Foundation Auditor Says the Natural History Museum May Be 'Faking' Records. The Museum Director Says 'No.'" *Los Angeles Times*, February 28, 1990.

Phelan, Marilyn E. 2014. *Museum Law: A Guide for Officers, Directors, and Counsel.* Latham, MD: Rowman & Littlefield.
Sokol, Brett. 2022. "After Basquiat Raid, Orlando Museum Faces Crisis of Credibility." *New York Times*, August, 12, 2022. https://www.nytimes.com/2022/08/12/arts/design/basquiat-raid-orlando-museum-rollins.html
Trachtenberg, Bruce S. 2010. "Fraud in Fruitlands – Museum Comes Late to Financial Controls." *Nonprofit Quarterly*, May 7, 2010. https://nonprofitquarterly.org/nonprofit-newswire-fraud-in-fruitlandsmuseum-comes-late-to-financial-controls/
United States v. Maurello. 23 CR 20 (N.D. Ill. January 23, 2023). https://www.justice.gov/d9/2023-01/indictment_maurello_0.pdf
Van Balgooy, Max. 2017. "Embezzlement: Is It Our Dirty Little Secret?" *History News* 72 (1): 20–5.
White, Jennifer L. 1996. "When It's OK to Sell the Monet: A Trustee-Fiduciary-Duty Framework for Analyzing the Deaccessioning of Art to Meet Museum Operating Expenses." *Art, Antiquity and Law* 1 (4): 375.

11

LEGAL AND ETHICAL CONSIDERATIONS

Marek Prokůpek

Introduction

Financial sustainability is now one of the main challenges for museums globally. They are pressured to diversify their income sources, engage more with the private commercial sector and individual donors, and implement more entrepreneurial spirit (Camarero and Garrido 2009; Lindqvist 2012; Woodward 2012; Tobelem 2013; Alexander 2018; Proteau 2018; Romolini et al. 2020; Pauget et al. 2021). Governments in the majority of countries have implemented several ways to encourage private investment in culture such as special tax treatment for cultural organizations, individuals, or businesses that provide donations to cultural institutions or their sponsors (Klamer et al. 2006).

In some cases, closer connections with the business sector created controversy, which led to some museums losing the confidence of the communities in which they served (Tobelem 2013; Chong 2019). Museums, in recent years, have faced increased scrutiny of their sources of funding, corporate partnerships and philanthropy (Prokůpek and Divíšková 2023). A number of museums have experienced demonstrations, happenings, and fierce criticism of environmental activists and community groups. Examples are the Tate Gallery for their partnership with British Petroleum, the Science Museums in London for cooperation with Shell and British Petrol, the Van Gogh Museum for relations with Shell, or the Guggenheim Museum and the Louvre Museum for donations received from the Sackler Trust. Ethical dilemmas in fundraising and philanthropy have become a focal point in the museum sector. Naturally, these controversies are mostly present in Western Europe and the United States, where museums are more dependent on private contributions and earned income. Partnership and cooperation with

DOI: 10.4324/9781003308003-14

the private sector have been, to a different extent in different countries, encouraged by legislation related mostly to tax incentives and diverse cultural policies. This chapter aims to provide an overview of tax and ethical consideration of museum financial management and how different models of legislation impact museum behavior. The chapter, furthermore, introduces ethical management tools in the form of codes of ethics that help museum professionals navigate their decisions in financial management.

Legislation and Diverse Taxation Landscape

Museums have different legal status in different parts of the world. In continental Europe, the majority of museums are state-subsidized organizations (sometimes called public benefit organizations), which means that there is a high degree of state involvement in financing and managing these museums. While state-subsidized museums benefit from relatively stable state subsidies, they do often struggle with a low level of autonomy and a high level of bureaucracy. In the United Kingdom and United States, as well as other countries, museums have charitable status (Varbanova 2013). Because of their status and their importance for society and development, governments all over the globe have gradually developed numerous ways to support museums, financially but also in other ways. Governmental support is provided via public subsidies, which can be divided into the direct and indirect subsidies categories. Direct subsidies are lump sum payments made to recipients by governments. Indirect subsidies are a form of compensation provided by tax codes (Buijze 2020). They are also known as tax expenditures or tax incentives. Less tax is paid by the taxpayer, which results in less tax revenue for the government (OECD 2020). There is no actual transfer of funds from the taxpayer to the government. However, the recipient organization ends up with more money, whereas the government ends up with less money than if there had not been any indirect subsidies. Preferential tax rates, income deductions, exemptions, and tax postponements are a few examples of indirect support. These actions are intended to affect taxpayer behavior in order to advance policy objectives (Buijze 2020).

Nonprofit status and tax-deductible charity contributions are the two main elements of tax codes that have the greatest direct influence on museums. Due to their nonprofit status, eligible institutions are tax exempt on most of the income they bring in. Moreover, donors contributing to museums may reduce their tax obligations based on the amount of their donations (OECD 2020). Different types of tax deductions in different countries are elaborated further in this chapter.

Tax Incentive to Support Private Donations

The arts and cultural heritage have traditionally benefited greatly from private initiatives. Even though the majority of European nations rely heavily on public support for their cultural institutions, private patronage has always been important. Directly or indirectly, European states frequently encourage the growth of charitable giving and fundraising efforts by employing a variety of strategies that help them accomplish their cultural policy goals. Tax incentives and tax benefits for contributors and beneficiaries are the most popular tools. They enable donors—individuals and corporations—to decrease their taxes in accordance with the size of their contributions (Prokůpek and Ballarini 2022). Planning is essential when developing tax incentives (Wu 2003), since each tax-deductible donation is a cloaked kind of government support.

There are numerous explanations why governments have actively encouraged private cultural patronage in recent years and established a variety of tax incentives to facilitate this. First, it is not possible for the government and institutions to preserve every piece of cultural material. This is especially true for historical structures and heritage sites, both of which are prevalent in Europe. Second, most museums do not receive enough government funding to cover the exorbitant costs of important works of art. Therefore, loans and donations from individual art collectors as well as private contributions of money and artwork continue to be crucial for museums. Additionally, many governments, in particular in Western Europe, actively push museums to secure private funding sources for some of their operations (Camarero and Garrido 2009; Lindqvist 2012; Woodward 2012; Tobelem 2013; Proteau 2018; Romolini et al. 2020; Pauget et al. 2021, Prokůpek et al. 2022). Governments want cultural organizations to be more attentive to their constituents, in addition to the fact that they have limited finances. Cultural institutions are forced to involve the public in their operations because they need to raise additional funds from the general population. Many European governments such as France, the United Kingdom, Italy, the Netherlands use tax incentives to support private initiatives in their campaigns to promote the value of cultural patronage (Daubeuf et al. 2020). In order to influence the private sector in a way that would otherwise be possible through direct subsidies, these incentives are made through special provisions in the tax legislation, such as a special deduction or exemption (OECD 2020). Even though tax benefits will almost never be people's primary motivation for supporting museums, they may encourage donations. Due to the fact that the tax incentive only lowers the costs of contributing, other motivations will predominate. The incentive, however, can provide donors more justification or a purpose to give more money (Hemels 2017). Compared to European museums, private and corporate donations are even more crucial for museums in the United States. According to the American Alliance of Museums (2020), on average 35% of museums' incomes come from private contributions.

Tax incentives for charitable giving frequently take the form of a deduction from taxable income, as in the United States, Japan, and Turkey, among other

TABLE 11.1 Donation deduction from taxable income in selected countries

Country	*Cap*	*Deductible gift*	*Tax benefit*	*Net cost of gift*
United States	50%	50,000	12,000 (24% tax rate)	48,000
Austria	10%	10,000	5,000 (50% tax rate)	55,000
Belgium	10%	10,000	5,000 (50% tax rate)	55,000
Germany	20%	20,000	8,400 (42% tax rate)	51,600
Netherlands	10%	10,000	4,950 (49.5% tax rate)	55,050
Netherlands (regular gift)	0%	60,000	29,700 (49.5% tax rate)	30,300

nations. The benefit to taxpayers is influenced by the tax system's progressivity, the applicable tax rate, and any applicable limitations (O'Hagan 2011). For instance, in the United States the cap is a 50% deduction of an individual's adjusted gross annual income, but 20% and 30% limitations apply in some cases such as donations to a private foundation (IRS 2023). In Germany, donations and membership fees amounting to up to 20% of a total annual income can be deducted from taxable income (EStG 2002). In the Netherlands, for gifts that are not regular, there is a 10% cap. However, if you are contracted to give routine payments for at least five years, there is no maximum offset (Hemels 2017).

As an example, an individual with an annual taxable income of $100,000 donates $60,000 to a museum that has a charitable status in selected countries. For simplicity, consider equal currency rates in these countries, no other personal allowances and deductions, and also consider only one tax rate in an income bracket.

Table 11.1 demonstrates a deductible gift, taking into account the caps of an annual taxable income, tax benefits and net cost of the gift for the individual. It shows that considering these selected countries, in the case of regular gifts, the Netherlands provides the largest tax benefits. On the other hand, in case of one-time donations, the United States offers the best tax deduction.

An alternative to tax deduction is tax credit. Tax credit lowers the amount of tax due, instead of a taxable income. For instance, 66% of the value of gifts is tax deductible in France, subject to a cap of 20% of taxable income (Service Public 2023). If an individual with an annual income of 100,000 donates 40,000 to an eligible organization, this person can reduce their tax obligation by 20,000 since there is a cap of 20% of an annual income. In the case of a donation of 20,000 given by an individual with the same income, this person can reduce their tax obligation by 13,200 (66% of the gift). Other countries such as Spain or Canada have also implemented a system of tax credit.

Another example of a tax credit is Art Bonus established by the Italian government in 2013 and operating since 2014. The Art Bonus program comprises substantial financial incentives for private individuals, who donate to state-subsidized cultural organizations. A tax credit equal to 65% of the donation makes up the art bonus, subject to the following annual caps: for companies, the maximum tax credit amount is 0.005% (five per thousand) of gross revenues; for individuals and non-profit organizations, the maximum credit amount is 15% of annual taxable income. The tax credit must be split into three equal annual installments. Firms can set off the tax credit against other taxes (Donelli et al. 2022). For example, take an individual with an annual income of 25,000 who pays tax on that of 6,250 (with the individual income tax rate of 25%). If this person makes a donation of 2,000, they will receive a tax credit of 1,300 (65% of 2,000), which means that they can reduce their tax obligation by 433 each year for the following three years. Consequently, the cost of 2,000 donations in cash terms is only 700.

A different type of tax incentive for charitable giving is based on a tax refund given to charities rather than to donors. The Gift Aid scheme established in the United Kingdom is an example of such incentives. UK charities are eligible to receive £0.25 from the government under the Gift Aid program for every pound of donations (Williams et al. 2020). It means that if a donor gives 100, a museum that has charitable status actually receives 125 (100 from the donor and 25 from the government).

Tax Benefits for Income-Generating Activities

Special nonprofit status of museums guarantees, in some countries, other tax benefits. These are benefits for the museums themselves, to be precise. Corporate income tax exemptions are a particularly popular exemption for charities. In the United States, tax exemptions for charities—not just the corporate income tax exemption but also the property tax exemption—have always been of paramount importance. Earned income is typically exempt from taxes for the museums in the United States; however, institutions that engage in commercial activities unrelated to their missions may be forced to pay Unrelated Business Income Tax (UBIT) on the resulting income (American Alliance of Museums 2020).

Similarly, in the United Kingdom, when a museum is a charity, it does not pay tax on most of its income and gains if those are used for charitable purposes, which is known as "charitable expenditure." This includes tax on donations, profit from trading, rental or investment income, profit when a museum sells assets, or when a museum buys a property (GOV.UK n.d.). States can choose between a full exemption model for charities (like in Australia, Ireland, and Hungary) and a partial exemption model where only non-business income is taxed. The second model is adopted by the vast majority of countries (Antón 2020).

Donations of Art Works

Gifts that are eligible for a tax advantage may be made in kind or in cash in some countries. Other nations have a unique system in place for gifts in kind. This is crucial for museums and heritage organizations since gifts in kind can be just as significant for these organizations as monetary gifts. For instance, a collector may choose to donate a priceless painting rather than sell it at auction if he is aware that he will receive a tax benefit (Hemels 2017).

In the United Kingdom, for example, the Cultural Gift Scheme, introduced in 2012, encourages UK taxpayers to donate important artworks and other national treasures to be made available to the public rather than sold through private sales. Applications for donations are made to the Arts Council and are considered by a panel of experts. In the case of application approval, in return, donors receive a tax reduction based on a set percentage of the value of the item they donate. The maximum value of the tax reduction for individuals is 30% of the agreed value of the object. In the case of companies, the cap is 20% of the agreed value of the object (Arts Council England n.d.).

The tax break appears to have encouraged art donations to museums in several instances. However, with this type of donation comes the issue of valuation of art works, since the value of art is often viewed as subjective. A high valuation of a work of art results in a substantial deduction for the donor (Hemels 2009). Moreover, accepting potential donations of antiquities or artworks also bears ethical considerations. A museum that accepts a donation of antiquities or artworks may be doing so on behalf of the public and thereby needs to be careful that the objects are not stolen goods (Yates 2015). Therefore, museums must have defined gift acceptance policies and procedures while accepting works of art and other objects.

Acceptance in Lieu of Tax: Pay Tax with Works of Art

Acceptance in lieu is a tax payment option that enables people who owe inheritance tax or one of its predecessor forms to settle their debt by giving significant cultural, scientific, or historical artifacts and archives to the country (Matassa 2011). Many European nations have provided the choice to pay inheritance tax, and in some cases other taxes. The United Kingdom, France, the Netherlands, Ireland, Italy, Belgium, and Spain are a few examples of European nations using this type of tax incentive. It is also feasible to pay inheritance tax in Japan using real estate, construction assets, or fine art. This is referred to as a "dation" in France and a "accepted in lieu of tax" in the United Kingdom (Hemels 2017).

In the UK scheme, instead of selling the same item and using the sale proceeds to pay the liability, an offeror can profit from a larger share of its worth. This is due to the method used to determine the credit the object generates. For example, if, in order to settle a tax liability, an estate sells an object valued at £100,000 on the open market, inheritance tax is generally payable at a rate of 40% and the estate receives £60,000 (100,000 – 40,000). If the same object is offered in lieu, 25% of the tax that would have been payable is remitted to the estate (25% of 40,000 = 10,000), with the result that the estate receives £70,000 for the object, the tax debt is paid off, and the country gains a significant object for the benefit of the general public. An owner therefore receives for the object around 17% more (increase from 60,000 to 70,000) if it is offered in lieu of tax than if it is sold on the open market at the same price (Arts Council England n.d.). In the Netherlands, a 20% discount applies. For example, if someone is required to pay €1,200,000 in inheritance taxes, they can settle the assessment by transferring works of art to the value of €1,000,000. The art becomes the property of the Dutch State, but can be released on permanent loan to a museum (Government of the Netherlands 2022).

The French dation scheme was initiated in 1968 and came into force in 1972. It enables one to pay all or part of a tax by offering the state a work of art or cultural property of heritage interest. Similar to the UK scheme, the value of the work is appraised by a specialized commission which determines whether it meets the required criteria. The work is then taken into account as a method of paying the tax if it is approved. The value of the work is subtracted from the amount of tax owed, and if the value of the object exceeds the amount of owed tax, the surplus can be carried over to the taxes of the following years, up to a maximum of five years (Ministère de la Culture n.d.). The success of the French incentive may be seen in the development of the Musée Picasso in Paris, which was created as a direct result of the application of the dation following the deaths of Picasso and later his wife, Jacqueline, in the following years (Hemels 2017).

Ethical Aspects of Museum Finance

Apart from the legal considerations museums face, they also need to pay attention to many ethical issues when it comes to their financial management. This is especially the case in recent years, when stronger cooperation between museums and the private sector and development of more market-oriented strategies have been encouraged by museums' governing bodies or museums themselves. In several cases, these tendencies sparked controversies and intense debate, and even attracted the attention of the mainstream media. For example, instances where Shell or British Petrol (BP) sponsored the Science Museum in London or the British Museum. Similarly, American artist Nan Goldin protested against the Sackler Trust (members of the family-run trust who own Purdue Pharma, a company selling the prescription painkiller OxyContin) funding several museums (Prokůpek and Divíšková 2023). Why do these partnerships create controversies? In the case of fossil fuel companies such as British Petrol, Shell or Total, activists argue that these companies, while causing significant environmental damages, wash their brands through partnerships with public cultural organizations (Evans 2015). Furthermore, when the London Science Museum's relationships with fossil fuel companies came under scrutiny, an alarming example was revealed. Information surfaced in 2015 that Shell, one of the sponsors of the Science Museum, had made efforts to influence the museum's Atmosphere exhibition, which explored climate science. The collaboration with Shell, BP, and Statoil sparked controversy, and a group that included many climate scientists claimed that it compromised the museum's credibility as a scientific institution (Vaughan 2018). Such activities may have a permanent negative effect on museums' reputation and may result in a decrease in public, professional, and peer confidence. Other sponsors, some less controversial, may stop funding a museum in response to such a circumstance.

The partnership between Sackler Trust and several museums worldwide sparked protests, mostly by an activist group called PAIN, initiated by the artist Nan Goldin. The Sackler family has received a lot of criticism for contributing to the opioid epidemic by allowing Purdue Pharma to produce the addictive medication OxyContin. Members of the Sackler family not only ran this business but made large donations to museums all around the world. Nan Goldin, who herself developed an addiction to OxyContin, refused to organize her retrospective exhibition in the National Portrait Gallery in London, if the museum were to accept a gift of £1 million from Sackler family. After this statement, the National Portrait Gallery became the first major art institution to give up a grant from the Sackler family. Consequently, many other institutions have removed the Sackler name from their walls and said they will no longer accept gifts from the family, largely as a result of PAIN's advocacy (Greenberger 2023). These are just a few examples of partnerships between companies and museums that cause controversies. Currently, museums face increasing scrutiny of their sources of finance, while at the same time struggling with often declining public funding and increasing competition in fundraising. The line between what is acceptable and what is not may be thin, therefore navigations, standards, and recommendations in fundraising decision-making may help museum leaders to avoid controversies and loss of their trust.

Facing Funding Ethical Dilemmas

As the examples above show, museums constantly face funding dilemmas. They are forced to be more entrepreneurial and cooperate more with the private sector yet, on the other hand, they are required, and should, behave ethically. What is ethical and what is not is not simple to define. How can museums improve their decision-making when it comes to the acceptance of support from companies or private individuals? Even if every problematic situation has unique characteristics, Yerkovish (2016) suggests that there are two stages to overcoming an ethical dilemma. The decision-maker is guided toward the best outcome by a sharp separation between the study of the challenge and the solution proposal. In the first phase, decision-makers formulate the problem, such as whether to accept a donation from a fossil fuel company. This first phase includes the collection of all facts, both soft (feelings, opinions, attitudes of people involved) as well as hard (established details and data). In this case, the decision-maker must discuss this donation with their colleagues and governing body to see what their opinions are, but they must also do research about business activities of the company, to see if it has supported other organizations and what reaction was, as well as look at the image of the company and its values and other available information. Furthermore, a differentiation between relevant and irrelevant facts should be made and irrelevant data eliminated. In this first phase, they should also identify the people and institutions involved, both internal and external such as colleagues, community groups, media, governing body, donors and funders, and experts, depending on the circumstances. Based on this information, the decision-maker can then formulate the ethical problem. Last but not least, relevant codes of ethics (such as codes in the museum sector as well as particular institutional codes) are to be reviewed, and other museums or organizations that have faced similar situations should be consulted. In the second phase of dealing with an ethical dilemma, Yerkovish (2016) proposes to establish possible solutions and actions. In this phase, the decision-maker should first formulate possible options for resolving the problem, consult any relevant laws as well as codes of ethics to make sure that the proposed solution is not against them, and consider potential consequences, both internal and external. In this moment, they should also identify the best and the worst scenarios and possible responses to these and develop a strategy to deal with negative responses. Lastly, feedback should be obtained from their colleagues and used to assess the decision and make necessary corrections. With regards to the case at hand, it would mean that the decision-maker would formulate options such as accepting donations and delineating the conditions of the deal, or refusing donations or other solutions, while consulting relevant codes and laws. The reaction of the stakeholders must be identified both in the case of accepting and rejecting the donation. There can be positive and negative responses in both cases, since diverse stakeholders may have conflicting goals. Community groups may be opposed to the partnership, while the governing body may support such cooperation. It is paramount to develop a strategy for all scenarios and prepare a communication strategy. What is important is to have a discussion about these options with other museum staff and implement their relevant comments. Of course, this case is simplified; each museum is specific with unique missions, values, stakeholders, and conditions. Therefore, while applying this framework, numerous characteristics need to be taken into account.

Navigation with Codes of Ethics and Fundraising Policies

In many facets of our society and in professional settings, codes of ethics are essential. Naturally, they do not offer a solution to every risky situation, nor they are universally applicable. Their main objectives are to develop professional standards and act as a guide for behavior. The museum industry has numerous codes of ethics that have been created by museum associations, organizations, and the museums themselves. A wide range of museum activities and operations are covered by museum ethics, and these organizations offer their established standards for universal access to museums.

Codes of ethics formalize a set of standards that are inherent to any individual who respects them and conducts themselves ethically. Codes of ethics are intended to control an individual's behavior within a system, offer direction when an individual is confronted with an ethical issue, and serve as a tool to deter unethical behavior. There is not a single code that can be applied to all occupations. On the contrary, each profession needs a clear strategy that takes into account its unique traits. Additionally, ethics codes need to be revised to reflect modern inclinations. Currently, having a code of conduct is viewed as a competitive advantage since it inspires confidence in stakeholders, consumers, and employees (Prokůpek and Divíšková 2023).

The first ethical guidelines for museums appeared in the United States. The first code was approved in 1925 by the American Alliance of Museums, formerly known as the American Association of Museums (Bounia 2014). The breadth and content of the many codes now in effect for the American museum sector varies. Inadvertently, however, their quantity, variety, and mutual meaning overlap could present difficulties for museum staff in the form of confusion about what conduct is truly ethical (Edson 1997).

The International Council of Museum's (ICOM) code of ethics is among the most significant in the museum industry. The 15th General Assembly in Buenos Aires first established this code on November 4, 1986, and the 21st General Assembly in Seoul last updated it in 2004. The organization decided to study and, if required, update the code following the 2019 25th ICOM General Conference, which was held in Kyoto. A draft of the Code of Ethics will be created by the Standing Committee on Ethics (ETHCOM) and will be the subject of consultation in 2024. By the triennial conference in 2025, ETHCOM anticipates having the updated Code of Ethics ready for adoption (ICOM 2023). A very small portion is used for fundraising. According to the ICOM code, "the governing body should ensure that there are sufficient funds to carry out and develop the activities of the museums and that all funds must be accounted for in a professional manner" (ICOM 2017, 4). The

ICOM Code of Ethics for Museums was supplemented by new fundraising standards, which were introduced in March 2022, further supporting the ethical concerns surrounding museum fundraising. This document highlights that each museum should have a fundraising policy that addresses the legal and ethical principles and professional responsibilities involved in accepting such donations. Furthermore, it says that the museum's governing body should have participated in the development of, and given final approval for, the fundraising policy before it is made public (ICOM 2022).

Many museums have implemented their own policies in different forms and under different names such as fundraising policy, acceptance policy, donation policy, or charts. According to Rich Cohen (2002), these documents should respond to the following three key issues:

1 What kind of businesses and industries will a museum seek funding from, and what types will it avoid or reject?
2 What limitations or conditions, if any, will the museum accept from the potential sponsor or donor?
3 How does the museum plan to assess its business partners and private donors?

The same as with codes of ethics, the missions and values of museums serve as the foundation for these policies and charts. Each museum should have an acceptance policy for a number of reasons. First of all, such a document inspires museum employees and serves as a reminder of the organization's values and ideas; as a result, museum employees should be included in the policy's creation. Second, it encourages museums to be transparent and accountable to all parties involved, including the government, businesses that fund them, private donors, their peers, museum associations, and the general public.

Conclusion

In the museum sector, even in countries with a strong tradition of public funding such as continental Europe, private contributions and cooperation with the private sector is gradually promoted and encouraged through a diverse set of policies and legislation. Different tax legislation, either for donors who can reduce their taxes based on the donation, or museums, who have special favorable tax obligations, aims to encourage stronger ties between museums, the private sector and entrepreneurial activities. While private contribution is encouraged for museums, increasing scrutiny of museum funding is present and the expectation that museums will respond to societal issues is growing.

It is becoming more and more required of museums to play a more active role in society and address a range of themes, such as gender concerns, environmental challenges, and sociological contexts at national, regional, and local levels. More and more, it is critical to have a common set of values and a strong ethical foundation (Sandahl 2019; Prokůpek and Divišíková 2023).

Legal and ethical considerations of financial museum management are therefore more important than ever before. Museums and governments are gradually developing new tools and legislation. Moreover, it is expected that due to the consequences of the COVID-19 pandemic in the form of increased national debts in the majority of countries, governments will decrease public spending in arts and culture and therefore encourage even more private support for museums and stimulate financial self-sustainability in the museum sector.

References

Alexander, D. Victoria. 2018. "Enterprise Culture and the Arts: Neoliberal Values and British Art Institutions." In *Art and the Challenge of Markets Volume 1*, edited by Victoria D. Alexander, 67–93. Cham: Palgrave McMillan.

American Alliance of Museums. 2020. *Trends Watch: The Future of Financial Sustainability*. American Alliance of Museums.

Antón, Ricardo García. 2020. "Cultural Heritage and Sustainable Taxation—Empowering Communities in the COVID-19 Times." *Revista de Estudios Jurídicos y Criminológicos*: 123–44.

Arts Council England. n.d. "Cultural Gift Scheme." Accessed July 4, 2023. https://www.artscouncil.org.uk/sites/default/files/download-file/Cultural_Gifts_Scheme_leaflet.p

Bounia, Alexandra. 2014. "Codes of Ethics and Museum Research." *Journal of Conservation and Museum Studies*, 12 (1): 1–7. 10.5334/jcms.1021214

Buijze, Renate. 2020. "Tax Incentives for International Giving to the Cultural Sector." In *Teaching Cultural Economics*, edited by Trine Bille, Anna Mignosa, and Ruth Towse, 86–90. Cheltenham: Edward Elgar Publishing.

Camarero, Carmen and María-José Garrido. 2009. "Improving Museums' Performance through Custodial, Sales, and Customer Orientations." *Nonprofit and Voluntary Sector Quarterly* 38 (5): 846–68. 10.1177/0899764008319230

Chong, Derrick. 2019. "Art, Finance, Politics, and the Art Museum as a Public Institution." In *Museum Marketizationm Cultural Institutions in the Neoliberal Era*, edited by Karin M. Ekström, 98–114. London: Routledge.

Cohen, Rick. 2002. "Fundraising Medicine: Creating Gift Acceptance Policies." *Grassroots Fundraising Journalm* 21 (1): 11–13.

Daubeuf, Clémentine, Andy Pratt, Elisabetta Airaghi, and Teodora Pletosu. 2020. *Enumerating the Role of Incentives in CCI Production Chains*. CICERONE publication.

Donelli, Chiara Carolina, Isabella Mozzoni, Francesco Badia, and Simone Fanelli. 2022. "Financing Sustainability in the Arts Sector: The Case of the Art Bonus Public Crowdfunding Campaign in Italy." *Sustainability* 14 (3): 1641. 10.3390/su14031641

Edson, Gary. 1997. *Museum Ethics*. London: Taylor & Francis.

EStG (Einkommensteuergesetz/Income Tax, Germany). 2002. "The Fiscal Code of Germany." Accessed July 4, 2023. https://www.gesetze-im-internet.de/estg/__10b.html

Evans, Mel. 2015. *Artwash: Big Oil and the Arts*. London: Pluto Press.

GOV.UK. n.d. "Charities and Tax." Accessed July 4, 2023. https://www.gov.uk/charities-and-tax/tax-reliefs.
Government of the Netherlands. 2022. "Inheritance tax." Accessed July 4, 2023. https://www.government.nl/topics/inheritance-tax/filing-an-inheritance-tax-return
Greenberger, Alexander. 2023. "Nan Goldin's PAIN Group Takes Its Anti-Sackler Protests to Harvard's Art Museums, Again." *ArtNews*. April 21, Accessed July 4, 2023. https://www.artnews.com/art-news/news/nan-goldin-pain-anti-sackler-protest-harvard-art-museums-1234665217/
Hemels, Sigrid. 2009. "From Private to Public with the Help of Tax Incentives: How Tax Legislation Can Support Private Patronage of the Arts and Cultural Heritage." *Japan Journal of Cultural Economics*: 1–8.
Hemels, Sigrid. 2017. "Tax Incentives for Museums and Cultural Heritage." In *Tax Incentives for the Creative Industries*, edited by Sigrid Hemels and Kazuko Goto, 107–35. Singapore: Springer.
International Council of Museums (ICOM). 2017. *ICOM Codes of Ethics for Museums*. Paris: ICOM.
International Council of Museums (ICOM). 2022. *Standards on Fundraising of the International Council of Museums*. Paris: ICOM.
International Council of Museums (ICOM). 2023. "Participate in the Revision of ICOM's Code of Ethics for Museums!" *ICOM*, 6 June 2023. Accessed July 4, 2023. https://icom.museum/en/news/participate-in-the-revision-of-icoms-code-of-ethics-for-museums/
International Revenue Service (IRS). 2023. "Tax Exempt Organization Search: Deductibility Status Codes." Accessed July 4, 2023. https://www.irs.gov/charities-non-profits/tax-exempt-organization-search-deductibility-status-codes
Klamer, Arjo, Lyudmilla Petrova, Anna Mignosa, Stichting Economie, and Cultuur. 2006. *Financing the Arts and Culture in the EU*. Brussels: European Parliament.
Lindqvist, Katja. 2012. "Museum Finances: Challenges Beyond Economic Crises." *Museum Management and Curatorship* 27 (1): 1–15. 10.1080/09647775.2012.644693
Matassa, Freda. 2011. *Museum Collections Management*. London: Facet Publishing.
Ministère de la Culture. n.d. "Measures to Encourage Individual Giving." Accessed July 4, 2023. https://www.culture.gouv.fr/en/Thematic/Patronage/Individuals/Measures-to-Encourage-Individual-Giving
OECD. 2020. "Taxation and Philanthropy." *OECD Tax Policy Studies*, No. 27, Paris: OECD Publishing. 10.1787/df434a77-en
O'Hagan, John. 2011. "Tax Concessions." In *A Handbook of Cultural Economics*, 2nd ed., 408–12, Cheltenham: Edward Elgar.
Pauget, Bertrand, Jean-Michel Tobelem, and Jean-Philippe Bootz. 2021. "The Future of French Museums in 2030." *Technological Forecasting and Social Change* 162: 120384. 10.1016/j.techfore.2020.120384
Prokůpek, Marek, and Bára Divíšková. 2023. "Ethics in Museum Fundraising: Evidence from the Czech Republic." *The Journal of Arts Management, Law, and Society* 53 (1): 42–61. 10.1080/10632921.2022.2135654
Prokůpek, Marek, Ellen Loots, and Diana Betzler. 2022. "Emergency or Emerging Financing Strategies of Art Museums in the Context of a Pandemic?" *Museum Management and Curatorship*, 1–18. 10.1080/09647775.2022.2111327
Prokůpek, Marek and Marie Ballarini. 2022. "Comparative Study of European Policies for Ethical Museum Fundraising and Philanthropy." In *Accomplishing Cultural Policy in Europe*, edited by Christopher Mathieu and Valerie Visanich, 123–40. London: Routledge.
Proteau, Jasmine. 2018. "Reducing Risky Relationships: Criteria for Forming Positive Museum-Corporate Sponsorships." *Museum Management and Curatorship* 33 (3): 235–42. 10.1080/09647775.2018.1467274

Romolini, Alberto, Silvia Fissi, Elena Gori, and Marco Contri. 2020. "Financing Museums: Towards Alternative Solutions? Evidence from Italy." In *Management, Participation and Entrepreneurship in the Cultural and Creative Sector*, edited by Martin Piber, 11–32. Cham: Springer.

Sandahl, Jette. 2019. "Addressing Societal Responsibilities through Core Museum Functions and Methods: The Museum Definition, Prospects and Potentials." *Museum International* 71 (1-2): iv. 10.1080/13500775.2019.1638016

Service Public. 2023. "Income tax—Donations to General Interest Associations and Organizations." Accessed July 4, 2023. https://www.service-public.fr/particuliers/vosdroits/F426?lang=en

Tobelem, Jean-Michel. 2013. "The Arts and Culture: A Financial Burden or a Way Out of the Crisis." *ENCATC Journal of Cultural Management and Policy* 3 (1): 52–60.

Varbanova, Lidia. 2013. *Strategic Management in the Arts*. London: Routledge.

Vaughan, Adam. 2018. "Science Museum under Pressure to Shun Big Oil Sponsorship." *The Guardian*, July 4, 2018. Accessed July 4, 2023. https://www.theguardian.com/business/2018/jul/04/science-museum-under-pressure-to-shun-big-oil-sponsorship

Williams, M. David, Salaheddin Darwish, Steve Schneider, and David R. Michael. 2020. "Legislation-Driven Development of a Gift Aid System Using Event-B." *Formal Aspects of Computing*, 32 (2-3): 251–73.

Woodward, Simon. 2012. "Funding Museum Agendas: Challenges and Opportunities." *Managing Leisure* 17 (1): 14–28. 10.1080/13606719.2011.638202

Wu, Chin-Tao. 2003. *Privatising Culture: Corporate Art Intervention since the 1980s*. London: Verso.

Yates, Donna. 2015. "Museums, Collectors, and Value Manipulation: Tax Fraud through Donation of Antiquities." *Journal of Financial Crime* 23 (1): 173–86. 10.1108/JFC-11-2014-0051

Yerkovich, Sally. 2016. *A Practical Guide to Museum Ethics*. London: Rowman & Littlefield Publishers.

12

MUSEUM FINANCES

Accounting for Capacity and Sustainability

Daniel Hummel[1] *and Leigh Hersey*[2]

[1]Assistant Professor of Political Science, University of Louisiana Monroe in Monroe, Louisiana, USA; [2]Associate Professor of Political Science, University of Louisiana Monroe in Monroe, Louisiana, USA

Introduction

In this chapter, we will explore an assessment of the financial condition of nonprofit museums in the United States. Nonprofit organizations are funded through three primary revenue sources—private giving, government grants and contracts, and earned income. Additionally, 60% (Calabrese and Ely 2017) of arts-oriented nonprofit organizations also depend on endowments. Referred to by some as a "mixed economy" (Anheier 2005), this variety of revenue sources is one characteristic of nonprofit organizations that makes the sector different from both government agencies and for-profit organizations (Grønbjerg 1991). Some argue that this diverse revenue portfolio helps provide these organizations with financial stability (Tuckman and Chang 1991; Kingma 1993; Association of Art Museum Directors 2018). While having a variety of funding sources can prevent a nonprofit organization from depending too much on one source, it also can give nonprofit organizations less ability to control their revenue streams than government or for-profit organizations (Grønbjerg 1991). A meta-analysis by Hung and Hager (2019) demonstrated that a diversified revenue portfolio has a small, but statistically significant positive impact on the financial health of nonprofit organizations. In general, art museums have a diversified revenue portfolio with 33% of total revenue generated from private giving, 27% from earned income, 22% from endowment income, and 15% coming from government support (Association of Art Museum Directors 2018).

The performance of nonprofit organizations, such as museums, depends on how well the organization achieves its mission. Financial health plays an important role in this assessment. For example, Kim (2017) references the

DOI: 10.4324/9781003308003-15

need for both stability and growth for the nonprofit. In this work, Kim references Bowman (2011) in which financial capacity is described as having the resources that enable the organization to act, presumably on its mission. Further, capacity is assumed to contribute to financial sustainability in which the organization can meet its financial obligations and cover expenses not only in the short term but also in the long term (Bowman 2011; Park and Matkin 2021).

Much of the nonprofit financial management literature has focused on financial health and condition. Ratios have been relied upon because, "financial ratio analysis is considered the most useful for nonprofits in order to assess distinct aspects of financial sustainability over the short term and long term" (Park and Matkin 2021, 547). Typically, these ratios have emphasized liquidity,[1] solvency,[2] margins, and profitability (Prentice 2016). The different kinds of ratios are detailed in the next section.

Financial Ratios for Nonprofits

The most popular financial ratios to assess the financial condition of nonprofits were developed by Tuckman and Chang (1991), expanded on by Bowman (2011), and employed frequently in the literature (McNeal 2013; Moore 2015; Yan and Sloan 2016; Kim 2017; Searing 2018). Tuckman and Chang's (1991) measure included ratios that captured revenue diversification and concentration (Hirshman-Herfindahl Index),[3] administrative expenses (compared to program expenses of total expenses), operating margin (revenue over expenses), and equity balance (net assets of total revenue).

Bowman (2011) expanded upon the measures of Tuckman and Chang (1991) with more detailed ratios separated by short-term and long-term financial objectives. Short-term objectives focused on resiliency to financial shocks by determining months of spending and changes in unrestricted net assets (Bowman 2011). Long-term objectives focus on equity and return on assets in which net assets and total assets were considered the most important criteria (Bowman 2011).

Based on these foundational studies as well as other literature on the topic, there are four definable solvency areas: cash, budget, equity, and fiscal slack. Cash solvency emphasizes liquidity and having cash on hand. Chabotar (1989, 193) described this as an "available funds ratio." One commonly used ratio in this area is the liquid unrestricted net assets ratio, which separates illiquid net assets[4] from total unrestricted net assets over monthly operating expenses (Antonelli 2016). Another ratio applied to this area is the quick ratio which considers receivables[5] in addition to other current assets as a proportion of monthly expenses (Greenlee and Bukovinsky 1998). At the core of these measures is an effort to understand how current assets compare to current liabilities[6] (Maguire 2016; Park and Matkin 2021).

Budget solvency was one of the initial ratios developed by Tuckman and Chang (1991) and used by Bowman (2011) in a return on assets ratio. Revenues are considered over expenses in comparison to total revenues or total expenses. This measure has been adopted in much of the literature on this topic (Greenlee and Trussel 2000; Ritchey and Kolodinsky 2003; Levine and Zahradnik 2012).

Equity[7] solvency has been measured in different ways. Net assets have been compared to total assets or total revenue (Tuckman and Chang 1991; Bowman 2011, 40). The focus is not on debt, but on whether a nonprofit could hold debt sustainably. Some research considers debt directly such as Andres-Alonso et al. (2016) who looked at total assets to total debt as well as current assets to total debt.

The final solvency measure considers fiscal slack.[8] Kirk and Nolan (2010) measured an overhead ratio which was general expenses and fundraising expenses over total revenue. Kim (2017) established an operating efficiency measure in which program expenses[9] were compared to total expenses. These ratios have been interpreted differently. For example, an increase in spending on programs is assumed to increase donations and improve financial condition or can limit administrative slack which would give fewer options to make cuts during times of financial stress which would decrease financial condition (Kim 2017). This assumption on administrative slack was noted by Tuckman and Chang (1991, 453) who argued that "nonprofits with high administrative costs (relative to others in their category) are assumed to have the greatest opportunity to cut back on administrative costs without reducing programs."

In museums and other arts organizations, cutting back on administrative costs may hamper reaching mission-driven goals. In their research on arts and cultural nonprofit organizations, Altamimi and Liu (2022) found that the relationship between the overhead cost ratio and program outcomes is an inverted U. Their findings suggest that too little spent on overhead deprives the organization of vital capacity-building strategies. However, too much money spent on overhead can lead to inefficiency.

These four solvency areas and the ratios that represent them can present a clearer picture of the financial condition of nonprofit organizations such as museums in both the short term and long term. Unfortunately, it is rare to use these measures in conjunction with one another and some consider these measures to be interchangeable. Altamimi and Liu (2022) recommend moving away from the "one ratio suits all" (1341) mentality. The following section outlines the development of a measure used in this study on museums.

A Comprehensive Measure of Financial Condition

We developed a theoretical framework that uses ten financial ratios based on the four solvency areas to assess the fiscal health of nonprofit museums.

We tested this framework using IRS Form 990 data from a sample of 60 nonprofit museums. For each ratio, an increase in the ratio value increases the financial condition of the museum. Although financial ratios are found in nonprofit rating systems, such as Charity Navigator, this framework represents the most comprehensive set of ratios that explore the different solvency areas present in a nonprofit organization.

For cash solvency, there are several items that can be used to create a set of ratios. On the asset side, these include cash, cash equivalents, investments, and receivables on a monthly average. On the liability side, average monthly expenses provide a good standard of the short-term liabilities for the organization. The emphasis on monthly current assets and liabilities is due to the monthly emphasis on nonprofit operations (Greenlee and Bukovinsky 1998; Bowman 2011). From these items two ratios can be calculated, the cash ratio (Equation 1) and the quick ratio (Equation 2).

Equation 1: Cash Ratio

Monthly average (cash + cash equivalents[10] *+ investments*[11]*)/*

Average monthly expenses

Equation 2: Quick Ratio

Monthly average (cash + cash equivalents + investments + receivables)/

Average monthly expenses

Further, the liquid unrestricted net assets (LUNA) ratio is an appropriate measure of cash solvency. This includes the total unrestricted net assets minus the total illiquid net assets averaged over 12 months (Equation 3). The difference is considered in proportion to the average monthly expenses. These three ratios can be averaged and equally weighted to produce a cash solvency score.

Equation 3: LUNA Ratio

Monthly average (total unrestricted net assets–total illiquid net assets)/

Average monthly expenses

Two ratios define most of the budget solvency measures. There is the operating ratio (Equation 4), which includes revenues and expenses. Additionally, there is the change in net assets ratio (Equation 5) which considers the monthly average of the surplus or deficit over the monthly average of total revenues. As with cash solvency, both ratios can be averaged and equally weighted to produce the budget solvency score.

Equation 4: Operating Ratio

$$Revenues/Expenses$$

Equation 5: Change in Net Assets Ratio

$$Monthly\ average\ of\ surplus(deficit)/Monthly\ average\ of\ total\ revenue$$

Equity solvency can be assessed through three separate ratios using net restricted and unrestricted assets along with total assets, total revenue, and total liabilities. The net asset ratio (Equation 6) considers net restricted assets plus net unrestricted assets in proportion to total assets. The equity ratio (Equation 7) considers net assets (total assets minus total liabilities) in proportion to total assets. Further, the equity ratio (Equation 8) can be shifted to consider the net assets in proportion to total revenues. The equity solvency score is a long-term financial condition measure; therefore, it is not necessary to average the components of the measure by 12 months.

Equation 6: Net Asset Ratio

$$Net\ restricted\ assets + Net\ unrestricted\ net\ assets/Total\ assets$$

Equation 7: Equity Ratio

$$Total\ assets - Total\ liabilities/Total\ assets$$

Equation 8: Equity Ratio per Revenue

$$Total\ assets - Total\ liabilities/Total\ revenue$$

The final solvency measure considered for this study is the fiscal slack score which evaluates program expenses and revenue. Given the contradictory opinions on the impact of spending on overhead versus programs, this measure attempted to be as inclusive as possible of these two perspectives. Equation 9 includes the program expenses to total expenses. This measure was reverse-scored so that an increase in this ratio would indicate an improving financial condition. Equation 10 determines the amount of revenue dedicated to programs of total revenue. Nonprogram salaries and benefits and fundraising fees were all deducted from total revenue to determine program-only dedicated revenue. The averaging of these ratios along with the equal weighting produced the fiscal slack score.

Equation 9: Program Expenses per Total Expenses

$$1/(Program\ expenses/Total\ expenses)$$

TABLE 12.1 Equation summary

Equation	*Measure*
Equation 1: Cash ratio	Monthly average (cash + cash equivalents + investments)/Average monthly expenses
Equation 2: Quick ratio	Monthly average (cash + cash equivalents + investments + receivables)/Average monthly expenses
Equation 3: LUNA ratio	Monthly average (total unrestricted net assets − total illiquid net assets)/Average monthly expenses
Equation 4: Operating ratio	Revenues/Expenses
Equation 5: Change in net assets ratio	Monthly average of surplus (deficit)/Monthly average of total revenue
Equation 6: Net asset ratio	Net restricted assets + Net unrestricted net assets/Total assets
Equation 7: Equity ratio	Total assets − Total liabilities/Total assets
Equation 8: Equity ratio per revenue	Total assets − Total liabilities/Total revenue
Equation 9: Program expenses per total expenses	1/(Program expenses/Total expenses)
Equation 10: Revenue for programs	Revenue − (Benefits paid + Nonprogram salaries + Fundraising fees)/Total revenue

Equation 10: Revenue for Programs

$$Revenue-(Benefit\ spaid^{12} + Nonprogram\ salaries + Fundraising\ fees^{13})/Total\ revenue$$

These four scores can be summed to create a comprehensive financial condition score that is comparative in nature; in other words, it determines the range of scores based on the sample. This avoids the problem of creating empirically unverifiable benchmarks and allows an organization to track its financial condition in comparison to other similar organizations such as museums. It also allows organizations that have larger total revenue and assets to be compared to other organizations with lower levels of revenue and assets. Table 12.1 provides a summary of these ten ratios.

Museum Selection and Study Design

To test this framework, we used IRS Form 990 data to compare a sample of museums across a range of three years to determine changes in financial condition before and going into the COVID-19 pandemic. The IRS requires any tax-exempt organization with gross receipts greater than or equal to $200,000 or with total assets greater than or equal to $500,000 to submit an annual Form 990 (Form 990 Instructions 2021, 2). Even small nonprofit organizations and religious institutions who are not required to submit a Form 990 choose to submit these forms to maintain transparency and accountability. There are other versions of the 990 such as the Form 990-EZ and Form 990-N, which are abbreviated versions of the full form, that are required to be submitted by some smaller organizations. These are less useful for acquiring the data needed to assess financial condition.

It is common to rely on IRS Form 990 data for nonprofit financial information (Kirk and Nolan 2010; Lam and McDougle 2016; Maguire 2016; Yan and Sloan 2016). The varied fiscal years of nonprofit organizations lead to varied submission times of the form. At the time of this study, 2020 Form 990s were digitally available for a little more than 2,000 museums. In 2018, the Institute of Museum and Library Services identified more than 33,000 museums in the United States (Frehill and Pelczar 2018). Among these museums, a random sample of 100 museums was selected for this study. Of these 100 museums, 60 had financial data for all three years of the study, from 2018 to 2020. These included the years prior to the pandemic and the first year of the pandemic. Based on an a priori sample size[14] estimate, a random sample of 60 is more than adequate at an acceptable probability level[15] of .05 with an effect size[16] (Cohen's D) of .7 and statistical power[17] of .8. To increase the robustness of these results, bootstrapping[18] was also used in the analysis. Further, additional analysis was also done with 2019 data only since there were more forms submitted that year.

The random sample represented a range of museums across the United States. In 2019, the total revenues in these museums ranged from more than $120 million to less than $25,000. Several museums were well below the minimum revenue or asset benchmark required to submit a Form 990. This wide range was also evident with total assets in which some museums had more than $800 million in total assets while others had less than $35,000 in total assets.

Due to these ranges, the standard deviation was quite high. Given that the selected financial condition measure is standardized and weighted, this did not influence any analysis of the sample. It is beneficial to have a diverse pool of museums represented in the sample so that aggregate trends in the sector can be detected while also allowing the organizations to be compared based on revenue and asset quartiles. Additionally, the museums in the sample represent a diverse pool of different kinds of museums from general museums to art museums to natural history museums. The descriptive statistics are in Table 12.2.

Of particular interest in this study is how the financial condition has changed for museums from 2018 to 2020. Since the measure is comparative, the sample may reveal aggregate trends of increasing/decreasing financial condition or a growing gap between those at the bottom of the scale and those at the top. This can also be separated based on the different solvency measures to see the source of this gap. In addition, these differences can be

TABLE 12.2 Descriptive statistics (2019)

	Mean	*SD*	*Min*	*Max*
Cash solvency	0	0.2014	−0.6006	0.9615
Budget solvency	0	0.221	−0.9347	0.8972
Equity solvency	0	0.1634	−0.5505	0.5204
Fiscal slack	0	0.1674	−0.8995	1.17
Financial condition	0	0.437	−2.14	1.17
Revenues	36,52,198	1,33,76,785	24,790	12,31,49,099
Assets	1,95,74,284	8,61,26,828	34,155	81,29,60,498

Note: N = 96. $\bar{x}$ is 0 because of standardization (mean-centering) for the financial condition measure.

assessed statistically through differences of means tests across quarters based on total revenues and assets.

Another interest of this study is the change in revenue from 2018 to 2020 across the four categories of revenues in the Form 990. These include contributions and grants, program service revenue, investment income, and other revenue. Given the centrality of revenues in the discussion on nonprofit financial condition, changes in revenues are considered an important aspect of changes in financial condition. These results are discussed in the following section.

Results

In most cases, the revenues were higher in 2018 or 2019 than in 2020. This was true for contributions and grants, program service revenue, and other revenue. The differences were statistically significant based on a pairwise mean comparison (Table 12.3). The year 2019 was an especially good year for the museums in the sample. The only revenue category that improved over previous years in 2020 was investment income. The significantly higher revenues in the years before the pandemic may be an indication of the effects of the pandemic on a critical aspect of financial condition for museums. These differences were significant even though foundations initially helped struggling nonprofits by expanding their grant making at the beginning of the pandemic (Chronicle of Philanthropy 2022, 5).

Interestingly, the gap between museums at the upper end of financial condition and the lower end shrunk from 2018 to 2020 indicating a convergence in the sample of museums. Those museums that were better off in the sample saw their financial condition decline while those museums at the lower end of the sample improved over 2019 (Figure 12.1). The different solvency scores contributed in unique ways to the overall financial condition score. Each solvency score is explored separately in order to understand these unique contributions.

The gap widened between the museums on cash solvency (Figure 12.2) in which those at the lower end of the index saw a decline in cash solvency going

TABLE 12.3 Pairwise mean comparison of revenues (2018–20)

			Confidence interval		
	Mean	*SD*	*Lower*	*Upper*	*Cohen's D*
Contributions & grants					
2018–19	20,40,598*	64,76,787	8,34,514.47	37,56,364	0.315
2018–20	16,55,678*	76,79,620	18,497.359	35,76,584	0.216
2019–20	−3,84,920	38,01,017	−17,38,638	2,86,399	−0.101
Program service revenue					
2018–19	−24,56,531*	69,00,478	−44,93,044	−9,27,617	−0.356
2018–20	−1,35,873.467	15,65,277	−4,93,174	2,77,278	−0.087
2019–20	23,20,658*	66,21,253	9,55,925	40,92,299	0.35
Investment income					
2018–19	−5,34,643	58,83,357	−22,31,380	4,76,102	−0.091
2018–20	−21,37,919*	52,93,908	36,53,158	−9,22,116	−0.404
2019–20	−16,03,276*	43,93,601	−27,72,936	−4,91,102	−0.365
Other revenue					
2018–19	34,367	13,83,587	−3,43,748.	3,67,034	0.025
2018–20	1,83,879*	5,94,269	68,610	3,41,143	0.309
2019–20	1,49,512	12,13,276	−72,211	4,43,716	0.123

Notes: N = 60; *df* = 59; *p ≤ .05; CI = bootstrapped (5,000 samples).

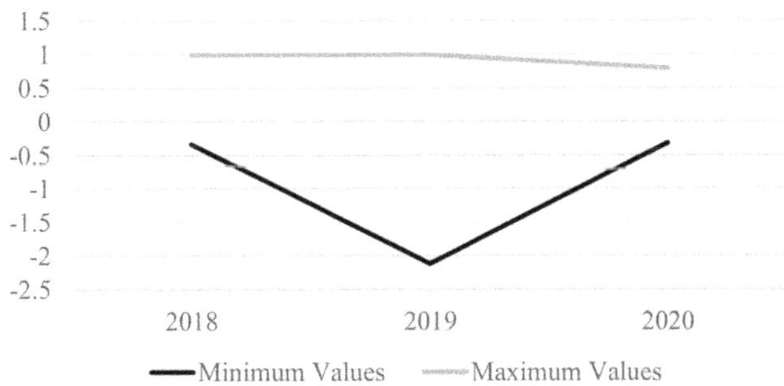

FIGURE 12.1 Financial condition.

into the pandemic while those at the upper end of the index saw continual improvement. Those better-off museums may have had more cash on hand going into the pandemic which would have prepared them more for the lockdowns while they made cuts in their short-term liabilities.

In both budget solvency (Figure 12.3) and equity solvency (Figure 12.4), the trend remained consistent between museums that were financially stable

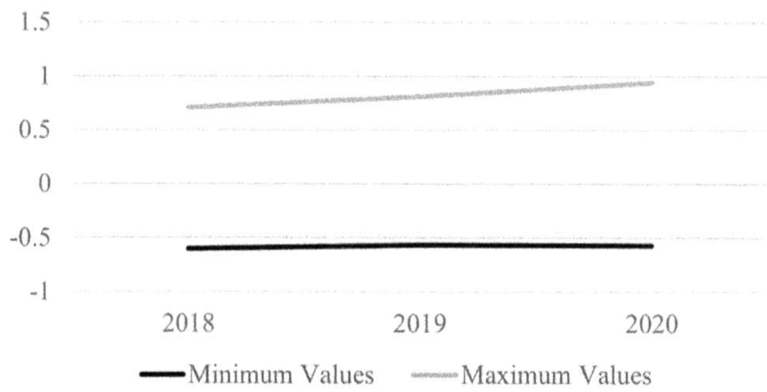

FIGURE 12.2 Cash solvency.

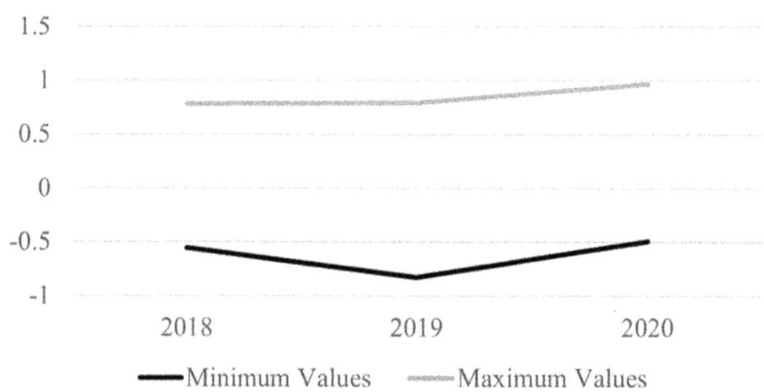

FIGURE 12.3 Budget solvency.

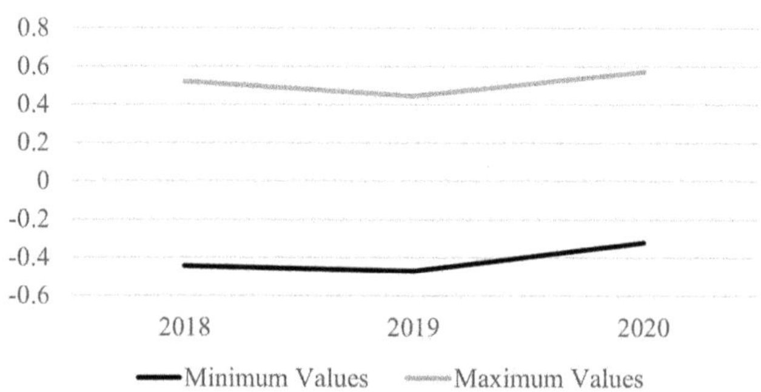

FIGURE 12.4 Equity solvency.

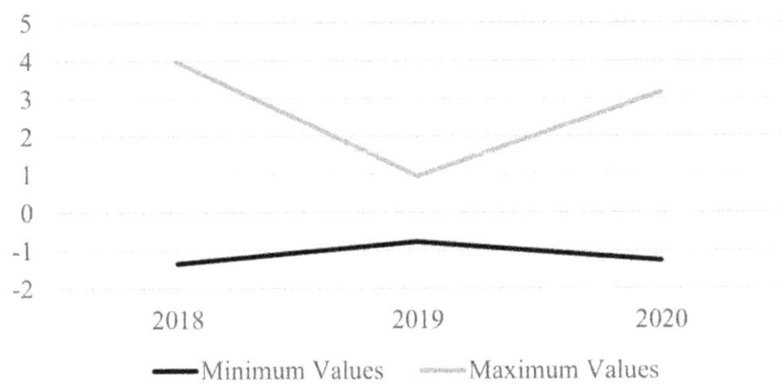

FIGURE 12.5 Fiscal slack.

and those that were less so. In both cases, the solvency score improved in 2020 over 2019 and 2018 even though revenue sources declined except for investment income. It can be assumed that these organizations made adequate adjustments such as cutting costs in response to the pandemic-induced lockdowns that improved budget solvency and equity solvency.

The gap in fiscal slack (Figure 12.5) between better-off and worse-off museums widened in 2020 in which the better-off organizations increased their fiscal slack score while worse-off museums decreased their fiscal slack score. Fiscal slack is a measure of commitment to administrative expenses and program revenues. It is possible that the museums in the sample increased or maintained administrative expenses at least in comparison to total expenses while increasing the share of revenues committed to programs. Those at the lower end of the scale may have cut administrative expenses while also committing less revenue to programs which would be a sign of greater fiscal stress.

Separately, a comparison of mean financial condition scores between different quarters of revenue and total assets in the sample provided further evidence that the differences between the museums with greater levels of assets and revenues and those with lower levels are insignificant on the measure of financial condition. These quarters are based on total assets and total revenue in 2020 in which higher quarters represent organizations with more assets and more revenue. The results were the same in 2019 as in 2020. See Tables 12.4 and 12.5.

In Tables 12.4 and 12.5, the only significant difference was between those organizations in the middle quarters for revenues and assets with those in the top quarter. This indicates that the divide between the museums in the sample is really between the middle-tier organizations and the upper-tier organizations while those at the bottom seem to be managing their lower levels of assets and revenues better than those in the middle. One assumption that can

TABLE 12.4 Financial condition by revenue quarter 2020

	Qtr 1	*Qtr 2*	*Qtr 3*	*Qtr 4*
Qtr 1		.2033 −.0465, .4646	.2887* .0562, .5396	.0373 −.2747, .3634
Qtr 2			.0854 −.1092, .2772	−.1660 −.4755, .1330
Qtr 3				−.2514 −.5473, .0285

Notes: N = 60; *df* = 56; $^*\rho \leq .05$; F = 1.946 ($\rho \leq .133$); $\omega^2 = .045$ (fixed); post-hoc tests based on Games-Howell estimation; bootstrapped at 5,000 samples.

TABLE 12.5 Financial condition by asset quarter 2020

	Qtr 1	*Qtr 2*	*Qtr 3*	*Qtr 4*
Qtr 1		.2951* .0365, .5617	.2656* .0025, .5334	.2688 −.0321, .5701
Qtr 2			−.0295 −.2628, .1959	−.0264 −.3081, .2584
Qtr 3				.0031 −.2790, .2805

Notes: N = 60; *df* = 56; $^*\rho \leq .05$; F = 2.017 ($\rho \leq .122$); $\omega^2 = .048$ (fixed); post-hoc tests based on Games-Howell estimation; bootstrapped at 5,000 samples.

be made based on these results is that even during the pandemic, smaller nonprofit museums are managing their resources to increase capacity and sustainability and therefore may be at less risk for financial failure. Leaders of nonprofit museums can use this information when speaking to potential funders to promote their organization's stability and growth opportunities.

Discussion and Conclusion

The results of this analysis show that having more resources (greater levels of assets and revenues) does not necessarily translate into better financial conditions in comparison to other organizations. There is certainly less margin for error with smaller nonprofit museums, but simply being small did not predict a lower financial condition. The real issue seemed to be with the average-sized organizations in comparison to the top organizations. These are interesting results from a managerial perspective.

The first year of the COVID pandemic seemed to be an important year among the three years included in the analysis. The range of financial condition scores narrowed as the top scores shrunk and the bottom scores increased over the prior year (2019). At the same time, revenues declined in three of the four categories. While the gap increased for cash holdings over current liabilities and with fiscal slack, there was a general improvement in budget solvency and equity solvency across the range of organizations in the sample. As mentioned previously, this may be evidence of managerial excellence in the first year of the pandemic, especially for those organizations with poorer financial conditions.

However, this does not say anything about program delivery and accomplishing the museum's mission. Although fiscal slack measures expenses committed to administration and revenues committed to programs, it does not measure goal accomplishment/outcomes which may have suffered in the first year of the pandemic. This financial conditional analysis can only be interpreted as that the museums at the lower end of the scale included in this study were in a better financial position than before the pandemic. Those organizations at the upper end of the scale did see their financial condition decline slightly over the prior year.

This analysis is limited to the first year of the pandemic and it is not known how the prolonged COVID restrictions influenced the museums' finances. Once the 2021 IRS Form 990s are released, a more complete picture can be depicted. This analysis is also not causal and only determines the differences from year to year and between levels of revenues and assets.

The measure adopted in this study is based upon best practices with various studies on nonprofit financial conditions. The ratios included and the method to aggregate those ratios to create solvency scores and through weighting an aggregate financial condition score have been established in the literature. However, there are other measures that have not been utilized in this assessment. The discussion on appropriate measures of nonprofit financial condition will likely continue in the future along with the contribution of this study.

Another limitation of this study is the dependence on IRS Form 990 data. Research has shown that the data on nonprofit IRS Form 990 is subject to measurement error (Krishnan et al. 2006; Andreoni and Payne 2003, 2008). In their comparison of 990s and audited financial statements, Froelich et al. (2000) found that more than 50% of their sample showed discrepancies of 10% or more for management expenses and program service revenue. Furthermore, they found that these discrepancies vary by subsector with arts and culture and educational organizations exhibiting larger discrepancies than the other subsectors. Although these discrepancies may seem small on an individual level, they could lead to much larger values when aggregated.

In this chapter, we have presented a group of financial ratios that collectively can be used to assess the fiscal health of nonprofit museums. We tested this framework with 60 nonprofit museums to demonstrate the validity of the ratios. Further research should be conducted to test this framework, not only with museums but with other nonprofit subsectors. The use of financial data for decision-making should be strategic for both the organization and potential donors. Additional research should survey museum directors and donors to see how they used this information and if it was helpful.

Notes

1 Liquidity defines how close an asset is to being cash.
2 Solvency is determined by the financial security of an organization, which can be defined in several ways. The most basic definition is having greater levels of revenue compared to expenses.
3 The Hirshman-Herfindahl Index (HHI) is typically used to measure market concentration but has been used to measure revenue concentration in nonprofit organizations. It captures the number of revenue sources as well as the proportion of the revenue compared to all revenue. A score of "0" means equal revenues from many sources while a score of "1" is a complete concentration of all revenue from one source.
4 Assets are anything of value to the organization and can include both short-term (cash or something close to cash) within a year and long-term for those assets available over a year. Net assets are those assets remaining after subtracting liabilities. For nonprofit organizations, they can be both restricted with donor-imposed restrictions on use such as gifts and endowments, and unrestricted which do not have those restrictions and can be used for any purpose in the organization.
5 Receivables are assets that are owned to the organization, but not yet received from those other parties.
6 Liabilities are anything owed outside the organization. They can be both short-term (due within a year) and long-term (due in one year or more).
7 Equity denotes the ownership of assets which can be creditors. A greater level of equity or potential for equity indicates a financially healthy organization.
8 Administrative support has been defined as a type of financial revenue, that is, slack resources (Park and Matkin 2021). An increase in program expenses has signaled less flexibility in making administrative adjustments during a time of financial hardship. However, an increase in revenue dedicated to programs has also been considered advantageous to nonprofits because it increases confidence and sustainability for those programs. Both are captured in the fiscal slack score.
9 Program expenses are used for program activities that further the organization's mission.
10 Cash equivalents are short-term investments that can easily be converted into cash.
11 These are investments with returns in the short term, that is, within the year.
12 Payments made by the organization for employee benefits such as health insurance or life insurance.
13 Professional fundraising fees for fundraising services such as solicitation campaigns and consulting services.
14 Sample size calculated before the study is conducted and/or before the design and planning of the study.
15 The likelihood of an event if there truly is no effect.
16 The strength of a relationship between two variables in a sample.
17 The probability of finding an effect if there truly is an effect.
18 A statistical process of resampling the original sample to produce more reliable standard errors and confidence intervals.
19 https://apps.irs.gov/app/eos/

References

Altamimi, H., & Liu, Q. 2022. "The Nonprofit Starvation Cycle: Does Overhead Spending Really Impact Program Outcomes?" *Nonprofit and Voluntary Sector Quarterly* 51 (6): 1324–48.

Andreoni, J., & Payne, A. A. 2003. "Do Government Grants to Private Charities Crowd Out Giving or Fund-Raising? [Electronic version]." *The American Economic Review* 93: 792–812.

Andreoni, J., & Payne, A. A. 2008. *Crowding Out Both Sides of the Philanthropy Market: Evidence from a Panel of Charities [Working Paper]*. Available from Jim Andreoni Web site, http://econ.ucsd.edu/~jandreon/

Andres-Alonso, P., Garcia-Rodriguez, I., & Romero-Merino, M. 2016. "Disentangling the Financial Vulnerability of Nonprofits." *Voluntas: International Journal of Voluntary & Nonprofit Organizations* 27 (6): 2539–60. 10.1007/s11266-016-9764-6

Anheier, H. K. 2005. *Nonprofit Organizations: Theory, Management, Policy*. New York: Routledge.

Antonelli, A. 2016, October 12. *Best Practices for Nonprofit Financial Health, Part One: Top 3 Measures of Financial Health*. Nonprofit Finance Fund. https://nff.org/blog/best-practices-nonprofit-financial-health-part-one-top-3-measures-financial-health

Association of Art Museum Directors. 2018. Art Museums by the Numbers 2018. https://aamd.org/sites/default/files/document/Art%20Museums%20by%20the%20Numbers%202018.pdf

Bowman, W. 2011. "Financial Capacity and Sustainability of Ordinary Nonprofits." *Nonprofit Management & Leadership* 22 (1): 37–51. 10.1002/nml.20039

Calabrese, T. D., & Ely, T. L. 2017. "Understanding and Measuring Endowment in Public Charities." *Nonprofit and Voluntary Sector Quarterly* 46 (4): 859–73.

Chabotar, K. J. 1989. "Financial Ratio Analysis Comes to Nonprofits." *The Journal of Higher Education* 60 (2): 188. 10.2307/1982176

Chronicle of Philanthropy. 2022. *Embracing the Future: Nonprofit Leaders Keep Adapting to a Changing World*. Washington, DC: The Chronicle of Philanthropy.

Frehill, L. M., & Pelczar, M. 2018. *Data File Documentation: Museum Data Files, FY 2018 Release*. Washington, DC: Institute of Museum and Library Services.

Froelich, K. A., Knoepfle, T. W., & Pollak, T. H. 2000. "Financial Measures in Nonprofit Organization Research: Comparing IRS 990 Return and Audited Financial Statement Data." *Nonprofit and Voluntary Sector Quarterly* 29: 232–54.

Greenlee, J. S., & Bukovinsky, D. 1998. "Financial Ratios for Use in the Analytical Review of Charitable Organizations." *The Ohio CPA Journal* 57: 32–8.

Greenlee, J. S., & Trussel, J. M. 2000. "Predicting the Financial Vulnerability of Charitable Organizations." *Nonprofit Management and Leadership* 11 (2): 199–210.

Grønbjerg, K. 1991. "Managing Grants and Contracts: The Case of Four Nonprofit Social Service Organizations." *Nonprofit and Voluntary Sector Quarterly* 20 (1): 5–24. 10.1177/089976409102000103

Hung, C., & Hager, M. A. 2019. "The Impact of Revenue Diversification on Nonprofit Financial Health: A Meta-Analysis." *Nonprofit and Voluntary Sector Quarterly* 48 (1): 5–27.

Instructions for Form 990 Return of Organization Exempt from Income Tax. 2021, December 8. Department of Treasury—Internal Revenue Service. chrome-extension://efaidnbmnnnibpcajpcglclefindmkaj/https://www.irs.gov/pub/irs-pdf/i990.pdf

Kim, M. 2017. "The Relationship of Nonprofits' Financial Health to Program Outcomes: Empirical Evidence from Nonprofit Arts Organizations." *Nonprofit & Voluntary Sector Quarterly* 46 (3): 525–48. 10.1177/0899764016662914

Kingma, B. R. 1993. "Portfolio Theory and Nonprofit Financial Stability." *Nonprofit and Voluntary Sector Quarterly* 22: 105–19.

Kirk, G., & Beth Nolan, S. 2010. "Nonprofit Mission Statement Focus and Financial Performance." *Nonprofit Management & Leadership* 20 (4): 473–90. 10.1002/nml.20006

Krishnan, R., Yetman, M. H., & Yetman, R. J. 2006. "Expense Misreporting in Nonprofit Organizations." *The Accounting Review* 81 (2): 399–420.
Lam, M., & McDougle, L. 2016. "Community Variation in the Financial Health of Nonprofit Human Service Organizations." *Nonprofit & Voluntary Sector Quarterly* 45 (3): 500–25. 10.1177/0899764015591365
Levine, H., & Zahradnik, A. 2012. "Online Media, Market Orientation, and Financial Performance in Nonprofits." *Journal of Nonprofit & Public Sector Marketing* 24 (1): 26–42. 10.1080/10495142.2012.652908
Maguire, K. A. 2016. "Nonprofit Financial Assessment and Research Service Learning: Evaluating the Performance of an Animal Welfare Nonprofit Organization." *Cogent Business & Management* 3(1). 10.1080/23311975.2016.1149958
McNeal, B. G. 2013. *Measuring the Financial Vulnerability of Membership-Based Nonprofit Business Leagues Using Accounting Ratios*. (2013-99010-282). Retrieved from https://ulm.idm.oclc.org/login?url=https://search.ebscohost.com/login.aspx?direct=true&db=psyh&AN=2013-99010-282&site=eds-live
Moore, M. S. B. 2015. *Community Engagement and Financial Vulnerability during an Economic Crisis*. Retrieved from https://ulm.idm.oclc.org/login?url=https://search.ebscohost.com/login.aspx?direct=true&db=ddu&AN=E176070B48115AFF&site=eds-live
Park, Y. J., & Matkin, D. S. T. 2021. *The Demise of the Overhead Myth: Administrative Capacity and Financial Sustainability in Nonprofit Nursing Homes*. 10.1111/puar.13269
Prentice, C. R. 2016. "Why So Many Measures of Nonprofit Financial Performance? Analyzing and Improving the Use of Financial Measures in Nonprofit Research." *Nonprofit & Voluntary Sector Quarterly* 45 (4): 715–40. 10.1177/0899764015595722
Ritchie, W. J., & Kolodinsky, R. W. 2003. "Nonprofit Organization Financial Performance Measurement: An Evaluation of New and Existing Financial Performance Measures." *Nonprofit Management & Leadership* 13 (4): 367. 10.1002/nml.5
Searing, E. A. M. 2018. "Determinants of the Recovery of Financially Distressed Nnonprofits." *Nonprofit Management & Leadership* 28 (3): 313–28. 10.1002/nml.21296
Tuckman, H. P., & Chang, C. F. 1991. "A Methodology for Measuring the Financial Vulnerability of Charitable Nonprofit Organizations." *Nonprofit and Voluntary Sector Quarterly* 20 (4): 445–60. 10.1177/089976409102000407
Yan, W., & Sloan, M. F. 2016. "The Impact of Employee Compensation and Financial Performance on Nonprofit Organization Donations." *The American Review of Public Administration* 46 (2): 243–58. 10.1177/0275074014554000

Appendix

To better understand the financial condition measure used in this chapter, an example has been provided in this appendix. The data for this demonstration is from one of the nonprofit museums included in this study, Ohr-O'Keefe Museum of Art, based in Biloxi, Mississippi. The Form 990 for 2019 can be located on the IRS website.[19] The data are located on the balance sheet (Part X), the statement of functional expenses (Part IX), and the reconciliation of net assets (Part XI).

Measure	*Form 990 location*	*Calculation with Ohr-O'Keefe Museum of Art*
Cash ratio: Monthly average (cash + cash equivalents + investments)/Average monthly expenses	Part X: Line 1 + Line 2 Part XI: Line 2	((1,16,736 + 18,955)/12)/ (20,99,896/12) = .0646
Quick ratio: Monthly average (cash + cash equivalents + investments + receivables)/Average monthly expenses	Part X: Line 1 + Line 2 + Line 3 + Line 4 Part XI: Line 2	((1,16,736 + 18,955)/12)/ (20,99,896/12) = .0646
LUNA ratio: Monthly average (total unrestricted net assets – total illiquid net assets)/ Average monthly expenses	Part X: Line 27 – ((Line 16 – (Line 1 + Line 2)) – Line 26) Part XI: Line 2	(1,75,32,433 – ((3,98,91,892 – (1,16,736 + 18,955)) – 4,73,556))/12/ (20,99,896/12) = −10.36
Operating ratio: Revenues/Expenses	Part XI: Line 1/Line 2	16,90,743/20,99,896 = .8052
Change in net assets ratio: Monthly average of surplus (deficit)/ Monthly average of total revenue	Part XI: Line 1 – Line 2 Part XI: Line 1	(16,90,743 – 20,99,896)/ (16,90,743/12) = −.2420
Net asset ratio: Net restricted assets + Net unrestricted net assets/Total assets	Part X: (Line 27 + Line 28)/ Line 16	(2,18,85,903 + 1,75,32,433)/ 3,98,91,892 = .9881

(*Continued*)

(Continued)

Measure	*Form 990 location*	*Calculation with Ohr-O'Keefe Museum of Art*
Equity ratio: Total assets − Total liabilities/Total assets	Part X: (Line 16 − Line 26)/ Line 16	(3,98,91,892 − 47,35,56)/ 3,98,91,892 = .9881
Equity ratio per revenue: Total assets − Total liabilities/Total revenue	Part X: Line 16 − Line 26 Part XI: Line 1	(3,98,91,892 − 4,73,556)/ 16,90,743 = 23.31
Program expenses per total expenses: 1/(Program expenses/ Total expenses)	Part IX: Line 25(B)/Line 25(A)	1/(19,18,842/20,99,896) = 1.094
Revenue for programs: Revenue − (Benefits paid + Nonprogram salaries + Fundraising fees)/Total revenue	Part XI: Line 1 Part IX: Line 4(C) + Line 4(D) + Line 5(C) + Line 5(D) + Line 6(C) + Line 6(D) + Line 7(C) + Line 7(D) + Line 8(C) + Line 8(D) + Line 9(C) + Line 9(D) + Line 11e(D)	(16,90,743 − (1,17,001))/ 16,90,743 = .9308

These ratios are then standardized, equally weighted, and averaged for each of the solvency scores. The cash, quick, and LUNA ratios are averaged for the cash solvency index score. The operating and change in net assets ratios are averaged for the budget solvency index score. The net asset, equity, and equity per revenue ratios are averaged for the equity score. The program expenses per total expenses and revenue for programs ratios are averaged for the fiscal slack score. These averages are summed to produce the overall financial condition score. This makes the measure comparative and summative in which a higher score indicates a better financial condition in comparison to the other organizations.

PART 4

Innovative Museum Funding Practices

13

NONPROFIT DOES NOT MEAN "NO PROFIT"

An Overview of Smithsonian Enterprises (Formerly Smithsonian Business Ventures)

C. Lorenzo Evans III

Introduction

The United States museum industry comprises for-profit and nonprofit organizations with a projected value of $20 billion in 2023 (Statista Research Department 2021). With a wide array of funding models to support their operations, many museums employ innovative business models that generate revenue to support the advancement of mission-aligned exhibits, programs, community activities, and business operations. In the nonprofit museum sector, fundraising activities and earned revenue are the most significant sources of revenue, representing 60% and 40%, respectively (Sotheby's Institute of Art 2018). While nonprofit museums receive most of their funding from fundraising activities, much of this revenue consists of gifts or grants restricted by time or programmatic activity. Competition for grant and philanthropic funding among museums in this sector is highly competitive and comes at a high cost to the organizations. Alongside the competition funding in the industry, the need for unencumbered revenue to support administration, programming, fundraising, and other operating expenses is of great importance. Unrestricted revenue serves a critical purpose in nonprofit organizations and can be designated at the discretion of organizational leadership, often covering essential costs that fall outside of restricted funding parameters.

As the world's largest museum institution, the Smithsonian Institution is a nonprofit organization that derives most of its funding from federal appropriations, constituting over 50% of its annual budget. Other sources of revenue for the Smithsonian Institution include fundraising revenue, endowment proceeds, business activities revenue, and other revenue (Smithsonian Institution, Annual

DOI: 10.4324/9781003308003-17

Reports 2016–21). This chapter explores the Smithsonian Institution's business activities known as Smithsonian Enterprises and how the profitability of this unique nonprofit business model serves a critical funding need for the institution. Smithsonian Enterprises was instituted by the Smithsonian Board of Regents in 1999 to consolidate all of the institution's businesses into one operating unit. While Smithsonian Enterprises generates significant unrestricted funding for the Smithsonian Institution through the organization's retail, food and beverage, theaters, publications, travel, and media businesses, it is not a separate entity from the Smithsonian Institution. Income generated by Smithsonian Enterprises' business activities provides funding for signature Smithsonian Institution programs and activities. These programs include but are not limited to the world's largest traveling museum service, the Smithsonian's relationships with its 200 affiliate museums, lectures, trips, and funding to support the annual Smithsonian Folklife Festival and other initiatives (Hearing on Smithsonian Institution Business Ventures 2006).

Smithsonian Institution Overview

Established by the United States Congress in 1846 with a landmark bequest by English chemist and mineralogist James Smithson, the Smithsonian Institution is the world's largest museum, education, and research complex and has amassed approximately 155 million artifacts and specimens in its over 176-year history (Smithsonian Institution Archives n.d. a; Smithsonian Institution n.d. d). The US Federal Government designated the Smithsonian Institution as "trust instrumentality," reflecting its authority to exercise the authority of the United States in carrying out the responsibilities that Congress undertook upon accepting the bequest of James Smithson in 1846 (Smithsonian Institution n.d. b). While not part of the Executive Branch of the US Federal Government, the Smithsonian Institution is governed by a congressionally appointed Board of Regents that is composed of the chief justice of the US Supreme Court, vice president of the United States, three members of the US Senate and US House of Representatives, respectively, and nine citizen members (Smithsonian Institution n.d. a). The Smithsonian Board of Regents is appointed to oversee the administration and governance of the institution, ensuring that its founding mission for the "increase and diffusion of knowledge" is carried out in all of its operations. In addition to its designation as a public trust, the Smithsonian Institution is classified by the Internal Revenue Service as a 501(c)3 tax-exempt educational organization (Smithsonian Institution n.d. b).

Home to 21 museums in Washington, DC, and New York, NY, the National Zoo, nine research facilities worldwide, and over 200 affiliate organizations in the United States and Puerto Rico, the Smithsonian hosted more than 20 million annual visitors in the years that preceded the COVID-19 pandemic.

While museum closures resulting from COVID-19 caused an interruption in visitation in 2020 and 2021, the Smithsonian resumed a more traditional schedule in 2022, hosting 8.9 million visitors as of July 2022 (Smithsonian Institution n.d. f).

Smithsonian Financial Overview 6-Years (Fiscal Years 2016–21)

The Smithsonian Institution has an annual operating budget of approximately $1.5 billion and receives its funding from two primary sources; federal appropriations and income generated from gifts, revenue-generating activities, and investments—referred to as "trust funds" (Smithsonian Institution n.d. b). In fiscal years 2016–21, federal appropriations represented 54% of the organization's budget, and trust funds composed the other 46%. Of its trust revenue, contributions and grants represented 21% of total revenue, followed by combined business activities and other revenue at 18%, and endowment revenue at 5% (Smithsonian Institution, Annual Reports 2016–21) (see Figure 13.1).

The Smithsonian Institution's annual expense budget reflects a 49% allocation to salaries and employee benefits, 26% to organizational operating expenses, 16% to capital expenditures, and 8% to business activities. Per the

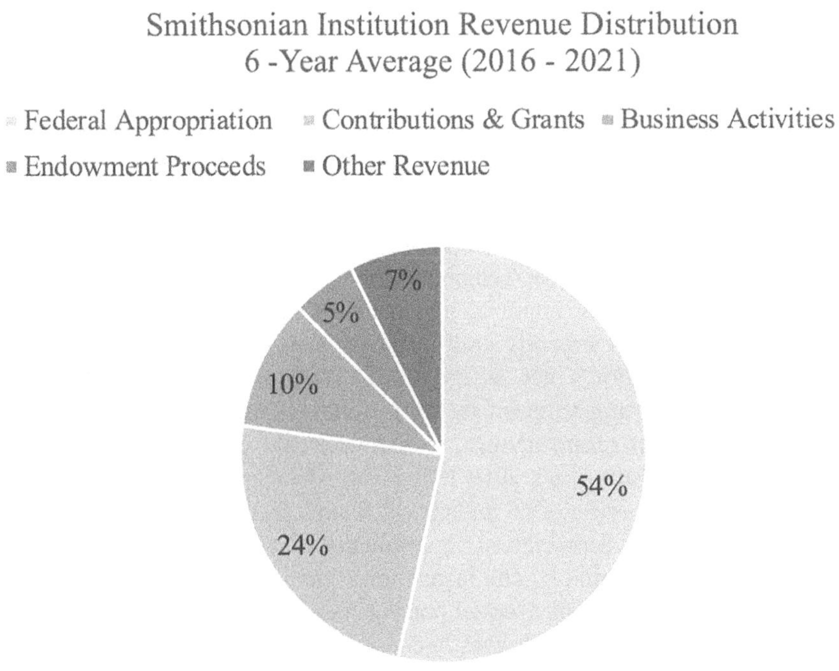

FIGURE 13.1 Smithsonian Institute revenue distribution.

Source: Smithsonian Institution Annual Reports for Fiscal Years 2016–21.

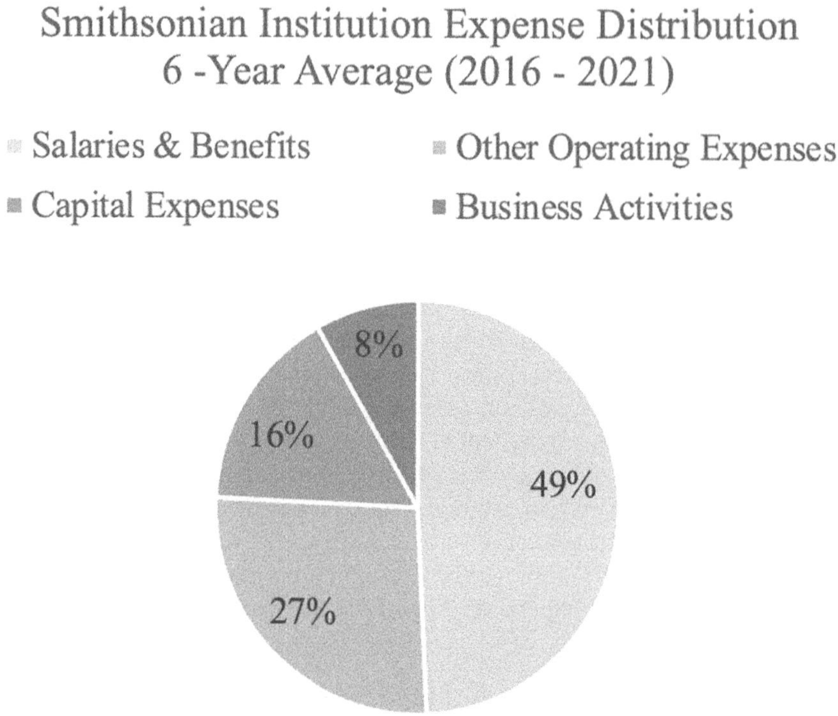

FIGURE 13.2 Smithsonian Institute expense distribution.

Source: Smithsonian Institution Annual Reports for Fiscal Years 2016–21.

organization's 990 IRS filings, most expenses are programmatic 75%, with administration and fundraising costs composing 21% and 3% of the budget, respectively (see Figure 13.2). In fiscal years 2016–20, the Smithsonian Institution reported surpluses ranging from $75 to $167 million, reflecting the organization's strong financial management given its unique organizational structure. With executive authority over its land and grounds, the Smithsonian Institution's net assets totaled $4.6 million in 2019, which reflected the accounting value of its land, buildings and equipment, investments, current assets (cash, savings, receivables), and liabilities. A review of the Smithsonian Institution's 2019 IRS Form 990 (Smithsonian Institution 2020b) reflects total assets of $6 million, with land, buildings, and equipment of $2.7 billion after depreciation, investments of $2.04 billion, and total current assets of $1.2 billion. The institution's liabilities in the tax year 2019 totaled $1.4 million and represented current liabilities of $972 million, bond liabilities of $94 million, mortgages and notes payable of $296 million, and other liabilities of $51.6. Per its 2021 annual report, Smithsonian Enterprise's net assets reached $5.4 million (Smithsonian Institution 2020b; Smithsonian Institution, Annual Reports 2021a) (see Figure 13.3).

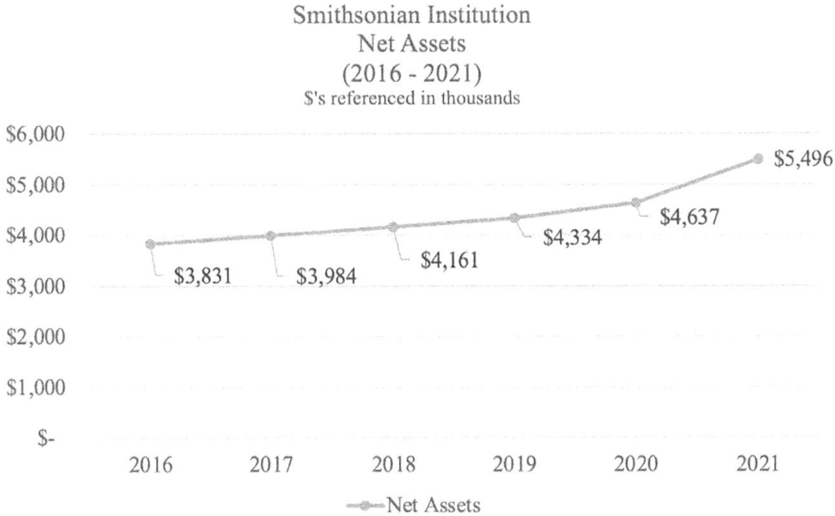

FIGURE 13.3 Smithsonian Institute net assets.

Source: Smithsonian Institution Annual Reports for Fiscal Years 2016–21.

Smithsonian Institution Revenue Overview

While the Smithsonian Institution receives its funding from primary sources, the most significant share of its annual revenue is restricted or designated for a specific purpose.

Federal Appropriations

Federal appropriations represent 54% of the Smithsonian Institution's operating budget. As of its 2023 fiscal year, US federal government appropriated $1.144 billion to the Smithsonian Institution, and the funds are designated as follows:

- $892.8 million for salaries and expenses, including pay raises for institutional staff, improvements in information technology infrastructure, and $2 million each for the institution's newest museums—the National Museum of the American Latino and Smithsonian American Women's History Museum.
- $251 million for facilities capital that covers the renovation and revitalization of some of the institution's most historic buildings, the construction of new buildings, and the development of future projects (Smithsonian Institution 2023).

Contributions and Grants

The Smithsonian Institution's second most significant revenue stream is contributions and grants. The contributions and grants category includes

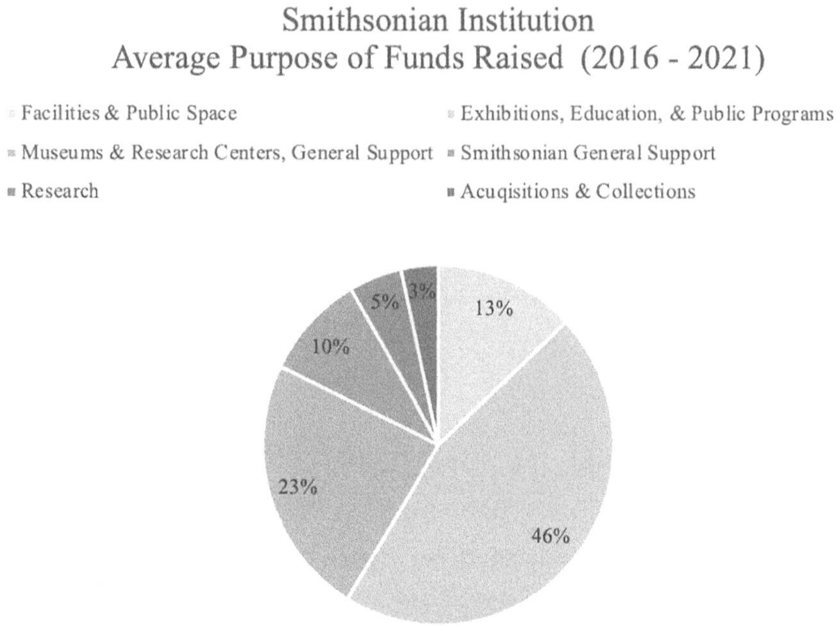

FIGURE 13.4 Average purpose of funds raised.

Source: Smithsonian Institution Annual Reports for Fiscal Years 2016–21.

funding from individual contributions, corporations, foundations, and other contributors. Individual contributions lead the Smithsonian's fundraising efforts and represent over 50% of funds raised annually. Funds are designated in the following categories and often restricted for the purposes (see Figure 13.4):

- Exhibitions, education, and public programs—46% average (2016–21)
- Museums & Research Centers, General Support—24% average (2016–21)
- Facilities and Public Space—17% average (2016–21)
- Smithsonian General Support—10% average (2016–21)
- Research—5% average (2016–21)
- Acquisitions & Collections—4% average (2016–21)

Notable among nonprofit organizations is the Smithsonian Institution's average fundraising efficiency of 97%, reflecting its low cost of fundraising in relationship to philanthropic revenue. Regarding fundraising, the organization retains an average of $.97 of each $1 earned in the contributions and grants category, per its 2016–19 IRS tax filings (Smithsonian Institution, Annual Reports 2016–21; Smithsonian Institution *IRS Form 990s* for FYs 2016–19).

Endowment Proceeds

Dating back to its first endowment in 1846, the Smithsonian Institution has focused on its long-term sustainability. As such, the institution's endowment has grown to $2.5 billion as of 2021. Since its 2006 inception, the Smithsonian Institution's Office of Investments has seen a $1.663 billion or 66% growth in its endowment assets. The Smithsonian Institution's endowment ensures the organization's long-term sustainability and offers short-term revenue to support its operations. As of 2021, the Smithsonian Institution's endowment proceeds constituted 5% of the organization's annual operating revenue. The current endowment is a diversified investment portfolio of private equity and venture capital funds, global equity, real assets, emerging markets, marketable alternatives, and fixed income/cash that has exceeded planned growth benchmarks. In 2021, the Smithsonian Institution allocated its endowment revenue as follows (Smithsonian Institution, Annual Reports 2016–21) (see Figure 13.5):

- Facilities and general support—$22.5 million or 25%
- Exhibitions, education, and public programs—20.9 million or 24%
- Centers general support—$17 million or 20%

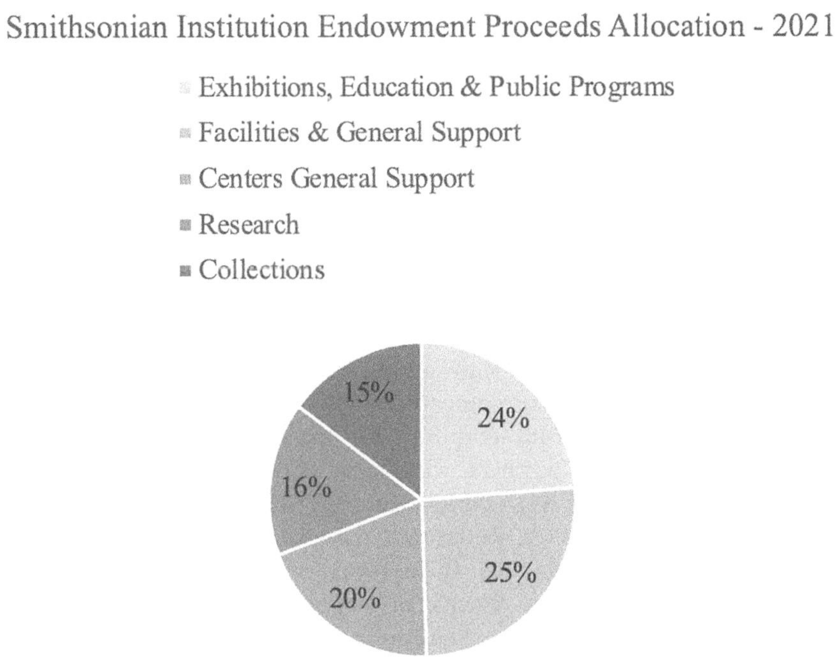

FIGURE 13.5 Endowment proceeds allocations.

Source: Smithsonian Institution Annual Reports for Fiscal Years 2016–21.

- Research—$13.8 million or 16%
- Collections—$13 million or 15%

Unrestricted Funds

The Smithsonian Institution's business activities revenue represents 11% of its annual budget and half its unrestricted revenue. Critical to the institution's funding is income generated from all of its business activities as it provides funding for institutional partnerships, lectures, traveling exhibits, affiliations, the annual Smithsonian Folklife Festival, and other mission-aligned initiatives (Hearing on Smithsonian Institution Business Ventures 2006). The Smithsonian Institution's business operations are led by Smithsonian Enterprises. This division oversees the combined operations of the institution's retail, media, and travel operations, yielding more that $35 million of income annually prior to the COVID-19 pandemic. Museum closures related to the COVID-19 pandemic drastically reduced the Smithsonian Enterprises' net income as it reported a year-over-year reduction of −$34 million per its 2020 financial reporting (KPMG 2021).

Smithsonian Enterprises History and Organizational Structure

With a mission to "engage in successful and profitable revenue-generating business activities that support and extend the Smithsonian's mission, values and reputation," Smithsonian Enterprises fills a vital funding need for the Smithsonian Institution as its activities compose half of the organization's unrestricted revenue (Smithsonian Enterprises n.d. a). Smithsonian Business Ventures, as initially named, brought together the institution's museum shops, restaurants, movie theaters, travel businesses, and *Smithsonian* magazine to operate as a single business unit in 1997 (Abruzzese 2008). Smithsonian Enterprises is an unincorporated operating division of the Smithsonian Institution and reports directly to the Smithsonian Board of Regents. With a professional staff of over 350 employees, Smithsonian Enterprises operates in several competitive markets and faces many of the same challenges as for-profit corporations operating in similar sectors. Smithsonian Enterprises partners with such corporations as Columbia Broadcasting System (CBS), Showtime, IMAX, the Quality Value Convenience Network (QVC), Restaurant Associates, and a host of others in the operation of its businesses. In its fiscal years 2016–20, Smithsonian Enterprises generated average revenue of more than $140 million from its three distinct operating groups, Smithsonian Enterprises' Retail Group, Smithsonian Enterprises Media Group, and Smithsonian Enterprises Travel Group (KPMG 2017, 2018, 2019, 2020, 2021). Appointed to the role of president in 2018, Carol LeBlanc shared that "the Smithsonian is one of the most trusted organizations in the world … [which] … allows [Smithsonian Enterprises] to translate the Smithsonian's brand, assets and intellectual property into compelling businesses, products, and services" (Smithsonian Institution 2018b).

Smithsonian Enterprises Retail Group

The Smithsonian Enterprises Retail Group manages the retail, food and beverage, concessions, theater, and parking operations across the Smithsonian Institution. It is home to Smithsonian Retail & Concessions, Smithsonian Store, Smithsonian Theaters, Smithsonian Licensed Products, and Smithsonian Books, which composed an average of 54% of Smithsonian Enterprises' annual revenue in fiscal years 2016–20 (KPMG 2017, 2018, 2019, 2020, 2021) (see Figure 13.6).

Smithsonian Retail and Stores

Smithsonian Enterprises Retail Group operates 35 stores across the Smithsonian Institution, with stores in 13 museums, Smithsonian Store online, the National Zoo, and Ronald Reagan Washington National Airport. Smithsonian retail stores contain merchandise and licensed products that are curated to reflect the artifacts and exhibitions of the Smithsonian Institution (Smithsonian Enterprises n.d. b). Smithsonian Enterprises staff manages the sourcing, buying, and pricing of all store-related merchandise and partners with

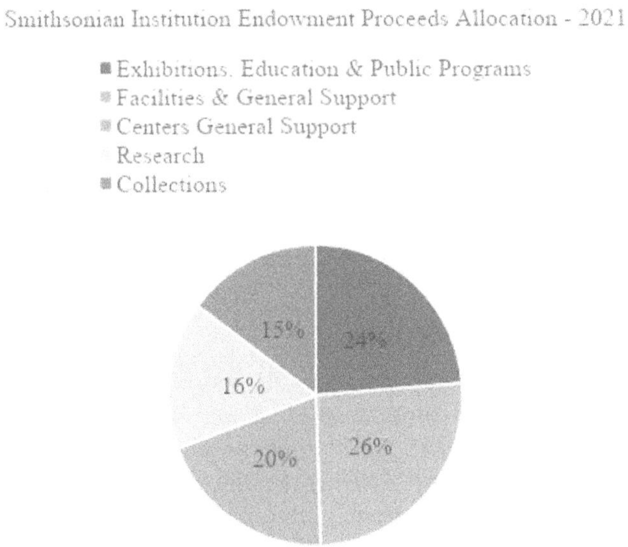

FIGURE 13.6 Endowment proceeds allocations.

museum staff on implementing curated items, store design/renovations, and retail location implementation. The Smithsonian Enterprises Retail Group's focus on profitability centers the store operations on efficiency, productivity, and economies of scale across all of its product lines. As such, Smithsonian Enterprises Retail Group manages its administrative costs by outsourcing various aspects of its operations to third-party vendors, including its store merchandise distribution (KPMG 2017, 2018, 2019, 2020, 2021).

In the retail trade sector, several key metrics are used to manage profitability and ensure the sustainability of store operations. Some of the metrics that Smithsonian Enterprises Retail Group employs to assess its operations are gross margin, average transaction value, foot & online traffic, conversion rate, and inventory turnover (Tableau n.d.), for example:

- Gross margin measures an organization's total net sales minus the cost of goods sold. This figure details how much net sales an organization retains from selling its merchandise.
- Average transaction value is the average amount a customer spends on each transaction. In retail operations, the goal is for the average transaction value to be as high as possible. This metric could also indicate customer price sensitivity if the average transaction value is lower than the average merchandise price.
- Foot and online traffic indicate how many potential customers enter a retail space or visit an organization's website. These can be leading and lagging indicators of many facets of a retail operation, such as store location, time of day, day of the week, time of year, museum visitation, the popularity of merchandise relating to exhibits, web traffic, online user experience, online shopping cart abandonment, etc.
- Conversion rate indicates how many store/online visitors make a purchase. Conversion is encouraged through engaged customer service, increased value proposition to customers, sales, and other incentives.
- Inventory turnover measures how efficiently a company sells its inventory, as unsold inventory could result in future write-downs or losses for an organization (Bloomenthal 2022).

Smithsonian Food and Beverage & Concessions

Smithsonian Enterprises Retail Group manages its food, beverage, and concessions operations across the institution, offering convenient and high-quality food options and entertainment for its millions of annual visitors. Smithsonian Enterprises Retail group delivers a wide array of dining experiences that include award-winning specialty restaurants, cafes, cafeteria style, and grab-and-go options through its partnership with hospitality company Restaurant Associates. In addition to its signature restaurants and cafes, the Smithsonian Enterprises Retail Group's food and beverage offerings include such popular chains as Elevation Burger, Auntie Anne's, Carvel, Ben & Jerry's, and Dippin' Dots. Smithsonian Enterprises' concessions include management of the institution's parking operations, ride, and flight simulators, virtual reality experiences, and other guest amenities. Smithsonian Enterprises Retail Group ensures the profitability of its food and beverage and concessions operations by prioritizing the guest experience at every interaction, ensuring the cleanliness and accessibility of all of its dining spaces, and delivering innovative and guest-engaging attractions to drive sales. Museum visitation is the most significant driver of the food and beverage and concessions operation (Washington.org. n.d.)

Smithsonian Theaters

Smithsonian Enterprises Retail Group operates world-class IMAX theaters and a planetarium that attracts visitors worldwide. The Lockheed Martin IMAX Theater, AIRBUS IMAX Theater, and the Albert Einstein Planetarium offer remarkable and immersive experiences for guests of the Smithsonian Institution's National Air and Space Museum and the National Air and Space Steven F. Udvar-Hazy Center. Some of the features of the Smithsonian Theaters include dual 4K laser projection and two- and three-dimensional presentations and giant screens that measure up to six stories tall. Leveraging remarkable and immersive movie-going experience, Smithsonian Enterprises Retail Group presents a wide array of mission-aligned films, programs, and custom viewing experiences that generate revenue through ticket and group sales annually (Smithsonian Institution n.d. e).

Smithsonian Licensing

Smithsonian Licensing is the storytelling arm of Smithsonian Enterprises Retail Group, as its best-in-class partnerships develop Smithsonian-branded products and promotions that are an extension of the organization's mission, history, and legacy. Defined by their unique quality, value, and ability to create a mission-aligned consumer experience, Smithsonian Licensing products consist of toys, games, interactives, publishing and graphics, home décor, apparel, jewelry, and accessories, collectibles, and licensed promotions. Smithsonian-branded products are the centerpiece of the merchandise sold within its stores and are also available in retail outlets outside the institution through various revenue-generating licensing agreements (Smithsonian Enterprises n.d. b).

Smithsonian Books

Leveraging the Smithsonian Institution's unparalleled authority in history, science, space, military, art, and culture, Smithsonian Books is a collection of trade nonfiction and signature illustrated books that are available wherever books are sold. Published through a partnership with Penguin Random House Publisher Services, Smithsonian Books builds on the institution's mission, making its titles available to the world (Smithsonian Books n.d.).

Smithsonian Enterprises Media Group

Smithsonian Enterprises Media Group comprises the business operations of Smithsonian Air Space Magazines and Smithsonian Channel (Smithsonian Enterprises n.d. b).

Smithsonian Air and Space Magazine

Smithsonian Air and Space Magazine features articles and online content that present the Smithsonian Institution's research in science, history, arts & culture, travel, popular culture, and innovation to a diverse readership of over 8 million monthly readers. *Smithsonian* magazine's revenue is generated through subscriptions and third-party advertisements. As related to cost, Smithsonian Enterprises incurs marketing and production costs alongside having subcontracted fulfillment services for its magazine circulation.

Smithsonian Channel

Smithsonian Channel is the institution's cable TV offering that was created as an innovative expansion of the Smithsonian Institution's mission. With a unique offering of documentaries and shows exploring history, science, nature, aviation, space, and popular culture, Smithsonian Channel has developed an expansive array of programming that earned it the ranking of 77th most popular channel on television as of January 2023 (U.S. TV Database n.d.). In 2006, Smithsonian Enterprises entered into a joint venture with CBS Showtime Networks to launch the channel's first iteration, Smithsonian Networks, and Smithsonian on Demand in 2007 (Hearing on Smithsonian Institution Business Ventures 2006). Smithsonian Channel is available via a wide array of cable networks. It has since grown to develop such popular programs as Aerial America, Air Disasters, Ice Airport Alaska, and Inside the Factory. In keeping with the evolution of streaming technology and content viewership, Smithsonian Channel launched Smithsonian Channel Plus. This ad-free, on-demand platform gives subscribers unlimited access to over 1,000 hours of content for a monthly fee.

In its original agreement with CBS Showtime, the Smithsonian owned a 10% stake in the Smithsonian Networks venture. Its initial revenue distribution from CBS Showtime was a minimum fee of $500k per year, with a percentage of revenue generated over $500k (Hearing on Smithsonian Institution Business Ventures 2006). Since its inception in 2007, Smithsonian Enterprises has

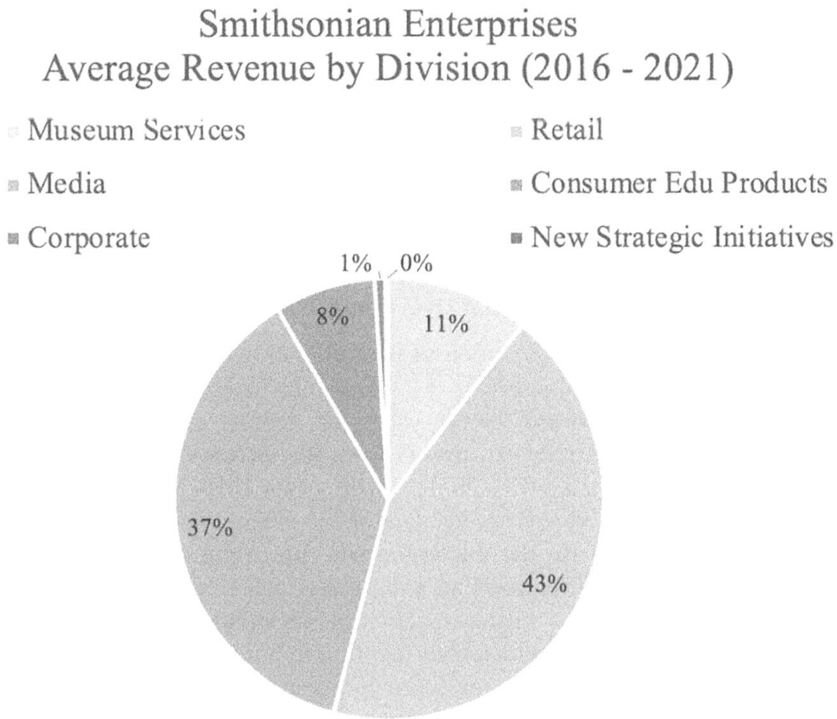

FIGURE 13.7 Average revenue by distribution.

Source: KPMG Statements of Net Gain for 2016–20.

invested in Smithsonian Channel, earning it larger shares of ownership. In 2017, Smithsonian Enterprises sold a portion of its investment in Smithsonian Channel to its partner Showtime Networks Inc. for $24.6 million, and its remaining interest in 2019 for $25.5 million (KPMG 2019, 2020). The Smithsonian Channel trademark is part of the Smithsonian Enterprises division that contributed an average of 37% to its revenue in 2016–20 (KPMG 2017, 2018, 2019, 2020, 2021) (see Figure 13.7).

Smithsonian Enterprises Travel Group

Smithsonian Enterprises Travel Group oversees the operations of Smithsonian Journeys and Smithsonian Student Travel (Smithsonian Enterprise n.d. b).

Smithsonian Journeys

Smithsonian Journeys is the global leader in educational travel. As an extension of the Smithsonian Institution's heritage and community, Smithsonian Journeys offers educational trips to destinations worldwide.

Led by world-class travel and cultural experts, Smithsonian Journeys offers land, cruise, and private jet tours for small groups, families, and independent travelers at varying price points.

Student Travel

Smithsonian Student Travel is the institution's signature travel service for students.

Smithsonian Enterprises Financial Overview (Fiscal Years 2016–20)

Generating profits at the intersection of institutional mission alignment and competitive business landscapes is a unique challenge for Smithsonian Enterprises. Profit is defined as the excess of returns over expenditure. Smithsonian Enterprises refers to profits from its operations as "net gain" (KPMG 2017, 2018, 2019, 2020, 2021). In the years 2016–20, Smithsonian Enterprises contributed an average net gain of $35 million to the Smithsonian Institution's budget, with the highest years preceding the COVID-19 pandemic. Net gain for Smithsonian Enterprises includes all revenue and expenditures related to its business activities, including certain expenses allocated directly from the Smithsonian Institution. Smithsonian Enterprises' annual statement of *net gain* is produced by its auditing firm KPMG and details its business performance by the operating group. Smithsonian Institution's financial statements are reported on the accrual basis of accounting per the US Generally Accepted Accounting Principles (GAAP). As a tax-exempt organization, the net gain from Smithsonian Enterprises is not subject to federal income taxes. However, revenue generated from unrelated business activities is subject to unrelated business income taxes or UBIT. As such, advertising revenue generated from Smithsonian Enterprises' Media Group is considered unrelated business and taxed accordingly (KPMG 2017, 2018, 2019, 2020, 2021).

Smithsonian Enterprises Revenue

Smithsonian Enterprises' revenue is classified as *Merchandise Sales*, *Media Revenue*, and *Concessions*, *Licensing*, & *Other Revenue*. In 2016–20, average merchandise sales and media revenue composed 34% and 39% of the unit's total revenue, respectively.

Concessions revenue composed 27%. Smithsonian Enterprises reports its three working groups across four main categories: *Museum Services, Museum Retail, Media,* and *Consumer Education Products*. The organization also has auxiliary classes that it identifies as *Corporate*, and *New Strategic Initiatives*, which are reserved for non-operating business activities (KPMG 2017, 2018, 2019, 2020, 2021) (see Figure 13.8).

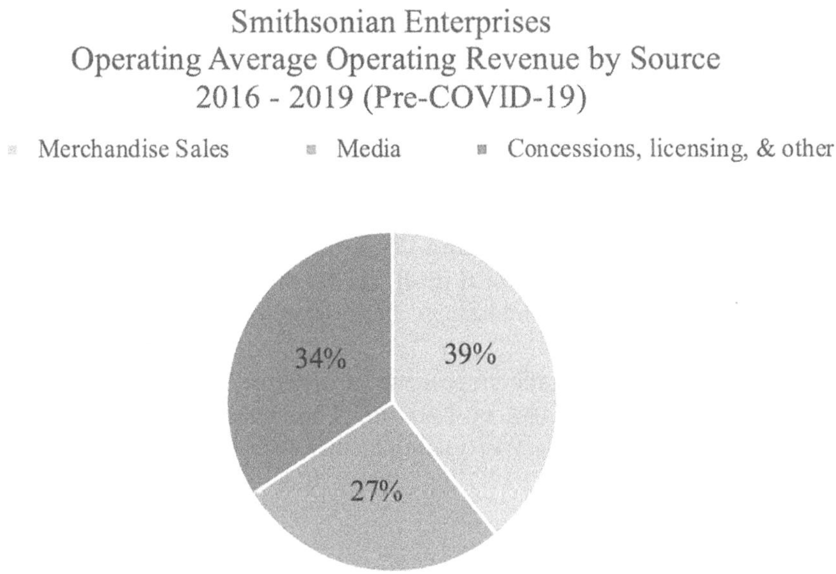

FIGURE 13.8 Operating average operating revenue by source.

Source: KPMG Statements of Net Gain for 2016–20.

For the five years under review, museum retail revenue composes the most significant overall revenue share at 43%. Following closely behind museum retail are media at 37%, museum services, and consumer education products, representing 11% and 8% of revenue, respectively. Smithsonian Enterprises' corporate and new strategic initiatives were not major revenue drivers for the division and generated an average of just over 1% of total revenue (KPMG 2017, 2018, 2019, 2020, 2021).

Smithsonian Enterprises Expenses

Smithsonian Enterprises' expenses are organized by *Selling, General, and Administrative Costs, Cost of Goods Sold, Production Costs, Circulation Costs,* and *Depreciation and Amortization* (KPMG 2017, 2018, 2019, 2020, 2021).

- Selling, general, and administrative costs led the organization's expenses to reflect an average of 51% of the total budget in 2016–20. These costs include Smithsonian Enterprises' staffing, administrative, and product fulfillment costs, with museum retail reflecting the highest expenditure in the years under review (KPMG 2017, 2018, 2019, 2020, 2021).
- Smithsonian Enterprises' cost of goods sold reflects the cost of merchandise/inventory for products sold in Smithsonian Stores and via licensing agreements. Cost of goods sold represented an average of 24% of the unit's

expense budget in 2016–20 and was primarily driven by the museum retail area. In retail operations, the cost of goods sold is a critical factor in determining an enterprise's gross margin or return on sales. Smithsonian Enterprises reported an average gross margin of 48% in the years under review, indicating that the organization retained $.48 of every $1 made on the sale of its products (KPMG 2017, 2018, 2019, 2020, 2021).

- Circulation and production costs comprised 10% and 12% of Smithsonian Enterprises' expense budget in 2016–20. In the years under review, these costs were most heavily reflected in the media area as they represent the direct operating costs of *Smithsonian* magazine (KPMG 2017, 2018, 2019, 2020, 2021).
- Depreciation and amortization represented an average of 3% of Smithsonian Enterprises' expense budget in 2016–20. This reflects the straight-line depreciation on the unit's property, equipment, and leasehold improvements to its operating facilities (KPMG 2017, 2018, 2019, 2020, 2021).

Net Gain Overview 2016–20

As previously mentioned, Smithsonian Enterprises' average net gain for 2016–20 is $35 million. In the years under review, Smithsonian Enterprises' media division contributed the highest percentage of net gain at $15 million or 43% of the total. Museum retail and museum services compose 36% and 34% of total net gain, respectively, and consumer education products were 14%. As insignificant revenue contributors to revenue, Smithsonian Enterprises' corporate and new strategic initiatives categories composed −28% of the unit's net gain (KPMG 2017, 2018, 2019, 2020, 2021) (see Figures 13.9 and 13.10).

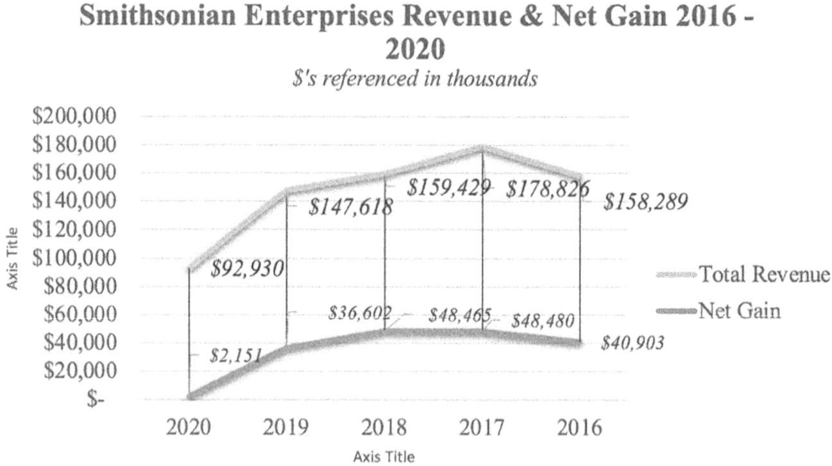

FIGURE 13.9 Smithsonian Enterprises revenue + net gain.

Source: KPMG Statements of Net Gain for 2016–20.

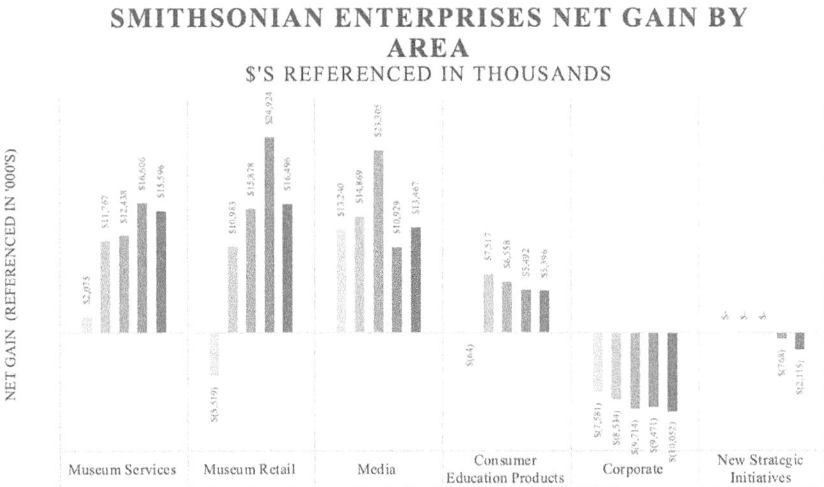

	Museum Services	Museum Retail	Media	Consumer Education Products	Corporate	New Strategic Initiatives
2020	$2,075	$(5,519)	$13,240	$(64)	$(7,581)	$-
2019	$11,767	$10,983	$14,869	$7,517	$(8,534)	$-
2018	$12,438	$15,878	$23,305	$6,558	$(9,714)	$-
2017	$16,606	$24,924	$10,929	$5,492	$(9,471)	$(768)
2016	$15,596	$16,496	$13,467	$5,396	$(10,052)	$(2,115)

FIGURE 13.10 Smithsonian Enterprises net gain by area.

Source: KPMG Statements of Net Gain for 2016–20.

While the media and retail operations generate the most net gain by dollar volume, profit margins for museum services and consumer education products are significantly higher at 73% and 43%, respectively. Smithsonian Enterprises has implemented cost savings measures to include outsourcing, licensing agreements, and partnerships to keep the costs of managing its most profitable ventures low. Profit margins for museum retail operations and media are 19% and 29%, respectively, indicating the high operating costs of managing the institution's stores and media. Smithsonian Enterprises actively manages operating costs for all divisions, ensuring optimal leveraging of fixed costs and nimble administration of variable costs throughout the organization (KPMG 2017, 2018, 2019, 2020, 2021).

Smithsonian Institution Key Business Drivers and Challenges—COVID-19 Impacts

Museum Visitation and COVID-19 Impacts

Museum visitation is the key driver of Smithsonian Enterprises' operations, as the trend in net gain was closely correlated to museum visitation in the years 2016–20. The unit's food and beverage, concessions, and retail operations are most significantly impacted by visitation, as museum visitors are the target customers of these operations. Museum closures relating to the

COVID-19 pandemic caused precipitous year-over-year declines in museum visitation and net gain for Smithsonian Enterprises (Smithsonian Institution n.d. f; KPMG 2017, 2018, 2019, 2020, 2021).

Smithsonian Enterprises' retail and travel groups were the most severely impacted by COVID-19, as museums were closed for nearly one year, and international travel was interrupted between 2020 and 2022. The year 2020 reflected the most significant reduction in both visitation and net gain as each experienced losses of 88% and 91%, respectively, compared to pre-pandemic averages (2016–19) (Smithsonian Institution n.d. f; KPMG 2017, 2018, 2019, 2020, 2021). With such a drastic reduction in net gain, Smithsonian Enterprises implemented a net loss mitigation plan that included the reduction of 237 of its retail, food and beverage, and theater workers and salary reductions for its staff that earned over $100k annually (McGlone 2020). The Smithsonian Institution implemented a museum reopening plan in May of 2021 and reported annual visitation of 5.9 million in 2021 and partial year visitation of 8.9 million as of July 2022 (Smithsonian Institution 2021b). While the Smithsonian Institution rebounds from the COVID-19 pandemic, new profitability challenges have arisen for Smithsonian Enterprises. Speaking on the financial impact of COVID-19 on the Smithsonian Retail Group, its director Ed Howell told *The Washington Post* that the unit "... tried to retain as many [employees] as [it] possibly could ... but ... financially, it was a real struggle" (McGlone 2020).

Smithsonian Institution Strategic Initiatives

While COVID-19 caused significant interruptions for the Smithsonian Institution and its adjoining business operations, the organization entered 2022 with a renewed focus on advancing critical initiatives from its 2017 strategic plan. Looking ahead to 2027, the organization's key priorities include transitioning to digital platforms and outlets; implementing nimble administrative processes; remaining a trusted source for what it means to be an American; and deepening its investment in science and education initiatives (Smithsonian Institution n.d. c). In addition to these priorities, the institution has committed funds to renovate many of its existing museums, the construction of the National Museum of the American Latino, and the American Women's History Museums. Smithsonian Enterprises' net gains will continue to fund its initiatives as it endeavors to "... meet challenges and opportunities of a rapidly changing world" (Smithsonian Institution n.d. c).

Conclusion

As the world's largest museum, education, and research complex, the Smithsonian Institution relies heavily on funding from various sources, many of which are specifically designated or restricted for a purpose. Restrictions on funding limit the organization's ability to meet some of its general operating, strategic, and programmatic initiatives. Smithsonian Enterprises serves a critical role as it manages the business operations that generate unrestricted funding for the institution. As an extension of the Smithsonian Institution, Smithsonian Enterprises leverages the institution's legacy and expands it in the profitable operation of its retail, food, and beverage, concessions, theaters, media, licensing, and travel businesses. Smithsonian Enterprises' business model supports the concept of profitability within a nonprofit context, indicating that nonprofit does not mean "no profit." Profit, or net gain from the Smithsonian Institution's businesses is essential to its sustainability and the furtherance of its mission.

The Smithsonian Institution is a shining example of how a nonprofit museum can employ profit-generating strategies that diversify revenue and provide resources to support its wide-ranging activities. An enterprising approach to profit generation within a nonprofit museum can deliver resources that diversify funding streams and offer opportunities to enhance the visitor experience through retail, food and beverage, entertainment, and other revenue-generating means. By thinking creatively about how a nonprofit museum can generate unrestricted revenue, there are endless opportunities to implement innovative business strategies that strengthen the organizational brand, enhance the visitor experience, and develop funding to ensure sustainability.

References

Abruzzese, Sarah. 2008. "Smithsonian Unit Is Revamped." *The New York Times*, June 21, 2008. https://www.nytimes.com/2008/06/21/arts/21arts-SMITHSONIANU_BRF.html.

Bloomenthal, Andrew. 2022. "Gross Margin: Definition, Example, and Formula for How to Calculate." *Investopedia*. July 9, 2022. https://www.investopedia.com/terms/g/grossmargin.asp.

Hearing on Smithsonian Institution Business Ventures: Hearing before the Committee on House Administration. 2006. 109th Cong. §. 28-299.

KPMG. 2017. *Smithsonian Enterprises Statement of Net Gain*. Washington, DC.

KPMG. 2018. *Smithsonian Enterprises Statement of Net Gain*. Washington, DC.

KPMG. 2019. *Smithsonian Enterprises Statement of Net Gain*. Washington, DC.

KPMG. 2020. *Smithsonian Enterprises Statement of Net Gain*. Washington, DC.

KPMG. 2021. *Smithsonian Enterprises Statement of Net Gain*. Washington, DC.

McGlone, Peggy. 2020. "Smithsonian Lays off 237 as Covid-19 Continues to Limit Operations." *The Washington Post*, October 1, 2020. https://www.washingtonpost.com/entertainment/museums/smithsonian-layoffs-pandemic/2020/10/01/8f2093ae-0418-11eb-a2db-417cddf4816a_story.html.

Smithsonian Books. n.d. "Welcome to Smithsonian Books." *Smithsonian Books Store*. Accessed January 31, 2023. https://www.smithsonianbooks.com/.

Smithsonian Enterprises. n.d. a. "About." *Smithsonian.com*. Accessed January 31, 2023. https://www.smithsonian.com/about/.

Smithsonian Enterprises. n.d. b. "Businesses." *Smithsonian.com*. Accessed January 31, 2023. https://www.smithsonian.com/about/our-businesses/.

Smithsonian Institution. 2017a. *2016 Annual Report*. Washington, DC. https://www.si.edu/sites/default/files/about/2016siannualreport.pdf.

Smithsonian Institution. 2017b. Internal Revenue Service Form 990 2016. https://www.si.edu/sites/default/files/about/2016-990-publicdisclosure-v1.pdf

Smithsonian Institution. 2018a. *2017 Annual Report*. Washington, DC. https://www.si.edu/sites/default/files/about/smithsoniannannualreport2017.pdf.

Smithsonian Institution. 2018b. "Carol Leblanc Named President of Smithsonian Enterprises." *Press release*, December 3, 2018. https://www.si.edu/newsdesk/releases/carol-leblanc-named-president-smithsonian-enterprises.

Smithsonian Institution. 2018c. Internal Revenue Service Form 990 2017. https://www.si.edu/sites/default/files/about/fy2018-990.pdf

Smithsonian Institution. 2019a. *2018 Annual Report*. Washington, DC. https://www.si.edu/sites/default/files/oa/annualreport_050719-upd072920.pdf.

Smithsonian Institution. 2019b. Internal Revenue Service 990 2018. https://www.si.edu/sites/default/files/about/2019-form-990.pdf

Smithsonian Institution. 2020a. *2019 Annual Report*. Washington, DC. https://www.si.edu/sites/default/files/oa/ar19-spreads-081820-smaller.pdf.

Smithsonian Institution. 2020b. Internal Revenue Service 990 2019. https://www.si.edu/sites/default/files/about/2019-form-990.pdf

Smithsonian Institution. 2021a. *2020 Annual Report*. Washington, DC. https://www.si.edu/sites/default/files/oa/smithsonian_2020_annual_report_071521.pdf.

Smithsonian Institution. 2021b. "Smithsonian to Fully Reopen Museums." *Smithsonian Institution*, May 26, 2021. https://www.si.edu/newsdesk/releases/smithsonian-fully-reopen-museums.

Smithsonian Institution. 2022. *2021 Annual Report*. Washington, DC. https://www.si.edu/sites/default/files/oa/smithsonian_2021_accessible-smaller.pdf.

Smithsonian Institution. 2023. "Smithsonian Fiscal Year 2023 Federal Budget Totals More than $1 Billion." *Smithsonian Institution*, January 9, 2023. https://www.si.edu/newsdesk/releases/smithsonian-fiscal-year-2023-federal-budget-totals-more-1-billion.

Smithsonian Institution. n.d. a. "The Board of Regents." *Smithsonian Institution*. Accessed January 31, 2023. https://www.si.edu/regents.

Smithsonian Institution. n.d. b. "Legal History." *Smithsonian Institution*. Accessed January 31, 2023. https://www.si.edu/ogc/legalhistory.

Smithsonian Institution. n.d. c. "Our Shared Future: Smithsonian 2027." *Smithsonian Institution*. Accessed February 3, 2023. https://www.si.edu/strategicplan-2027.

Smithsonian Institution. n.d. d. "Smithsonian Collections." *Smithsonian Institution*. Accessed January 31, 2023. https://www.si.edu/newsdesk/factsheets/smithsonian-collections.

Smithsonian Institution. n.d. e. "Smithsonian Theaters." *Smithsonian Institution*. Accessed January 31, 2023. https://www.si.edu/imax.

Smithsonian Institution. n.d. f. "Visitor Stats: 2022." *Smithsonian Institution*. Accessed January 31, 2023. https://www.si.edu/newsdesk/about/stats.

Smithsonian Institution Archives. n.d. "General History." *Smithsonian Institution Archives*. https://siarchives.si.edu/history/general-history.

Sotheby's Institute of Art. 2018. "The Business Model of the Nonprofit Museum." *Sotheby's Institute of Art*, January 9, 2018. https://www.sothebysinstitute.com/news-and-events/news/the-business-model-of-the-nonprofit-museum/.

Statista Research Department. 2021. "Museums – Statistics & Facts." *Statista*. September 15, 2021. www.statista.com/topics/1509/museums/#editorsPicks (site updated with more recent statistics as of June 30, 2023).
Tableau. n.d. "8 Important Metrics for Retail Industry KPIs." *Tableau*. Accessed January 31, 2023. https://www.tableau.com/learn/articles/retail-industry-metrics-kpis.
U.S. TV Database. n.d. "Smithsonian Channel Ratings – Kwayisi." Accessed January 31, 2023. https://ustvdb.com/networks/smithsonian/.
Washington.org. n.d. "Smithsonian Dining." Washington.org. Accessed January 31, 2023. https://washington.org/find-dc-listings/smithsonian-dining.

14

ALTERNATIVE FINANCING AND FUNDING STRUCTURES AND STRATEGIES

Marek Prokůpek

Introduction

Museums have always experienced financial difficulties; there has never been a period of economic prosperity for museums. Beginning in the early nineteenth century, museums managed by the state or municipal governments experienced difficulties with public funding and the effects of recessions in subsequent economic cycles (Greffe et al. 2017). But in the last decades, the financial pressure has been exacerbated by decreasing public and private funding especially in the Western part of the world (Prokůpek et al. 2022). Museums have therefore been forced to assess and innovate their business models in order not only survive but thrive in the fast changing and evolving environment. Declining art public funding, financial crises, COVID-19 pandemic, terrorism, and many other external and internal factors made museum leaders think about new unprecedented funding models and how to develop and implement a more entrepreneurial spirit (Camarero and Garrido 2009; Lindqvist 2012; Woodward 2012; Tobelem 2013; Alexander 2018; Proteau 2018; Odding 2020; Romolini et al. 2020; Pauget et al. 2021; Prokůpek and Divíšková 2023).

Several museums, particularly large ones, have implemented diverse more market-oriented activities and strategies previously used exclusively in the commercial sector, such as franchising in the case of the Guggenheim Foundation, the Louvre Museum, Centre Pompidou, and others. Institutions such as the Van Gogh Museum in Amsterdam and Centre Pompidou in Paris offer consulting services to private art collectors and other institutions in order to diversify their funding sources. The Louvre Museum in Paris in 2020 organized an auction in cooperation with auction houses Christie's and Drouot

DOI: 10.4324/9781003308003-18

and collected more than two million euros to cover the financial loss caused by the COVID-19 pandemic. Another trend is the cooperation between museums and brands, such as the Museum of Modern Art in New York and fashion chain Uniqlo and the Museum of Contemporary Art, Los Angeles where they dropped Keith Haring Levis jackets. We can find many other examples of such cooperation and product development. Some museums also actively reacted to the newest trend of non-fungible tokens (NFTs). The State Hermitage Museum in St. Petersburg, as well as the Uffizi Gallery in Florence, addressed blockchain technology. Specifically, they "tokenized" some of their precious artworks into NFTs (Prokůpek et al. 2022).

This chapter, based on an extensive review of academic and secondary resources and observations of the museum sector and media monitoring, provides an overview of non-traditional museum funding strategies, income-generating activities, and structures demonstrated with examples from the global museum sector.

Shifting Funding Structures

Traditionally, we can distinguish three models of cultural policies that influence ways museums are funded: the continental Europe model, the British model, and the American model (Vicente et al. 2012). These models differ mainly in the extent of the government involvement in the cultural sector. American museums are more independent from the government, unlike European museums, and in particular those in continental Europe that rely heavily on state support. Museums in continental Europe therefore did not feel a strong pressure to innovate their funding structures and implement alternative financing until recently. In the British model, the government intervenes sparingly and works to maintain cultural autonomy at an arm's length. The distinctions between the three models have become more blurred in recent years, and many museums in Europe have begun to use a mixed model that combines public funding, private donations, and self-generated income (Johnson and Thomas 1998; Frey and Meier 2006; Camarero and Garrido 2009; Lindqvist 2012; Zarobell 2017; Romolini et al. 2020; Loots et al. 2022) to create a hybrid funding structure. Many European museums are likely to keep their current status since they are traditionally conservative institutions whose nonprofit status encourages their fiduciary duty. However, the expansion of commercial and fundraising initiatives inside the museum sector has appealed to their enterprising inclinations (Odding 2020).

The activities of museums are supported by a variety of sources of funding (Johnson and Thomas 1998; Camarero and Garrido 2009), including earned income, and governmental and private contributions (Lindqvist 2012). This three-funding structure model mostly prevails in museums in Europe. The majority of their American counterparts also add the fourth category of income, investment income, since the large American museums have endowment funds. The norm for US museums is to have 5% of the endowment income accessible for spending each year, with the remaining 95% invested in a variety of equities, bonds, and other financial instruments that are chosen to ensure the endowment's continued growth. On average, US museums derive nearly 12% of revenue from investments (American Alliance of Museums 2020).

The exact funding structure of one museum differs from that of another, even if they are the same type, but in general, we can say that the overall average funding mix of state-subsidized museums in continental Europe consists of a maximum of 20% of earned income, with around 10% coming from private contributions and around 70% from public subsidies (Pauget et al. 2021). For example, the Musée d'Orsay, state-subsidized museum's overall budget for 2021 was €89.24 million, of which 4% came from donations, sponsorships, and partnerships, 11.5% from ticket sales, and 6.2% from other sources of generated income. Public funding provided 78.3% of the total museum budget in 2021. It should be noted that public subsidies increased in 2021 compared to prior years to offset losses brought on by the museum's closure in 2020 due to the pandemic (Musées d'Orsay et de l'Orangerie 2022). Musée d'Orsay is one of the most visited museums in France, therefore, smaller regional or municipal museums have even lower earned income and income from private contributions. The funding structure of American museums is different compared to their European counterparts. According to the American Alliance of Museums (2020), most private nonprofit museums combine in their funding structure approximately 19% from governmental funding, 11% investment income, around 35% from earned income, and 35% from private contribution.

Due to the changes in public art funding and its decreasing trends, a stronger focus on performance indicators, as well as changing philanthropic environment, museums, even those in continental Europe, have been adopting more entrepreneurial spirit and methods in recent decades (Toepler and Dewees 2005; Alexander 2019; Brenton and Bouckaert 2020). These factors worked together to covertly introduce the idea of social entrepreneurship to the museum sector (Toepler and Dewees 2005; Eid 2019), which raises hopes for the advantages that entrepreneurial endeavors may have in the future (Murphy 2018). Being commercial and entrepreneurial does not necessarily mean departing from the museum's core values, even though the most common applications of entrepreneurship seem to consist in diversifying income, raising money through entrepreneurial endeavors, or engaging in business-like activities (Toepler and Dewees 2005). In this context, Brendan Ciecko (2019), CEO and founder of Cuseum, came up with the term *museopreneur* to describe an institution that "embraces or assumes characteristics of an entrepreneur to advance their museum's business model and general operations" (18).

Alternative Innovative Financing Strategies

Any traditional source of revenue eventually reaches its limits. Beyond the leveling-off point, the effort needed to improve performance even further might outweigh the advantages. In these circumstances, a sideways leap—experimenting with whole new methods of monetizing the museum's assets—is more advantageous. The following are examples of such experiments and innovative financing strategies museums have implemented in recent years.

Capitalizing Knowledge

Since its opening, Amsterdam's main tourist destination has been the Van Gogh Museum, which houses the largest collection of the artist's works. The museum has excellent staff and has figured out a method to profit from their expertise. Employees at the Van Gogh Museum may devote between 5% and 10% of their working hours to helping commercial clients with collection conservation, temperature control systems, museum management, and educational initiatives. The program began in 2016 with the aim of contributing around 5% of annual revenue—a much-needed injection to make up for the reductions in state support and a regional downturn in tourism (Ciecko 2019).

The Toledo Museum of Art served as an example of how many fundamental ideas about arts education may be used in other fields. In order to extend training in visual literacy to industrial settings like occupational safety, it developed a company called the Center of Visual Expertise. They also maintain a partnership with the Campbell Institute at the National Safety Council. The Center of Visual Expertise brings in more cash, but does so in a way that supports the museum's mission and introduces art and novel ideas to new audiences (Ciecko 2019).

Capitalizing Brand

Franchise museums have become more prevalent in the museum sector throughout the years, sweeping the cultural scene off its feet. These museums' brands are a result of the shifts they underwent over the past few decades that shaped their function as social agents, as well as the impact of globalization, which changed the paradigm of what museums fundamentally are, and ultimately gave rise to their new function as diplomatic agents (Figueruelo 2022). Museums such as the Guggenheim or the Louvre Museum capitalized their brands and sold the license to use it to the city of Bilbao in the case of Guggenheim, and to Abu Dhabi in the case of both of these museums. With regards to the Louvre Museum, the decision to sell the license was in the hands of the Ministry of Culture, whereas the Guggenheim is an independent nonprofit foundation with complete autonomy, and is therefore able to keep the income from licensing. The part of the income from the licensing to use the Louvre brand for the development of a museum in Abu Dhabi was used to establish Louvre Endowment Fund, which made the Louvre Museum the first museum in France with this funding mechanism (Gombault and Selles 2018).

Capitalizing the Collection

Collections are the backbones of museums, and thus their main assets. Recent technological developments have created new opportunities for monetizing digitized museum collections. In recent years, non-fungible tokens (NFTs), a unique digital identifier that allows for the ownership and trade of any type of digital asset, have drawn a growing amount of interest. The possibility of cryptocurrency collectibles is already being investigated by the museum industry (Valeonti et al. 2021). The Uffizi Gallery in Florence was one of the first major art museums to sell NFTs (Prokůpek et al. 2022). It offered a tokenized version of the painting The Doni Tondo, one of Michelangelo masterpieces from the museum's collection. This sale provoked a strong reaction from the Italian government. It appeared as though the Gallery had discovered a significant new source of income when it sold an NFT of the painting for €240,000 in 2021. However, it turns out that the museum only received €70,000 of the total since the technological company it teamed with to make the digital work charged so much in fees. Consequently, the Italian ministry in charge of overseeing the nation's museums requested that organizations temporarily halt their agreements with NFTs suppliers (Batycka 2022). The number of museums exploring NFTs is still relatively low, since they have a tendency to be risk-averse. Despite a variety of obstacles, NFTs are unexplored resources with potential for further use in museums (Jung 2022).

The recent introduction of MetaRembrandt by the Rembrandt Heritage Foundation and HODL Finance aims to "make Rembrandt's oeuvre accessible and illuminating to everyone." The Foundation, through MetaRembrandt, has produced an 8,000 piece NFT collection of Rembrandt's well-known picture "The Night Watch," which is available for purchase on their website. Anyone can buy a virtual replica of the painting together with many special advantages for 0.15 ethereum, which equates to approximately US$270, plus a gas fee of 0.006 ethereum (US$10). The "Night Watch" NFT grants owners lifetime access to the collection and entitles them to founder membership in the MetaRembrandt museum. The 8,000 founding members will also have their names on the wall of fame in the MetaRembrandt museum, be able to rent out their NFTs to make passive income, have access to the entire collection of Rembrandt's works, be able to attend exclusive events in the MetaRembrandt museum and real life, and have access to the "founder's" chat. The most notable of these benefits is the restricted entry to the MetaRembrandt museum available only to NFT buyers. The statement says that the aim is to make Rembrandt's work accessible to everyone, but of course, not everyone can afford to pay US$270 for NFTs. The goal of MetaRembrandt is to virtually preserve Rembrandt's art as well as the exclusive and elitist attitudes that surround it, not to make his works available to everyone. Evidently, the MetaRembrandt project's driving force is profit, not increasing accessibility (Taylor 2022).

Even more recent development and a competitor to NFTs are Art Security Tokens, which combine the blockchain's technological prowess with the legal security provided by a cutting-edge new approach to digital securities. The financial legislation and the supervision of this by the regulatory agencies are constrained by the issue of Art Security Tokens. This separates Art Security Tokens from uncontrolled tokens like Bitcoin and NFTs, which typically still lack a defined legal structure. In the case of Art Security Tokens, a target company purchases an artwork and must have the appropriate financial resources to do so. The artwork serves as collateral for the target company in order to get the financial resources. The payment rights for the piece, known as art security tokens, are divided into numerous equal portions, just as the artwork is divided into many equal parts. These Art Security Tokens are issued by the target company, and investors who subscribe to them become indirect owners of the works of art (Rubey n.d.).

The first museum in Europe to apply this cutting-edge funding strategy to increase its collection is the Royal Museum of Fine Arts Antwerp (KMSKA). In this way, the public and art enthusiasts can jointly invest and own James Ensor's Carnaval de Binche that will be provided on loan to KMSKA. This gives everyone a chance to invest in art while also enabling the museum to strengthen its collection. In order for interested parties to invest in a portion of the masterpiece starting at €150, the Art Security Tokens are made available for purchase. The masterwork will be sold following a ten-year custodianship in the KMSKA. The actual token owners will divide any potential earnings (KMSKA n.d.).

Capitalizing Space

Bringing culture-related businesses on-site through co-working and innovation spaces is an interesting trend in the museum sector's adoption of the start-up mentality. NEW INC at the New Museum in New York City is one such audacious concept. The first "museum-led incubator" in the world, NEW INC opened its doors in 2014 (Ciecko 2019). The museum selects a 100-person interdisciplinary cohort through a competitive procedure, offering them workspace, mentorship, professional development training, and access to media production and a fabrication lab during the course of the program's one-year duration. In 2023, there were around 350 program alumni. Over 175 enterprises and 390 jobs have been produced by the participants, who also raised over US$17 million and earned US$19.6 million in revenue. The museum receives funding from resident fees as well as corporate and philanthropic donations (American Alliance of Museums 2020).

As Ciecko (2019) points out, these kinds of initiatives can benefit museums in multiple ways. They create a favorable environment for partnerships and collaborations by opening the institutions to a variety of new contacts. They also make it possible for museums to foster a fresh, forward-thinking community that serves as a steady source of income.

Experimenting with Admission Fee

It is common for museums to struggle between the need to be accessible and the need to generate enough revenue to cover expenses. These factors do not necessarily conflict; some visitors to the museum might be able and willing to pay more than the admission price the institution has established. Museums can develop a range of demand-based pricing solutions thanks to increasingly complex algorithms. This strategy covers a wide range of tactics, including buy-ahead pricing (providing discounts for in-advance purchases with the assurance that the price will not go any lower), dynamic pricing (which changes based on real-time data), and premium access for specific, constrained times (American Alliance of Museums 2020).

Dynamic pricing, increasing prices for special projects or for programs during peak time, is commonly employed in the performing arts, but it is rarely used in the museum sector. However, several museums started to test dynamic or demand-based pricing in an effort to increase their profits. For instance, the San Francisco Museum of Modern Art raised admission by US$2 for the final four weeks of operation before renovations started, and there were no objections from visitors (van Balgooy 2014).

Dynamic pricing reduces crowding gives budget-conscious visitors more options, and prevents the museum from having empty galleries at particular hours. It can also help with income stability because the museum can modify its marketing efforts in accordance with what has already been reserved. Additionally, it can ensure that the museum is not losing money by charging admission prices that are below what patrons can afford (American Alliance of Museums 2020).

Crowdfunding

Since 2008, museums have utilized crowd-sourced and new media tools (such as social media, blogs, and wikis) to interact, engage, and cooperate with online visitors (Proctor 2010). These online connections have influenced new business models and procedures, including the use of crowdfunding and crowdsourcing. Museums are able to adopt fresh, inventive, and interesting methods of approaching online fundraising efforts thanks to crowd-sourced formats. There are already many examples of museums adopting crowd-funding methods to increase income. One of such example is the Louvre Museum that launched a campaign in 2010 to purchase Lucas Cranach's The Three Graces for the museum collection. Since then, "*Become a Patron!*" campaigns have become a major annual event.

Each year, several thousand people contribute to the conservation or acquisition of important works of art such as The Winged Victory of Samothrace in 2013. Here, the phrase "*Tous mécènes*" from the Louvre Museum's crowdfunding campaign is instructive. The exclamation mark elevates the significance of cultural almsgiving: we are all patrons!

The Hermitage Amsterdam, an independent cultural institution, serves as an inspiring model of a crowdfunding campaign. To make up for the significant losses the museum suffered as a result of its closure during the pandemic, it started a crowdfunding effort. Tickets sales typically account for 70% of the organization's budget. The Hermitage Amsterdam started the crowdfunding campaign in the first quarter of 2021, and it was able to raise close to one million euros from modest to substantial contributions. The general public was inspired to donate by putting together a special week that drew attention to the Hermitage Amsterdam, and by enlisting ambassadors for the cause. Starting such a focused period for the museum resulted in financial assistance as well as new levels energy amongst staff members (Prokůpek et al. 2022).

Innovative Partnership with Brands

Traditional ways of partnership between museums and companies may no longer be attractive, as companies tend to express the desire to be more involved in the content creation rather than being just a passive donor. In recent decades, several museums have built cooperations with brands in order to develop products or services that lead to increased income and the strengthening of brands of both cooperating entities.

The Louvre Museum in Paris and the Museum of Modern Art in New York, both developed cooperation with fashion chain Uniqlo and created editions of T-shirts, sweatshirts, and other clothes with the motives of artworks from museums' collections. The Van Gogh Museum, since its opening, created products together with brands such as Vans, Daily Papers, Samsonite, and others. Licensing is one method that museums might benefit financially from these collaborations. According to the Van Gogh Museum, collaborations in the form of licensed goods offer a chance to enter new markets and educate consumers around the globe about the Dutch painter's work and life. The Van Gogh Museum Amsterdam brand is expanded by licensing companies by looking into new markets in places like Asia and the United States (Prokůpek et al. 2022).

An even more unprecedented type of partnership, at least in the European context, was adopted by the Louvre Museum. Together with auction houses Christie's and Drouot, The Louvre Museum hosted an auction in December 2020 where participants could bid on donated artwork from artists like Pierre Soulages and Jean-Michel Othoniel as well as a variety of museum-related events like the chance to see the Mona Lisa's yearly examination. Over 2.3 million euros were made during the auction, which equates to about 1% of the museum's annual budget (Prokůpek et al. 2022).

Innovations in Public Funding

Innovations in funding mechanisms and structures are not initiated only by museums themselves. Many European nations, particularly in Western Europe, have seen a transition from direct support, such as in the form of lump sum subsidies, to the development of entrepreneurship in the arts and culture. Along with this, there are tools like start-up financing, programs to promote innovation and exports, and incubation centers (Prokůpek et al. 2022). Public venture capital funds aim to produce society advantages in addition to financial profits, frequently in the form of regional development, job creation, and other favorable externalities (Block et al. 2018).

Several countries launched matching funding, a merging policymaking and a technique, in which a commercial or public organization provides additional cash to cultural projects that have been pre-approved by independent donors through small monetary donations. This strategy is implemented through Internet platforms that match project creators with potential audiences as well as with institutional donors (Dalla Chiesa and Alexopoulou 2022). Some countries implemented matching funding schemes for one or more years to motivate museums and other cultural organizations to raise money from individuals and corporations. Depending on the scheme, governments provide either the same or double the amount of money a museum is able to raise on its own.

Conclusion

By choice or necessity, the need for innovative financing and funding structures increased earned income and private contribution has expanded in the museum sector. Even in the parts of the world where museums have benefited from significant public support, new income-generating strategies have been implemented. Museums all over the world have adopted entrepreneurial behaviors, while trying to stay true to their missions and nonprofit statuses.

Based on this observation, it is mostly large museums with strong brands, located in major cities, that are pioneers in innovative financing strategies. This may be due to their resources allowing them to develop and implement such strategies. In some cases, these steps led to the criticism that museums have become too commercial, too customer- and market-oriented, and that in some cases they have shifted away from their missions. Museums selling licenses to use the brand have been criticized for behaving like fast food companies; McDonaldization of culture or McGuggenheimization are terms that appeared in such a context. Museums are therefore in a difficult situation, encountering the need to be more financially independent while facing a scrutiny of their entrepreneurial activities. Nonetheless, several examples highlighted in this chapter show that being entrepreneurial and developing income-generating activities does not have to mean compromising the museum's mission and public status.

Due to the challenging economic times the whole world is facing now, it can be expected that public subsidies will shrink and companies will reconsider their sponsorship and philanthropic budgets. Museums, therefore, will need to continue to experiment with new financing strategies and look for non-traditional sources of income.

References

Alexander, D. Victoria. 2018. "Enterprise Culture and the Arts: Neoliberal Values and British Art Institutions." In *Art and the Challenge of Markets Volume 1*, edited by Victoria D. Alexander, 67–93. Cham: Palgrave McMillan.

Alexander, D. Victoria. 2019. "Cultural Policy Effects on the Marketing Orientation in London Art Museums." In *Museum Marketization*, edited by Karin M. Ekström, 81–97. Abingdon: Routledge.

American Alliance of Museums. 2020. *Trends Watch: The Future of Financial Sustainability*. American Alliance of Museums.

Batycka, Dorian. 2022. "Italy Instructs Museums to Halt Contracts with NFT Companies, Citing 'Unregulated' Terms That Could Affect the Country's Cultural Heritage." *Artnet*, May 14. Accessed January 25, 2023. https://news.artnet.com/market/cinello-nft-michaelangelo-2145003

Block, Joern H., Massimo G. Colombo, Douglas J. Cumming, and Silvio Vismara. 2018. "New Players in Entrepreneurial Finance and Why They Are There." *Small Business Economics* 50 (2): 239–50. doi: 10.1007/s11187-016-9826-6

Brenton, Scott and Geert Bouckaert. 2020. "Managing Public Museums Appropriately and Consequentially: The Distinctiveness and Diversity of Leading Organization." *Public Administration Review* 81 (4): 715–27. doi: 10.1111/puar.13323

Camarero, Carmen and María-José Garrido. 2009. "Improving Museums' Performance through Custodial, Sales, and Customer Orientations." *Nonprofit and Voluntary Sector Quarterly* 38 (5): 846–68. doi: 10.1177/0899764008319230

Ciecko, Brendan. 2019. "Museopreneur: How Museums Are Leaping into New Business Models with Entrepreneurial Spirit." *American Alliance of Museums* 2019: 17–21.

Dalla Chiesa, Carolina and Andriani Alexopoulou. 2022. "Matchfunding Goes Digital: The Benefits of Matching Policymaking with the Crowd's Wisdom."

European Journal of Cultural Management and Policy, 1. doi: 10.3389/ejcmp.2022.11090
Eid, Haitham. 2019. *Museum Innovation and Social Entrepreneurship: A New Model for a Challenging Era*. London, England: Routledge.
Figueruelo, Alejandra Linares. 2022. "Cultural Franchises or Franchising Cultures?" *Museum International* 74 (1-2): 120–33. doi: 10.1080/13500775.2022.2157570
Frey, Bruno S. and Stephan Meier. 2006. "The Economics of Museums." In *Handbook of the Economics of Art and Culture* (Vol. 1), edited by Victor A. Ginsburgh and David Thorsby, 1017–47. Amsterdam: Elsevier.
Gombault, Anne and Didier Selles. 2018. "Company Profile: Louvre Abu Dhabi: A Radical Innovation, But What Future for French Cultural Influence?" *International Journal of Arts Management* 20 (3): 83–94.
Greffe, Xavier, Anne Krebs, and Sylvie Pflieger. 2017. "The Future of the Museum in the Twenty-First Century: Recent Clues from France." *Museum Management and Curatorship* 32 (4): 319–34. doi: 10.1080/09647775.2017.1313126
Johnson, Peter and Barry Thomas. 1998. "The Economics of Museums: A Research Perspective." *Journal of Cultural Economics* 22 (2): 75–85. doi: 10.1023/A:1007537500352
Jung, Yuha. 2022. "Current Use Cases, Benefits and Challenges of NFTs in the Museum Sector: Toward Common Pool Model of NFT Sharing for Educational Purposes." *Museum Management and Curatorship*, 1–17. doi: 10.1080/09647775.2022.2132995
KMSKA. n.d. KMSKA Is the First European Museum to Use Art Security Tokens to Make a Masterpiece Publicly Accessible. Accessed July 4, 2023. https://kmska.be/en/kmska-first-european-museum-use-art-security-tokens-make-masterpiece-publicly-accessible
Lindqvist, Katja. 2012. "Museum Finances: Challenges beyond Economic Crises." *Museum Management and Curatorship* 27 (1): 1–15. doi: 10.1080/09647775.2012.644693
Loots, Ellen, Diana Betzler, Trine Bille, Boram Lee, and Karol Borowiecki. 2022. "New Forms of Finance and Funding in Creative Industries." *Journal of Cultural Economics* 46 (2): 205–30. doi: 10.1007/s10824-022-09450-x
Murphy, Oonagh. 2018. "Coworking Spaces, Accelerators and Incubators: Emerging Forms of Museum Practice in an Increasingly Digital World." *Museum International* 70 (1-2): 62–75. doi: 10.1111/muse.12193
Musées d'Orsay et de l'Orangerie. 2022. "Rapport d'activité 2021 Musées d'Orsay et de l'Orangerie." Accessed January 20, 2023. https://www.epmo-musees.fr/sites/default/files/2022-07/RAMO-2021_web.pdf
Odding, Arnoud. 2020. "Museum Entrepreneurship in the Times of Corona." *Rijksmuseum*, December 14. Accessed January 20, 2023. https://www.rijksmuseumtwenthe.nl/content/2850/en/museum-entrepreneurship-in-thetimes-of-corona
Pauget, Bertrand, Jean-Michel Tobelem, and Jean-Philippe Bootz. 2021. "The Future of French Museums in 2030." *Technological Forecasting and Social Change* 162: 120384. doi: 10.1016/j.techfore.2020.120384
Proctor, Nancy. 2010. "Digital: Museum as Platform, Curator as Champion, in the Age of Social Media." *Curator: The Museum Journal* 53 (1): 35. doi: 10.1111/j.2151-6952.2009.00006.x
Prokůpek, Marek and Bára Divíšková. 2023. "Ethics in Museum Fundraising: Evidence from the Czech Republic." *The Journal of Arts Management, Law, and Society* 53 (1): 42–61. doi: 10.1080/10632921.2022.2135654
Prokůpek, Marek, Ellen Loots, and Diana Betzler. 2022. "Emergency or Emerging Financing Strategies of Art Museums in the Context of a Pandemic?" *Museum Management and Curatorship*, 1–18. doi: 10.1080/09647775.2022.2111327

Proteau, Jasmine. 2018. "Reducing Risky Relationships: Criteria for Forming Positive Museum-Corporate Sponsorships." *Museum Management and Curatorship* 33 (3): 235–42. doi: 10.1080/09647775.2018.1467274

Romolini, Alberto, Silvia Fissi, Elena Gori, and Marco Contri. 2020. "Financing Museums: Towards Alternative Solutions? Evidence from Italy." In *Management, Participation and Entrepreneurship in the Cultural and Creative Sector*, edited by Martin Piber, 11–32. Cham: Springer.

Rubey. n.d. What Are Art Security Tokens? Accessed July 4, 2023. https://www.rubey.be/en/

Taylor, Kyson. 2022. "What the Hell Happened: MetaRembrandt." Accessed July 4, 2023. https://www.thecrimson.com/article/2022/11/1/metarembrandt-thinkpiece-hodl-finance-nft-launch-2022/

Tobelem, Jean-Michel. 2013. "The Arts and Culture: A Financial Burden or a Way Out of the Crisis." *ENCATC Journal of Cultural Management and Policy* 3 (1): 52–60.

Toepler, Stefan, and Sarah Dewees. 2005. "Are There Limits to Financing Culture through the Market? Evidence from the US Museum Field." *International Journal of Public Administration* 28 (1–2): 131–46. doi: 10.1081/PAD-200044548

Valeonti, Foteini, Antonis Bikakis, Melissa Terras, Chris Speed, Andrew Hudson-Smith, and Konstantinos Chalkias. 2021. "Crypto Collectibles, Museum Funding and OpenGLAM: Challenges, Opportunities and the Potential of Non-Fungible Tokens (NFTs)." *Applied Sciences* 11 (21): 9931. doi: 10.3390/app11219931

van Balgooy, Max. 2014. "How Museums Can Optimize Revenue through Dynamic Pricing." Accessed July 4, 2023. https://engagingplaces.net/2014/07/02/how-museums-can-optimize-revenue-through-dynamic-pricing/

Vicente, Eva, Carmen Camarero, and María-José Garrido. 2012. "Insights into Innovation in European Museums: The Impact of Cultural Policy and Museum Characteristics." *Public Management Review* 14 (5): 649–79. doi: 10.1080/14719037.2011.642566

Woodward, Simon. 2012. "Funding Museum Agendas: Challenges and Opportunities." *Managing Leisure* 17 (1): 14–28. doi: 10.1080/13606719.2011.638202

Zarobell, John. 2017. "Museum Funding: Who Shapes Institutions?" In *Art and the Global Economy*, edited by John Zarobell, 35–58. Oakland: University of California Press.

15

UNIQUE, ONE-TIME, OR TEMPORARY FUNDING OPPORTUNITIES

Mega-Event Legacy Activities as Funding Opportunities for Museums

Tiffany Bourgeois

Introduction

This chapter offers a case study of Super Bowl 50 as a special revenue strategy for museums. Specifically, it uses mega-event legacy theory (Preuss 2007, 2015) as a lens to understand the sports mega-event as an alternative funding source for museums due to its temporary nature and as an alternative to well-established granting institutions. The temporary structure of Super Bowl host committees and events desire to have lasting impact. This inquiry examines the Children's Discovery Museum of San Jose, California Indian Museum and Cultural Center, Habitot Children's Museum, and Asian Art Museum as grant recipients from the 50 Fund, which is the legacy fund of the San Francisco Bay Area Super Bowl 50 Host Committee. This study, using mega-event legacy theory, offers a particular perspective on alternative funding sources for museums that highlights how museum administrators can prepare for and take advantage of this unique funding opportunity during future Super Bowls. By reviewing literature on mega-events, urban development, the Olympics, and Super Bowls, this work examines the funding structure of the San Francisco Bay Area Super Bowl 50 Host Committee and investigates the museums and programs that received funds. Mega-event legacy theory provides a theoretical framework to understand the relationship between the mega-event and the region that hosts it by examining the lasting effects on the region.

Mega-events are large-scale cultural, commercial, and sporting events that have a dramatic character, mass popular appeal, and international significance and are organized by a combination of national, governmental, international, and nongovernmental organizations (Roche 2000). The Super

DOI: 10.4324/9781003308003-19

Bowl fits within the mega-event framework due to its short-term and spectacular nature. Donald Getz's explanation of mega-events links them to soft power: "Indeed, many countries have used mega events to gain legitimacy and prestige, draw attention to their accomplishments, foster trade and tourism, or to help open their countries to global influences" (2008, 414). Museums as grant recipients from these funding opportunities are an example of an institution that can benefit from the mega-event.

The special revenue strategy embodies the mega-event characteristic of drawing attention to accomplishments because the San Francisco Bay Area Super Bowl Host Committee highlights the distribution of funds as an intended legacy. In general, this reflects historical funding trends from Super Bowl host committees. Super Bowl 50's attempt to be the most philanthropic and giving Super Bowl ever make this alternative funding structure and the amount of grants unique (50 Fund n.d.). Mega-events can be utilized as vehicles of financial support for the region, the city, and local museums. The focus on the Super Bowl as an alternative funding structure for museums emphasizes the significance of the opportunity due to its annual timeline. This case study focuses on funds received by the Children's Discovery Museum of San Jose, California Indian Museum and Cultural Center, Habitot Children's Museum, and Asian Art Museum to highlight the specific funding outcomes for museums. It also explores the goals of the San Francisco Bay Area Super Bowl 50 Host Committee and analyzes the activities and the funding structure of the 50 Fund. Lastly, the chapter contextualizes the impact of this alternative funding structure by noting how museums fit within the greater Super Bowl funding framework.

About the San Francisco Bay Area Super Bowl 50 Host Committee

Before museums were even awarded any grants, Super Bowl 50 was grounded in a unique context. For the first time in decades, the National Football League (NFL) did not use Roman numerals to denote the game. The NFL decided to use "50" instead of the Roman number "L" because it was thought to be more appealing to audiences for the 50th anniversary of the game and to address the negative connotation in sports associated with getting an "L," or losing a game.

The Super Bowl host committee is responsible for the planning and execution of the game. "Working in partnership with Bay Area public officials and the NFL, the San Francisco Bay Area Super Bowl 50 Host Committee is responsible for Super Bowl 50 and its celebration elements, including the Super Bowl Village, public exhibits and planning of game day logistics" (San Francisco Bay Area Super Bowl 50 Host Committee n.d.). The host committee is also accountable to local responses to the lead up and execution of the game. Not all of the residents in the area were in support of hosting the game. "In a city divided over gentrification, sky-high housing prices and the technology industry's influence on local government, even the nation's biggest party has become a battleground" (Lovett 2016, paragraph 2). Environmental and social justice issues are commonly associated with sports mega-events and Super Bowl 50 was not immune to these issues. "To tidy up for the tourists, the city's large homeless population has been swept out of view, which some people here see as evidence that this city, long a seat of leftist activism, has sold itself to corporate interests" (Lovett 2016, paragraph 3). Although the negative consequences of a sports mega-event are well documented, the host committee attempted to lay the groundwork for a positive legacy: "The Host Committee seeks to make Super Bowl 50 the most giving ever, and is investing in Bay Area community initiatives and high-performing nonprofits through the 50 Fund, its signature philanthropic fund" (Business Wire 2016, paragraph 9). This initiative is the crux of the inquiry, because it provides an opportunity for museums to take advantage of their city or region hosting the game. The 50 Fund had a variety of grant programs and community initiatives to support its goals. This investigation highlights awards given to museums through the Game Changer, Playmaker, and PLAY 60, Play On programs.

Theoretical Framework

This work emphasizes how museums use alternative funding sources by noting how museums fit within the greater framework of mega-event legacies and outcomes using case study methodology (Creswell 2007; Ying 2009, 2018). Specifically, funding from the Super Bowl host committee is designed to support event-related changes for local organizations and the community. Preuss's (2015) theory indicates a specific structure that is helpful in understanding the special revenue strategy for museums that can be described as unique, one-time, or temporary funding opportunities. Although this chapter focuses on Super Bowl 50, there are other examples, such as the Olympics and the World Cup, that support similar cultural outcomes through arts and cultural programming. Preuss's framework includes components to determine a mega-event legacy: specifically, what constitutes an event-related change, who is affected by the change, how the legacy affects a particular stakeholder, and when a legacy begins and how long it lasts (2015, 649). Although the distribution of funds is an economic transaction, the outcomes of the transaction are related to cultural experiences and activities. This work implements this framework to better understand how museums are impacted by this change. Scholars like Mueller (2015) and Hiller (1995) provide structures for understanding mega-events. Garcia (2008) and Bourgeois (2019) focus on the cultural outcomes of the Olympics, which are relevant for this study in understanding how arts and cultural outcomes function for sports mega-events. Although the Olympics are an international mega-event while the Super Bowl includes only US teams, the two events are similar because both include cultural programming elements like the Super Bowl Fanfest and the Olympic Arts Festival. The economic and financial components of sports mega-events are explored by Zimbalist (2012) and Andranovich and Burbank (2011). Additionally, other scholars have focused on Super Bowl—specific outcomes (David et al. 2008; Inoue and Havard 2014). The content of these works explicitly connects to this investigation of Super Bowl 50. Matheson (2005), Matheson and Baade (2006), Baumann and Matheson (2018), and Kim and Walker (2012) add to the perspective on the Super Bowl's economic impact, its effects on tourism, and its social impact. Lastly, Bourgeois and Socolof (2022) provide a unique perspective that specifically highlights the relationship between the Super Bowl host committees and arts and cultural institutions.

Mega-Event Legacy Theory

Mega-event legacy theory stems from a variety of impacts and outcomes related to large-scale events. This approach is relevant for this work because it allows for a comprehensive perspective on potential outcomes. For instance, the concept of leveraging, which can be considered like legacy, emphasizes how the initiatives can be used to extend the reach of the event to other domains (Smith 2014). Chalip (2006) focuses on the economic value and social impact of sports mega-events as instances of legacy. Legacy can fit within diverse categories, such as political and cultural (Veal et al. 2012). The diversity in approaches to understanding legacy is reflected in a diversity of scholarly works. Thomson et al. (2020) noted opportunities to develop methodological approaches that reflect the "soft" nature of social legacies, which fits this examination of the cultural organizations. This work is grounded in Preuss's (2015) approach to legacy that notes what constitutes a legacy, who is affected, how stakeholders experience the legacy, for how long, and how long a legacy can last.

Funding distributed by the Super Bowl 50 Host Committee can be described as event-related changes. Specifically, through the 50 Fund, the host committee effects change by supporting different initiatives from nonprofits. The process includes nonprofits applying to the program and the 50 Fund choosing recipients and distributing funds. This is an event-related change because it is a one-time or unique funding structure that was created by the host committee in conjunction with the National Football League for Super Bowl 50. Due to the Super Bowl changing host cities each year and the event-specific funding, it exemplifies an event-related change that fits within Preuss's (2015) mega-event legacy framework.

Although examination of the funding patterns for Super Bowls is linked to economic impact discussions, this work uses a cultural outcomes lens to investigate the distribution of awards because the organizations involved produce, exhibit, or support arts and culture. The framework for understanding how museums take advantage of the unique funding source from the 50 Fund is grounded in Preuss's (2015) legacy framework. Preuss included six characteristics within his definition of legacy: time, new initiatives, value, tangibility, space, and intention. The funds distributed by the 50 Fund for programming post the Super Bowl fit the criterion that requires a legacy to last longer than the event. There is also the creation of new programmatic opportunities due to the awards. Preuss's discussion of value consists of changes that bring positive and negative impacts. This concept relates explicitly to organizations that received funds as positive impacts and those that did not receive funds as negative impacts (Bourgeois and Socolof 2022). The 50 Fund supported programming and the construction of physical spaces. The dispersion of funds within the Bay Area fits within Preuss's framework that highlights a specific space required for legacy. According to Bourgeois and Socolof, "There could also be unintentional consequences based on the unpredictable nature of people and their experiences during programming" (2022, 6). The 50 Fund and the awards given to the Children's Discovery Museum of San Jose, California Indian Museum and Cultural Center, Habitot Children's Museum, and Asian Art Museum to support programming represent a unique and temporary funding opportunity framework that other museums can implement during future Super Bowls.

Museums

Museums provide a unique opportunity to examine the legacies associated with sports mega-events. They play vital economic and cultural roles in their communities. According to the American Alliance of Museums (AAM), "The economic activity of museums generates over $12 billion in tax revenue, one-third of it going to state and local governments. Each job created by the museum sector results in $16,495 in additional tax revenue" (2018, section 2). Museums are also an essential part of the cultural landscape. "More people visited an art museum, science center, historic house or site, zoo, or aquarium in 2018 than attended a professional sporting event" (AAM 2018, section 4). Using mega-event legacy theory as a lens to understand the 50 Fund as a unique funding source for museums provides a framework for museum administrators in cities that may host future Super Bowls.

California Indian Museum and Cultural Center

The California Indian Museum and Cultural Center was founded in 1996 with the purpose of educating the public about the history, culture, and contemporary life of California Indians and to honor their contributions to civilization (CIMCC n.d.). It received a Playmaker grant and a PLAY 60, Play On grant. It is the only museum in this study that is the recipient of multiple awards from the 50 Fund. The Playmaker grant program provides $10,000 grants to community-based organizations with a passionate advocate and a specific, compelling need for the grant in order to provide an immediate community impact (50 Fund n.d. b). The grant was awarded to support the development of CIMCC's Tribal Youth Ambassadors arts micro-enterprise through a one-year project to increase the youths' native arts micro-enterprise skills and improve K–12 visitors' and the public's understanding of local tribal cultures through native arts. The expansion of the Playmaker program was supported through a $250,000 grant from the StubHub Foundation (Business Wire 2016). This program affirms the values of the 50 Fund. Specifically, the host committee demonstrated that it was committed to investing in young people, their families, and their communities because its members believed they were investing in the future of the Bay Area (50 Fund n.d. b). The additional award, PLAY 60, Play On, also focused on children. Specifically, the $40,000 award was used to create Indigenous Play for Active Lives, an interactive and portable sidewalk display that engages kids and families in play and physical activities while teaching them to sing, count, and speak in Native American languages. During fiscal year 2015, CIMCC's revenue was $420,925 and in 2016 it was $387,729 (ProPublica 2016b). Based on the calendar for the fiscal year, the awards comprised approximately 10% of the museum's total revenue.

Children's Discovery Museum of San Jose

The Children's Discovery Museum of San Jose's mission is to "inspire creativity, curiosity and lifelong learning" (n.d.). One of the organization's aspirations is for children to find joy in play and discovery, which relates to the grant awarded by the 50 Fund through its Game Changer program. The Children's Discovery Museum of San Jose was one of only a few organizations that won the large award. An article in *Forbes* magazine observed, "The 50 Fund kicked off its giving 50 weeks before the Super Bowl, awarding $500,000 worth of grants to five 'Game Changers' out of an applicant pool of 147" (Carter 2016, paragraph 13). Interestingly, the article also observed that the Game Changer had been expanded to include more than five organizations: "Thanks to well-received fundraising efforts, the 50 Fund was able to extend its Game Changer initiative and award nine additional $200,000 grants focusing on community-building and the environment" (Carter 2016, paragraph 15). Specifically, the 50 Fund awarded $258,860 to the Children's Discovery Museum of San Jose to address the lack of connection to the natural world in nearby densely urban neighborhoods. The goal was to build an outdoor play space that would be a bridge to nature, combining interactive experiences in a natural setting with conservation, demonstrations, and educational programs that would respond to the learning needs of diverse families (50 Fund n.d.). The award was approximately 2–3% of the museum's revenue for that fiscal year. In addition to the 50 Fund award, the program was supported by other funding sources, which will ensure the initiative is supported over the long term. The award supported the development of Bill's Backyard, a half-acre of welcoming and safe nature exploration. This space includes a Jr. Ranger Station, Look Out Tower and Tunnel, Dig Pit and Dry Creek, which all allow children to engage with natural features and encourage physical activity and design through play (Children's Discovery Museum of San Jose n.d.). This event-related change functions as a legacy due to the facility still being in use years after the Super Bowl took place.

Habitot Children's Museum

The Habitot Children's Museum, located in Berkeley, California, received a PLAY 60, Play On grant for $32,000. The organization's mission "is to help parents and caregivers—from as broad an audience as possible—as they raise creative, curious, and confident children" (Habitot Children's Museum 2020, paragraph 1). The grant was used to temporarily transform an underused 3,600-square-foot parking lot into a popup play space. This space featured a giant sandbox, interactive art, a play-based recycling center exhibit, loose part play pieces, and plenty of tools for digging, excavating, and shaping. Specifically, it was a "one-week popup Sand Zone that Habitot created by transforming a 3,600 square foot parking lot at Adeline [Street] and Alcatraz [Avenue] in Berkeley into a giant sandbox to promote active play for children of all ages" (Berkeleyside Staff 2016, paragraph 1). In 2016, the revenue for the organization was $573,595 (ProPublica 2016c). The gift was approximately 6% of the museum's total revenue for that year. This project is unique among the ones discussed in this chapter because it was temporary in nature. Yet, it continued to support the host committee's goal of creating a legacy for Super Bowl 50 by receiving funding through the legacy fund.

Asian Art Museum

The Asian Art Museum, situated in the heart of San Francisco, celebrates, preserves, and promotes Asian and Asian American art and cultures for local and global audiences. The organization provides a dynamic forum for exchanging ideas, inviting collaboration, and fueling imagination to deepen understanding and empathy among people of all backgrounds (Asian Art Museum n.d.). Interestingly, the museum was celebrating its 50th anniversary during Super Bowl 50. The Asian Art Museum received a $17,000 grant under the PLAY 60, Play On program to create the Living Innovation Zone experience. This was an inviting, playful sidewalk intervention lined with interactive art installations that celebrated and encouraged human creativity in all its forms and provide safe and engaging play experience for all ages. The purpose of this program was to close the opportunity gap for kids in the Bay Area and provide a catalyst to inspire communities to rethink play in order to ensure all kids get the play they need to thrive (PLAY 60, Play On n.d.). The grant supported the Village Artist Corner initiative. *The Journey* (سفر) is the final mural on the Village Artist Corner, a project of the Asian Art Museum and the San Francisco Public Library supported by numerous area organizations and individuals like the Family of Tania Vonelleese Seymour, Housing-Related Parks Program from the State of California, San Francisco Recreation and Parks Department, the Hearst Foundations, California Arts Council, the NFL Foundation, 50 Fund, and the legacy fund of the Super Bowl 50 Host Committee (Asian Art Museum 2022). The year the Asian Art Museum was awarded the grant (fiscal year 2016), its operating budget was $28.4 million (Asian Art Museum 2023). That is the equivalent of 0.06% of the museum's entire operating budget, which is relatively a small portion. Also, the grant supported a program that was in operation for approximately five years. The established nature of the program and the small amount of the grant relative to the operating budget is unique. The total revenue for the Asian Art Museum's fiscal year 2015 was $47,767,323; in 2016 it was $41,703,058; and in 2017 it was $31,478,868 (ProPublica 2015; ProPublica 2016a; ProPublica 2017). Given the revenue history of the organization, the grant of $17,000 was monetarily insignificant, but its receipt of funds from the 50 Fund still represented a unique funding opportunity. The museum used those funds in conjunction with other donors to support its Village Artist Corner, which fell in line with the goals for PLAY 60, Play On that intended to support initiatives that encouraged playful transformations of sidewalks and spaces to encourage active play.

The museums discussed in this chapter are diverse in size, budget, and mission. The grant amounts awarded to them and the initiatives funded by the grants are different. Yet each museum is part of the legacy designed by the host committee. The 50 Fund's temporary funding sources aligned the goals of the host committee with the missions of the museums to create a legacy for Super Bowl 50.

Discussion

The museums associated with this study reveal the diverse opportunities related to Super Bowl 50. In general, museums with larger budgets have the capacity to employ more arts administrators to secure funding. Specifically, smaller institutions do not have the same capacity to have the same access to funding.

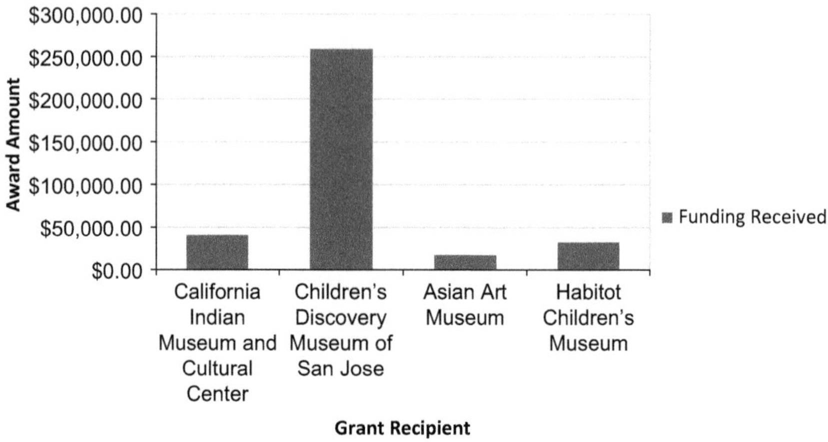

FIGURE 15.1 Museums that received grants from the 50 Funds.

These organizations highlight the host committee's diversity and variety in its gift amounts and the differing programs it chose to support. The temporary funding opportunities from Super Bowl 50 resulted in the support of unique programs and organizations. For instance, the Asian Art Museum is the oldest institution in our sample and has the largest budget, yet it received the smallest grant. Also, some of the funds delivered to the institutions were in conjunction with other funds for the programs. Figure 15.1 outlines the award amount received by each museum from the 50 Fund.

The City of San Jose, along with at least six other entities, joined the 50 Fund to give a significant amount at either the visionary or benefactor level to support Bill's Backyard at the San Jose Children's Museum (Children's Discovery Museum of San Jose 2022a, 2022b). The legacy associated with the program is strengthened because the funds are from the 50 Fund in conjunction with other community and funding support. I assert that this highlights how the 50 Fund supported programming that was relevant to other stakeholders in the communities the museums served. It demonstrates that the Super Bowl can support initiatives that already are relevant to communities that host the game. The diversity of the programs that were supported highlights the diversity of the organizations and broad spectrum of support from the Super Bowl host committee.

The application process and award process to secure funds highlight the limited support of arts organizations and even specifically museums. The preparation for a sports mega-event can demonstrate the manner in which museums can note how Super Bowl host committees provide funding opportunities. The specific granting programs can vary by games due to the goals of the city and host committee. Using Preuss's (2015) framework for legacy exemplifies potential goals for future Super Bowl host committees that will allow museums to take advantage of a unique source of funds. This chapter analyzes the activities and the funding structure of the 50 Fund and recognizes the six characteristics that Preuss (2015) includes within his definition of legacy: time, new initiatives, value, tangibility, space, and intention.

The funds distributed by the 50 Fund for programming post the Super Bowl fit the criteria that requires a legacy to last longer than the event. There is also the creation of new programmatic opportunities due to the awards that were implemented by the California Indian Museum and Cultural Center. Preuss's discussion of value consists of changes that bring positive and negative impacts. This concept relates explicitly to organizations that received funds as positive impacts and those that did not receive funds as negative impacts (Bourgeois and Socolof 2022). The 50 Fund supported programming and the construction of physical spaces like the Sand Zone at Habitot Children's Museum. The dispersion of funds within the Bay Area fits within Preuss's framework that highlights a specific space required for legacy. According to Bourgeois and Socolof, "There could also be unintentional consequences based on the unpredictable nature of people and their experiences during programming" (2022, 6). The 50 Fund and the awards given to the Children's Discovery Museum of San Jose, California Indian Museum and Cultural Center, Habitot Children's Museum, and Asian Art Museum to support their programming represent a unique funding opportunity framework that museums can implement during future Super Bowls.

Conclusion

In conclusion, this chapter uses mega-event legacy theory (Preuss 2015) as a lens to understand how Super Bowl 50 provided a special revenue strategy for museums in the Bay Area of California. Specifically, the Children's Discovery Museum of San Jose, California Indian Museum and Cultural Center, Habitot Children's Museum, and Asian Art Museum received funds from the 50 Fund as part of the legacy initiative. There are differences in museums, amounts awarded, and supported initiatives. Yet, all of the museums received a one-time and unique funding opportunity that supports the legacy of Super Bowl 50. The next step in this work includes examining the Super Bowl before and after Super Bowl 50 to determine how its host committees engage museums with their legacy initiatives. Mega-events are associated with a variety of social justice and environmental concerns. This work would provide additional context for the sports mega-event related to the arts and culture sector. This would allow arts administrators to prepare for and take advantage of an alternative funding source associated with the temporary event.

References

50 Fund. n.d. *The Legacy Fund of the San Francisco Bay Area Super Bowl 50 Host Committee*. https://www.50fund.org.

American Alliance of Museums. 2018. "Museum Facts & Data." https://www.aam-us.org/programs/about-museums/museum-facts-data/#_edn13.

Andranovich, G. and M. J. Burbank. 2011. "Contextualizing Olympic Legacies." *Urban Geography* 32 (6): 823–44. 10.2747/0272-3638.32.6.823.

Asian Art Museum. 2022. "The Journey Mural Unveiling." https://calendar.asianart.org/event/the-journey-%D8%B3%D9%81%D8%B1-mural-unveiling/.

Asian Art Museum. 2023. "About." https://about.asianart.org/about-the-asian-art-museum/governance/.

Asian Art Museum. n.d. "About." Accessed February 22, 2023. https://about.asianart.org.

Baumann, R. and V. Matheson. 2018. "Mega-Events and Tourism: The Case of Brazil." *Contemporary Economic Policy* 36 (2): 292–301. 10.1111/coep.12270.

Berkeleyside Staff. 2016, January 22. "The It List: Five Things to Do This Weekend in Berkeley." *Berkeleyside*. https://www.berkeleyside.org/2016/01/22/the-it-list-five-things-to-do-this-weekend-in-berkeley-4.

Bourgeois, T. 2019. "London 2012 Olympics: Exercises in Cultural Diplomacy." *Place Branding and Public Diplomacy* 15: 198–205. 10.1057/s41254-017-0084-4.

Bourgeois, T. and J. Socolof. 2022. "Super Bowl LII: Rural Arts and Cultural Institution Engagement." *American Journal of Arts Management* 10: 1–14.

Business Wire. 2016. "StubHub Foundation Provides $250,000 Grant to 50 Fund to Extend Impact of Playmaker Program." January 20, 2016. https://www.businesswire.com/news/home/20160120005448/en/StubHub-Foundation-Provides-250000-Grant-to-50-Fund-to-Extend-Impact-of-Playmaker-Program.

California Indian Museum and Cultural Center. n.d. https://cimcc.org/

Carter, A. 2016. "Super Bowl 50 Hosts Reinvent Philanthropic Vision For NFL." *Forbes*, February 3, 2016. https://www.forbes.com/sites/alikocarter/2016/02/03/super-bowl-50-hosts-reinvent-philanthropic-vision-for-nfl/?sh=3d201f037999.

Chalip, Laurence (2006). Towards Social Leverage of Sport Events. *Journal of Sport & Tourism*, 11, 109–12710.1080/14775080601155126.

Children's Discovery Museum of San Jose. 2022a. "Bill's Backyard." Accessed February 22, 2023. https://www.cdm.org/visit/exhibits/bills-backyard/.

Children's Discovery Museum of San Jose. 2022b. "Bill's Backyard Sponsors." https://www.cdm.org/visit/exhibits/bills-backyard/bills-backyard-sponsors/.

Children's Discovery Museum of San Jose. n.d. "Mission." Accessed February 22, 2023. https://www.cdm.org/about/mission/.

Creswell, J. 2007. *Qualitative Inquiry & Research Design: Choosing among Five Approaches*. 2nd ed. Thousand Oaks, CA: Sage Publishing.

David, P., B. Horton, and T. German. 2008. "Dynamics of Entertainment and Affect in a Super Bowl Audience: A Multilevel Approach." *Communication Research* 35 (3): 398–420. 10.1177/0093650208315965.

Garcia, B. 2008. "One Hundred Years of Cultural Programming within the Olympic Games (1912–2012): Origins, Evolution and Projections." *International Journal of Cultural Policy* 14 (4): 361–76. 10.1080/10286630802445849.

Getz, D. 2008. "Event Tourism: Definition, Evolution, and Research." *Tourism Management* 29 (3): 403–28. 10.1016/j.tourman.2007.07.017.

Habitot Children's Museum. 2020. "Our Mission." https://www.habitot.org/our-mission.

Hiller, H. H. 1995. "Conventions as Mega-Events: A New Model for Convention-Host City Relationships." *Tourism Management* 16 (5): 375–9. 10.1016/0261-5177(95)00041-L.

Inoue, Y. and C. T. Havard. 2014. "Determinants and Consequences of the Perceived Social Impact of a Sport Event." *Journal of Sport Management* 28 (3): 295–310. 10.1123/jsm.2013-0136.

Kim, W. and M. Walker. 2012. "Measuring the Social Impacts Associated with Super Bowl XLIII: Preliminary Development of a Psychic Income Scale." *Sport Management Review* 15 (1): 91–108. 10.1016/j.smr.2011.05.007.

Lovett, I. 2016, February 4. "Super Bowl 50 Further Divides San Francisco." *The New York Times*. https://www.nytimes.com/2016/02/05/us/super bowl 50 further divides-san-francisco.html.

Matheson, V. A. 2005. "Contrary Evidence on the Economic Effect of the Super Bowl on the Victorious City." *Journal of Sports Economics* 6 (4): 420–8. 10.1177/1527002504267489.

Matheson, V. A. and R. A. Baade. 2006. "Padding Required: Assessing the Economic Impact of the Super Bowl." *European Sport Management Quarterly* 6 (4): 353–74. 10.1080/16184740601154490.

Müller, M. 2015. "What Makes an Event a Mega-Event? Definitions and Sizes." *Leisure Studies* 34 (6): 627–42. 10.1080/02614367.2014.993333.

PLAY 60, Play On. n.d. "PLAY 60, Play On." Accessed February 22, 2023. https://www.play60playon.org/.

Preuss, H. 2007. "The Conceptualisation and Measurement of Mega Sport Event Legacies." *Journal of Sport & Tourism* 12 (3–4): 207–28. 10.1080/14775080701736957.

Preuss, H. 2015. "A Framework for Identifying the Legacies of a Mega Sport Event." *Leisure Studies* 34 (no.mac_mac): 643–64. 10.1080/02614367.2014.994552.

ProPublica. 2015. "Asian Art Museum Foundation of San Francisco" [tax form 990]. https://projects.propublica.org/nonprofits/organizations/941704765.

ProPublica. 2016a. "Asian Art Museum Foundation of San Francisco" [tax form 990]. https://projects.propublica.org/nonprofits/organizations/941704765.

ProPublica. 2016b. "California Indian Museum and Cultural Center" [tax form 990]. https://projects.propublica.org/nonprofits/organizations/943244506.

ProPublica. 2016c. "Habitot Childrens Museum: Full Text of 'Full Filing' for Fiscal Year Ending Dec. 2016" [tax form 990]. https://projects.propublica.org/nonprofits/organizations/943191605/201712419349301136/full.

ProPublica. 2017. "Asian Art Museum Foundation of San Francisco" [tax form 990]. https://projects.propublica.org/nonprofits/organizations/941704765.

Roche, M. 2000. *Mega-Events and Modernity: Olympics and Expos in the Growth of Global Culture*. London: Routledge.

San Francisco Bay Area Super Bowl 50 Host Committee. n.d. "About." LinkedIn. Accessed February 22, 2023. https://www.linkedin.com/company/san-francisco-bay-area-super-bowl-50-hostcommittee/about/.

Smith, Andrew (2014). Leveraging sport mega-events: new model or convenient justification? *Journal of Policy Research in Tourism, Leisure and Events*, 6, 15–30. 10.1080/19407963.2013.823976

Thomson, Alana, Kennelly, Millicent, & Toohey, Kristine (2020). A systematic quantitative literature review of empirical research on large-scale sport events' social legacies. *Leisure Studies*, 39, 859–876. 10.1080/02614367.2020.1800804

Veal, A. J., Toohey, Kristine, & Frawley, Stephen (2012). The sport participation legacy of the Sydney 2000 Olympic Games and other international sporting events hosted in Australia. *Journal of Policy Research in Tourism, Leisure and Events*, 4, 155–184. 10.1080/19407963.2012.662619

Yin, R. K. 2009. *Case Study Research: Design and Methods*. Vol. 5. Thousand Oaks, CA: Sage Publishing.

Yin, R. K. 2018. *Case Study Research and Applications*. Thousand Oaks, CA: Sage Publishing.

Zimbalist, A. (Ed.). 2012. *Comparative Economic Systems: An Assessment of Knowledge, Theory and Method*. Vol. 3. Berlin, Germany: Springer Science & Business Media.

16

MISSION-BASED, SOCIALLY DRIVEN INVESTMENT STRATEGIES

Rebekah Beaulieu

Recognized as cornerstones of the global cultural sector, museums are invaluable resources that offer access to historical artifacts, priceless works of art, and unmatched experiential educational offerings. Yet museums are often underestimated in their definition as mission-driven, nonprofit organizations, when they also function as businesses that invest millions in local, national, and global economies. Though museums' economic interests in the free market may be seen as incongruous with their social and cultural value, we increasingly recognize the complementary tracks of mission-relevant and business interests. This chapter elucidates how nonprofit cultural institutions can assert values, mission, and their role as civic and economic drivers through investing in socially conscious opportunities.

Recent History of Museum Endowment Management

Museum investing activities take place through the establishment and management of endowment funds. While the concept of an endowment dates back centuries, the modern endowment structure dates only to the early 20th century. Accumulations of massive individual results were the basis for national tax reform in a number of countries; in America, the Revenue Tax Act of 1935 placed a 70% federal income tax on large inheritances, for example (Beaulieu 2022). Such tax reforms placed a burden on the generational growth and transfer of wealth between individuals, and many established nonprofit centers, such as foundations, to house their wealth. The Ford Foundation, for example, was founded in 1936 as a vehicle to support civic interests in automobile manufacturer Henry Ford's home state of Michigan, while simultaneously benefiting him by relocating his massive

DOI: 10.4324/9781003308003-20

wealth in a nonprofit, income-tax resistant structure. Such early funds are incongruous with our modern understanding of foundations as well-structured and public facing entities; in fact, the Ford Foundation only formalized its funding priorities for national "areas of action" in 1950 (McCarthy 2010). The endowment structure has increasingly standardized across nonprofit fields over the past 60 years, and today, we typically define museum endowments as "assets that have been given to the museum on the condition that the principal of the gift is to be kept intact and that only the investment income it produces can be used to meet the museum's needs." The essence of the endowment is the protection of the principal and the use of the investment income it produces to benefit the institution.

Impact investing is a modern concept and is defined by the Global Impact Investing Network (n.d.) as an investment "made with the intention to generate positive, measurable social and environmental impact alongside a financial return." The earliest examples of impact investing are not from the academic arena but are from religious organizations (Moerschbaucher 2001). In the United States, the first example of impact investing dates to 1970: the Socially Responsible Investment Guidelines were published by the United States Conference of Catholic Bishops (USCCB) and disseminated by the Confraternity of Christian Doctrine, based in Washington, DC. The USCCB guidelines include conventional language regarding financial returns, but also delineate stipulations that comprise a social doctrine as well:

> Economic decisions have human consequences and moral content; they help or hurt people, strengthen or weaken family life, advance or diminish the quality of justice of our land … to proclaim the Gospel in such a complex economic world requires a prudent strategy where decisions are made by following the moral teaching of the Church. In her teaching, the Church offers crucial and valuable principles to apply to specific situations and questions. (USCCB 2021, 4)

The USCCB guidelines evidence a commitment to both financial sustainability as well as to metrics that align with church doctrine and are revised periodically to update the acceptable investment activities. The 2021 revision, for instance, defines strategies to support care for the environment, protection of human life, and divestment from interests deemed harmful, such as tobacco and the manufacturing of firearms (USCCB 2021, 9).

The prevalence of impact investing has grown exponentially in recent years, particularly in the secular sector.[1] In 2021, the CFA Institute—the international accrediting body for Chartered Financial Analysts—produced the first global guidelines for impact investing, the "Global ESF Disclosure Standards for Investment Products" (CFA Institute 2021). The document outlines objectives, process, and stewardship for environmental, social, and governance-oriented (ESG) investments and represents the first time ESG protocols are included in ethics and standards for fund managers.

Such a crystallization of standards is welcome news for the cultural sector, within which impact investing has grown over the past decade in particular (Callanan 2022). A 2022 article by Laura Callanan of UpStart Co-Lab published on the American Alliance of Museums (AAM) website traces the original locus for impact investing in museums to a 2013 TED Talk by Seth Miller, in which he stated that "every time you spend a dollar, you are creating the world you live in" (Callanan 2022). Conversations regarding impact investing have gained traction in the nonprofit sphere: as of 2022, 47% of universities employ an impact strategy, as do 51% of foundations (Callanan 2022).

Notably, museums have lagged in the implementation of guidelines to invest with a social and environmental impact. A 2022 study by Callanan's UpStart Co-Lab, an organization that studies impact investing and the creative economy, cites their 2021 study in which only 13% of museums self-identify as employing impact investing tactics (Callanan 2022). The UpStart Co-Lab study, entitled "Cultural Capital: The State of Museums and their Investing" was co-published by the Association for Art Museum Directors and the Black Trustee Alliance for Art Museums, and explains that museums are only in the early era of impact investing (Upstart Co-Lab 2022). The results are heartening, however: of the 13% of museums with formal impact investing protocols, 90% of museums report that values alignment is a critical driver in investing strategy, and 35% share that at least a portion of their endowment is managed by BIPOC, or women fund managers.

Impact Investing Methods and Structures

As more museums consider impact investing strategies, specific methodologies and forms of impact investing have been identified (Demmert 2019). "Impact investing" is the most inclusive of terminology, with further designations relevant to different content-specific strategies:

- *ESG investing*: investment in environmental, social, and/or governance-oriented funds. Such investments typically reflect specific social themes and/or advocacy, such as the mitigation of environmental risks, or in business dealings with firms owned by women or historically marginalized or culturally specific populations.
- *Mission-centric investing*: thematic investment in funds that reflect a specific set of priorities and/or direct mission orientation. While a commonly used phrase in the nonprofit world, mission-centric investing is not interchangeable with ESG investing or with impact investing as a

whole. Most common in human rights and social services organizations, mission-centric investments take the form of investing in firms or products that directly benefit the industry of the nonprofit. For instance, a nonprofit organization whose mission is nature conservation investing in biodiversity industry and research.

- *Micro-economic investing*: investment directly in the local and regional economy of a specific industry sector or geographical area. Micro-economic investing is designed to create a structure to support a local economy through progressive socioeconomic development of a particular region. An institution that invests in local BIPOC-owned businesses is an example of micro-economic investing.

As the museum sector acclimates to impact investing strategies, museums employ a variety of strategies to integrate impact investing into their policies. The following comprise a list of basic impact investing systems, of which none are mutually exclusive, and some are more feasible for museums than others:

- *Exclusionary screening*: the exclusion from an investment portfolio representation from specific companies, industries, and/or countries whose economic structure is incompatible with the philosophy of the organization.
- *Positive screening*: the active investment in specific companies, industries, and/or countries whose economic structure is compatible with the philosophy of the organization.
- *ESG integration*: the incorporation of ESG data points with conventional financial analysis to ensure ESG considerations do not diminish the return on investment. This method is particularly popular with smaller organizations or more fiscally conservative investment committees.
- *Active ownership*: the direct engagement of an investor with the company and control of voting shares to initiate changes to company policy and management. While not typically an option for most nonprofit organizations, it is worth mentioning as an investment strategy more common in the for-profit world.[2]

Case Studies in Museum Impact Investing

Walters Art Museum (Baltimore, Maryland)

Originally founded as the Walters Art Gallery in 1934, the Walters Art Museum mission is as follows:

> To bring art and people together for enjoyment, discovery, and learning. We create a place where people of every background can be touched by art. We engage and strengthen our community by collecting, preserving, and interpreting art. (Walters Art Museum n.d.)

A 1931 bequest by founder Henry Walters to the City of Baltimore included 22,000 objects, two buildings, and an endowment. Today, the museum consists of five buildings, three of which are owned by the City of Baltimore, and a collection of 35,000 objects. The current collection is composed of objects from a variety of cultures, periods, and representative of world geography, a marked expansion from Walters' original collection of primarily European objects. Between 1931 and 1934, the Walters utilized the original endowment bequest to transition from a publicly accessible private exhibition space to a fully public institution by its opening.

The Walters Art Museum underwent a substantial endowment campaign between 2008 and 2015, ultimately raising $30 million and with the intention to implement a new investment policy. In 2015, the Walters established a diverse fund manager strategy in which 10% of the endowment is invested with firms owned by women and people of color as a commitment to diversity, equity, accessibility, and inclusion and in alignment with the institutional strategic plan. The annual distribution rate was increased to 5% of the twelve-quarter valuation average to accommodate the diversity initiative and to support long-overdue capital maintenance. The adjusted draw, while still within industry best practices of 4–5% of the average, allowed the Walters to use the endowment distribution for current operational needs while preserving the fund principal (Callanan 2021).

Julia Marciari-Alexander, director of the Walters Art Museum since 2016, explains that the strategy was not without its challenges. Like many negotiations with donors, the Walters sought to attract gifts with minimal restrictions, with the acknowledgment that "who we are is not who we will be in twenty-five years" (Julia Marciari-Alexander, interview with author, June 23, 2021). Furthermore, donor expectations now included impact strategies, which had to be managed along with any concerns regarding financial returns. The Walters Art Museum staff were in the position to navigate conversations about the content of the institutional investments, their dedication to market-rate financial returns, and consistent attention to spending considerations.

By 2021, the Walters Art Museum held endowment investments totaling $200 million, which consist of unrestricted funds to underwrite operations, as well as funds restricted to endowed positions, publication projects, and exhibitions. Almost 50% of the annual operating budget is allocated from institutional investments and 21% of the endowment is invested in minority- and women-owned funds. The Investment Committee now includes a subcommittee dedicated to socially responsible investing strategy, which functions in tandem with the Museum's DEAI working group of staff and board members. The next step in the impact investing strategy of the Walters Art Museum is to invest in Baltimore-based organizations to demonstrate the Museum's dedication to community and interest in the local economy. In this way, the Walters Art Museum creates alignment between internal organizational goals and its impact investing strategy to support the economic development of Baltimore.

The Massachusetts Museum of Contemporary Art (North Adams, Massachusetts)

Located on a 16-acre site in Western Massachusetts, the Massachusetts Museum of Contemporary Art (MASS MoCA) is in the home of a former industrial mill, which encompasses 26 buildings that were in use for commercial purposes until 1985. In 1986, MASS MoCA was founded to expand contemporary exhibition space for the nearby Williams College Museum of Art in Williamstown, Massachusetts. The space eventually evolved into a stand-alone institution by its opening in 1999, and from an exhibition space to a center for changing exhibitions, performing arts, and art making. Today, MASS MoCA is the largest contemporary art museum in the United States and maintains an annual operating budget of approximately $17 million, of which its endowment of $27 million provides 7.5% of support. The organization received additional support from the Commonwealth of Massachusetts, private contributions, and earned revenue through admissions and other activities such as the leasing of commercial space. The Mass MoCA mission states the following:

> Through innovative collaborations, MASS MoCA helps artists and their supporters create and show important new work, bringing to our visitors bold visual and performing art in all stages of production, while also creating a stimulating center of creativity and commerce that brings life and economic vibrancy to its hometown. (MASS MoCA n.d.)

In recent years, the organization has implemented ESG and mission-relevant investment strategies. North Adams was a booming industrial town until the Great Depression, and lingering effects of the Depression caused the closure of clothing manufacturer Oliver Arnold & Company in 1942, at that time the largest employer in the area and housed in the site MASS MoCA now occupies. The Sprague Electric Company took ownership of the property until its closure in 1985, a move that devastated the local economy and caused a steep population decline (Dobrowolski 2013).

The development of the former mill into an arts center was originally a way to re-use the vast complex, and MASS MoCA today serves as the anchor of a vibrant arts community in the Berkshire Mountains. Recognizing the institution's role as an economic driver, the leadership of MASS MoCA prioritizes regional development such as affordable housing, which also provides housing for artists working at the museum. The investment policy includes the prioritization of investments in environmental sustainability and positive screening for ESG alignment. Today, MASS MoCA is viewed as an example of micro-economic investment and ESG strategy implementation (Raginskaya 2020).

The Louvre Museum (Paris, France)

The Louvre Museum is the most widely visited museum in the world, with over ten million visitors each year and almost 72,000 meters of exhibition space. Located in a former royal residence and founded over eight hundred years ago, the Louvre has been a public museum since 1974 and is owned by the French government. Today, the Louvre functions on a budget of €250 million, almost half of which is funded directly by the French government. The remainder of the budget is met through a combination of earned revenue, direct contributions, and institutionally held funds.

The endowment structure is a relatively new one for the French financial landscape, introduced into law in 2008 and loosely based on American precedent. The Louvre Endowment Fund was established shortly thereafter in 2009, and today functions as the largest capitalized structure managed by a cultural institution in Europe (Moreolo 2018). The fund currently consists of €240 million, with 5% of the total fund invested using impact investment strategies. Incorporated with its own CEO and staff separate from the government-owned Louvre, the Louvre Endowment Fund functions without the aid of external investment consultants. The fund allocates 3% of its returns to Louvre operations, and practices impact strategies such as exclusionary screening, prohibiting investment in sectors such as weapons manufacturing, as well as a documented focus on socially conscious investments that align with the Louvre's priorities of art, education, and heritage. For example, the investments include educational systems and French companies in the crafts sector.

France is one of the first companies to establish corporate social responsibility (CSR) protocols into law. In both the United Kingdom and in Europe, such policies have been enacted to support ESG and impact investing interests; investments in countries of the European Union, for instance, are subject to the EU Sustainable Finance Disclosure Regulation (SFDR). The SFDR is designed to ensure transparency in the business activities of companies that self-designate as ESG compliant, establishing thresholds for ESG best practices and holding such companies accountable to an objective standard. As of 2021, 31% of the transferable securities market in Europe, or €1.6 billion, is allocated to responsible investments and subject to SFDR (ESMA, n.d.). The advent of the endowment investment structure as well as impact strategies and new oversight models demonstrate that like the United States, Europe is exploring innovative and content-oriented investment systems.

Together, these case studies provide evidence that the implementation of impact investing is a seismic shift for any museum and an evolution that must be managed carefully. Because impact investing underscores the institutional commitment to social consciousness and transparency, the timely and relevant disbursement of financial data is paramount. The correspondence of impact relevance and financial returns is a new conversation with many donors, and unimpeachable financial reporting may ease any concerns that new modes and metrics diminish the core objective of adept and return-driven investing. Similarly, each institution profiled has a policy in place that documents a commitment to impact investing, but on a small scale in comparison to their investments in total. These sensitivities to return on investments, donor relations, and the proportion of an impact invested amount versus the fund total elucidate that questions about impact investing and its tenability remain.

Opportunities for the Future of Impact Investing in Museums

Impact investing and its various sub forms comprise an innovative mission for social consciousness and mission activation in museums, yet concerns linger regarding its logistics and benefit.

Unlike conventional investing of museum endowment funds, those invested with an impact interest require strong oversight and additional metrics for success. Because of the low valuation of museum endowments in the global market of traded securities, museum endowments are traditionally managed using a passive investing method, in which funds are managed to keep pace with market trends and are often invested in amalgamated index funds, through which there is little oversight of individual companies. In the active investing method, however, investments are managed more aggressively and individually, usually with the goal of outpacing market performance. Active investing requires additional management of the fund, often in the form of research on individual companies' performance in the market, as well as higher management fees. Most museums have invested using the passive method given the interest in reducing fees and simply keeping pace with the market. Yet since the advent of impact investing, more museums are taking a more active role in managing investment activities, for the traditional investment in index funds does not allow for support (or lack thereof) of specific companies.

The increased focus on impact investing has encouraged many museums to review where and in what companies and/or business interests their funds are held. Many museum professionals and board members may be surprised to learn that a typical passive investment in the index often includes investment in tobacco, weapons manufacturing, and other industries potentially misaligned with organizational mission or ESG interests. In recent years, new tactics and investment methods have developed to help museums and other ESG-/impact-minded institutions more confidently invest. There now exist ESG-compliant index funds, such as the MSCI KLD 400 Social Index and the S&P 500 ESG Index, both of which exclude companies with known negative social and environmental impact (Callanan 2019). Another tactic is to invest in exchange traded funds (EFTs) with explicit ESG goals. EFT funds are diversified holdings, which include stock, commodities, bonds, and other securities, and now exist with ESG metrics available. In this way, museums can easily invest in funds that align with mission, values, and social consciousness.

Another question that is common with museum impact investing is if it tests the limitations of financial return and the capacity of individual organizations. In terms of return on investment (ROI), there is no evidence to support the misconception that taking an interest in ESG-minded funds reduces ROI. We can look at the success of foundations as a model, such as the Ford Foundation and the Rockefeller Brothers Fund, for explicit success in the market alongside impact investing strategies. In fact, the volatility of the marketplace in 2020 and 2021 during the upheaval of early COVID uncertainty did little to negatively influence the performance of ESG funds. ESG funds actually performed better than traditionally invested funds in 2020 (Hale 2020).

In addition to performance concerns, some in the museum field may wonder if impact investing is an option for small- and mid-sized institutions. If the Louvre is considered a small fund at a €240 million valuation, what about the local art and history museums scattered throughout the world that have infinitely smaller funds? Endowments are not a requirement for American museums, though they are more prevalent than in the asset structure of their European and Asian peers. Yet museums that maintain endowments are beholden to strict regulations, as previously noted, defined by state and federal law as well as donor intent. Institutions with endowments of $1–$10 million may see little benefit to impact investing given the increase in fees and oversight that may be considered untenable with their organizational capacity. Museum professionals and academics are, however, already seeing investing options available to smaller- and mid-sized museums: pooled investing, for instance, is a strategy in which modestly scaled funds from multiple organizations are collectivized and invested for greater market share, financial return, and impact (Saab 2014). The collectivization of resources is especially prevalent in the post-COVID era, with smaller museums pooling resources to build capacity, share expense burdens, and leverage staff and financial resources.[3] In this way, museums of all sizes can participate in impact investing.

Recommendations and Resources for Impact Investing

As museums consider implementation of impact investing strategies, there are actionable steps to integrate such activities into museum operations and governance. The most important consideration is the alignment of impact investing with institutional priorities and communication at all levels.

Internally, the prioritization of impact investing must be shared by both staff and members of the governing body, which includes committees related to investment and finance matters. Because impact investing is reflective of institutional values and accurately understood to be an advocacy measure, it is imperative to have collective awareness of any activities at all levels of the organization. Alongside parameters for the expectations for spending and for financial returns, the investment policy and committee charter should articulate language related to the areas of interest in impact investing (Beaulieu 2017, 50). An organization's institutional plan, which is typically revised every three to five years, is another vehicle in which impact investing can be documented. In fact, the institutional plan is the most valuable roadmap for any institution for its ability to marry mission values and governance with operational tactics. For this reason, impact investing can be cited as an avenue by which a museum is forwarding its goals regarding civic engagement and/or DEAI.

Externally, museum leadership will want to consider how best to message its impact investing strategy. Collaboration with external firms, particularly those specializing in impact investing, can ensure that museums are following best practices while ensuring as strong an ROI as possible. Museum board and management leadership should consider how to promote such a strategy to demonstrate a commitment to specific values, though with an awareness that such statements cannot be simply performative: because museums are non-profit institutions, their financial disclosures are available for public inspection; guidance by external fund management firms can be a vital guide for drafting, following, and monitoring investments for external transparency.

The increase in interest in impact investing has resulted in a growing treasury of resources to support organizations as they consider the strategy. Investment fund managers of all sizes are expected to be fluent in impact investing and ESG content, and museums are increasingly seeking partnerships with firms who collaborate with mission-oriented organizations and can help guide mission-aligned investment activities. The Upstart Co-Lab is a thought leader in impact investing in the cultural sector with a strong online presence, and other resources serve as a reference for international clientele, such as the British Business Bank, the French Responsible Investment Forum, and France Invest.

While the momentum of impact investing is a strong presence in European and American markets, it is only now gaining momentum in Asia, mainly due to a lack of similarly structured protocols and skill resources. Yet we are seeing remarkable growth in ESG interest in the Asian market (China issued $84 billion in ESG bonds in 2022), which no doubt will soon create an avenue for impact investing in Asian museums. Already, the Asian Venture Resource

Network and the Asia Pacific Risk Center are building a repository of advisory materials for organizations interested in exploring impact investing.

As we look to the future, impact investing in museums—whether activated through ESG screening, mission relevance, or community/economy building—cannot be underestimated. Rarely has a financial management tool so readily accommodated mission and values alignment, advocacy, and civic responsibility. The world of impact investing is a new one for museums, yet we can already observe that with strong oversight and policy, it provides a new and unmatched path for museums to articulate their power as cultural leaders and economic drivers.

Notes

1 Impact investing as a general concept is undiscussed until the early 2010s in books on nonprofit management. Even texts such as Diana S. Newman's *Nonprofit Essentials: Endowment Building* (2005) and Easton et al.'s *Financial Accounting for MBAs* (2008) make no mention of impact investing.

2 For more detail regarding suggestions on the integration of impact investing into historical policy, see Kumar et al.'s *Understanding & Comparing ESG Terminology* (2018).

3 Children's museums are a particular example of the pooled resources method. See "Museums in a Pandemic: Diversifying Funding Streams" by the Association of Children's Museums (2021).

References

Association of Children's Museums. 2021. "Museums in a Pandemic: Diversifying Funding Streams," *News & Blog*. February 9, 2021. https://childrensmuseums.org/2021/02/09/museums-in-a-pandemic-diversifying-funding-streams/.

Beaulieu, Rebekah. 2017. *Financial Fundamentals for Historic House Museums*. Washington, DC: Rowman & Littlefield.

Beaulieu, Rebekah. 2022. *Endowment Essentials for Museums*. Washington, DC: Rowman & Littlefield.

Callanan, Laura. 2019. "Museums Should Lead in Socially Responsible Investing." *Financial Times* (London), September 20, 2019. https://www.ft.com/content/b7328400-c432-11e9-ae6e-a26d1d0455f4.

Callanan, Laura. 2021. "How Museums Can Ethically Invest Their Money." *The Art Newspaper*, March 30, 2021. https://www.theartnewspaper.com/2021/03/30/how-museums-can-ethically-invest-their-money.

Callanan, Laura. 2022. "Museums Discover Impact Investing." *Center for the Future of Museums Blog, American Alliance of Museums*. July 27, 2022. https://www.aam-us.org/2022/07/27/museums-discover-impact-investing/.

CFA Institute. 2021. "Global ESG Disclosure Standards for Investment Products." *Research and Policy Center*. Accessed March 15, 2023. www.cfainstitute.org/en/ethics-standards/codes/esg-standards.

Demmert, James E. 2019. *The Sustainable Endowment*. Los Angeles, CA: New Insights Press.

Dobrowolski, Tony. 2013. "John L. Sprague Reflects on Past, Present Economy." *Berkshire Eagle* (Pittsfield, MA), May 28, 2013. https://www.berkshireeagle.com/

news/local/john-l-sprague-reflects-on-past-present-economy/article_534a96af-a0e3-5bc2-87f6-dc0199c58178.html.

Easton, Peter D., John J. Wild, Robert F. Halsey, and Mary Lea McAnally. 2008. *Financial Accounting for MBAs*. New York: Cambridge Business Publishers.

ESMA (European Securities and Markets Authority). n.d. "ESG Fund Management." *ESMA's Activities*. Accessed March 15, 2023. https://www.esma.europa.eu/esmas-activities/investors-and-issuers/fund-management.

Global Impact Investing Network. n.d. "What You Need to Know about Impact Investing." *About Impact Investing*. Accessed March 15, 2023. https://thegiin.org/impact-investing/need-to-know/.

Hale, Jon. 2020. "Sustainable Funds Weather the First Quarter Better than Conventional Funds." *Morningstar, Inc.*, April 3, 2020. https://www.morningstar.com/articles/976361/sustainable-funds-weather-the-first-quarter-better-than-conventional-funds.

Kumar, Rakhi, Natasha Dayaramani, and James D. Rocha. 2018. "Understanding & Comparing ESG Terminology." *State Street Global Advisors*. https://www.ssga.com/investment-topics/environmentalsocial-governance/2018/10/esg-terminology.pdf

Mass MoCA (Massachusetts Museum of Contemporary Art). n.d. "About: What We Do." Accessed March 15, 2023. https://massmoca.org/about/#:~:text=We%20thrive%20on%20helping%20artists,enjoy%20their%20time%20with%20us.

McCarthy, Anna. 2010. *The Citizen Machine: Governing by Television in 1950s America*. New York: New Press.

Moerschbaucher, Lynda S. 2001. *Building an Endowment Right from the Start*. Chicago, IL: Precept Press.

Moreolo, Carlo Svaluto. 2018. "How We Run Our Money: Louvre Endowment Fund." *IPE Magazine*, May 2018. https://www.ipe.com/how-we-run-our-money-louvre-endowment-fund/10024408.article.

Newman, Diana S. 2005. *Nonprofit Essentials: Endowment Building*. Hoboken, NJ: John Wiley & Sons.

Raginskaya, Anna. 2020. "Art Museums Should Use Their Endowments to Help Battle Climate Change." *The Art Newspaper*, May 21, 2020. https://www.theartnewspaper.com/2020/05/21/art-museums-should-use-their-endowments-to-help-battle-climate-change.

Saab, Elise M. 2014. "Pooled Vehicles: The New Investment Frontier for Small to Midsized Museums." (Master's thesis, Harvard University Extension School). https://www.proquest.com/openview/822f376ce83a671882f5447943873f2a/1?pq-origsite=gscholar&cbl=18750&diss=y.

Upstart Co-Lab. 2022. *Cultural Capital: The State of Museums and Their Investing*. June 2022. https://upstartco-lab.org/wp-content/uploads/2022/06/Cultural-Capital-Museums-and-Investing-1.pdf.

USCCB (United States Conference of Catholic Bishops). 2021. *Socially Responsible Investment Guidelines for the United States Conference of Catholic Bishops*. Washington, DC: USCCB. https://www.usccb.org/resources/Socially%20Responsible%20Investment%20Guidelines%202021%20(003).pdf.

Walters Art Museum. n.d. "Mission & Vision." About. Accessed March 15, 2023. https://thewalters.org/about/mission/#:~:text=The%20mission%20of%20the%20Walters,%2C%20preserving%2C%20and%20interpreting%20art.

17

PROS AND CONS OF CORPORATE SPONSORSHIP AT THE NATIONAL MUSEUM OF MODERN AND CONTEMPORARY ART IN KOREA

Geuntae Park

Introduction

The National Museum of Modern and Contemporary Art (MMCA) is the only national museum in Korea dedicated to art, architecture, and design. Over the last decade, it has attracted substantial sponsorship from several large enterprises in Korea for its exhibitions and programs. Since 2012, MMCA has been organizing the Korea Artist Prize with the support of SBS Culture Foundation, the satellite organization of a major broadcasting company for art and culture. Hyundai Motor Company has also been sponsoring a ten-year project, Hyundai Motor Series, since 2014 to organize exhibitions for established Korean artists. In addition, Hyundai Card collaborated with MMCA for the Young Architects Program (YAP) from 2014 to 2017 to find young talents and grant them an opportunity to create a summer pavilion at MMCA's courtyard, which was a part of the global YAP network by Museum of Modern Art (MoMA) PS1. Although private sector investment is currently common in the global contemporary art scene (Martorella 1996; Rectanus 2002), occasionally inviting controversial debates (Charlesworth 2018; Harris 2019), this phenomenon in Korea has drawn widespread attention because MMCA is one of few museums that enjoys corporate sponsorship. This chapter aims to explore this phenomenon further to identify the pros and cons of corporate sponsorship at this national art museum.

While collaboration between MMCA and companies may seem impressive and it makes the staff and management of other museums envious, the following questions need to be addressed through further studies: what are the benefits and risks to MMCA from sponsorships and how does the museum maintain a balance? Are there only win-win effects as expected? As a

DOI: 10.4324/9781003308003-21

state agency under such strong financial and administrative control of the central government, with a stable budget that is an outstanding privilege of the institution, why does MMCA still attract sponsorships? To answer these questions, this chapter first quickly explores the current issues surrounding corporate sponsorship at art museums through documentary resources, particularly in terms of a transition from *sponsorship* to *partnership*, which would work as an overarching framework for the whole phenomenon and the article. It will then examine how this rationale is working in a specific case in Korea. For this, functional divisions of MMCA, mainly its curatorial and education/public programs, were examined to investigate multiple perspectives regarding the impact of corporate sponsorship on the museum. Therefore, this research is mainly based on a collection of interviews with MMCA professionals that are supported by other materials, such as academic articles, museum reports, and media coverage.

Art Museum and Corporate Sponsorship: A Transition from Sponsorship to Partnership

Sponsorship was traditionally understood as a marketing tool or business strategy that provides some financial support to a certain individual or organization to help them achieve their goals and perform their activities, seeking increased global perception or awareness in return (De Astous and Blitz 1995; Meenaghan and Shipley 1999; Olkkonen and Tuominen 2006; Cobbs 2011; Lewandowska 2016). Art sponsorship as a typology of sponsorship has become part of this marketing strategy since the early 1990s. This was also when arts management began to emerge as an independent professional field (McNicholas 2004). Ever since, the arts sector has actively introduced business minds to its practice, which has incorporated marketing as a central concept of its management (Evrard and Colbert 2000; McNicholas 2004). Private sector investments in art reflect the recognition of arts organizations as business partners, not just a beneficiary entity (Lewandowska 2015).

However, this commercial approach, providing financial support for enhanced public perception, has encountered many challenges, most of which are related to ethical controversies that emerge from audience groups (Bal et al. 2010; Lewandowska 2015). Some of the most commonly discussed issues related to art sponsorship include the sponsoring company's intervention in art organizations, influence on contents, negative reaction from the public and artist communities, ethical issues, and the financial status of art organizations (Davidsson and Sørensen 2010). For example, in the Museum of Contemporary Art in Los Angeles, the artists rejected a tobacco company Philip Morris's sponsorship due to the unhealthy effects of tobacco (Lidström 2004) and artist-activists made Tate cancel British oil company BP's sponsorship of the museum (Charlesworth 2018). In Korea, MMCA also raised concerns on whether it endowed a privilege on specific companies that sponsored the museum (e.g., through free or discounted admissions for the company's customers) and whether a sponsorship focused on MMCA would stimulate the polarization of financial status among art museums because small- and medium-sized art institutions do not attract much sponsorship (Wang 2014; Jang 2020).

In order to address these controversial features and focus on creating more mutually constructive relationships, the concept of partnership has replaced that of sponsorship over the last few decades in defining the nature of a relationship between the art sector and companies. Sponsorship has evolved to encourage mutual benefits based on the comparative advantage at each party such as money, technology, or services from companies and knowledge, education, or perspectives from art institutions (Lidström 2004). McNicholas (2004) also maintained that the relationship between art and business can be further developed by both parties to grow together over a long time. Thus, sponsorship is not adequate to describe the changes to relationships between art and corporate entities when taking into account that arts and cultural organizations have developed a new framework in collaboration with the business sector to achieve a more upgraded relationship, not merely commercial support (McNicholas 2004; Lewandowsak 2016). With this new approach, called a partnership, apart from meeting financial resources, art organizations get a better understanding of the audience and external relations, and both parties achieve common goals through artistic and educational programs for the public (McGuigan 2004; Thomas et al. 2009). McNicholas (2004) stated that a partnership has become the most contemporary form of arts and business relations, evolving from the historical philanthropic approach mainly based on financial support in the 1980s and 1990s (donation or patronage) to the synergy of artistic and business objectives and strong mutual engagement in the 21st century, which exceeds public relations and branding to become a broader, overall business strategy for both parties.

This trend of adopting partnerships has occurred somewhat differently in MMCA since the boundaries of sponsorship and partnership are still not clear and both concepts are widely used in defining relationships. MMCA professionals still use the term *corporate-sponsored* exhibitions even though companies sometimes list (or hope to list) their names as co-organizers of the exhibition, not simply as a sponsor. When discussing the possibility of sponsorship at the early stage, establishing the relationship, and working on the press release, both parties (MMCA and the company) share the vision and agree with constructive cooperation as partners, which sets the background against which to create the partnership. However, MMCA professionals, in particular curatorial staff members, tend to consider it a more financially focused relationship (Curator A, personal communication, January 9, 2023[1]; Curator B, personal communication, January 10, 2023; Curator C, personal communication, January 11, 2023; Curator D, personal communication, January 13, 2023; Curator E, personal communication, January 21, 2023; Designer A, personal communication, January 15, 2023). Thus, there exists a gap in recognition of partnership and sponsorship among MMCA people. Behind this recognition, there is also concern about the company's intervention in the museum's activities, which may be interpreted as an attempt to defend its unique role and position as an art museum. In other words, it clearly reveals MMCA's bottom line that it will never allow companies to get involved in handling the *contents* of an exhibition (out of concern that partnerships may allow this intervention). However, unlike the initial stage when the art sector and companies in Korea first began to collaborate, most companies now better understand and respect MMCA's professionalism and do not get too involved in any content-related issue, suggesting a transition toward advanced partnerships (Curator A, personal communication, January 9, 2023; Curator B, personal communication, January 10, 2023). Simultaneously, MMCA professionals also began to realize that working closely with companies can help promote the museum and attract greater audiences, particularly for large-budget projects, a recent trend in contemporary art.

Corporate Partnership as a Way of Meeting the Ever-Changing Contemporary Art Scene

Since 2000, arts sponsorships have greatly increased globally (IEG 2015), with the MMCA also showing this trend. After MMCA opened its Seoul branch in 2013,[2] there has been obvious growth in corporate sponsorship[3] in terms of the size and number of companies expressing interest. MMCA Seoul, located in the heart of the capital city, has a geographical advantage to attract public attention. Its symbolic identity as the only national museum in Korea dedicated to contemporary art has also contributed to getting sponsorship from companies. In response to this interest, the MMCA established the National Museum of Modern and Contemporary Art Foundation (the Foundation hereafter),[4] one of whose main responsibilities is to handle relationships with the private sector including sponsorship. In addition, some large corporations in Korea have begun gradually launching sponsorship activities to world-renowned art organizations. This global expansion could also be regarded as a background to MMCA's sponsorship offers. For example, Hyundai Motors has been sponsoring Hyundai Commission at Tate Modern, an annual program that supports an exhibition project in its Turbine Hall, and the establishment of the Hyundai Tate Research Centre: Transnational in 2019 is also part of the company's long-term partnership with Tate.

Regarding corporate sponsorship, the curators at MMCA first discuss financial assistance as the most significant benefit (Curator A, personal communication, January 9, 2023; Curator B, personal communication, January 10, 2023; Curator C, personal communication, January 11, 2023; Curator D, personal communication, January 13, 2023; Curator E, personal communication, January 21, 2023), but it is also important to investigate other features related to MMCA's positioning as a contemporary art organization in today's changing art field. In monetary terms, the proportion of budget allocation for a single sponsored project is generally bigger than the institution's own exhibition budget. This difference allows MMCA more room for scaled up exhibitions. Also, in a practical manner for MMCA, the sponsorship is being handled by the Foundation, so the budget execution process is relatively quicker and less complicated than running the museum itself. Since the MMCA belongs to a governmental department (Ministry of Culture, Sports and Tourism), the budget execution process is slow and it is challenging and complex to modify it when the need arises. Thus, some practical matters such as hiring contractors, budget planning or modifying, etc. become a lighter burden for MMCA professionals and sponsored artists to carry. This financial and practical benefit was mentioned by not only the curatorial team but also other teams including education and design (Curator A, personal communication, January 9, 2023; Curator B, personal communication, January 10, 2023; Curator C, personal communication, January 11, 2023; Educator A, personal communication, January 11, 2023; Designer A, personal communication, January 15, 2023).

However, curators also argue that it is necessary to consider the current contemporary art scene to better understand the nature of corporate sponsorship and the reason why MMCA is seeking external funding opportunities (Curator A, personal communication, January 9, 2023; Curator B, personal communication, January 10, 2023). Many exhibitions at the museum these days are categorized into installations, performances, and various other types of media/digital art. Their size and/or quality are closely related to the amount of the project budget and mostly need to be supported by advanced technologies. The current MMCA budget size may not meet all these requirements. Therefore, corporate sponsorship is particularly useful in such contemporary projects to both art museums and artists. A large on-site installation or size-specific artwork generally requires a huge budget, so public museums such as the MMCA tend to seek external funding to figure out its financial burden. Along with the global trend of increasing corporate sponsorship, it is significant to understand the nature of current contemporary art works as a background to this phenomenon. One curator (Curator B, personal communication, January 10, 2023) interviewed for the article regarded this aspect as an extended platform diversifying the context of museum exhibition by exhibiting a totally different approach from previous exhibitions.

An additional advantage apart from financial support to create new art works that is frequently mentioned is promotion or marketing (Curator C, personal communication, January 11, 2023; Curator D, personal communication, January 13, 2023). Along with MMCA's public relations department, the sponsoring company's established network with media, know-how in marketing/branding, and customer management will create more impacts when promoting the exhibitions. Due to this collaboration, public awareness increases, attracting more participants when organizing related events, whose satisfaction is also generally high (Educator B, personal communication, January 13, 2023). For example, when MMCA organized the Young Architects Program along with Hyundai Card, it was observed that the programs targeting this company's card holders were quite successful each year in terms of the number of participants. It was interesting to watch how the company took advantage of using the museum programs as a chance to encourage customer loyalty.

In addition, what needs attention in MMCA's current sponsorship is the emergence of sponsored activities in the education department. Sponsored education activities are a very recent phenomenon, which began around 2020, and focuses on improving the general public's cultural accessibility and enhancing their cultural enjoyment. Most sponsoring projects have focused and still focus on exhibitions that are easier to get public attention. As a main function of the museum, exhibitions have been the best target for companies to maximize attention and the impact of sponsorship. From MMCA's perspective, the activity that requires the largest budget is also an exhibition, so it is more efficient to get sponsorship for exhibition projects. However, starting a few years ago, the education department has worked in partnership with companies for its various activities. A common goal is to provide high-quality education programs for the public, including under-represented or marginalized groups. In spite of its advantage of attracting high attention, most exhibitions are short-term projects (usually within a few months). However, the nature of sustainability in education programs is now appealing to sponsoring companies. Although MMCA has more secured budgets for education programs than do other museums in the country, their size and flexibility are very limited when compared to that of exhibitions. Considering a wide spectrum of education programs, segmented by various categories based on lifecycle, that are continuing—not completed within a short-term, this situation has restricted the possibility to meet all needs (Educator A, personal communication, January 11, 2023).

In this situation, corporate sponsorship has widened possibilities and increased the accessibility of public art. For example, MMCA recently worked with KT Skylife, a communication-media company, to develop education materials for school teenagers' career counseling. It was closely related to the public education curriculum and national educational policy, provided students with an understanding of professions in the art sector, and ultimately contributed to enhancing their appreciation of contemporary art. The materials were distributed all across the country, including areas that were culturally excluded due to their geographic location. The company and MMCA shared their vision of conducting a future generation targeted program, aiming at a long-term impact not a short-sighted outcome. For the sponsoring company, this sustainable education program works to bring a positive branding image to the public in a way that is different from exhibitions. Unlike exhibitions, the effect of sponsoring education programs is not immediately visible. However, it certainly enriches MMCA education programs and contributes to the company's corporate social responsibility. One of the MMCA educators mentioned that corporate sponsorship enabled MMCA to explore further opportunities of conducting programs for the public regardless of their location or level of cultural capital (Educator A, personal communication, January 11, 2023). In particular, it is very useful for areas that require huge budgets but have no quick visible outcome, such as programs for people with disabilities. Although it is one of MMCA's responsibilities as a national organization, a limited budget cannot adequately meet this need. In this category, sponsorship works particularly well (and also contributes to enhancing the company's corporate social responsibility more than through mere exhibitions). For example, a sign language video and audio-aided exhibition materials could be the projects that benefit from sponsorship.

Concern about Curatorial Roles and Institutional Identities

It is interesting to witness that the concerns of corporate sponsorship (mainly in curatorial matters) share their roots with its benefits. While current trends for a large-sized installation or media art have enabled MMCA to seek external financial help, it has also highlighted some fundamental challenges with curators in relation to their profession (Curator A, personal communication, January 9, 2023; Curator B, personal communication, January 10, 2023; Curator D, personal communication, January 13, 2023). In many cases, the role of curator in a large-sized sponsored exhibition becomes less visible when compared to other exhibitions. From the artist selection to installation, a lot of external people (reviewers, advisors, committee members, etc.) get involved in the project, which occasionally results in limiting the traditional roles of curators that include discussing the concept of the work, developing the exhibition narrative and framework, and working as a mediator between the artist and the institution. For example, if the sponsored project involves a competition process to select artists, curators are less involved in the artist selection. Sometimes, a designated curator for the exhibition is excluded from the selection process to ensure fair selection. While the most unique roles of curators include the process of developing the project and their position as a liaison between the artist and the museum, sponsored projects certainly limit curators' roles. In a traditional art museum setting, the close relationship between curator and artist is essential to create a good-quality exhibition. Their communication on the concept, space, display and installation, design, related programs, and even budget is critical when developing an exhibition. However, in a sponsored exhibition, the relationship between the sponsor and artist is also regarded important since, in many cases, the sponsored project supports the artist in creating new works.

In relation to this, the tension between the artist and museum is occasionally observed (Curator A, personal communication, January 9, 2023). This tension usually stems from two aspects—the quality or completeness of the new artwork and the practical matters in executing the budget. Regarding the former, it is also related to the system of many sponsored exhibition projects. As mentioned earlier, since there is not much room for curators to get involved in the process of the creation, it becomes more challenging to produce the best-quality artwork. A selection through competition for new artwork is based on a plan, not on real work; thus, it requires a thorough process to create a plan that best fits within the exhibition space. Sponsored projects lack this aspect, which can raise concerns about the completeness of the new work. The practical matter in handling a huge budget is also observed. While sponsored projects provide a great opportunity to both the museum and artist, it is also a rare chance for artists to manage a huge budget by themselves. Thus, the execution of the budget according to the institutional guidelines is sometimes challenging.

Although this changing role of curator is discussed as a challenging issue in this section, many curators agree that this huge project with several developing stages and professionals is also necessary for MMCA as a leading art institution in the country (Curator A, personal communication, January 9, 2023; Curator B, personal communication, January 10, 2023; Curator E, personal communication, January 21, 2023). They believe that sponsored exhibitions are essential for current contemporary arts exhibitions; thus, although they could be challenging, they are unavoidable. For the museum's sake, this situation is an opportunity to expand its role as a platform for various exhibitions, which, for a curator, could also present a chance to act as a project manager handling more diverse matters.

In relation to the project itself, there are growing voice asking whether the large size of a one-off installation project is really necessary and meaningful and, more importantly, whether it contributes to the general art community (Curator A, personal communication, January 9, 2023; Curator B, personal communication, January 10, 2023). For a sponsored company, artist, and museum, it would result in an outstanding outcome, but a critical perspective views this phenomenon simply as a money feast. From the quality of the sponsored artwork to its validity, this voice indicates whether the system can prove its impact and value to a general art sector, which echoes concerns toward large international biennales regarding its effectiveness.[5]

Another concern at sponsored exhibitions relates to the different expectations of sponsoring companies (Curator B, personal communication, January 10, 2023). Although it is not about the project itself, the different levels of expectation are somewhat challenging since many companies still regard sponsoring a museum as an extended or different marketing strategy, not as a long-term partnership. In this case, they hope to see short-term, visible outcomes, which do not always align with the museum's goals. For example, when the sponsoring company focuses on the popularity of the project and evaluates it mainly by the level of attention or issue making, it creates tension among museum professionals, the artist, and the company. In a similar context, too much reliance on sponsorship would result in increased chances for activities that are more popular and attractive to the market (Lidström 2004).

Finally, there is a practical issue in branding and promotion (Curator C, personal communication, January 11, 2023; Curator D, personal communication, January 13, 2023). Although it is less frequent, there still exist traditional conflicts such as how to showcase the company's logo and how much and where to display its brand identities. Since companies have their own promotion and public relation guidelines, a conflict between MMCA and sponsoring companies occasionally occurs. During the sponsored project, all release materials from MMCA are supposed to be agreed upon by the sponsored company in advance, which means MMCA should be careful regarding the details of the materials and has to prepare them as early as possible. However, this issue could be addressed when both parties spend enough time during an early stage when discussing the sponsorship (contents, press release, etc.) and reach an agreement.

Conclusion

Thompson (2012) argues that every successful non-profit and corporate relationship has mutual recognition at its core, which creates a win-win situation. This relationship is only possible when both parties seriously examine the benefit to each side that cannot be acquired without the partnership and that begins with finding an answer to how both parties can aim for more realistic expectations for the sponsored project's outcome (Butterfield 2001; Thompson 2012; Proteau 2018). Museums Association (n.d.) in the United Kingdom also advises museums to conduct thorough research based on evidence to understand the company's business and corporate culture before beginning a partnership project. The partnerships with an art institution gives companies cultural and social resources, which can enhance their brand value. It also contributes to strengthening the relationships with its customers (current and potential) by creating and sharing artistic, more broadly cultural values (Lund and Greyser 2015). For a museum, the partnership expands its capacity to realize the goals of the organization and also extends the network of museum partners and potential donors.

Everyone who was interviewed for this article indicated that MMCA has certainly enjoyed its unique status in the country. According to them, MMCA's stable status as a national institution along with its long history and experience of conducting exhibitions results in sponsoring companies being more trusting of MMCA as an investment target compared to other cultural organizations. Its location, in particular, MMCA Seoul, where most sponsored projects have been conducted, has enjoyed the benefits over other venues in terms of attracting audiences and the branding impact. MMCA Seoul has now become a place where the museum's and companies' interest overlap, and it seems to be enjoying this privilege.

Based on interviews with MMCA professionals, the most outstanding benefit of sponsorship is its financial assistance, meaning not only the amount of budget allocated for the project but also its convenience and practical advantage in executing the budget. However, interestingly, the curatorial challenges are also related to this financial advantage that allows a bigger and more complex project. This is because it somehow limits traditional curatorial roles in its project development process. Rather than developing a concept and contemplating installation and display together with the artist, curators serve as managers who overview and monitor the whole process for a smooth delivery. Another interesting aspect in corporate sponsorship is the growing support for educational programs. Unlike short-term events and exhibitions, education programs are being conducted with a long-term perspective and reach a much wider audience. In addition, their sustainable effect and social meaning can give companies a more enhanced brand perception. MMCA also can expand its service to a wider audience group, including the ones not currently represented in the museum. It was also interesting to observe that companies these days appreciate that they are not supposed to get involved in the *contents* of an exhibition.

The challenges of corporate sponsorship were mainly general ones concerning its intervention and lack of understating art organization (mainly in practical matters, such as promotions or press releases), all of which are currently being handled by both MMCA and the sponsoring company through discussions before they conduct a partnership project. However, apart from these practical matters, MMCA needs to appreciate more fundamental assignments for the future. One of the curators interviewed for the article emphasized the stage before MMCA embarks on any kind of sponsored project (Curator D, personal communication, January 13, 2023). She argued that MMCA should be ready with more systematic operations in managing sponsorship, suggesting that there should be a clear agenda regarding which types of projects (supporting experimental attempts, international promotion, social responsibility, etc.) target which level of artists (emerging, experienced, or master's) with what kinds of sponsorship. Her argument is noteworthy since, based on this agenda, MMCA could work better with companies to maximize the benefits to both parties. In this case, sponsoring projects would not be one-off events, but a presentation of a constructive partnership between two vastly different organizations.

While this chapter examines a specific case of MMCA to identify the pros and cons of corporate sponsorship at this museum, the attempts to identify the challenges and opportunities revealed from the case should be applicable to a wider discussion of the topic since it interprets corporate sponsorship as a way of meeting the ever-changing contemporary art scene in a global context and achieving the goals of the organization.

Acknowledgment

I appreciate the staff of the MMCA who participated in the interviews for this chapter. Names were anonymized.

Notes

1 The interviews were conducted several times and each date refers to the date of the most recent interview with each professional.
2 MMCA has currently four branches at Gwacheon (main one), Deoksugung, Seoul, and Cheongju. Deoksugung and Seoul branches are located in Seoul. The former focuses on modern period and the latter mainly deals with contemporary art.
3 "Sponsorship" is more commonly used by MMCA professionals when describing MMCA's relationships with sponsoring companies. Although the nature of this relationship is shifting toward "partnership" in the long-term, "sponsorship" is still widely used in communication including written materials. For example, "sponsored by" or "supported by" is in most cases used in corporate-sponsored exhibitions when defining the positioning of sponsored company. In this article, "sponsorship" is used when describing the MMCA case.
4 The National Museum of Modern and Contemporary Art Foundation was established in 2013, around the same time as was MMCA Seoul, to serve as a bridge between MMCA and private sectors. It handles all sponsorship-related matters and also manages museum's shops, restaurants, etc.
5 Since this is currently a growing opinion, there will be more chances to discuss this topic in the future.

References

Bal, Charles, Pascale Quester, and Carolin Plewa. 2010. "Emotions and Sponsorship: A Key to Global Effectiveness? A Comparative Study of Australia and France." *Asia Pacific Journal of Marketing and Logistics* 22 (1): 40–54. DOI: 10.1108/13555851011013146

Butterfield, Anne. 2001. "Museums, Public Service, and Funding: Today's Conundrum, Tomorrow's Partnership?" *Curator* 44 (1): 35–46. DOI: 10.1111/j.2151-6952.2001.tb00028.x

Charlesworth, J. J. 2018. "The Ethics of Sponsorship in Art: Is There Such a Thing as Bad Money?" *ArtReview*, December 17, 2018. https://artreview.com/ar-september-2018-feature-aesthetic-judgement/

Cobbs, Joe B. 2011. "The Dynamics of Relationship Marketing in International Sponsorship Networks." *Journal of Business and Industrial Marketing* 26 (8): 590–601. DOI: 10.1108/08858621111179868

Davidsson, Eva and Helene Sørensen. 2010. "Sponsorship and Exhibitions at Nordic Science Centres and Museums." *Museum Management and Curatorship* 25 (4): 345–60. DOI: 10.1080/09647775.2010.525399

De Astous, Alain and Pierre Bitz. 1995. "Consumer Evaluations of Sponsorship Programmes." *European Journal of Marketing* 29 (12): 6–22. DOI: 10.1108/03090569510102504

Evrard, Yves and François Colbert. 2000. "Arts Management: A New Discipline Entering the Millennium?" *International Journal of Arts Management* 2 (2): 4–13.

Harris, Gareth. 2019. "British Museum Director Endorses Controversial Sponsor BP as Part of Future Vision." *The Art Newspaper*, July 8, 2019. https://www.theartnewspaper.com/2019/07/08/british-museum-director-endorses-controversial-sponsor-bp-as-part-of-future-vision

IEG. 2015. "Sponsorship Spending Report." Accessed November 18, 2022. https://www.sponsorship.com/ieg/files/4e/4e525456-b2b1-4049-bd51-03d9c35ac507.pdf

Jang, Heesun. 2020. "A Study on the Change of Corporate Sponsorship Method in Art Museum through MMCA Hyundai Motor Series." Master diss., Kyung Hee University.

Lewandowska, Kamila. 2015. "From Sponsorship to Partnership in Arts and Business Relations." *Journal of Arts Management, Law, and Society* 45 (1): 33–50. DOI: 10.1080/10632921.2014.964818

Lewandowska, Kamila. 2016. "It's Not All about the Profit: An Analysis of Changes in Arts and Business Relations." *Economics and Business Review EBR* 16 (1): 107–26. DOI: 10.18559/ebr.2016.1.7

Lidström, Bengt. 2004. "Arts and Business: Attitudes Towards Arts Sponsorship." Accessed November 18, 2022. http://neumann.hec.ca/iccpr/PDF_Texts/Lidstrom_Bengt.pdf

Lund, Ragnar and Stephen A. Greyser. 2015. "Corporate Sponsorship in Culture – a Case of Partnership in Relationship Building and Collaborative Marketing by a Global Financial Institution and a Major Art Museum." *Harvard Business School Working Paper* 16-041. Accessed November 18, 2022. https://www.hbs.edu/ris/Publication%20Files/16-041_0a81dd11-2e2f-459c-8eca-008f24bb313e.pdf

Martorella, Rosanne. 1996. "Art and Business: An International Approach on Sponsorship." In *Art and Business*, edited by Rosanne Martorella, 3–16. Westport: Praeger.

McGuigan, Jim. 2004. *Rethinking Cultural Policy*. Berkshire: Open University Press.

McNicholas, Bernadette. 2004. "Arts, Culture and Business: A Relationship Transformation, a Nascent Field." *International Journal of Art Management* 7 (1): 57–69.

Meenaghan, Tony and David Shipley. 1999. "Media Effect in Commercial Sponsorship." *European Journal of Marketing* 33 (3/4): 328–48. DOI: 10.1108/03090569910253170

Museums Association. n.d. "Ethics: Sponsorship." Accessed November, 4, 2022. https://www.museumsassociation.org/campaigns/ethics/sponsorship/

Olkkonen, Rami and Pekka Tuominen. 2006. "Understanding Relationship Fading in Cultural Sponsorships." *Corporate Communications: An International Journal* 11 (1): 64–77. DOI: 10.1108/13563280610643561

Proteau, Jasmine. 2018. "Reducing Risky Relationships: Criteria for Forming Positive Museum-Corporate Sponsorships." *Museum Management and Curatorship* 33 (3): 235–42. DOI: 10.1080/09647775.2018.1467274

Rectanus, Mark. 2002. *Culture Incorporated: Museums, Artists, and Corporate Sponsorship*. Minneapolis, MN: University of Minnesota Press.

Thomas, Sarah R., Simon J. Pervan, and Peter J. Nuttall. 2009. "Marketing Orientation and Arts Organisations: The Case for Business Sponsorship." *Marketing Intelligence & Planning* 27 (6): 736–52. DOI: 10.1108/02634500910988654

Thompson, Frederick. 2012. "Corporate Partnership for Nonprofits: A Match Made in Heaven?" *Nonprofit World* 30 (2): 6–9.

Wang, Jinoh. 2014. "gungnipyeondaemisulgwan, eokdae muryoipjang harin hyetaek nollan" [MMCA controversy over billions free admission discount] CNB NEWS, September 30, 2014. https://www.cnbnews.com/news/article.html?no=266375

PART 5

External Influences and Technological Innovations

18

UNDERSTANDING THE FINANCIAL IMPACT OF DEACCESSIONING

Rachel Shane[1] *and Chris Burgess*[2]
[1]University of Kentucky; [2]College of Charleston

Introduction

Museums throughout the world collect, care, and exhibit art, artifacts, and objects. As custodians of cultural heritage, the preservation and safeguarding of the museum collection are paramount. While preservation and conservation are often considered the first role of the museum, there are times when a museum may determine that pieces within the collection should no longer be cared for by that museum. The formalized removal of objects from a museum collection, often through the sale or transfer to another entity, is known as deaccessioning. This activity enables the museum to shift or scale its collection. Specifically in the case of sales, proceeds of deaccessioning are subject to overarching policy guidelines dictating how the revenue might be used. Thus, deaccessioning may appear to be a function only of the curatorial or artistic side of the museum, but the evolution of deaccessioning policy has actually resulted in considerable transformation of fiscal policy and financial practice.

This chapter explores those changes employing John Kingdon's Multiple Streams Framework to three US case studies in order to answer the research questions: What is the evolution of deaccessioning fiscal policy and practice over time? What external pressures contributed to change? How have those changes altered financial reporting and practice at US museums?

What Is Deaccessioning?

The process of deaccessioning is an important aspect of maintaining a relevant, high-quality, mission-driven collection that represents the dynamic nature of museum curatorial and conservation approaches. The scale of deaccessioning collections differs by museum structure and design but

DOI: 10.4324/9781003308003-23

typically represents a critical part of how the organization operates. Though there have been some controversial cases within this area for individual institutions, particularly over the last 50 years, deaccessioning is nevertheless a fundamental aspect of museum administrative practices, including the funding of acquisitions and the direct care of the collection. Definitionally, there is clear agreement across the museum sector, both domestically and internationally, on what is meant by the term itself:

> *The American Alliance for Museums (AAM)*: The act of formally removing [an] object from the museum's permanent collection (American Alliance of Museums, n.d.).
>
> *Association of Art Museum Directors (AAMD)*: The process by which a work of art or other object (collectively, a "work"), wholly or in part, is permanently removed from a museum's collection (Association of Art Museum Directors 2010).
>
> *International Council of Museums (ICOM)*: The act of lawfully removing an object from a museum's collections ("Guidelines on Deaccessioning of the International Council of Museums" 2019).

Museums may deaccession because an object is no longer a fit for the curatorial vision of the organization, the mission might have evolved over time thus making the object superfluous, or, the object could be damaged. Circumstances differ and the unique nature of collections management on an institutional level must be considered in any overarching framework. Museums approach deaccessioning through carefully defined policy guidelines providing the mechanism of disposal or disposition.

For instance, the Museum of Modern Art (MoMA) in New York City lists the following as part of their Collections Management Policy guide approved in April 2020 and is indicative of many such approaches within the art museum world, whether large or small in nature:

> The decision to deaccession should be made cautiously and follow generally accepted museum practices. Works of art may be deaccessioned for a variety of reasons, including but not limited to the following:
>
> 1 The object is not relevant to the mission of the museum or has little value in the museum's collection.
> 2 The object is redundant or is a duplicate and is not necessary for research purposes.
> 3 The object is of lesser quality than other objects of the same type either already in the collection or about to be acquired.
> 4 The authenticity, attribution, or genuineness of the object is questionable or determined to be false or fraudulent.

5 The object lacks sufficient esthetic merit or art historical importance to warrant retention.
6 The museum is unable to conserve the object in a responsible manner or it is determined that it has decomposed.
7 The object is the subject of a claim related to title or provenance that requires its deaccessioning and dispersal (Museum of Modern Art 2020, 7).

Deaccessioning Stakeholders and Financial Reporting

Through the continued use of MoMA as an institutional example, we can consider the financial impact of collection management practices by examining the museum's financial documents. According to MoMA's 2022 audited financial statements, the museum sold artwork that resulted in revenue of $9,902,000 through deaccessioning activities (Price Waterhouse Cooper LLP 2022). Remember, this is not unusual as museums sell work for a variety of reasons thereby creating revenue from the transaction. However, the museum also spent $16,694,000 on new acquisitions (Price Waterhouse Cooper LLP 2022). Once again, this is a normal aspect of collections management. Both acquisition and deaccessioning expenses are shown within the museum financial statements to allow those interested to gain insight into collection activities of the organization from a financial perspective as well as to potentially track fiscal impact. As mentioned previously though, the revenue gained is subject to specific policy framework parameters dictating how it might actually be used across the organization.

This financial policy has been set by professional associations, not legal entities (such as local, state, or federal government). When this occurs, it is known as a "pseudo-regulatory framework." The pseudo-regulatory framework, in this case pertaining to use of deaccessioning proceeds, now guides the activities of the museum industry. While the associations do not have any legal authority to enforce these policies, the internal penalties to member museums are significant and result in museums conforming to the regulations.

This regulatory role of these associations (AAM, AAMD, and ICOM) is a modern phenomenon. Prior to the 1970s, museums controlled aspects pertaining to deaccessioning internally. The cases that triggered this regulatory change are discussed in detail below. The cases themselves were controversial and, subsequently, led to notable fiscal policy changes within the museum industry.

As part of the establishment of this pseudo-regulatory framework, each association has provided definitions of deaccessioning (as reviewed above) as well as value propositions of museums, collections, and deaccessioning. The approach to these value propositions results in financial implications for museums.

For instance, as part of its ethical guidelines, AAM specifies that the value of the collection is beyond a monetary benefit:

> Museums acquire items of cultural or scientific value for their collections through donation, purchase, rescue or field research and hold these items for the benefit of present and future generations. Although **these items may have a monetary value**, once they become part of a museum's permanent collection, **that value becomes secondary** to their importance as a means to enhance understanding of our world and ourselves. Consequently, **museum collections are considered cultural—not financial—assets, to be held for the public benefit**. (American Alliance of Museums 2016, 5)

Similarly, AAMD stipulates that collections cannot be treated as assets or capitalized on financial statements:

> The collections the museum holds in public trust are **not financial assets** and **may not be converted to cash for operating or capital needs**. No collection or portion thereof may be pledged as collateral for a loan, except that a museum may grant a security interest in a work that it is acquiring in order to secure the payment of the balance of the purchase price. To present fairly the museum's financial position, **collections should not be capitalized**. (Association of Art Museum Directors 2011, 11)

Correspondingly, the constructs set forth by AAM and AAMD in the United States extend to international environments through the International Council of Museums (ICOM):

> Museum collections are held in public trust and may not be treated as a realisable asset. Money or compensation received from the deaccessioning and disposal of objects and specimens from a museum collection should be used solely for the benefit of the collection and usually for acquisitions to that same collection. (International Council of Museums 2017, 12)[1]

Since museum collections are not treated as capital assets by member organizations due to these guidelines, as a result, the monetary value of a collection would not be found on an organization's balance sheet. Importantly, a museum's collection is not financially accounted for as an asset in the same way as other assets, such as land or investments, and, thus, is not written as a line item within an organization's financial documentation. This should not be interpreted to mean that objects in a collection do not have specific monetary value and financial significance. An examination of a contemporary art auction dispels that notion quickly. However, museums are required to treat collection objects differently than a collector.

This approach is due to the constraints placed on museums as part of the professional association framework which limits the use of deaccessioning funds for member organizations as well as the fundamental philosophy that a collection is not a financial asset to be drawn upon when needed but rather a "cultural asset" as described earlier by the AAM with the institution in the role of public stewardship. This distinction is critical as it places limitations on a museum's financial management by dictating how certain assets might be used, when, and in what capacity. There may be museums that do choose to profit from a collection and use the proceeds as they see fit, but they are not the norm within the museum industry and are acting outside of the pseudo-regulatory framework.

While collections are typically not reported as a full asset on financial statements of museums due to the capital asset limitations, deaccessioning and accessioning activities are often listed (as in the MoMA example above). Typically, the museum will report on its collection acquisitions and sales in its audited financial statements and/or its IRS Form 990. It should be noted that there is no comprehensive legal requirement that museums report this activity with any level of detail, but many museums see this as an important area for transparency.

Below is an example of what deaccessioning/accessioning reporting looks like on an audited financial statement from the Metropolitan Museum of Art noted as "purchases of art" and "proceeds from sales of art."

Figure 18.1 includes an audit note detailing the accounting for collections as well as the role of a legal (non-pseudo) regulatory for the museum, the New York Board of Regents:

The Metropolitan Museum of Art
Statement of Activities

for the year ended June 30, 2019, with summarized financial information for the year ended June 30, 2018 (in thousands)

	Without Donor Restrictions	*With Donor Restrictions*	*Total 2019*	*Total 2018*
OPERATING				
REVENUE AND SUPPORT:				
Admissions	$ 55,059	$	$ 55,059	$ 48,148
Membership	29,091		29,091	28,650
Gifts and grants	29,482	30,057	59,539	67,368
Operating appropriations from the City of New York (Note A)	26,822		26,822	25,446
Endowment support for current activities (Note G)	80,826	25,027	105,853	103,185
Retail and other auxiliary activities	85,842		85,842	88,117
Other income	8,232		8,232	8,357
Net assets released from donor restrictions to fund operating expenses	58,730	(58,730)		
TOTAL REVENUE AND SUPPORT	374,084	(3,646)	370,438	369,251
EXPENSES:				
Program Services	222,898		222,898	226,672
Auxiliary Activities	84,826		84,826	86,720
Supporting Services	82,618		82,618	79,595
TOTAL EXPENSES	390,342		390,342	392,987
Transfer of non-operating funds	14,358	(6,362)	7,996	20,049
CHANGE IN NET ASSETS FROM OPERATING ACTIVITIES	(1,900)	(10,008)	(11,908)	(3,687)
NON-OPERATING				
Museum-designated and donor-restricted gifts	10,687	91,871	102,558	89,747
Endowment gifts (includes board-designated endowments)	10,652	77,066	87,718	39,033
Endowment support for current activities (Note G)	23,469	24,728	48,197	47,426
Investment return in excess of current support (Note G)	15,778	14,179	29,957	177,307
Change in value of split interest agreements (Note H)	(380)	(18,544)	(18,924)	2,032
Depreciation and non-capitalized expenditures (Notes E and F)	(47,932)		(47,932)	(48,348)
Interest expense on bonds and interest rate swaps (Notes A and K)	(12,748)		(12,748)	(12,793)
Realized and change in unrealized gains on 2015 bond proceeds	5,806		5,806	12,106
Transfer of designated non-operating funds to operating and other	(39,310)	32,115	(7,195)	(18,154)
Net assets released from donor restrictions	6,006	(6,006)		
Change in net assets before collection items not capitalized and other adjustments	(29,872)	205,401	[illegible]	284,669
Purchases of art (Note D)	(88,932)		(88,932)	(89,481)
Proceeds from sales of art		6,182	6,182	2,115
Net assets released from donor restrictions to fund acquisitions of art	82,539	(82,539)		
Pension-related changes other than NPPC (Note I)	(20,953)		(20,953)	35,122
Change in fair value of interest rate exchange agreements (Notes G and K)	(8,709)		(8,709)	7,284
CHANGE IN NET ASSETS	$ (65,927)	$ 129,044	$ 63,117	$ 237,709
NET ASSETS AT THE BEGINNING OF THE YEAR (Note A)	$ 1,127,923	$2,544,083	$ 3,672,006	$ 3,434,297
NET ASSETS AT THE END OF THE YEAR	$ 1,061,996	$2,673,127	$ 3,735,123	$ 3,672,006

New York Board of Regents

Collections - In conformity with accounting policies generally followed by art museums, the value of the Museum's collections has been excluded from the Statement of Financial Position, and gifts of art objects are excluded from revenue in the Statement of Activities. Purchases of art objects by the Museum are recorded as decreases in net assets in the Statement of Activities. Pursuant to state law and Museum policy, proceeds from the sale of art and related insurance settlements are recorded as net assets with donor restrictions for the acquisition of art.

FIGURE 18.1 Metropolitan Museum of Art, Audited Financial Statement, FY 2019.

Form 990 (2018) Page 2

Part III Statement of Program Service Accomplishments

Check if Schedule O contains a response or note to any line in this Part III . . . . . ☑

1 Briefly describe the organization's mission

THE METROPOLITAN MUSEUM OF ART COLLECTS, STUDIES, CONSERVES, AND PRESENTS SIGNIFICANT WORKS OF ART ACROSS ALL TIMES AND CULTURES IN ORDER TO CONNECT PEOPLE TO CREATIVITY, KNOWLEDGE, AND IDEAS

2 Did the organization undertake any significant program services during the year which were not listed on the prior Form 990 or 990-EZ? . . . . . ☐ Yes ☑ No

If "Yes," describe these new services on Schedule O

3 Did the organization cease conducting, or make significant changes in how it conducts, any program services? . . . . . ☐ Yes ☑ No

If "Yes," describe these changes on Schedule O

4 Describe the organization's program service accomplishments for each of its three largest program services, as measured by expenses Section 501(c)(3) and 501(c)(4) organizations are required to report the amount of grants and allocations to others, the total expenses, and revenue, if any, for each program service reported

4a (Code) (Expenses $ 165,662,723 including grants of $ 2,965,533) (Revenue $ 6,295,448)
See Additional Data

4b (Code) (Expenses $ 88,932,148 including grants of $) (Revenue $ 6,181,633)
See Additional Data

4c (Code) (Expenses $ 56,868,560 including grants of $) (Revenue $)
See Additional Data

See Additional Data Table

4d Other program services (Describe in Schedule O)
(Expenses $ 111,491,441 including grants of $) (Revenue $ 3,577,218)

4e **Total program service expenses ▶** 422,954,872

Form **990** (2018)

Form 990, Part III, Line 4b:
ACQUISITIONS AND SALES OF ART - SEE SCHEDULE O FOR MORE INFORMATION

FIGURE 18.2 Metropolitan Museum of Art, IRS Form 990, FY 2019.

> In conformity with accounting policies generally followed by art museums, the value of the Museum's collections have been excluded from the Statement of Financial Position, and gifts of art objects are excluded from revenue in the Statement of Activities. Purchases of art objects by the Museum are recorded as decreases in net assets in the Statement of Activities. Pursuant to state law and Museum policy, proceeds from the sale of art and related insurance settlements are recorded as new assets with donor restrictions for the acquisition of art.[2]

In Figure 18.2 from the same fiscal year, the IRS Form 990 categorizes the accessioning and deaccessioning of artwork as part of the museum's programming under Program Service Accomplishments. Thus, the sale and purchasing of art is simply a programmatic activity within the organization's budget.

Both types of financial reporting statements illustrate the unique nature of a collection's financial treatment, and by extension, accessioning and deaccessioning.

Theoretical Framework

When viewing the various cases involved in the deaccessioning evolution narrative and its financial implications, it is helpful to apply an organizing framework rooted in public policy theory, particularly one which is relatively straightforward and lends itself well to operationalizing events and actions over time. The framework provides the tools needed to understand in context the actions and outcomes of these events in which issues arise and force significant interaction among a diverse group of stakeholders, not just those within the museum industry, in working through policy development and implementation.

John Kingdon's Multiple Streams Framework provides an ideal approach in this scenario as it is designed to break apart the processes involved in policy development with an eye toward highlighting the importance and practice of problem definition, the development of policy alternatives as well as feasibility, and the substantial role of an evolving political environment involving actor receptivity (Kingdon 1995). Kingdon builds on the "organized anarchies garbage can model" of Cohen et al. (1972) and highlights the problem stream, the policy stream, and the political stream all of which run independently from one another until a policy window opens in either the problem stream or the political stream as a result of a focusing event. The framework has been applied across numerous industries over the last few decades but is not often employed within the arts though this seems to be changing as the sector looks deeper into how cultural policy adapts, changes, and grows across time. This is particularly helpful when we consider the financial implications of these changes and their far-reaching impact, issues we are particularly sensitive to as part of the deaccessioning debate.

The model itself is intuitive and can be distilled down here into a quick overview of the framework fundamentals. According to Kingdon, the problem stream is largely where problem definition occurs. Essentially, what exactly is the problem to be addressed? And whose definition of the problem is used to frame the debate? The latter question is vital, as those who successfully define the problem are often those who are able to shop for their preferred solution with the most success. The policy stream is where policy alternatives/policy proposals are generated and live waiting for an appropriate political climate. These are solutions in search of problems and they run along a continuum of feasibility and practicality. The political stream involves public opinion, administration turnover, or philosophical changes which all impact actor receptiveness to specific alternatives or problem definition. Essentially, is the environment conducive to intervention? As these streams run separately over time, inevitably a focusing event takes place which draws direct attention to an issue and pushes it onto the decision agenda. Thus a window of opportunity is opened which allows for potential action in the form of viable policy alternatives.

As the cases below will demonstrate, the model provides a guiding framework to critically analyze the controversies as well as the various stakeholders involved, the numerous policy alternatives in play, and the environment in which all of these developments took place. Without question windows opened, and the industry was forced to consider what types of changes needed to take place if any. Inaction can be a viable policy alternative as well, but it is the choice itself that is critical in that it is the culmination of problem definition winners and losers as well as the environment in which the decisions are made.

Finally, the framework is presented here not only as a lens through which to view these cases as past events which shape the current reality. It is also presented as a tool by which those within the museum industry understand how policy change occurs and can thus pay attention to the environment in which they operate with a particular eye on changing policy landscapes and policy alternative generation. The model itself is not predictive, but can easily be used to institutionally strategically position and anticipate when windows might be on the verge of opening. At that point, those who are paying attention can lead the problem definition conversation and thereby influence, at least to some degree, the direction of the field.

Case #1: Formation of Policy Communities

While deaccessioning historically was a common practice for decades at all museums, it was not until the 1970s that the general public was made aware of the concept. In 1972, John Canaday, New York Times art critic, published a piece entitled, "Very Quiet and Very Dangerous" (Canaday 1972, D21), regarding the potential sale of several artworks from the collection of the Metropolitan Museum of Art. Canaday questioned the ethics of any museum professional who sold work from a collection. He argued that these sales happen quietly in order not to draw attention to the museum attempting to raise "hard to find" cash (ibid.). Canaday contended that museums should never sell artwork:

> Art museums are neither merchandise marts nor esthetic stock exchanges. They are repositories of precious records. Nothing worth buying or accepting as a gift in the first place ever becomes less than part of the record of a phase of our culture, even if it also represents a curatorial idiocy. (Canaday 1972, D21)

"Very Quiet and Very Dangerous" ignited the first public discussion about deaccessioning—Kingdon's Focusing Event (see Figure 18.3). The first response came from Thomas Hoving, the Metropolitan Museum of Art's director. In his editorial, "Very Inaccurate and Very Dangerous," Hoving retorted, "The Metropolitan is not a Library of Congress of works of art, not an archive similar to an etymological collection of a natural history museum"

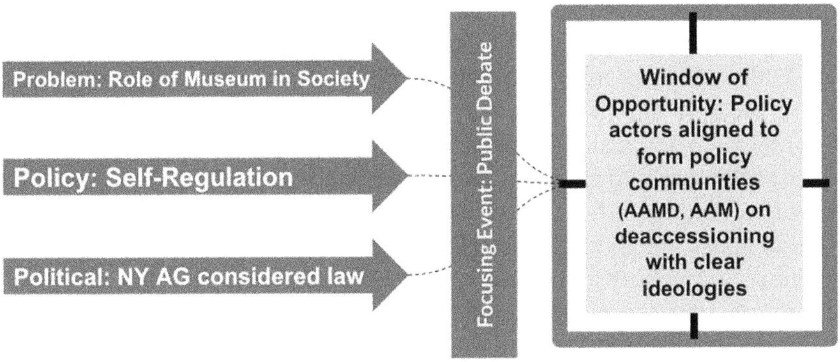

FIGURE 18.3 Formation of policy communities.

(Hoving 1972, D21). And so began a public debate on the nature of a museum's purpose and societal role—Kingdon's Problem Stream (see Figure 18.3). This debate would lead to the formalizing of nascent policy communities that would, in turn, develop deaccessioning policies.

Following the public strike, New York State Attorney General, Louis Lefkowitz, brought various stakeholders together to consider policy formation (Political Stream): "To what extent should the disposition procedures agreed to by the Metropolitan Museum of Art be adopted by other museums?" (Garfield 1997, 17). Museum professionals supported self-regulation over governmental intervention (policy stream).

Within one month, the first formalized deaccessioning policy was adopted by the College Art Association (CAA). Subsequently, the CAA put forth several criteria pertaining to deaccessioning, including a requirement that museums establish clear deaccessioning policies that are publically available (College Art Association Board of Directors 1973). Subsequently, AAM and AAMD also established policies pertaining to deaccessioning, although it would take years for the policies to be released.

Examining the incident utilizing Kingdon's Multiple Streams Framework, the three streams came together through the focusing event of the public discourse on deaccessioning. This led to the window of opportunity opening for various policy actors to advocate for self-regulation and then move to establish such policies which would support organizational ideologies rather than formal regulatory political intervention.

While the CAA was the first to release guidelines, these simply stated that museums must have a deaccessioning policy available to the public. However, the AAMD and the AAM put forth policies that were more restrictive and specified the financial treatment of deaccessioning proceeds.

First, in 1987, the AAMD released "Considerations for Formulating a Policy for Deaccessioning and Disposal." This document identified acceptable reasons and appropriate methods for accessioning and disposal. Several years later, in 1991, AAMD added a clause to its code of ethics that forbade the selling of artwork to cover operations or capital expenses. This marked the first time in US history that a policy was formally established indicating the relationship between museum art deaccessioning activity and the use of the resulting proceeds. Soon after AADM restricted deaccessioning proceeds, so too did AAM. In this case, the association restricted "the use of proceeds from the sale of collection materials ... to the acquisition of collections" (American Association of Museums, 1993).

Lastly, in 1993 the AAM updated the 1991 policy to "proceeds from the sale of nonliving collections are to be used consistent with the established standards of the museum's discipline, but in no event shall they be used for anything other than the acquisition or **direct care of collections**" (emphasis added, American Association of Museums 1993). Meeting minutes state that proceeds could NOT be used for operating costs (including salaries) or as a remedy in a financial crisis. However, "direct care" was left undefined. This is the first time we see the term "direct care" used in association policy documents. However, the issue of "direct care" will not be formally addressed again by AAM until 2020.

This first case study, which began in the 1970s with a controversy at the Metropolitan Museum of Art (focusing event), led to the development of policy committees that established policy both on deaccessioning and the resulting proceeds (window of opportunity). Thus, a formal policy was never enacted through the legislative branches.

Nonetheless, this pseudo-regulatory policy established by the museum professional associations led quickly to the adaptation of financial accounting standards set forth by the Financial Accounting Standards Board (FASB). In 1993, FASB established the following policy:

> Contributions of works of art, historical treasures, and similar assets **need not be recognized as revenue or capitalized** if the donated items are added to collections that are
>
> a held for public exhibition, education, or research in furtherance of public service;
> b protected, kept unencumbered, cared for, and preserved; and
> c subject to an organizational policy that requires the proceeds from sales of collection items to be used to acquire other items for the collection. (emphasis added, Financial Accounting Standards Board 1993)

Thus, by the early 1990s, the US museum field had formalized deaccessioning policies as well as accounting standards in which the financial treatment of collections and the works thereof are at the center.

Case #2: Policy Enforcement & Sanctions

It would be nearly 40 more years before deaccessioning entered the public forum again. This case, also in New York City, transpired when the National Academy sought to sell two paintings. Founded in 1825, the National Academy is an honorary association of professional artists, a school of fine arts, and a museum. The collection of the National Academy consisted of more than 7,000 works of what the organization called "diploma pieces." Diploma pieces were given to the Academy by artists upon their induction. The works represented a "who's who" of great American artists including Chuck Close, Thomas Eakins, Helen Frankenthaler, Frank Gehry, Horatio Greenough, Winslow Homer, Jasper Johns, Maya Lin, Tom Otterness, I. M. Pei, Robert Rauschenberg, Dorothea Rockburne, John Singer Sargent, Frank Lloyd Wright, and Andrew Wyeth.

Despite the prestige of the National Academy, it had been facing significant financial hardships for numerous years. From 2003 to 2008, the Academy ran a deficit. In order to shore up its financial circumstances, the membership considered the sale of the institution's six-story mansion on Fifth Avenue and 89th Street. However, in 2007, the Academy members voted against selling the building.

By 2008, the Academy turned to selling its artwork to mitigate the deficit. Its members voted to sell two Hudson River School paintings to shore up operating expenses. The works proposed were not part of the significant "diploma works" collection but did hold considerable value and were sold for $13.5 million.

As established by the policies set forth in the 1990s, the sale of the paintings themselves wasn't controversial. After all, deaccessioning is a regular museum practice. Rather, it was the use of the proceeds that sparked a firestorm. In this case, the National Academy used the proceeds to offset the debts of the organization. As described by the interim director of the Academy, Carmine Branagan [If not for the sale] "the academy would close and that is an honest and sincere statement" (Kennedy 2008).

The AAMD did not accept the Academy's rationale for the use of the proceeds.

> The National Academy is now breaching one of the most basic and important principles of the museum world by treating its collection as a financial asset, rather than the cornerstone of research, exhibition and public programming, a record of human creativity held in trust for people now and in the future. (Kennedy 2008)

Correspondingly, the AAMD issued sanctions against the Academy which included the banning of any AAMD members involved in loaning or program collaborations with the National Academy. The Academy withdrew its membership from AAMD as a result of those sanctions. In effect, they were now in the wilderness.

The sanctions worked. "Sanctions really hurt. You're completely incapable of designing exhibition programming going forward because you can't loan and you can't get loans, and sanctions also affect funding. Sanctions were very, very painful" (Pogrebin 2010, C2N). Nearly two years later, the AAMD lifted the sanctions against the National Academy which was then barred from selling any of its art until the organization came up with a clear financial plan for the use of the proceeds. Additionally, the Academy was required to create an ethics committee to review its policies and procedures.

The National Academy controversy, combined with several other high-profile sales, rekindled the debate of the establishment of formal regulations regarding deaccessioning. The New York State Board of Regents issued an emergency injunction to ban cultural institutions under its authority from selling pieces of collections.

By March 2009, Assemblyman Richard L. Brodsky, the New York State Board of Regents, and the Museum Association of New York proposed a bill that would ban deaccessioning to pay for general museum expenses. "These collections were not created as reservoirs of capital to be used for the benefit of the institution. You keep selling paintings to keep the doors open and eventually, you have open doors and no paintings" (Pogrebin 2009, C1N).

Yet, by 2010, the bill was shelved. The Board of Regents said that after hearing from museums statewide, "there was no consensus on the efficacy of those emergency regulations … those regulations will be allowed to expire, allowing the prior regulations regarding museum collections to once again take effect" (Pogrebin 2010).

Brodsky was disappointed with this failure to make the emergency regulations banning cultural institutions from selling pieces of the collection to pay for institutional expenses, enacted in 2008, permanent: "This removes a substantial obstacle to the monetization of art held in the public trust and to the transfer of art from public hands to private hands" (Pogrebin 2010) (Figure 18.4).

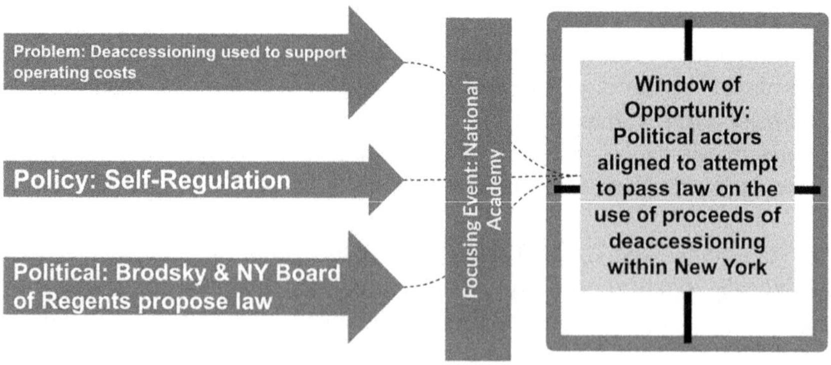

FIGURE 18.4 Attempt to shift policy enforcement.

Case #3: Direct Care Debate

The debate over deaccessioning funds used toward the direct care of collections has long been a part of the policy alternatives stream, with some arguing for more institutional discretion, thereby allowing for maintenance and preservation allowances, and others advocating for a more narrow approach in which proceeds only be used toward acquisitions.

In effect, the problem was never really clearly defined, there was no real agreement on policy alternatives among actors involved, and there was no consistent momentum within the political stream to place the issue on a decision agenda. This changed in 2020 with the advent of the COVID pandemic, but can also be traced back to a relatively overlooked move by the AAM in 2016 which finally provided some clarification to what it considered to be direct care within the industry thereby providing a workable definitional framework.

AAM has included direct care as an acceptable use of deaccessioning proceeds since its 1993 Code of Ethics revision but had been glaringly ambiguous as to what that meant exactly thus placing institutions at a fundamental disadvantage relating to interpretation complications. By 2016, this shifted when a more operationally workable framework was established. As a result, in 2019 the Financial Accounting Standards Board (FASB) changed its language to allow for "the direct care of existing collections," and required museums to disclose the policy on the use of deaccessioning funds, as well as the associated definition of direct care, if applicable. Clearly, a window was opening.

However, it was not until 2020 that the AAMB announced it would loosen sanction activity leading to more financial discretion for institutions in navigating the unprecedented pandemic challenges. To be clear though, the policy shift was not intended to be permanent at the time but rather a temporary measure designed to end in 2022 that would immediately assist museums in a time of unequivocal need. As a result, a number of museums announced plans to take advantage of this opportunity, including the Baltimore Museum of Art (BMA) which signaled intentions to sell three works in order to raise approximately $65 million toward the "Endowment for the Future," an initiative supporting staff pay raises, diversity programming, acquisitions of underrepresented artists, collection management costs, as well as free admission to special exhibitions (Baltimore Museum of Art 2020).

While all commendable goals, a portion of these plans were a significant diversion from previous ethical standards guiding deaccessioning fund destination and led to pushback among some institutional stakeholders as well as some in the industry, leading the BMA to temporarily halt the sale. Indeed, of the expected $65 million, $54.5 million was to be earmarked as an endowment for the direct care of their collection, something that would have been a major stretch under previous AAMD guidelines. At this point, the window is fully open as policy alternatives are widely and intentionally under discussion by stakeholders across the industry within an environment conducive to change and it is clear that this was an opportunity to act.

Finally, in September 2022, AAMD permanently backed the direct care provision for the use of deaccessioning funds but went a step further by providing substantial definitional parameters:

> Funds received from the disposal of a deaccessioned work of art including any earnings and appreciation thereon, may be used only for the acquisition of works of art in a manner consistent with the museum's policy on the use of restricted acquisition funds or for direct care of works of art. Direct care for purposes of this section means the direct costs associated with the storage or preservation of works of art. Such direct costs include for example those for (i) conservation and restoration treatments (including packing and transportation for such conservation or restoration) and (ii) materials required for storage of all classifications of works of art, such as, acid-free paper, folders, matboard, frames, mounts, and digital media migration. Funds received from the disposal of a deaccessioned work of art shall not be used for operations or capital expenses except as provided above. Direct care does not include (a) salaries of staff or (b) costs incurred for the sole purpose of temporary exhibition display. (Association of Art Museum Directors 2022)

The language is direct, unambiguous, and provides institutions the guidance needed to properly handle funds generated from deaccessioning activities while also staying in full compliance with the professional agencies acting in a regulatory capacity, although one which is not legally binding as discussed in previous sections. That said, violation sanctions are significant, and agreement among institutions and agencies sets the stage for future financial health and stability across the museum industry while also encouraging capacity building. The direct care debate and, ultimately, the overall consensus has laid the groundwork for stronger financial management approaches as museums better understand both the constraints and possibilities facing their future financial health and the role collections management, and specifically deaccessioning, plays in their path to sustainability and growth (Figure 18.5).

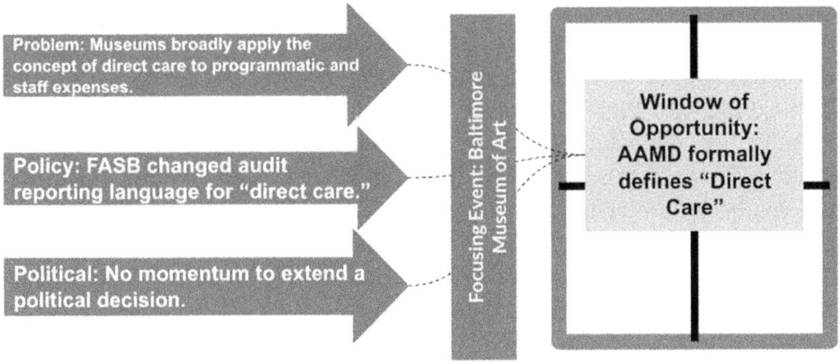

FIGURE 18.5 Direct care definition.

Considerations

The examination of the previous three cases illustrates a museum field that has sought to control its own policy frameworks and set its own guidelines for the treatment of collections financially.

The first case in the 1970s introduced the concept of deaccessioning to the general public and ignited the first broad debate about deaccessioning. This resulted in the consideration of legal solutions but ended with the formation of organized policy communities with actionable alternatives. Subsequently, these communities developed viable deaccessioning policies aligned with organizational values and impacted the financial treatment of the proceeds from the sale of artworks.

Nearly 40 years later, deaccessioning entered the public forum again when the National Academy sought to sell two paintings. The National Academy used the proceeds—nearly $13.5 million—to offset the debts of the organization. Using the proceeds in such a way was considered unethical due to the policies in place at the time within the pseudo-regulatory framework installed by the primary industry professional associations. The National Academy faced sanctions from the museum world and New York considered a true regulatory legal response once again.

In 2020, in the final case, the Baltimore Museum of Art (BMA) sought to sell artworks in order to provide pay raises, diversity programming, acquire works from underrepresented artists, collection management costs, and provide free admission to special exhibitions. BMA argued to some degree that many of these uses were within the scope of "direct care"—a concept that has been included in museum association policy since 1993. Policy developers disagreed, at least in relation to the broad scope of the approach. The result was a tightening of fiscal policy guidelines to coincide with a formal definition of "direct care" thereby significantly reducing a great deal of uncertainty within the field.

Combined, these three case studies articulate the transformation of fiscal deaccessioning policy impacting US museums over a period of 50 years. While professional associations have largely maintained policy control in collaboration with their membership, each of the cases has also involved a tightening of financial parameters associated with deaccessioning for museums. There is less ambiguity in the field as a result of this evolution. Museums better understand the financial parameters under which they must operate when deaccessioning works and now engage in more comprehensive collections management practices that will ultimately continue to benefit the industry and the public moving forward.

Notes

1 While ICOM provides similar guidance as AAM and AAMD to museums around the world, due to the funding structures of museums throughout Europe and Asia, national governments play a more authoritative role in deaccessioning policy outside of the United States.
2 The New York Board of Regents charters museums in New York State and has governing authority over those organizations. Its rules for museums are in alignment with AAM.

References

American Alliance of Museums. 2016. *Direct Care of Collections: Ethics, Guidelines, and Recommendations*. Washington, DC: AAM.

American Alliance of Museums. n.d. “Deaccessioning and Disposal – American Alliance of Museums.” *American Alliance of Museums*. Accessed April 18, 2023. https://www.aam-us.org/programs/resource-library/collections-stewardship-resources/deaccessioning-disposal/.

American Association of Museums. 1993. “AAM Code of Ethics for Museums – American Alliance of Museums.” *American Alliance of Museums*. https://www.aam-us.org/programs/ethics-standards-and-professional-practices/code-of-ethics-for-museums/.

Association of Art Museum Directors. 2010. “AAMD Policy on Deaccessioning June 9, 2010.” *Association of Art Museum Directors*. https://aamd.org/sites/default/files/document/AAMD%20Policy%20on%20Deaccessioning%20website_0.pdf.

Association of Art Museum Directors. 2011. *Professional Practices of Art Museums*. New York City, NY: AAMD.

Association of Art Museum Directors. 2022. “Membership of AAMD Approves Change to Deaccessioning Rule, Bringing Policy in Line with American Alliance of Museums (AAM) and Financial Accounting Standards Board (FASB).” *Association of Art Museum Directors*. https://aamd.org/for-the-media/press-release/membership-of-aamd-approves-change-to-deaccessioning-rule-bringing.

Baltimore Museum of Art. 2020. “The Baltimore Museum of Arts Announces Ambitions Plan to Secure and Increase Staff Salaries, Improve Community Access, and Continue to Diversify its Collection.” *Baltimore Museum of Art*. https://cdn.artbma.org/2021/04/01052815/NEWSRELEASE_Endowment_for_the_Future_final.pdf.

Canaday, John. 1972. “Very Quiet and Very Dangerous.” *New York Times* (New York City), February 27, 1972, D21.

Cohen, Michael D., James G. March, and Johan P. Olsen. 1972. "A Garbage Can Model of Organizational Choice." *Administrative Science Quarterly* 17 (1): 1–25. 10.2307/2392088.
College Art Association Board of Directors. 1973. *Resolution Concerning the Sale and Exchange of Works of Art by Museums*. n.p.: College Art Association.
Financial Accounting Standards Board. 1993. "Superseded Standards – Summary of Statement No. 116." *FASB*. https://www.fasb.org/page/PageContent?pageId=/reference-library/superseded-standards/summary-of-statement-no-116.html&bcpath=tff.
Garfield, D. 1997. "Deaccessioning Goes Public." In *A Deaccession Reader*, 11–22. Washington, DC: American Association of Museums.
"Guidelines on Deaccessioning of the International Council of Museums." 2019. ICOM Museum. https://icom.museum/wp-content/uploads/2019/08/20170503_ICOM_standards_deaccessioning_final_EN-v2.pdf.
Hoving, Thomas. 1972. "Very Inaccurate and Very Dangerous." *New York Times* (New York City), March 5, 1972, D21.
International Council of Museums. 2017. *ICOM Code of Ethics for Museums*. Paris: ICOM.
Kennedy, Randy. 2008. "National Academy Sells Two Hudson River School Paintings to Bolster Its Finances (Published 2008)." *The New York Times*, December 5, 2008. https://www.nytimes.com/2008/12/06/arts/design/06acad.html.
Kingdon, John. 1995. *Agendas, Alternatives, and Public Policies*. New York: Longman.
Museum of Modern Art. 2020. *Collections Management Policy*. https://www.moma.org/momaorg/shared/pdfs/docs/about/Collections-Management-Policy-2020-04-20.pdf
Pogrebin, Robin. 2009. "Bill Seeks to Regulate Museums' Art Sales." *New York Times*, March 18, 2009, C1N.
Pogrebin, Robin. 2010a. "ArtsBeat: Board of Regents Ending Injunction against Museums' Art Sales." *New York Times*, September 14, 2010. https://archive.nytimes.com/artsbeat.blogs.nytimes.com/2010/09/14/board-of-regents-to-allow-special-rules-on-museums-sales-of-art-to-expire/.
Pogrebin, Robin. 2010b. "Sanctions End for National Academy, Which Sold Paintings." *New York Times*, October 19, 2010, C2N.
Price Waterhouse Cooper LLP. 2022. "Consolidated Financial Statements, June 30, 2022 and 2021." *MoMA*. https://www.moma.org/momaorg/shared/pdfs/docs/about/MoMAFY_22.pdf.

19

FUNDING THROUGH POLICY ATTACHMENT

An Examination of Funding for the Dawson City Museum

Robin Nelson

Support for community museums—that is, municipal and nonprofit museums focused on local heritage—in what we colonially call Canada is not the designated responsibility of any one level of government. Within this multi-level governance framework, museums can receive support targeting them from all levels of government and through professional associations. At the same time, museum activities intersect with a variety of policy areas, such as reconciliation or education. Museums can, therefore, receive support through a variety of departments, agencies, and associations relating to their programming objectives. To that end, they engage in policy attachment, making connections between their programs and diverse funding or policy initiatives to get the support they need to operate.

Using the Dawson City Museum as a case study, this chapter considers the ways community museums engage in policy attachment to maximize the support they receive. After discussing research on policy attachment, the chapter describes the Dawson City Museum case study. Examples of policy attachment related to economic objectives are provided within three themes—tourism, employment, and celebration. The discussion highlights how policy attachment enabled the Museum to grow their budget and expand their operations. However, connections to temporary objectives and programs encouraged growth beyond what was sustainable with more targeted programs and earned revenues. Policy attachment is a valuable strategy, but relies on the availability of labor for a variety of projects and a perceived need for the work of policy attachment, as well as the relevancy of diverse policy objectives to museum work.

DOI: 10.4324/9781003308003-24

Understanding Policy Attachment

According to Gray (2002), policy attachment is "the idea that policy development in certain policy areas takes place through the attachment of that area to other policy concerns" (80). Small and politically weak sectors like culture use attachment strategies to attract political attention, economic support, status, and/or social support (Doustaly and Gray 2008). These strategies are often described as reactive responses that use culture and shift policy focus from internal concerns to the detriment of the sector as part of instrumentalism. More broadly, instrumentalism involves the use of so-called instrumental objectives, such as those related to the economy like tourism, to justify cultural expenditures. Nisbett (2013) has complicated conceptions of both instrumentalism and policy attachment, arguing reality is more nuanced than is often portrayed. Her research demonstrates museums can proactively advocate for policy and justify cultural spending in so-called instrumental terms for projects that further their own mission and objectives. Building on Nisbett's understanding, this chapter uses the concept of policy attachment but does not assume strategies are reactive or necessarily detrimental to the sector.

In addition to considering policy attachment as a nuanced strategy, the chapter addresses a gap in the levels of government typically considered in policy attachment research. The literature on policy attachment is most robust when considering the local level (Gray 2017; Robinson 2018; Dick et al. 2021). However, policy attachment can and does occur at other levels. Notably, within what is now known as Canada,[1] community museums operate within a multilevel governance framework, which is considered herein.

As staff engage in policy attachment, they do not necessarily identify their work as attachment strategies (e.g., Dewinter et al. 2020). For example, community museums and their associations engage in redefinitions of museum roles as part of both policy attachment *and* changing understandings within the community regarding priorities (Nelson 2021). Further, there is no agreement regarding what museum objectives are core or intrinsic and which are "instrumental" (Gibson 2008). As a result, the chapter does not discuss the intentionality of museum workers or argue policy attachment necessitates a move from core objectives. Instead, it focuses on examples where the Museum has sought funding or attention outside initiatives specifically targeting museums, such as grants associated with Yukon's museums policy or the federal Museums Assistance Program, with work connected to explicitly economic objectives, such as tourism.

Case Study: The Dawson City Museum

The Dawson City Museum (DCM) is a nonprofit community museum in Dawson City, Yukon.[2] It was established by the Klondike Tourist Bureau (now the Klondike Visitors Association or KVA) in 1953 then founded as an independent museum in 1957 and incorporated as a nonprofit in 1959. The Museum is housed in a government building—the Old Territorial Administration Building—for a fee of only 4,000 Canadian dollars (CAD) a year from the territorial government. It operated primarily through volunteer labor with some seasonal paid staff until 1975 when the board began hiring year-round employees, including a curator that acted as the director, thanks to a federal employment program. Staffing has fluctuated dramatically depending on the number of projects underway and the season due to the need for more staff during the summer when tourism causes an influx of visitors to Dawson City. Generally, the Museum has employed an executive director or similar position, one other year-round full-time employee (e.g., curator) as well as a variety of part time or contract staff. At its peak, the Museum's operating budget was just under a million dollars in 1994–5. However, the Museum's budget is more typically between 300,000 and 400,000 CAD. Prior to hiring a full-time, year-round staff person in 1975, the Museum operated on less than 5,000 CAD a year.

Until the 1980s, the largest single source of funding for the DCM was admissions. Other sources of earned income include an annual auction and gift shop revenues. The Museum is eligible for funding from the federal, territorial, and municipal governments as well as some nonprofit associations. In one instance, they even received a grant from a self-governing First Nation government—that is, the Tr'ondëk Hwëch'in. They have received an operating grant targeting museums or museums as a kind of tourist organization from the federal or territorial governments since the 1950s. The federal and territorial governments have also provided support through project funding targeting museums since the 1970s or 1980s, respectively. More importantly for a chapter on policy attachment, the Museum has received a variety of grants that do not directly target museums as they attach their activities to government or professional organizations' policy objectives outside of a heritage branch/department or museum associations.

The chapter relies on research conducted for the Dawson City Museum Project (Nelson 2023), asking: How has the Dawson City Museum evolved in relation to government policy and community action? We conducted 15 interviews with people that have had a relationship with the museum as an employee, volunteer, board member, and/or civil servant in the territorial government or Parks Canada. We also conducted archival research in the Dawson City Museum's extensive corporate archive, which contains records from the Museum's inception to today. Drawing on both the interviews and archival data, the chapter considers the Dawson City Museum as a case study to examine policy attachment in a relatively small community museum.

Policy Attachment at the Dawson City Museum

Before considering examples where the Museum attached itself to policy objectives not specific to museums for attention or funding, it is important to discuss why the DCM became incorporated as a museum. In the early 1950s, the Klondike Tourism Bureau opened the Museum as a tourist attraction that also preserved artifacts. Opening the Museum was a deliberate strategy for community member's plans to develop the tourism industry around the Klondike Gold Rush. Volunteers applied for and received a grant from the federal government for museums in the Yukon, but the check was written to the Museum and not the tourism bureau. Community members founded the Museum as an independent organization and incorporated to continue receiving and cashing the 500-dollar operating grant from the federal then territorial governments. As a founding member recalled:

> The Klondike Visitor's Association were instigators of our Museum. They were the sponsors. I just ran [it], so what could we do? I went to the bank and I said, "how can we cash this cheque?" He says, "you can't, you have to deposit it." We had no account to deposit it, so I phoned our minister ... and I said, "I just formed a new society, you're the president and the secretary-treasurer." Knowing how I did things, he said "that's fine with me," so that was it. (Gaundroue and Gaundroue 1973)

At the time, the operating grant was the only government funding available that targeted community museums in the Yukon. While both the federal and territorial government eventually developed community museum funding programs in the 1970s and 1980s respectively, Museum volunteers and staff had to engage in forms of policy attachment to grow their budget and enable the Museum to operate year-round because earned revenues were not enough to support staff.

The first year-round full-time curator, hired through an employment grant in 1975, started the tradition of seeking funding from wherever possible. In 1980, a member of the Yukon Legislative Assembly wrote to the director, saying: "I know you'll be your ingenious self, finding grants where no one else could" (McCall 1980). Finding grants "where no one else could" involved attaching the Museum's work to a variety of areas where funding or attention was more easily available. In this chapter, we provide examples of attachment to economically oriented examples, including tourism, employment policy, and celebrations.

Tourism

As described above, tourism and serving as a tourist destination have been central to the DCM's work since its conception as part of a tourism bureau's activities. Importantly, the tourism industry is central to the development of community museums more broadly in Yukon. As stated in a 1980 report on the sector:

> Few Canadian Community Museums are as closely tied to the Tourist Industry as those located in Yukon. With visitors to the area outnumbering residents by, at least, ten to one, museum activities are chiefly tourist motivated, frequently at the expense of other museum responsibilities. (Kyte 1980, 4)

Considering museums' close ties to the tourism industry, this section outlines the ways that the museum sector's relationship to tourism in the Yukon has benefited the Dawson City Museum through increased funding or attention obtained through advocacy.

First, the connection to tourism, which occurred within government *and* the museum community, bolstered arguments for the development of a territorial support program specific to museums. When Yukon created a Tourism Branch in 1962, the Branch saw the preservation of historical resources as part of the development of the sector because a romanticized conception of Yukon's history was a key tourism resource. In Dawson City specifically, conceptions of the Klondike Gold Rush lured tourists to the region (Graham 1972). As a result, when the federal government stopped providing funding for Yukon museums in the 1960s, the Tourism Branch took over, providing community museums with an operating grant *if* they contributed to the development of tourism (Yukon 1976).

In the 1980s, arguments for a new territorial support program for community museums worked to elevate arguments about the inherent value of heritage and the value of heritage for Yukoners. However, the heritage community continued to also highlight the importance of tourism, which was key to their successful efforts. For example, a 1984 submission on heritage legislation from the Yukon Historical and Museums Association stated, "It is clear that the heritage of a local area is precisely what interests the tourist and it is the signs and flavour of the visible past that compensates the tourist for his expenditures" (3). The eventual Museum policy was released only after a commitment stressed in both the Yukon Economic Strategy and Yukon Tourism Action Plan. It emphasized both ideas—that is, museums are important socially for Yukoners and economically for tourism (Yukon Tourism 1989).

Second, an attachment to tourism provided the Dawson City Museum with the attention needed to argue for funding. Most notably, the Canada-Yukon Interim Subsidiary Agreement on Tourism Development was signed in 1980. The agreement emphasized the importance of tourism for Yukon as a sector that ranked below only mining in terms of its contributions to the economy

(Hawkins 1981). The DCM argued for and received funding to reconstruct the roof as part of the agreement (Ross 1982). Eventually, the Museum also received funding for the foundation (Dawson City Museum and Historical Society 1983), which started 2.9 million dollars in renovations in the mid-1980s. While the renovation funding did not come from the tourism agreement, the agreement contributed to the attention politician's paid to the DCM and its needs at the time.

An attachment to tourism objectives has also enabled the DCM to seek support from the Klondike Visitors' Association (KVA)—that is, the nonprofit tourism sector organization. For example, the KVA loaned the DCM money to purchase a collection in 1975 (Snowalter 1975). Then, the Museum received the KVA's first grant from the Community Trust Fund for Dawson nonprofits' capital projects (Whitehorse Star 1978).

In short, community museums' relationship to tourism, emphasized in advocacy documents, shaped the support they received and the development of a policy more specifically targeting museums. Looking at the Dawson City Museum more specifically, attachment to tourism has, at times, led to the attention needed to successfully advocate for funding. That being said, the connection to tourism is often assumed and is implicit within much of the support museums receive in the territory. As such, it differs from the following example—employment related funding—which has required more active work to (re)attach the Museum to specific policy objectives over time.

Employment Policy and Community Development

The DCM began accessing funding to address unemployment from the federal government starting in 1975. In the 1980s and 1990s, there were a range of employment funding opportunities available from the federal and territorial governments. Those opportunities have evolved overtime as seen with a shift from encouraging winter employment to student employment. Considering the different programs that the Museum has accessed, this section outlines the policy objectives to which the Museum has attached as it seeks out and applies for funding itself in the interest of increasing the staff at the DCM.

The Museum has actively sought out programs that provide funding for jobs targeting unemployed peoples and those on social assistance. Many of these programs were designed as counter-cyclical policy tools to address unemployment issues during periods of economic downturns (Roy and Wong 1998, 2000). For example, the Local Initiatives Program was a federal program that aimed to address unemployment in regions of deindustrialization during the 1970s. Other examples of programs the DCM accessed or attempted to access include Canada Works, Canada Community Development Projects,

Job Development (federal), Unemployment Insurance Job Creation Program (federal), and Local Employment Opportunities Program (territorial).

As the DCM applied for these grants and made a case for themselves in their applications, they became an active participant in the primary policy objective to keep people in the workforce and, as a result, help them avoid a reliance on social programs. As a former director noted,

> [The federal grants officer] talked to me about the importance of keeping people employed. The thing with social assistance is they're no longer tied to the workforce. [Through these programs] you keep people tied to the workforce; you continue them working … (Interview)

This policy objective worked well in Dawson City because it was a seasonal town without enough work for the population.

Reflecting the secondary policy objectives, funded projects were meant to provide useful services to communities, such as promoting economic recovery, improving community assets, or providing community services. These secondary goals aligned well with the Museum's needs. The Museum was able to argue for labor to support a variety of projects that would ultimately contribute to the professionalization of the organization from the 1970s to the 1990s, including capital projects, administrative work, and revenue-generating activities.

Relatedly, in 1989 the Yukon Government launched the Community Development Fund (CDF), which replaced the Local Employment Opportunities Program. While CDF is not exclusively an employment policy, it aims to "create employment opportunities" (Yukon 2023) continues to be a core objective. As seen with the employment programs, there are additional objectives, such as improving community services and providing training. The Museum has argued for and received CDF funding for projects that enhanced their ongoing work, such as the development of finding aids for photos, capital projects, and the creation of mannequins for the permanent exhibitions.

The DCM has also sought out funding to address youth unemployment and training needs. These programs first emerged in the 1970s when young baby boomers began entering the job market, causing an increase in youth unemployment. At the time, the federal government feared social unrest associated with youth unemployment (Roy and Wong 1998, 2000). The availability of funding to address youth unemployment expanded in the 1980s and 1990s as the federal government began incentivizing subnational governments to create their own programs. The DCM was able to argue for funding that ultimately expanded the summer programming for tourists. Due to the importance of summer employment to the often seasonal museum sector, in the late 1990s student summer employment programs functionally became part of federal museum policy with the Canadian Museums

Association administering Young Canada Works in Heritage. The Canadian Council of Archives and the Canadian Library Association also began administering programs, which the DCM has accessed due to its library and archival functions.

In short, direct employment programs developed in the 1970s to keep people in the workforce, avoid reliance on social programs, and prevent civil unrest associated with youth unemployment. At the DCM, staff actively engaged in relationship building with the responsible grants officer to attach their work to the changing secondary objectives. Interview participants working into the 1990s discussed ongoing efforts to learn about changing and new programs. As a result, they were able to attach projects they wanted to achieve, such as developing new exhibition cases, to a well-funded policy objective. In the 1990s, direct job creation programs were phased out at the federal level, and student employment programs began targeting museums, libraries, and archives through their associations. As a result, the use of employment programs to support winter employment and a variety of projects became less tenable as a strategy. That being said, the Community Development Fund and youth programs continue to be relevant today.

Anniversary Celebrations

The 1990s involved several important anniversaries in the Yukon, such as the 100th anniversary of the Klondike Gold Rush. The territory formed the Yukon Anniversaries Commission, which received funding from the tourism sub-agreement from the territorial government, as part of their tourism action plan (Yukon 1988). Anniversary celebrations are included separate from tourism due to the Commission's goal to also increase Yukoner's understanding of who they were. Following the Commission's creation, the DCM received a recommendation from a civil servant in the Heritage Branch to deliberately take advantage of the available funding and attention to celebrations (Dawson City Museum 1990). The museum related grants from the territory also began focusing on providing attractions to visitors during this period (Yukon 1994). As a result, the DCM actively used available grants for celebratory activities to gain attention and expand their operations.

Throughout the 1990s, the DCM positioned itself as a key actor in the territory's celebratory work, at first using the museum related funding available. For example, they focused exhibition development on anniversaries. Klondike Gold was a traveling exhibition celebrating the 100th anniversary of the Klondike Gold Rush. They also had temporary exhibitions on the centennial of the Yukon Order of Pioneers and Yukon civic government in relation to the anniversary of the Yukon Territory Act (Swackhammer 1997). Due in part to its anniversary related work, the Museum became active with local Centennial Anniversaries Committee to help plan activities that used the Yukon Government Tourism Infrastructure money. As a result, the Museum director was able to successfully argue for funding to subsidize student employment from the municipality, which contributed to an expansion of their summer offerings for tourists with costumed interpretation both within and outside their building.

The Dawson City Museum's active participation in a decade of celebratory activities through exhibitions, student interpretations for tourists, and participation on committees in Dawson City led to more attention paid to the Museum. The attention helped the Museum attract more funding, including donations from private individuals. One family's donation to commemorate a grandfather with a connection to the Klondike Gold Rush providing the initial support needed to fund a new exhibition space and storage. Importantly, the attention did not simply lead to financial support. For example, the Museum was able to argue for the use of necessary tools (laptop, fax machine, printer) from the Yukon Anniversaries Commission to support their work developing a database (Richthammer 1998). Notably, the projects developed expanded work the museum was already doing.

Discussion

The examples provided are nuanced. To some extent, they illustrate a top-down control of museum objectives according to the available funding. However, finding, accessing, and/or advocating for the funding programs discussed is an active process. In particular, the tourism example demonstrates advocacy work—that is, submitting briefs and making arguments to government officials—as important. Museum directors, contractors, and volunteers interviewed described the work and relationships building needed to seek out funding opportunities related to employment. Contributing to a policy objective with significant attention involved focusing some of the labor at the DCM toward that objective for a decade. Notably, the Museum was most successful at this policy attachment work from 1975 up to the end of the 1990s. There are several intersecting and overlapping explanations for the change.

First and most importantly, people with relevant skills and the time to invest in relationship building, finding funding opportunities outside of heritage branches within a multi-level governance framework, and applying for those grants are needed. From 1970s to the 1990s, there were multiple programs available to support labor at the Museum year-round, meaning core staff could engage in policy attachment work as temporary staff completed museum projects when they were less busy in the winter. The Museum developed a pool of trained individuals who were available to do and complete projects independently. Some of these people even filled their grant applications to support the projects they would lead (Interviews).

However, they were not hired and paid as full-time, year-round staff. Unfortunately for the DCM, several of these key individuals left Dawson City in the late 1990s or early 2000s. The limited number of permanent staff then took on responsibility for the projects, leaving little time for the work of policy attachment or multiple ongoing projects.

Second, with more museum operational funding, there is less of a need to engage in multiple projects to generate funding that would also incidentally support or indirectly enable earned revenues to support the Museum's core staff. From 2002 to 2023, the DCM's operational grant from Yukon government has increased from 23,500 to 130,000 CAD. With an additional annual special project grant and other earned revenues, the Museum is able to comfortably support two full-time, year-round staff members and pay for its operations. Comparatively, when the Museum hired its first year-round curator/director in 1975, the position was only possible due to an employment program. Since there is less of a need to seek funding outside the Yukon Heritage Branch, Museum staff are able to focus their time and effort on work seen as crucial to museum staff, such as developing stronger relationships with the Tr'ondëk Hwëch'in and completing a renewal of their permanent exhibitions. However, this also means the Museum engages in fewer projects and employs fewer people. As a result, it is seen as less of a community hub than it was in the 1990s (interviews).

Third, funding programs with objectives that did not explicitly target museums but aligned with the Dawson City Museum's objectives were available and more accessible to staff in the past. The 1990s saw an intersection in the availability of these programs, leading to increased attention and support that enabled the Museum to expand their activities. However, without these intersecting programs, the expansion was ultimately unsustainable. For example, as part of a donation of library and archival materials during celebrations for the anniversary of Klondike Gold Rush, the Museum committed to supporting this collection with a full-time librarian/archivist. The Museum has been unable to fulfill this promise into the 21st century.

Conclusion

In short, policy attachment is a key strategy that can enable museums to develop and expand their activities. However, it relies on the availability of personnel at the Museum to do the work of policy attachment and trained individuals in the community available for short-term contracts associated with project-based work. It also necessitates aligning government priorities with work that the Museum would like to or needs to do. The use of funding associated with diverse policy objectives can help museums expand their work, but without the continued availability of these programs and/or ongoing policy attachment strategies to (re)attach the museum to diverse objectives expansion can be unsustainable. Moreover, with sufficient operational funding for key staff, there is less of a need to engage in this work.

Notes

1 The chapter uses colonial terms for contemporary jurisdictions, including what is now commonly called Canada. However, the author acknowledges that Canada is a nation-state founded on the territory of many nations. The land has many names, depending on the region and Indigenous community consulted (e.g., Turtle Island).
2 What is now, Dawson City is on the traditional territory of the Tr'ondëk Hwëch'in.

References

Dawson City Museum. 1990, April 27. *AGM Minutes. Digital File*. Dawson City Museum Corporate Archives.

Dawson City Museum and Historical Society. 1983. "Dawson Museum News." *Newsletter* 13: 39–41.

Dewinter, Hanne, Kris Rutten, and Lieve Bradt. 2020. "Policy Attachment in the Arts: The Underlying Agendas of Arts' Social Role." *Cultural Trends* 29 (2): 96–111. 10.1080/09548963.2020.1763780

Dick, Ben, Sharon Jeannotte, and Kelly Hill. 2021. "Positioning Culture within Canadian Municipalities." *Culture and Local Governance* 6 (1): 1–75. 10.18192/clg-cgl.v6i1.4550

Doustaly, Cécile and Gray, Clive. 2008. "Labour and the Arts: Managing Transformations?" *Observatoire de la société britannique* 8: 319–38. 10.4000/osb.953

Gaundroue, Margretta and Elmer Gaundroue. 1973. Interview by Kathleen "Mike" Dalton. Dawson City, Yukon. August 19, 1973. Accessed: https://oharchives.library.uaf.edu/78/78-54-01_and_02.mp3

Gibson, Lisanne. 2008. "In Defence of Instrumentality." *Cultural Trends* 17 (4): 247–257.

Graham, R. D. 1972. Yukon Tourism 1972 Annual Report: A Review of the Yukon Travel Industry 1962–72.

Gray, Clive. 2002. "Local Government and the Arts." *Local Government Studies* 28 (1): 77–90. 10.1080/714004133

Gray, Clive. 2017. "Local Government and the Arts Revisited." *Local Government Studies* 43 (3): 315–22. 10.1080/03003930.2016.1269758

Hawkins, Lois. 1981. Manpower and Labour Branch. Consumer and Corporate Affairs. Canada. August 1981. Preliminary Draft: A Manpower Perspective on Yukon's Tourism Industry. Government of Canada.

Kyte, John E. 1980, November. Museums in Yukon: A Profile and Training Report. Prepared for Yukon Historical and Museums Association.

McCall, Meg. 1980, February 7. *Letter to Museum Director. 5.5.50. Box 5*. Dawson City Museum Corporate Archives.

Museum Director. 1979, July 23. *Director's Report. Digital File*. Dawson City Museum Corporate Archives.

Nelson, Robin. 2021. "Community Museum Governance: The (Re)Definition of Sectoral Representation and Policy Instruments in Ontario." PhD diss. (University of Ottawa, 2021).

Nelson, Robin. 2023. "The Dawson City Museum Project: A Community Engaged Research Project." *Museoception*. Accessed: https://museoception.ca/projects/dawson-city-museum-project/

Nisbett, Melissa. 2013. "New Perspectives on Instrumentalism: An Empirical Study of Cultural Diplomacy." *International Journal of Cultural Policy* 19 (5): 557–75. 10.1080/10286632.2012.704628
Ritchthammer, John. 1998. *Letter to the Yukon Anniversaries Commission. Correspondence Director 1997 1998. Box 25.* Dawson City Museum Corporate Archives.
Robinson, Helena. 2018. "Cultural Policy, Local Government and Museums: An Australian Perspective." *Local Government Studies* 44 (5): 719–38. 10.1080/03003930.2018.1488688
Ross, Brian. 1982, September. *Letter to the Deputy Minister of Tourism, Heritage and Cultural Affairs. 7.7.10. Box 5.* Dawson City Museum Corporate Archives.
Roy, Arun S. and Ging Wong. 1998, December. *Job Creation Programs: Evaluation Lessons.* https://publications.gc.ca/collections/collection_2013/rhdcc-hrsdc/RH64-103-1998-eng.pdf
Roy, Arun S. and Gina Wong. 2000. "Direct Job Creation Programs: Evaluation Lessons on Effectiveness." *Canadian Public Policy* 26 (2): 157–69.
Snowalter, Mirian. 1975, October 31. "Dawson Museum Society Finds Escape from Hole." *Whitehorse Daily Star*. p. 21.
Swackhammer, Mac. 1997, March 21. *Letter to the Legislative Assembly Office. Correspondence: Director 1997–1998. Box 25.* Dawson City Museum Corporate Archives.
Yukon. 1976, March 2. *Yukon Legislative Assembly Debates & Procedures.* https://yukonassembly.ca/sites/default/files/inline-files/Debates-Proceedings-23-5-1976-03-02-Number-9.pdf
Yukon. 1988. *Yukon Tourism Action Plan.*
Yukon. 1994, January 11. *Yukon Legislative Assembly Debates & Procedures.* https://yukonassembly.ca/sites/default/files/hansard/28-1-080.html
Yukon. 2023. "Community Development Fund Program: Guidelines and Application." Accessed: https://yukon.ca/sites/yukon.ca/files/ecdev/ecdev-forms/ecdev-community-development-fund-application-form-yg4665.pdf
Yukon Historical and Museums Association. 1984. *A Submission to the Government of Yukon Concerning the Proposed New Heritage Legislation.*
Yukon Historical and Museums Association. 1994, December. "Summary: Yukon Museum Activities." *YHMA Newsletter:* 5–6.
Yukon Tourism. 1989. *Museums Policy.* Accessed: https://emrlibrary.gov.yk.ca/yukon2000/museums-policy.pdf
Whitehorse Star. 1978, August. "Museum Gets First KVA Grant." *Whitehorse Star.*

20

CONTEXTUALIZING THE POTENTIAL OF NFTs IN FINANCIAL GOVERNANCE OF ART MUSEUMS

Wen Guo

Assistant Professor, Department of Art Education, Florida State University, Tallahassee, FL, USA

A non-fungible token (NFT) refers to a unique unit of data registered on a blockchain. As a form of digital ledger, it is proof of ownership of collective digital property. According to a study developed by Nonfungible.com[1] and L'Atelier owned by BNP Paribas,[2] sales of NFTs, including digital art, video game assets, and property/land in the metaverse spiked 21,000% to more than $17 billion in 2021 in comparison to a total of 82 million in 2020 (Brown 2022). Since "Quantum" (2014–21) of Kevin McCoy and "CryptoPunk" sold at $1.4 Million and $11.8 million, respectively, at the Sotheby's auction in 2021 (Liscia 2021), NFTs, as a new approach to proving the ownership and scarcity of digital art and experiences, have opened new pathways for creating, trading, collecting, and appreciating art.

In the past two years, many leading art institutions worldwide have hosted intriguing dialogs on the myth and future of NFTs. Pérez Art Museum Miami, Museum of Modern Art, Tampa Museum of Art, Brattleboro Museum & Art Center, and Asia Art Center in Taipei hosted instructional seminars on the production and trade of NFTs (CUSEUM 2022). Quite a few large institutions in the United States and Europe had taken the initiative to experiment with NFTs during the COVID pandemic when arts and cultural institutions were pushed to reexamine their resistance to digital technologies and strategize their digital transformation for a changing world. For instance, Uffizi in Florence sold an NFT rendition of Michelangelo's "Doni Tondo" (1504–6) (Mattei 2022). Smaller institutions like The Whitworth at the University of Manchester test alternative models of financing social art practice. They experimented with the new funding model using the sale proceeds of the NFT image of William Blake's *The Ancient of Days* to fund socially beneficial projects in collaboration with local communities (Harris 2021).

DOI: 10.4324/9781003308003-25

Moreover, two museums focusing on presenting NFT arts were established in 2022. The Seattle NFT Museum was launched by a partnership of two tech entrepreneurs, Jennifer Wong and Peter Hamilton, on January 14, 2022, to showcase original blockchain-based digital artworks. It is the first physical NFT museum to show NFT artworks created by international and local artists (Seymour 2022). Musee Dezentral is the world's first virtual NFT museum founded on a blockchain (CUSEUM 2022). The decentralized nature of the museum allows visitors to feature their own NFTs in its collection. Meanwhile, most museums are still held back from jumping on the bandwagon of the NFT craze by the current debates and controversies around the social, artistic, and financial implications of the NFTs.

This chapter attempts to review and discuss the burgeoning conversations of the new trend of NFT, focusing on its implications on the financial governance of museum management. By examining scholarly studies and gray literature, this chapter situates the emerging dialogs on NFTs at the intersection of existing research on funding strategies, digital transformation, technology adoption, and financial governance of art museums.

Introducing Blockchains, Smart Contracts, and NFTs

Blockchain and smart contracts are critical technical and economic innovations (Liebenau and Elaluf-Calderwood 2016) that enable the preservation and trading of NFTs. A blockchain is a shared ledger that continually and securely updates the record of digital property transactions across a peer-to-peer network. It is a reliable solution to transactions based on the assumption that no human or machine can be fully trusted (Morisse 2015). Blockchain reduces the time needed for transactions and solves the security problem in transaction processes by not allowing a single member across a distributed network to change the record of transactions (Liebenau and Elaluf-Calderwood 2016). The technology of blockchain enables the existence of cryptocurrency (e.g., Bitcoin, Ethereum, Tether). Smart contracts are computer programs or tokens developed and stored in blockchain technology (Giancaspro 2017). Similar to a real-world contract, a smart contract functions as a sale agreement that assigns and reassigns ownership in a trading process (Giancaspro 2017). As a self-executing computer program based on if-then logic, a smart contract removes the need for the involvement of an intermediary or trusted third parties for transactions (Giancaspro 2017).

NFTs are perceived as digital property traded with cryptocurrency and encoded with smart contracts of Ethereum on a blockchain (Liebenau and Elaluf-Calderwood 2016). Unlike cryptocurrencies, smart contracts allow each NFT work to be coded with unique I.P. and identity information deemed critical by creators (Giancaspro 2017). Thus, blockchain technology can reduce the probability of copyright infringements for digital artworks and make the history of ownership transparent (Vasan et al. 2022). NFTs are not only minted and traded as visual artworks. NFTs also include other items, including music, avatars and profile pictures (PFPs), photography, digital objects in games, domain names, event tickets, and membership passes that register on a blockchain, and much more (Valeonti et al. 2021). The various forms of NFTs imply their application of broader relevance in the museum in addition to the current focus on the exhibition and acquisition of NFT arts. These implications will be discussed shortly. Table 20.1 lists the definitions and examples of the most popular emerging forms of NFTs.

The Potential of NFTs in Changing Financial Governance of Art Museums

In general, most art museums around the globe have a revenue structure constituted by four pillars: various forms of philanthropic contributions from private donors, direct government subsidies and tax incentives, grants from public charity organizations and private philanthropic organizations, and earned income through sales of admission, merchandise, advertisement, and membership. Art museums in the United States follow a more business-like tradition (Anglo-American Model) that relies more on private donations and service pricing, while their European counterparts have a more public tradition based on a higher level of government funding (Camarero et al. 2011). The distribution of financial resources in the museum sector is highly inequitable. As the amount of donation highly correlates with the prestige of art museums (Shekhtman and Barabasi 2022), private donations tend to be concentrated in the few flagship and elite museums. Moreover, smaller museums also do not have the social capital and financial resources to compete with their more established counterparts for funding from foundations (Bellamy et al. 2015). The outbreak of COVID led to the loss of revenue from closing their physical space to the cancellation of donor gifts, memberships, and fundraising galas. More than 30% of Americans claimed to reduce their charitable giving in 2021 (Candid, 2023). Quite a few cultural institutions struggled with the slow recovery of their attendance, even post-COVID (American Alliance of Museums 2021; Small 2022). The disruptive public health disaster reminded the roughly 35,000 museums of their fragile development strategies that either highly rely on public support or compete for aging donors and the several hundred private philanthropic foundations. An article of Artnet News suggested that about 30% of Americans would reduce their charitable giving, and the top seven causes they would like to support did not include arts and cultural organizations (Wolf 2020).

In response to the changing landscape of fundraising catalyzed by the COVID crisis, several art museums have engaged with NFTs to develop new ways of generating earned income, raising funds, or enriching their collections. For example, during the opening of "Hokusai: The Great Picture Book

TABLE 20.1 Forms of NFT collectibles

Type of NFTs	*Definition*	*Sample collectible project*	*Sample marketplace (To mint, buy, or sell)*
One-of-one (1/1) artwork	In contrast with multi-edition NFTs, 1/1 refers to an artwork issued as a single or unique edition.	Beeple XCOPY	Opensea SuperRare Asyncmarket LaCollection
Multi-edition NFTs (Rare, limited, open edition)	Creators of a minted NFT can choose to issue more than one edition of their work. These editions look identical but have their unique edition number and/or token I.D. A rare digital creation may be sold and owned by no more than ten collectors at any given time. An open edition creation does not have a predetermined number of creations.	Max Pain and Frens (Open edition)	Opensea Zora Manifold LaCollection
Digital extension of original masterpieces	Digital ownership of collections in museums and cultural institutions.	SenseTime and Dunhuang Michelangelo's Doni Tondo (1505–6)	Cinello LaCollection
Generative art	Artworks created by artificial intelligence (AI), generative algorithms, or physical robots.	Naon Fidenza	Art Blocks Opensea
Music NFTs	NFTs linked to all kinds of music (e.g., single songs, albums, music videos, generative music).	Justin Blau (3LAU)	Royal
Profile Picture (PFP) and Avatar	Digital or algorithmically generated cartoonish or pixelated characters or designs. They are typically used as profile pictures for Web 2 and Web 3 social media platforms.	CryptoPunks	Opensea Reddit
NFT event tickets	Tickets on a blockchain that give access to live or virtual events.	Scope Art Show	Seatlab Yellow Heart GUTS Ticket

(Continued)

TABLE 20.1 (Continued)

Type of NFTs	*Definition*	*Sample collectible project*	*Sample marketplace (To mint, buy, or sell)*
NFT membership passes	Memberships on a blockchain that grant exclusive access to benefits, status, and perks of communities and brands.	Adidas Bored Ape Yacht Club (BAYC)	Hang.xyz
Domain names	Blockchain domain names independent of any third-party providers and the actual Internet.	.io.crypto.sol	Unstoppable domain Bonfida
Gamified NFTs	Gaming resources programmed as NFTs to be traded and exchanged for financial reward-winning outcomes.	Axie Infinity	RareRooms
Other Collectibles	Any digital files with unique identifiers to track down their transaction history and prove ownership.	NBA Top Shot	All websites mentioned above and others

of Everything" which displayed a collection of rare and rediscovered prints by artist Katsushika Hokusai, the British Museum launched a series of NFT postcards of his prints in collaboration with LaCollection, a service platform that mints, exhibits, and trades NFTs of masterpieces and original artworks for cultural institutions and collectors (Harris 2022). The museum sold the artist's first edition of "The Great Wave" for 10.6 ETH, which equaled approximately $45,000 at that time (Harris 2022). The museum continued its collaboration with LaCollection by selling 20 NFTs of J. M. W. Turner's watercolors. Partnering with Vastari Labs, the Whitworth Art Gallery in Manchester minted an NFT drop of *The Ancient of Days* by William Blake to sell it on a marketplace based on Tezo, an eco-friendly blockchain. The £30,000 (approximately $40,300) raised by selling the artwork was contributed to a fund for socially beneficial projects in the local community. In the United States, the Institute of Contemporary Art (ICA), Miami, and the San José Museum of Art (SJMA) added NFT artworks to their collections. A trustee of ICA gifted CryptoPunk 5293 to the museum (SJMA 2021; Whiddington 2022). The SJMA premiered a new NFT commission by Rashaad Newsome. In addition to directly incorporating NFTs into programs and exhibitions of museums, a small number of museums, such as MoMA, the Museum of Chinese in America (MOCA), and ICA, Miami, have also started accepting cryptocurrency donations (Lu, 2022).

The successful attempts of incorporating NFTs into programs and fundraising strategies of art museums resonate with the recent call for a fieldwide reimagination of arts funding and philanthropy to align with the core values and lifestyles of Millennial and Gen Z donors (Carr 2021; Wolf 2020). Integrating NFTs in the museum sector may transform museum visitor experiences, pricing, and promotion of their experiences, consumption, and donation behaviors of museum audiences. The immense potential of NFTs in changing the financial operation of art museums lies in their disruption of our established understanding of digital ownership, creation and distribution of value, authenticity, collector/visitor/donor/user status, and decentralized branding and distribution (Hofstetter et al. 2022). In particular, I would like to discuss the opportunities and challenges created by NFTs for the financial governance of art museums.

NFTs in Art Museums' Digital Transformation

The various forms of NFTs and blockchain technology could deepen the digital transformation of art museums to offer a better visitor experience in both their physical and virtual space. They may also provide solutions to lowering program and operational costs and new sources of income. For instance, the NFT ticket/membership purchases and cryptocurrency donations made by visitors and members can reduce transaction fees for museums.

It is worth noting that state-financed museums are generally not permitted to sell their artworks, with the exception of deaccessioning in American museums (Finkel 2009). However, it is possible for art museums to create and sell limited-edition NFTs of their collections, similar to other spin-off products based on their collections. NFT airdrop is known as the free distribution of NFTs to a specific group of people. One only needs to pay a gas fee[3] to mint an NFT airdrop (Gumelar 2023). NFTs airdropped by museums allow museum fans to trade in the secondary market as a way to build intimate relationships and share original stories or sentiments attached to the digital tokens sealed by museums. As creators of the NFTs, art museums or commissioned artists can use smart contracts to earn continuous royalties for each sale of their creation automatically. This new way of preserving one's museum experience may generate long-term value for both individuals and museums. The possibility of attaching rich ownership history to an NFT distinguishes it from the current merchandise offered by museums. The experience of museum visitors and donors can be preserved in perpetuity through digital tickets/memberships/donations unique to everyone. It has the potential to attract more digital natives to build new types of relationships with museums that transcend geographic boundaries. The added value of NFTs to visitors' experience is tokenized into an immutable and public part of the history of museums.

Moreover, art museums have invested more resources to enhance their digital offerings and make their physical experience more interactive. The decentralized nature of NFTs rewards and empowers creators of all kinds to generate and share their digital expressions on their terms. As user-generated content is crucial for the existence and sustainability of virtual worlds, museums may partner with blockchain platforms, marketplaces, or other Web3 tech companies, which refers to business establishments operated on the basis of various Internet applications of blockchain technology (Murray et al. 2023), to design affordable educational programs about user-generated content and their relationships with the expanding horizon of digital worlds.

Reimagine Funding Models Inspired by NFTs

The next generation of funders seeks to play an active role in solving global challenges through technology and creating positive social change through impact investment (Buntz 2022; Konstantinou and Jones 2022). The new generation of funders is yearning to see the role of the arts in challenging social injustice and changing how the social and economic system works (Wolf 2020). For example, the museum sector has been reflecting on their colonial history and taking measures carefully of their ownership of artifacts unjustly acquired from countries of the global south as well as the digital data associated with these artifacts. On top of the heated debates on ethical and legal concerns of restitutions, museums are currently challenged by financial constraints and the difficulty of identifying source communities. The fundamental moral and practical challenge lies in the dilemma between museums' mission of promoting and protecting cultural heritage and facilitating the radical redistribution of cultural heritage that belongs to all humankind (Matthes 2017). NFTs and blockchains may offer cost-effective and innovative solutions to build global partnerships to handle and present these artifacts and address the power imbalances and inequalities (Ali 2020). The cost can be shared among participating museums, public funders, and private donors based on the common pool model that treats museum digital resources as common goods that belong to us all (Jung 2022). The model emphasizes the educational mission of museums and allows them to "share collections and rights of use digitally in one centralized location among global museums" (Jung 2022, 2) by applying a variety of open licenses for reuse based on the fair use copyright principle.

Alternatively, museums can partner with a third party that represents the source community or the public to create, control, and/or manage the circulation and distribution of the ownership of digital copies of their collections. Looty, an NFT restitution project, used a legal process to render 3D NFT copies of looted artifacts in prominent institutions. They released a unique set of 1:1 designs of 25 NFTs of looted Benin Bronzes in the British Museum in May 2022. In total, 20% of the sale proceeds will be used to support artists under the age of 25 from the African continent (Abrams 2022). The sales data of the project is still unknown and ethical issues regarding digital ownership have emerged for further debate. However, this project inspires museums to consider innovative models of allocating and redistributing financial resources and build equitable partnerships through NFTs toward justice when the restitution process is still open to dialog.

The cuts in state funding for art museums have increased their reliance on the financial support of private donors (i.e., dealers, galleries, wealthy individuals, and corporate patrons). Such reliance creates exclusive circles of supporters who either become board members of art museums or control resource allocation through restricted funds (Zarobell 2017). This allows them to be involved in the decision-making of collections, exhibitions, programs, and critical governance aspects in art museums. Their exercise of power may damage the public integrity of art museums in carrying out their missions. Moreover, the status of an art museum is granted by its legacies rooted in mutually reinforcing colonialism, white supremacy, and capitalism that exploit and marginalize people of color.

The decentralized nature of NFTs resonates with the ongoing movement of disrupting the hierarchical, exclusive, opaque, and illiquid art market. NFTs make the art market more accessible and transparent for the public by connecting patrons and artists directly. The disintermediation[4] of traditional gatekeepers in the art market serves as a premise for art museums to reconsider their reliance on resources and assets held by the very few high-net-worth elite collectors/investors and institutions (i.e., galleries and auction houses) that represent their wealth and taste (Brown 2020). The proof-based marketplaces on blockchains can potentially lower transaction costs (i.e., circulation, insurance, conservation, fundraising, etc.). Art museums have been paying for discovering, presenting, and collecting artworks. Artists representing historically marginalized groups can gain direct access to global markets. They have started changing the wealth calculus[5] that has been Eurocentric and white-dominant (Whitaker 2019; Evans 2022). Thus, art museums that commit to decolonizing the global art ecosystem could better achieve their mission by identifying and supporting emerging artists, female artists, and artists of color through engaging with NFTs.

Moreover, the transparent record of historical ownership of artworks disrupts the opaque traditional art market. Therefore, art museums engaging with NFTs is an investment in the next generation of donors, investors, and audiences by supporting emerging artists, disrupting oppressive cultural norms, and driving innovation. It is a forward-looking conversation about democratizing pathways to wealth creation and healing the current art ecosystem.

The Myths and Challenges of NFTs for Financial Governance of Museums

The expanded adoption of NFTs across the museum sector is still questioned due to the lack of legal frameworks and proof of their long-term value. Before jumping on the bandwagon of NFTs, museums need to consider the financial implications of the following challenges. First, although the average price of most NFT art sold in 2021 remains largely unchanged (Vasan et al. 2022), the trade volumes of NFTs dropped by 97% as a part of the $2 trillion wipeouts in the crypto sector since January of 2022 (Sullivan 2022). A mix of unpredictable factors on the demand side sways the market pricing of cryptocurrencies and NFTs. In particular, the value of NFTs still hinges on the collective belief that they are a viable product category and can survive in the long term (Zhang 2022). In particular, standard metrics to assess the quality of NFTs are yet to be developed (Sharma et al. 2022). Collectors are still more inclined to own physical artworks. It is challenging to measure and predict the value of donations and gifts in the form of NFTs.

Second, in addition to the high and irreversible gas fees of minting NFTs, museums may be subject to paying for substantial hidden costs of NFTs due to the murky legal and regulatory frameworks for the technical, trading, and copyright aspects of NFTs. It is not rare to see trade washing, lazy minting, copyright infringement, and unfair trade cases that either inflate the NFT market or leave unprotected investors in the limbo of scams and hacking incidents. As a result, the Italian government halted sales of NFTs based on masterpieces from its public art institutions in July 2022 (Mattei 2022). The investors will also be likely to face large amounts of taxes once the market becomes regulated by governments (Chalmers et al. 2022). Meanwhile, domestic and international legislation on mining operations and trading behaviors of cryptocurrencies will also have a ripple effect on NFTs (Sharma et al. 2022). It takes legal consultation and financial advising for museums to make case-by-case decisions when engaging with any NFT purchases, fundraising, and programming.

Third, although many artists and scholars have found that NFTs can disrupt the power structure of the traditional art market, they do not guarantee to deliver equitable outcomes as branded. Early adopters of NFTs reap profits not only from cutting off the intermediaries but also by exploiting the gap between the emergence of new technologies and the formulation of regulations (Merritt 2023). The inequitable distribution of knowledge and information challenges newcomers and arts institutions that already struggle with resources and funding to keep up with the technology. The technological process of creating NFTs constitutes at least the following steps: setting up a crypto wallet,[6] acquiring and/or placing cryptocurrencies into the wallet, connecting the crypto wallet to an NFT marketplace, and, finally, minting NFTs (Sharma et al. 2022). The learning curve of the tech-heavy process requires museums to take extra money and resources to develop educational materials and tech support for their stakeholders to understand (Whitaker 2019). In addition, the environmental footprints of NFTs may undermine the brand asset of museums that promote their stance on environmental and social justice or at least oblige museums to find partners and solutions on eco-friendly blockchain platforms.

In Closing

With all the facts and discussions above, the chapter presents a mix of potentialities and risks brought by NFTs to the museum sector. The concepts and practices around Web3 technologies inspire museum administrators to envision bold integration of NFTs and digital art to transform traditional museum experiences by handing over more authority to the public and exploring the potentiality of technology in alleviating their funding issues. The discussion on the potentialities of NFTs above neither tries to propose a technological solutionism for museums to address their current challenges nor amplify the aforementioned risks that are common for any economic and technological innovations. Although the hype of the NFTs and the value of status represented by them have calmed down, the true value of digital art creation and technological solutions to the fair use and trade of the creation will keep evolving into broader and more compelling use cases. Thus, the controversial status of the NFTs presents a unique and generative point of departure for museums to explore their boundaries of resource allocation and public engagement toward a more decentralized and transnational model of operation through small-scale experiments, investments, and partnerships.

Acknowledgment

This chapter is made possible with the invaluable support of Elise Pertusati, Gift Officer of Corporations and Foundations at the Smithsonian American Art Museum and Renwick Gallery, and Liza Strelka, Manager of Exhibition and Curatorial Planning at Smithsonian's Hirshhorn Museum and Sculpture Garden. They have made a significant contribution to the writing process of the chapter. Their time and effort are greatly appreciated.

Notes

1 Nonfungible.com was founded in 2018. It tracks decentralized asset transactions in real time on the Ethereum blockchain and provides data analysis and information services for NFT enthusiasts.
2 L'Atelier is a subsidiary company founded in 1978 by BNP Paribas, a French international banking group. This company provides analysis and insight regarding opportunities associated with technological innovation.
3 Gas fee measures the computational resources used to execute transactions in Ethereum transactions, regardless of success or failure of transactions (Ghelani 2022).
4 Disintermediation, known as "cutting out of middlemen," refers to market behaviors of removing intermediaries that connect different parties between product and customers in business transactions. These intermediaries include distributors, wholesalers, brokers, and agents. In creative industries, disintermediation refers to the decline or transformation of "the longstanding vertical and horizontal structures of the creative industries" (Massi et al. 2020; Walzer 2023, 50).
5 Afro-Caribbean artist Itzel Yard (aka IX Shells) sold her work "Dreaming at Dusk" for $2 million, setting the record for female NFT artists to date.
6 A crypto wallet refers to a software program or online service that stores and accesses users' cryptocurrencies securely by holding private keys.

References

Abrams, Amah-Rose. 2022, May 26. "Meet Looty, a New Project That Infiltrates Museums, Makes NFTs from Stolen Objects, and Sells Them to Fund Young African Artists." *Artnet News*. https://news.artnet.com/art-world/looty-nfts-digital-restitution-of-stolen-objects-2121054.

Ali, Siobhan. 2020, May 25. https://www.roosevelt-group.org/quick-takes/should-we-repatriate-museum-artefacts-ethics-and-concerns."Should We Repatriate Museum Artefacts?: Ethics and Concerns." The Roosevelt Group

American Alliance of Museums. 2021, June 21. "Museum Recovery Expected to Take Years Due to Devastating Financial Losses, New Survey Reveals." *American Alliance of Museums*. https://www.aam-us.org/2021/06/01/museum-recovery-expected-to-take-years-due-to-devastating-financial-losses-new-survey-reveals/.

Bellamy, Sarah, Nate Young, Jonathon McCrory, Uri Sands, and Mikki Shepard. 2015, April 28. "Diversity in the Arts: The Past, Present, and Future of African American and Latino Museums, Dance Companies, and Theater Companies." *The Clarice*. DeVos Institute of Arts Management. https://theclarice.umd.edu/events/2015/future-field-african-american-dance-companies-theaters-and-museums.

Brown, Kathryn. 2020. "When Museums Meet Markets." *Journal of Visual Art Practice* 19 (3): 203–10. 10.1080/14702029.2020.1811488.

Buntz, L. A. 2022. "Diversity and Philanthropy—Engaging Women of Color and the Next Generation of Donors." In *Generosity and Gender: Philanthropic Models for Women Donors and the Fund Development Professionals Who Support Them*, 193–214. Cham: Springer International Publishing.

Camarero, Carmen, Mª José Garrido, and Eva Vicente. 2011. "How Cultural Organizations' Size and Funding Influence Innovation and Performance: The Case of Museums." *Journal of Cultural Economics* 35: 247–66.

Candid. 2023. "A Third of Americans Plan to Give Less or No Money to Charity in 2021 …" *Philanthropy News Digest. Candid.* Accessed January 30, 2023. https://philanthropynewsdigest.org/news/a-third-of-americans-plan-to-give-less-or-no-money-to-charity-in-2021.

Carr, Christina. 2021. "Board Age Diversity and the Future of Museum Leadership." *Curator: The Museum Journal* 64 (2): 237–52.

Chalmers, Dominic, Christian Fisch, Russell Matthews, William Quinn, and Jan Recker. 2022. "Beyond the Bubble: Will NFTs and Digital Proof of Ownership Empower Creative Industry Entrepreneurs?" *Journal of Business Venturing Insights* 17. 10.1016/j.jbvi.2022.e00309.

CUSEUM. 2022, May 25. "How Museums Are Interacting with NFTs in 2022." *CUSEUM*. https://cuseum.com/blog/2022/4/26/how-museums-are-interacting-with-nfts-in-2022.

Evans, Tonya M. 2022. "The Genesis of Creative Justice on the Blockchain to Disintermediate Creativity." *Lewis & Clark Law Review* 26: 219.

Finkel, Jori. 2009. "When, If Ever, Can Museums Sell Their Works?" *The New York Times*, January 1, 2009. https://www.nytimes.com/2009/01/03/arts/03iht-finkel.1.19031384.html#:~:text=The%20sale%20of%20artwork%20from.

Ghelani, Diptiben. 2022. "What Is Non-Fungible Token (NFT)? A Short Discussion about NFT Terms Used in NFT." *Authorea Preprints*. 10.22541/au.166490992.24247550/v1

Giancaspro, Mark. 2017. "Is a 'Smart Contract' Really a Smart Idea? Insights from a Legal Perspective." *Computer Law & Security Review* 33 (6): 825–35. 10.1016/j.clsr.2017.05.007.

Gumelar, Michael Sega. 2023. *What Is NFT for Beginners: NFT, NFT 2.0, NFT 3.0 Explore the Future of NFT Art*. An1mage.

Harris, Gareth. 2021, September 28. "The Whitworth Gallery in Manchester Mints a William Blake NFT in Aid of Community Causes." The Art Newspaper – International Art News and Events. https://www.theartnewspaper.com/2021/07/23/the-whitworth-gallery-in-manchester-mints-a-william-blake-nft-in-aid-of-community-causes.

Harris, Gareth. 2022, January 11. "British Museum Banks on Turner NFTS after Hokusai Initiative." The Art Newspaper – International Art News and Events. https://www.theartnewspaper.com/2022/01/11/british-museum-banks-on-turner-nfts-after-hokusai-initiative.

Hofstetter, Reto, Emanuel de Bellis, Leif Brandes, Melanie Clegg, Cait Lamberton, David Reibstein, Felicia Rohlfsen, Bernd Schmitt, and John Z. Zhang. 2022. "Crypto-Marketing: How Non-Fungible Tokens (NFTs) Challenge Traditional Marketing." *Marketing Letters* 33 (4): 705–11. 10.1007/s11002-022-09639-2.

Jung, Yuha. 2022. "Current Use Cases, Benefits and Challenges of NFTs in the Museum Sector: Toward Common Pool Model of NFT Sharing for Educational Purposes." *Museum Management and Curatorship*, 1–17. 10.1080/09647775.2022.2132995.

Konstantinou, Iro and Kate Jones. 2022. "Investigating Gen Z Attitudes to Charitable Giving and Donation Behaviour: Social Media, Peers and Authenticity." *Journal of Philanthropy and Marketing* 27 (3): e1764.

Liebenau, Jonathan and Silvia Elaluf-Calderwood. 2016, March 18. "Blockchain Innovation Beyond Bitcoin and Banking." Available at: https://ssrn.com/abstract=2749890.

Liscia, Valentina Di. 2021, June 11. "'First Ever NFT' Sells for $1.4 Million." *Hyperallergic*. https://hyperallergic.com/652671/kevin-mccoy-quantum-first-nft-created-sells-at-sothebys-for-over-one-million/.

Lu, Fei. 2022, September 30. "Why the Museum of Chinese in America Is Welcoming Crypto Donations." *Jing Culture & Crypto*. https://jingculturecrypto.com/museum-of-chinese-in-america-moca-giving-block-crypto-cryptocurrency/.

Massi, Marta, Marilena Vecco, and Yi Lin. 2020. "Digital Transformation in the Cultural and Creative Sectors." In *Digital Transformation in the Cultural and Creative Industries*, 1–9. Routledge.

Mattei, Shanti Escalante-De. 2022, July 8. "Italian Government Halts Sales of NFTs Based on Masterpieces from the Country's Museums." *ARTnews.com*. https://www.artnews.com/art-news/news/italian-government-halts-nfts-museums-1234633668/.

Matthes, Erich Hatala. 2017. "Repatriation and the Radical Redistribution of Art." *Ergo, an Open Access Journal of Philosophy* 4 (32). 10.3998/ergo.12405314.0004.032.

Merritt, Elizabeth. "NFTs, Cryptocurrency, and Museum Practice." American Alliance of Museums, July 6, 2023. https://www.aam-us.org/2022/03/09/nfts-cryptocurrency-and-museum-practice/.

Morisse, Marcel. 2015. "Cryptocurrencies and Bitcoin: Charting the Research Landscape." In: 21st Americas Conference on Information Systems, Fajardo. https://core.ac.uk/reader/301365720.

Murray, Alex, Dennie Kim, and Jordan Combs. 2023. "The Promise of a Decentralized Internet: What Is Web3 and How Can Firms Prepare?" *Business Horizons* 66 (2): 191–202.

San José Museum of Art. 2021. "SJMA Announces Auction and Virtual Benefit to Take Place on September 18, 2021." *San José Museum of Art*. Accessed January 30, 2023. https://sjmusart.org/press-release/sjma-gala-auction-2021.

Seymour, Tom. 2022, January 13. "NFTs IRL: Seattle to Be Home to First Museum Dedicated to Blockchain Art." *The Art Newspaper – International Art News and Events*. https://www.theartnewspaper.com/2022/01/13/nft-museum-opening-seattle-blockchain-art.

Sharma, T., Zhou, Z., Huang, Y. and Wang, Y. 2022. "It's a Blessing and a Curse": Unpacking Creators' Practices with Non-Fungible Tokens (NFTs) and Their Communities. *arXiv preprint arXiv:2201.13233*.

Shekhtman, Louis and Albert Laszlo Barabasi. 2022. "Philanthropy in Art: Locality, Donor Retention, and Prestige." 10.31235/osf.io/5ebjw.

Small, Zachary. 2022, July 6. "Once-Promising Attendance Figures at U.S. Museums Have Plateaued, Revealing the Pandemic's Enduring Grip on the Cultural Economy." *Artnet News*. https://news.artnet.com/art-world/us-museum-attendance-figures-2142562.

Sullivan, Terry. 2022, November 15. "The Rise and Fall of NFT Art." *Worth*. https://www.worth.com/the-rise-and-fall-of-nft-art/.

Valeonti, Foteini, Antonis Bikakis, Melissa Terras, Chris Speed, Andrew Hudson-Smith, and Konstantinos Chalkias. 2021. "Crypto Collectibles, Museum Funding and OpenGLAM: Challenges, Opportunities and the Potential of Non-Fungible Tokens (NFTs)." *Applied Sciences* 11 (21): 9931.

Vasan, Kishore, Milán Janosov, and Albert-László Barabási. 2022. "Quantifying NFT-Driven Networks in Crypto Art." *Scientific Reports* 12 (1). 10.1038/s41598-022-05146-6.

Walzer, Daniel. 2023. "Towards an Understanding of Creativity in Independent Music Production." *Creative Industries Journal* 16 (1): 42–55.

Whiddington, Richard. 2022, November 17. "Yuga Labs Has Gifted a Cryptopunk to ICA Miami, Kicking off the Company's Initiative to Place Its NFTs in Contemporary Art Museums." *Artnet News*. https://news.artnet.com/market/yuga-labs-cryptopunks-punk-legacy-project-ica-miami-2211586.

Whitaker, Amy. 2019. "Art and Blockchain: A Primer, History, and Taxonomy of Blockchain Use Cases in the Arts." *Artivate* 8 (2): 21–46. 10.1353/artv.2019.0008.

Wolf, Melissa Cowley. 2020, December 10. "Arts Funding Is Facing a Dire Crisis. To Survive, Cultural Organizations Must Change How They Frame Themselves to the Public." *Artnet News*. https://news.artnet.com/opinion/arts-funding-op-ed-melissa-cowley-wolf-1929365#:~:text=Arts%20Funding%20Is%20Facing%20an,donors%20increasingly%20disinterested%20in%20culture.

Zarobell, John. 2017. *Art and the Global Economy*. Oakland, CA: University of California Press.

Zhang, Z. John. 2022. "Cryptopricing: Whence Comes the Value for Cryptocurrencies and NFTs?" *International Journal of Research in Marketing*. 10.1016/j.ijresmar.2022.08.002.

21

THE DISTRIBUTED MUSEUM

Using Smart Contracts and NFTs to Find Financial Equity in Co-produced Exhibitions

Frances Liddell

Remuneration, Value, Collaboration

"Community engagement" is the practice of working collaboratively, often focused on a shared interest or issue. As a concept, it differs from ideas such as "community outreach," which focuses primarily on informing and relaying messages to a specific group of people or "community" (Behrooz 2012; Hasan 2022). Instead, community engagement aims to facilitate dialog, exchange ideas, and create long-term partnerships with specific communities (Crooke 2010; Morse and Munro 2018). In museums, community engagement can include activities such as recording oral histories (Frisch 1990), contemporary collecting (Knell 2016), and co-productive exhibitions (Simon 2010), and these aims to bring a multi-vocal perspective to institutional collecting and exhibition practices. In doing so, this type of work embodies "new museology" and the "participatory turn" that has taken place in museum practices that seeks to challenge the "unassailable voice of the museum" and views objects as polysemic in meaning (Vergo 1989; Walsh 1997; Hooper-Greenhill 2000). From the UK context, community engagement work also contributes to the political and economic understanding of museums as "agents of social inclusion" who support those marginalized within society by helping to build a sense of identity and strengthening ties among the community and between the institution and its wider locality (Sandell 1998; Scott 2009). As such, this type of work engages in practices of shared authority and participation to produce wider social impact.

However participant remuneration in work such as community engagement is a complex and ambiguous topic. In research ethics, financial remuneration remains a contentious subject which risks participant coercion or even "commercializing" the researcher-participant relationship (Dickert and Grady 1999;

DOI: 10.4324/9781003308003-26

Permuth-Wey and Borenstein 2009). This "commercialization" suggests that financial value could implicate the broader non-economic values of the project, an idea which is evident in discussion on museum community engagement where the financial value and social value could cause friction. Indeed, community engagement work provokes an "affective labor," which combines emotion and care into the practice of work (Morse 2020), and this can create tensions if a financial interest is apparent.

But a lack of financial remuneration risks undervaluing an individual's participation and could be understood as using as individuals a form of "resource extraction" (Onciul 2015; Romero 2019). As Helen Graham et al. (2012) highlight, community engagement work forms its legitimacy from the way it impacts the engaged community and the institution, but largely this can focus too heavily on the benefits for the museum. Lack of remuneration only fuels this problem and suggests that the community's investment into the project is merely a "contribution" to the project as opposed to working as a collaborator or partner with the institution (Simon 2010; Lynch 2011; Morse 2014, 2020). Indeed, this issue is noted across the cultural and arts sector including in arts participation (Harvie 2013), crowdsourcing projects (Mayer 2016; Kidd 2020), and consultations with Indigenous communities (McMullen 2008; Onciul 2015). Therefore, this highlights financial remuneration as a theme within an ethical museum practice which could have relational, knowledge, and economic implications (Kidd 2020). As such, fair remuneration that goes beyond the reimbursement of expenses should be understood as a core principle to creating more equitable participation (Giblin et al. 2023).

Of course, finances are a major factor in this conversation and COVID-19 has had a severe impact on museum finances across the sector. In 2021, UNESCO documented that national museums across the world reported on average 40–60% losses in revenue in comparison to 2019 (UNESCO 2021; Prokůpek et al. 2022). At the end of 2020, the American Alliance of Museums (AAM) found that 12% of museums were at "significant risk" of closing, with 60% of respondents to a 2022 survey reporting that they are still experiencing pandemic-related losses (AAM 2020, 2022).

In the United Kingdom, the sector faced financial difficulties prior to COVID-19 with the reduction in public and local government funding which has left the sector to explore alternatives, and this includes financial cuts and scaling back parts of the program which in some cases has included community engagement departments (Newman and Tourle 2011; Morse and Munro 2018). Indeed, community engagement work now tends to be funded outside of the main institutional budget with external funding sources, meaning that such work has a sense of precariousness and lives on the periphery of the institution rather than being central to operations (Lynch 2011).

Therefore, in this chapter, I propose alternative systems using web3 technologies that inform an ethically and financially sensitive remuneration in community engagement work. These systems collect and distribute value from the process of exhibiting to support financial remuneration, but it aims to do so through methods that do not compromise the finite budgets and the social value of community engagement work.

Web3 refers to a new phase of the Internet which is characterized by decentralization; it includes technologies such as Internet of things, metaverses, blockchains, smart contracts, and non-fungible tokens (NFTs) (Antonopoulos and Wood 2019). The focus of this chapter is on smart contracts and NFTs and the examples outlined build on previous research on web3 technologies in museum management (Whitaker et al. 2020; Valeonti et al. 2021; Liddell 2021, 2022). It does so by extending thinking through theorizing and implementing the "Distributed Museum" model, an idea that understands the museum as part of wider network that connects "people, ideas, and projects back into its collections and buildings, and connecting up its collections, ideas, and staff by moving out towards different community nodes" (Baran 1964; Morse 2014, 226). The "Distributed Museum" aims to progress understandings around community engagement by reimagining the complex power and value dynamics between an institution and community and explores the institution as a space of circulation where value flows in and beyond the museum walls to support the institution and its wider locality (Crooke 2008; Lynch and Alberti 2010; Dewdney et al. 2012; Morse 2014; Liddell 2022). In this respect, this chapter investigates examples that reflect this community engagement model include NFT ticketing, live minting, and smart donation boxes. These examples take the co-produced exhibition as the premise and consider how NFTs and smart contracts could support an equitable and ethical system of financial remuneration.

Smart Contracts, NFTs, and an Emerging Equitable Paradigm[1]

Smart contracts are a series of instructions in the form of code which can be programmed onto a blockchain and deployed through a transaction (Szabo 1997; Filippi et al. 2021). In other words, the technology reduces an agreement into self-executing code and this includes any agreement providing it can be clearly summarized to an if/when statement. A notable example in the context of NFTs is the use of smart contracts to implement resale right agreements for creators, which allows them to receive a percentage of any secondary sales of their work (Whitaker and Kräussl 2020).

However, the technology has been criticized by legal theorists for being neither "smart" nor even a "contract" in the context of the law (Levy, 2017; McKinney et al. 2017. Therefore, the key use value of smart contracts derives from the technology's ability to automate the distribution of value. For example, Nicola Bidwell et al. (2021) demonstrate how smart contracts could be implemented on a donation platform. Working in collaboration with

Oxfam Australia, the platform allows users to set conditions into the smart contract to trigger a donation, which might include actioning donations upon an earthquake or natural disaster in a specific location. In doing so, the smart contract automates donating to a specific charity when an urgent campaign is activated which demonstrates how smart contracts could enable immediate relief in a crisis.

Smart contracts also have the capacity to distribute value to multiple stakeholders through storing several wallets into the programmed code (McKinney et al. 2017). Wallets are used to control and access different tokens on a blockchain such as NFTs and cryptocurrencies, they act as a form of identity key in the web3 field (Antonopoulos and Wood 2019). *Trickle Down: A New Vertical Sovereignty* by Helen Knowles exemplifies this characteristic of the technology, which was originally presented at Arebyte Gallery, London in January 2020 and later at Hyundai Motorstudio, Beijing in November 2022.[2] The work questions the role of automation and technology in navigating wealth disparities and involved participants from four different markets including Her Majesty's Prison Altcourse in Merseyside, UK, a Sotheby's auction in London, the Ethereum Summit in New York 2018, and Openshaw Market in Manchester (Papadimitrou 2020). Each market is represented as part of a four-screen video installation, and this installation is deployed through a coin-slot machine at the center of the space, which also contains an Ethereum-backed smart contract (see Figures 21.1 and 21.2). Upon activation by the

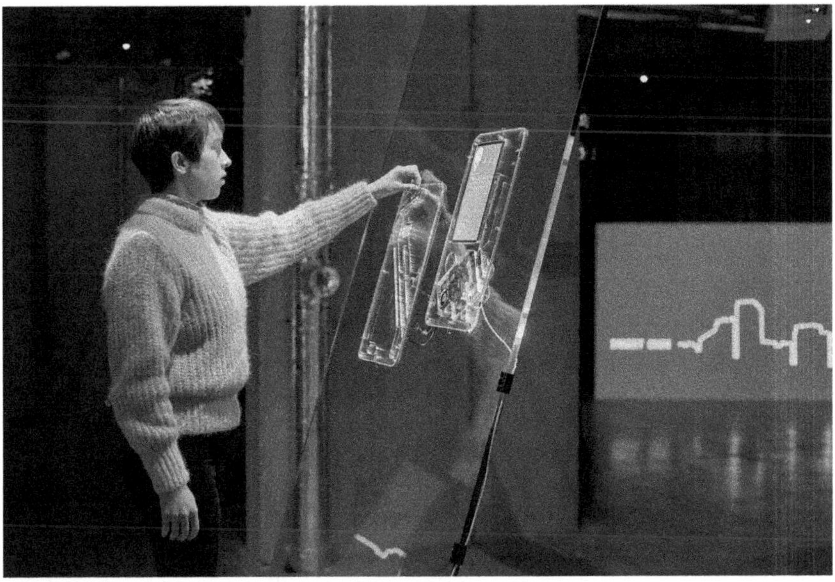

FIGURE 21.1 Arebyte Gallery/Trickle Down pt. 1.

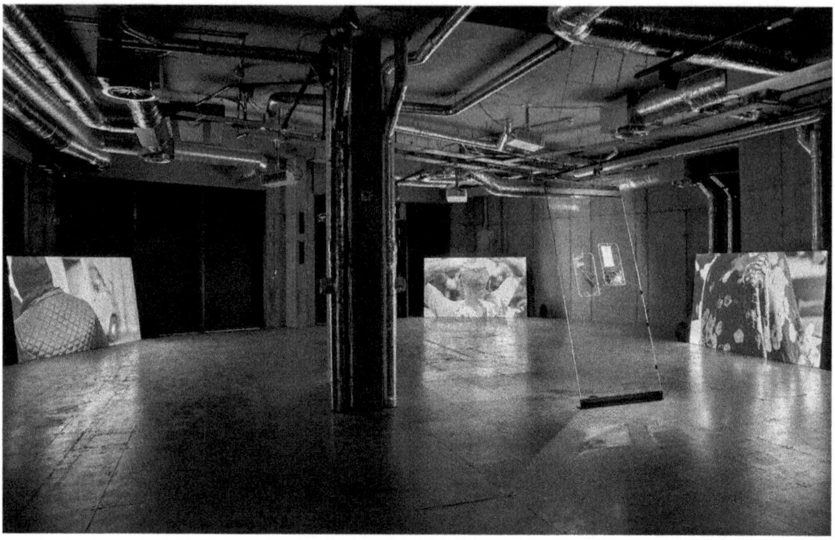

FIGURE 21.2 Arebyte Gallery/Trickle Down pt. 2.

pound coin, the contract exchanges and distributes this pound evenly among the participants of the project, each of whom was invited to create and register a wallet in the associated smart contract. In doing so, the work demonstrates how smart contracts evenly distributed funds to each individual, thus informing an equality-based model to compensation.

As noted earlier, smart contracts are vital to the management of NFTs, a type of digital asset that can be bought and sold via a blockchain.[3] NFTs simulate the idea of digital property by enforcing a sense of scarcity in digital content (Brekke and Fischer 2020), and this effect of digital scarcity has been pivotal for the digital art market as it commodifies the once "uncommodifiable" digital art (Reas 2019). A case in point is the now famous Christie's auction of Beeple's *First 5,000 Days* in March 2021 which fetched over 69 million dollars.[4] Smart contracts are essential to "minting" (creating) NFTs and as noted earlier, incorporate resale rights which enable artists to gain a continuous income stream through secondary sales. In practice, this is beneficial for sustaining artistic endeavors; on the other hand, this explicit commodification of art has created a "frenzy" of speculation that reduces the artwork to a mere investment strategy (O'Dwyer 2018; Beller 2021; Read et al. 2022). Furthermore, the infrastructure of this market has meant that many artists rely on NFT platforms and their smart contract model, which are often not fit for collaborative purposes (Kushnir 2021). Hence, this emerging NFT art market has only intensified the relationship between financialization and art, incorporated new middlemen, and created an infrastructure that limits, as opposed to liberates, the artist.

However, the artist community is reevaluating this current infrastructure and exploring alternatives that are more equitable and support social causes. For example, charity-based NFT auctions are commonplace and can raise large sums, a case in point is ArtBlocks, an NFT platform for generative art that has raised over 54 million dollars for charities since its launch in November 2020.[5] But other examples show how these technologies could inform equitable structures of remuneration. *Pieces of Me* is an online exhibition developed in 2021 by TRANSFER gallery and Left. Gallery made up of 50 digital artworks by different artists, each sold as an NFT upon exhibition launch using an Ethereum-based smart contract. This contract distributed the proceeds of every sale on a 70/30 split where the artist(s) of the work received 70% of the proceeds, and the other 30% being distributed to the other stakeholders of the exhibition, including the other artists, technologists, and curators (Transfer Gallery 2021). This ratio prioritizes the artist, who has invested the most to produce the work, but it also recognizes the numerous different stakeholders in the production of exhibitions. As such, the work takes a "solidarity" approach, showcasing how the technology can distribute financial equity based on labor invested into the project (Transfer Gallery 2021).

A similar approach was taken with *ECHOES,* an online exhibition by EPOCH gallery, the Art and Technology Lab at Los Angeles County Museum of Art (LACMA),[6] and UNCOPIED,[7] which launched in February 2022. The exhibition contains works by artists who have been previously funded by the Art and Technology Lab's artist fund and these are set within a virtual environment modeled to represent LACMA's East Campus. This entire environment was packaged as an NFT and sold using an Algorand-based smart contract upon the launch of the exhibition with the profits split representing 70% to the artists involved, 20% to LACMA, and 10% to EPOCH.[8] This example also demonstrates a "solidarity" or equity-based model to the technology and, in addition, shows a unique approach of selling the entire exhibition as an NFT rather than each work singularly. According to Peter Wu, founder and creator of EPOCH, this singular NFT has a powerful impact on collaborators by embedding feelings of co-creation,[9] which suggests that the technology has the potential to distribute financial and reinforce social connections through sales.

These examples highlight how smart contracts and NFTs can be tools to build new automated value distribution systems. Indeed, these cases illustrate an alternative paradigm within web3 that explores how the technology can embody a more socially valuable structure, an idea that aligns with the ethos of a "Distributed Museum" model. As noted in the introduction, the "Distributed Museum" aims to decenter the institution and reconsiders the museum and its communities as part of a shared network where value flows in and beyond the institution (Dewdney et al. 2012; Morse 2014; Liddell 2022). This idea is informed by notions of accountability and reciprocation where community engagement seeks to go beyond short-term impact and reflect on how this type of work can create a continuous stream of value that flows between the different nodes in the network. In what follows, I propose systems that focus primarily on the distribution of financial value to build long-term impact and social value among engaged communities. These systems explore how to extract value from the practice of exhibiting, an idea that I draw from Amy Whitaker et al.'s (2020) work, who propose a system of distribution using smart contracts in repatriation disputes where exhibiting the disputed artifact can support financial retribution for source communities. Similarly, I offer three cases that collect and distribute value to communities in co-produced exhibitions thus informing a "Distributed Museum" model. In doing so, my aim is to consider how outputs of community engagement can address the risk of undervaluing community participation. This is not to focus on making huge amounts of profits on the back of socially valuable projects but instead explore ways to ensure that fair and equitable compensation can occur when communities choose to invest time and effort into collaborating with museums.

Practical Applications of the Distributed Museum

NFT ticketing is a growing practice in the web3 space with start-ups such as Yellowheart[10] and Seatlab,[11] offering ready-made and user-friendly platforms to buy and exchange NFT tickets for events (Regner et al. 2022). Similarly, Ticketmaster has experimented with commemorative NFT tickets for the Super Bowl in February 2022 on the Polygon blockchain (Ticketmaster Business 2022), which has sold 70% of all available tickets.[12] Ticketmaster's success with NFT commemorative tickets suggests that this method could be a valuable tool with co-produced exhibitions, where projects sell NFT tickets as additional digital memorabilia to visitors. This practice would not replace the current ticketing system and instead provide a way to collect value from exhibiting. The associated smart contract to these NFTs would be used to distribute the sale of each NFT to the different participants using either the equality-based or equity-based models highlighted earlier, thereby creating a distributed structure that immediately remunerates participants for their time and effort. Furthermore, the NFT could replicate the concept shown in *ECHOES* by representing the entire exhibition in digital format to inform a sense of co-creation among collaborators. In doing so, this would both remunerate and reinforce the social connection produced during community engagement work.

NFT ticketing relies on visitors to have the confidence to download a digital wallet and purchase an NFT which creates a potential barrier. However, the emerging practice of live minting has shown how this barrier can be addressed with the use of alternative signup systems. Live minting is a process of minting an NFT while visiting a physical space. This can include working with generative art, where the NFT visual is randomly produced through programmed code upon minting (Droitcour 2021), and the recent partnership between the Art Basel art fair, the public blockchain Tezos and Tezos Foundation, and the NFT generative platform FxHash exemplifies this idea.[13] Visitors who attended the Tezos booth at Art Basel could mint a free NFT using a QR code, a Kukai wallet, a type of digital wallet, and their email address. Live minting can also use pre-designed NFTs, such as in NXT Museum's exhibition *UFO Unidentified Fluid Other*, which contained hidden NFTs around the physical space for visitors to mint as they progressed through the exhibit.[14] Specifically, *UFO* contained NFTs known as POAPs, which are "proof of attendance protocol" NFTs designed and minted on the POAP platform, and users only need to sign up with their email address to claim their token.[15] Both of these examples practice alternative signup methods that simplify the process, providing visitors possess an email address, a smartphone, and an understanding of QR codes.

In addition, live minting offers a more nuanced response to digital memorabilia as it combines the token with exhibition design. In doing so, the NFT has the potential to add another dimension to the visitor experience, for example, they could be used to guide visitors around the space in a specific direction or provide a more personalized experience as shown in LAS Foundation's recent exhibition with Ian Cheng, *Life after B.O.B.*[16] Furthermore, the smart contract associated with the NFT can incorporate multiple wallets and therefore distribute value to each participant. However, unlike NFT ticketing, live minting tends to be a free process as a means to lower access barriers. Therefore, the addition of resale rights can ensure that this practice draws out and distributes value to participants as each individual would gain a percentage from the secondary sale of these NFTs. This has shown to be a successful practice in collecting income, for example, Ada Ada Ada's *Klyft* was a free mint at the Art Basel Paris and to date has earned a total of 706 Tez from secondary sales since the initial mint.[17]

However, the practice of selling NFTs in museums was initially criticized by the sector with some arguing that it lacked value or was even a form of "digital deaccession" (Ledesma et al. 2021; Mittendorf and Smith 2021; Valeonti et al. 2021; McCarthy 2022; Paul 2022; Valeonti 2022). This perception appears to be changing (Nayeri 2022), particularly with the move toward the use of environmentally friendly blockchains such as Ethereum 2.0 and third generations such as Tezos and Algorand (Howson 2019; Ethereum Foundation 2022). Nevertheless, these NFT use cases could face similar criticism from the sector. Therefore, the final example shifts the focus away from NFTs and explores how smart contracts could be applied to donation boxes to collect and distribute value.

Donation boxes are a common micro-philanthropy tool used across the sector which provide physical prompts for visitors to donate as they explore the museum (Půček et al. 2021). Using this idea, donation boxes could be made "smart" with a smart contract and sensors as illustrated in *Trickle Down,* where visitors inserted a one-pound coin into the coin machine to activate the installation. Using similar tools, a smart donation box could be installed in the central space of a co-produced exhibition and collect and distribute donations to the different participants of the project. This practice relies on the effectiveness of donation boxes which is not always guaranteed particularly in cases where there is already an admission fee (Neuts 2020). Therefore, this would need additional support to encourage altruistic behavior, which could include interactivity and gamification (Tanaka et al. 2009), a recommended donation to support social norms (Agerström et al. 2016), or a clear message on what the donation supports to give a stronger sense of trust and transparency (Shang et al. 2019).

There are, however, practicalities to consider. Firstly, the technology creates a complex situation where fiat currency donations need to be transferred into cryptocurrency in order to be distributed by the technology. To address this issue, the *Trickle Down* smart contract held a deposit of Ethereum cryptocurrency (ETH) which was used to immediately distribute funds to the different wallets upon activation and to cover the transaction fee which is paid to the Ethereum network, known as a "gas" fee (Ethgasstation.info 2019). Meanwhile, the pound coins were collected and deposited into a bank account with Knowles even setting the project up with its own nonprofit status and an accountant to appropriately tax the income from the exhibition. In this respect, *Trickle Down* highlights the complex procedure needed to exchange between the "traditional" banking system and crypto, particularly when physical cash is involved. The use of contactless payments could ease the friction in this process and would also be more aligned with the changing monetary habits in a "post-COVID" era (Keating 2022). Platforms such as Stripe offer fiat to crypto payments using card, and this could be incorporated into a smart donation box to make a more streamlined approach that would not impact the visitor experience in donating.[18]

On the other hand, contactless donations do not solve the high volatility that many cryptocurrencies experience which has implications for the cost of transacting on-chain. Indeed, this is a problem that all three examples would be challenged with. To use *Trickle Down* as an example, the price of ETH rapidly increased during 2020, starting the year at an average of 165 dollars which rapidly increased to a peak of 408 dollars in August 2020 and this was attributed to the escalation of decentralized finance (DeFi) in the Ethereum network (Chong 2020; Young 2020).[19] Price impacts the cost of "gas" and transacting on-chain which can have implications for the entire process of distribution. "Gas" cost as little as 8.97 Gwei in January 2020 and reached a high of 78.9 Gwei in August 2020, a 780% increase over the year. For *Trickle Down,* this meant that the cost of distributing the one pound to the different participants cost as much as 7.26 dollars in certain cases,[20] making the method redundant in being able to distribute a one-pound coin to the different collaborators. However, newer third generation blockchains do not experience such levels of volatility in terms of transactions and therefore help to mitigate this flaw in using cryptocurrencies to distribute value. A case in point is Algorand which was used for the *ECHOES* exhibition and costs 0.00025 dollar to transact on thereby ensuring that little of a donation would be wasted on logistics.[21] Therefore, the choice of blockchain and the recommended amount to donate are critical to ensure smart donation boxes are an effective strategy for distributed remuneration.

Lastly, the use of cryptocurrencies and digital wallets could have tax and government benefit implications for the participants receiving the funds, which is a prevalent issue across community engagement work when reimbursing with fiat as well as an issue that cuts across all three examples presented in this chapter (Giblin et al. 2023). Under UK law, cryptocurrencies received as "non-cash" payments are liable to income and national insurance contributions, meaning that participants need to declare their contributions and any profits they make if they choose to invest and sell off their crypto assets into fiat (HMRC 2022), and a similar situation is evident in the United States (The Giving Block 2022). To elevate the process for individual participants, both NFT sales and smart donation boxes could be used to financially support specific charities or organizations that would in turn support the engaged community. This practice would not directly remunerate the individuals who participated in the project, but the charities supported can directly relate to the themes of the exhibition or directly support causes that are important for all stakeholders involved. A similar approach was taken in the online exhibition *Unprotected* at EPOCH gallery, which was an artist response to the overturn of Roe vs. Wade in the United States and was sold as an NFT with the proceeds supporting abortion rights groups.[22] Such a practice has a multiplier effect on the value collected from exhibiting, meaning that this value has a ripple effect that goes beyond the institution and into the wider community. Likewise, this could have a positive impact on giving behavior in visitors as it shows a direct connection between their donation and the social impact in society. Furthermore, this could have an impact on participants who might feel a stronger sense of investment into the project knowing that their labor and time are supporting a cause that they care for or indeed, care for them. This would still require organizations to be equipped with a digital wallet but companies such as The Giving Block offer charities the resources and support to accept crypto donations using a tax compliant and automated system,[23] for instance, the Museum of Moving Images already uses the platform to enable visitors to donate using cryptocurrencies.[24]

As such emerging platforms and tools such as The Giving Block highlight how the practicalities associated with live minting, NFT ticketing, and smart donation boxes can be addressed with more streamlined approaches. These do not completely mitigate the risk of using cryptocurrencies and web3 technologies. Indeed, there remains ambiguity over whether NFTs are considered a security or a form of art in financial law (Frye 2021), which could have implications for museums wishing to engage in this field. But these tools provide a way to embed these technologies into museum structures, support value distribution, whilst not impacting the visitor experience.

Conclusion

The web3 arts field highlights an emerging paradigm that challenges the current financial models found in the current NFT market. This paradigm supports a more equitable model of distribution that focuses on fairly and ethically remunerating artists and collaborators for their time and effort. In this chapter, I have explored how this emerging model might inform a more ethical and equitable practice in co-productive projects in museums which includes NFT ticketing, live minting, and smart donation boxes. Each of these methods shows how smart contracts could be deployed to distribute value to the different stakeholders of a project. In doing so, these tools highlight how value might flow from the exhibition, beyond the walls of the museum, and to the different collaborators, thereby connecting them in a distributed network and implementing a "Distributed Museum" model.

These practices are by no means conclusive, and the analysis presented here highlights some of the practicalities involved in engaging with the technology, not to mention the cost of implementing these structures which would likely require collaborations with web3 companies to help mitigate some of the process of development, as well as the changing financial policies and discourse which would require support from international lawyers and accountants. But underneath these practicalities, web3 technologies offer an insight into the practice of "decentralizing" the museum. The examples outlined in this chapter infiltrate notions of care, reciprocation, and accountability into the process of exhibiting and therefore use the technology to challenge what it means to truly "decentralize" a cultural institution. In this respect, this chapter presents cases that combine understandings of "new museology" (Vergo 1989), the "post-museum" (Hooper-Greenhill 2000), and distribution and offers an alternative perspective on web3 technologies that is more supportive of a museum practice.

Notes

1 An extended explanation of web3 technologies is beyond the scope of this chapter, I recommend readers turn to the following sources for further information (Drescher 2017; Antonopoulos and Wood 2019; DuPont 2019).
2 See https://www.helenknowles.com/index.php/work/trickle_down for further details.
3 For the purpose of this chapter, the focus is on NFTs recorded in the Ethereum and Algorand public blockchains.
4 https://onlineonly.christies.com/s/beeple-first-5000-days/beeple-b-1981-1/112924.

5 Generative art refers to work produced through computer code and in part produced through randomness and not under the artist's direct control (Boden and Edmonds 2009). See https://info.artblocks.io/about (Accessed January 28, 2023).
6 https://www.lacma.org/lab (Accessed November 23, 2022).
7 https://uncopied.art/about/chirograph/ (Accessed November 23, 2022).
8 Personal correspondence with the creators.
9 Personal correspondence with the creators.
10 https://yh.io/about/.
11 https://www.seatlabnft.com/.
12 Data accurate to 22/01/2023. See https://nfl.live-nfts.com/token/losangelesramsnflsuperbowllvichampions/all.
13 For further information for Art Basel see https://www.artbasel.com/?lang=en, for Tezos https://tezos.com/, for FxHash https://www.fxhash.xyz/ (Accessed April 13, 2023).
14 https://nxtmuseum.com/exhibition/ (Accessed January 2, 2022).
15 https://poap.xyz/ (Accessed January 2, 2022).
16 See https://lightartspace.org/programme/life-after-bob-the-chalice-study (Accessed January 28, 2023).
17 ($790, 28/01/2023), https://www.fxhash.xyz/marketplace/generative/20424 (Accessed January 28, 2023).
18 See https://stripe.com/gb (Accessed January 2, 2022).
19 Decentralised Finance (DeFi) refers to the financial cryptocurrency market. It uses blockchain technology to remove centralized institutions such as banks from financial transactions (Sharma 2023).
20 The following link connects to the *Trickle Down* smart contract, https://etherscan.io/tx/0xb29e2334930d3f7fd5ef01b90798911747da0d9ee4fde3c285c1a93706e26333 (Accessed January 9, 2023).
21 Accurate to January 28, 2023 https://algoexplorer.io/.
22 See https://epoch.gallery/unprotected/ (Access January 14, 2023).
23 See https://thegivingblock.com/crypto-fundraising-solution/ (Accessed January 9, 2023).
24 See https://thegivingblock.com/donate/museum-of-the-moving-image/ (Accessed January 14, 2023).

References

AAM. 2020. "National Snapshot of COVID-19 Impact on United States Museums (October 2020)." *American Alliance of Museums* (blog). 2020. https://www.aam-us.org/2020/11/17/national-snapshot-of-covid-19/.

AAM. 2022. "Museum Field Experiencing Compounding Financial Losses, New Survey Reveals." *American Alliance of Museums* (blog). February 8, 2022. https://www.aam-us.org/2022/02/08/museum-field-experiencing-compounding-financial-losses-new-survey-reveals/.

Agerström, Jens, Rickard Carlsson, Linda Nicklasson, and Linda Guntell. 2016. "Using Descriptive Social Norms to Increase Charitable Giving: The Power of Local Norms." *Journal of Economic Psychology* 52 (February): 147–53. 10.1016/j.joep.2015.12.007.

Antonopoulos, Andreas and Gavin Wood. 2019. *Mastering Ethereum*. Sebastopol: O'Reilly.

Baran, P. 1964. "On Distributed Communications Networks." *IEEE Transactions on Communications Systems* 12 (1): 1–9. 10.1109/TCOM.1964.1088883.

Behrooz, F. 2012. "A Guide to Community Engagement & Outreach." *Scarborough: Scarborough Civic Action Network*. https://connectedcommunities.ca/files/96/Scarborough-Civic-Action-Network-engagement-guide.pdf.

Beller, Jonathon. 2021. "NFT Does Not Stand for Non-Fascist Token, But It Should." *CoinDesk*, March 23, 2021. https://www.coindesk.com/fascism-blockchain-art-nfts.

Bidwell, Nicola J., Chris Elsden, Ludwig Trotter, Josh Hallwright, Sadie Moore, Kate Jeite-Delbridge, Mike Harding, et al. 2021. "A Right Time to Give: Beyond Saving Time in Automated Conditional Donations." In *Proceedings of the 2021 CHI Conference on Human Factors in Computing Systems*, 1–20. CHI '21. New York, NY, USA: Association for Computing Machinery. 10.1145/3411764.3445371.

Boden, Margaret A. and Ernest A. Edmonds. 2009. "What Is Generative Art?" *Digital Creativity* 20 (1–2): 21–46. 10.1080/14626260902867915.

Brekke, Jaya and Aron Fischer. 2020. "Digital Glossary of Decentralised Sociotechnical Systems." *Internet Policy Review* 10(2). https://doi.org/10.14763/2021.2.1548

Chong, Nick. 2020. "Ethereum Fees Just Hit a Multi-Year High, But There Are Solutions." *NewsBTC*, June 29, 2020. https://www.newsbtc.com/2020/06/29/ethereum-fees-multi-year-high-solutions/.

Crooke, Elizabeth. 2008. *Museums and Community: Ideas, Issues and Challenges*. 2nd ed. London & New York: Routledge.

Crooke, Elizabeth. 2010. "Museums and Community." In *A Companion to Museum Studies*, edited by Sharon Macdonald. Chichester, UK: John Wiley & Sons.

Dewdney, Andrew, David Dibosa, and Victoria Walsh. 2012. *Post Critical Museology: Theory and Practice in the Art Museum*. London, UK.

Dickert, Neal and Christine Grady. 1999. "What's the Price of a Research Subject? Approaches to Payment for Research Participation." *New England Journal of Medicine* 341 (3): 198–203. 10.1056/NEJM199907153410312.

Droitcour, Brian. 2021. "Generative Art and NFTs." *ARTnews.Com* (blog). March 11, 2021. https://www.artnews.com/list/art-in-america/features/generative-art-and-nfts-1234586572/.

Ethereum Foundation. 2022. "The Merge." *Ethereum.Org*. https://ethereum.org/en/upgrades/merge/.

Ethgasstation.info. 2019. "What Is Gas?" *ETH Gas Station* (blog). July 31, 2019. https://ethgasstation.info/blog/what-is-gas/.

Filippi, Primavera De, Chris Wray, and Giovanni Sileno. 2021. "Smart Contracts." *Internet Policy Review* 10(2). 10.14763/2021.2.1549

Frisch, Michael. 1990. *A Shared Authority: Essays on the Craft and Meaning of Oral and Public History*. New York: State University of New York Press.

Frye, Brian L. 2021. "How to Sell NFTs without Really Trying." *SSRN Scholarly Paper* ID 3930430. Rochester, NY: Social Science Research Network. https://papers.ssrn.com/abstract=3930430.

Giblin, John, Robert Blyth, Yahya Barry, Phoenix Archer, and Iona Diver. 2023. "Exchange: Community-Led Collection Research. Recommendations for More Equitable Participation." *National Museums Scotland & Royal Museums Greenwich*. https://www.nms.ac.uk/collections-research/collections-departments/global-arts-cultures-and-design/projects/exchange-community-led-collections-research/.

Graham, Helen, Rhiannon Mason, and Nigel Nayling. 2012. "'Earning Legitimacy': Participation, Intellectual Property and Informed Consent." Leeds, Newcastle, Swansea.

Harvie, J. 2013. *Fair Play – Art, Performance and Neoliberalism*. London, UK: Palgrave Macmillan UK.

Hasan, Mahbub. 2022. "Community Engagement and Outreach." In *Community Development Practice: From Canadian and Global Perspectives*. Open Library. https://ecampusontario.pressbooks.pub/communitydevelopmentpractice. Licensed CC BY-NC-SA 4.0.

HMRC. 2022. "CRYPTO20050 – Cryptoassets for Individuals: Which Taxes Apply – HMRC Internal Manual – GOV.UK." 2022. https://www.gov.uk/hmrc-internal-manuals/cryptoassets-manual/crypto20050.

Hooper-Greenhill, Eilean. 2000. *Museums and the Interpretation of Visual Culture*. London & New York: Routledge.
Howson, Peter. 2019. "Tackling Climate Change with Blockchain." *Nature Climate Change* 9 (9): 644–45. 10.1038/s41558-019-0567-9.
Keating, Mike. 2022. "Digital Impact in Museums and Galleries." *Arts Professional*. 2022. https://www.artsprofessional.co.uk/magazine/361/feature/digital-impact-museums-and-galleries.
Kidd, Jenny. 2020. "Infrastructure That Democratize? Citizen Participation and Digital Ethics." In *A History of Participation in Museums and Archives*, edited by Per Hetland, Palmyre Pierroux, and Line Esbord, 73–89. Abingdon & New York: Routledge, Taylor & Francis Group.
Knell, Simon J. 2016. *Museums and the Future of Collecting*. Florence, UK: Taylor & Francis Group.
Kushnir, Alana. 2021. *The Legal Ambiguities of Art Collaborations and Their Compatibility with NFTs*. London: Serpentine.
Ledesma, Andrea, Jeremy Munro, Erin Canning, and Claire Blechman. 2021. "MCN Insights: NFTs Are a Scam." *MCN*, 2021. https://mcn.edu/mcn-insights-nfts-are-a-scam/.
Levy, Karen E. C. 2017. "Book-Smart, Not Street-Smart: Blockchain-Based Smart Contracts and The Social Workings of Law." *Engaging Science, Technology, and Society*, 3: 1–15. 10.17351/ests2017.107.
Liddell, Frances. 2021. "Building Shared Guardianship through Blockchain Technology and Digital Museum Objects." *Museum and Society* 19 (2): 220–36. 10.29311/mas.v19i2.3495.
Liddell, Frances. 2022. "The Crypto-Museum: Investigating the Impact of Blockchain and NFTs on Digital Ownership, Authority, and Authenticity in Museums." Doctoral, Manchester, UK, University of Manchester. https://pure.manchester.ac.uk/ws/portalfiles/portal/216118534/FULL_TEXT.PDF.
Lynch, B. 2011. *Whose Cake Is It Anyway?: A Collaborative Investigation into Engagement and Participation in 12 Museums and Galleries in the UK*. London: Paul Hamlyn Foundation.
Lynch, B. and J. Alberti. 2010. "Legacies of Prejudice: Racism, Co-Production and Radical Trust in the Museum." *Museum Management and Curatorship* 25 (1): 13–25.
Mayer, Allana. 2016. "Crowdsourcing, Open Data and Precarious Labour." *Model View Culture* (blog). 2016. https://modelviewculture.com/pieces/crowdsourcing-open-data-and-precarious-labour.
McCarthy, Douglas. 2022. "Museums and NFTs – a Conflict of Interest?" *Douglas McCarthy* (blog). March 1, 2022. https://douglasmccarthy.com/2022/03/museums-and-nfts-a-conflict-of-interest/.
McKinney, Scott A., Rachel Landy, and Rachel Wilka. 2017. "Smart Contracts, Blockchain, and the Next Frontier of Transactional Law." *Washington Journal of Law, Technology & Arts* 13 (3): 313–47.
McMullen, Ann. 2008. "The Currency of Consultation and Collaboration." *Museum Anthropology Review* 2 (2): 54–87.
Mittendorf, Brian and Sean Stein Smith. 2021. "4 Reasons Why Museums Aren't Cashing in on NFTs Yet." *The Conversation*, 2021. http://theconversation.com/4-reasons-why-museums-arent-cashing-in-on-nfts-yet-171993.
Morse, Nuala. 2014. "Museums and Community Engagement: The Politics of Practice within Museum Organisations." Doctoral, Durham University. http://etheses.dur.ac.uk/10846/.
Morse, Nuala. 2020. *The Museum as a Space of Social Care*. London: Routledge. 10.4324/9781315461403.

Morse, Nuala and Ealasaid Munro. 2018. "Museums' Community Engagement Schemes, Austerity and Practices of Care in Two Local Museum Services." *Social & Cultural Geography* 19 (3): 357–78. 10.1080/14649365.2015.1089583.
Nayeri, Farah. 2022. "NFTs, on the Decline Elsewhere, Are Embraced by Some Museums." *The New York Times*, November 30, 2022, sec. Arts. https://www.nytimes.com/2022/11/30/arts/design/nfts-museums.html.
Neuts, Bart. 2020. "Mixed Pricing Strategies in Museums: Examining the Potential of Voluntary Contributions for Capturing Consumer Surplus." *Tourism Economics* 26 (1): 115–36. 10.1177/1354816619828223.
Newman, Kathryn and Paul Tourle. 2011. "The Impact of Cuts on UK Museums." *London: Museums Association.*
O'Dwyer, Rachel. 2018. "A Celestial Cyberdimension: Art Tokens and the Artwork as Derivative • Circa Art Magazine." *Circa Art Magazine*, December 3, 2018. https://circaartmagazine.net/a-celestial-cyberdimension-art-tokens-and-the-artwork-as-derivative/.
Onciul, Bryony. 2015. *Museums, Heritage and Indigenous Voice: Decolonizing Engagement*. Routledge Research in Museum Studies 10. New York: Routledge.
Papadimitrou, Irini. 2020. "Trickling Down Hide and Seek." *Arebyte Gallery* (blog). 2020. https://www.arebyte.com/text-trickling-down.
Paul, Christiane. 2022. "NFT Art—A Sales Mechanism or a Medium?" *The Art Newspaper – International Art News and Events*, February 18, 2022. https://www.theartnewspaper.com/2022/02/18/nfts-are-a-sales-mechanism-not-a-medium.
Permuth-Wey, Jennifer and Amy R. Borenstein. 2009. "Financial Remuneration for Clinical and Behavioral Research Participation: Ethical and Practical Considerations." *Annals of Epidemiology* 19 (4): 280–85. 10.1016/j.annepidem.2009.01.004.
Prokůpek, Marek, Ellen Loots, and Diana Betzler. 2022. "Emergency or Emerging Financing Strategies of Art Museums in the Context of a Pandemic?" *Museum Management and Curatorship* 38 (5): 1–18. 10.1080/09647775.2022.2111327.
Půček, Milan Jan, František Ochrana, and Michal Plaček. 2021. "Financial Management of the Museum." In *Museum Management: Opportunities and Threats for Successful Museums*, edited by Milan Jan Půček, František Ochrana, and Michal Plaček, 139–49. Arts, Research, Innovation and Society. Cham: Springer International Publishing. 10.1007/978-3-030-82028-2_6.
Read, Sparrow, Matt Kane, and Judy Mam. 2022. "Can Web3 Automate Equity?" *Right Click Save*, 2022. https://www.rightclicksave.com/article/can-web3-automate-equity.
Reas, Casey. 2019. "Collecting in the Age of Digital Reproduction." *Artnome*, 2019. https://www.artnome.com/news/2019/9/9/collecting-in-the-age-of-digital-reproduction.
Regner, Ferdinand, André Schweizer, and Nils Urbach. 2022. "Utilizing Non-Fungible Tokens for an Event Ticketing System." In *Blockchains and the Token Economy: Theory and Practice*, edited by Mary C. Lacity and Horst Treiblmaier, 315–43. Technology, Work and Globalization. Cham: Springer International Publishing. 10.1007/978-3-030-95108-5_12.
Romero, Anthony. 2019. "Museum Resolution: Build Social Relations over Property Relations." 2019. https://walkerart.org/magazine/soundboard-museum-resolutions-anthony-romero.
Sandell, Richard. 1998. "Museums as Agents of Social Inclusion." *Museum Management and Curatorship* 17 (4): 401–18. 10.1080/09647779800401704.
Scott, Carol A. 2009. "Exploring the Evidence Base for Museum Value." *Museum Management and Curatorship* 24 (3): 195–212. 10.1080/09647770903072823.
Shang, Jen, Adrian Sargeant, and Kathryn Carpenter. 2019. "Giving Intention versus Giving Behavior: How Differently Do Satisfaction, Trust, and Commitment Relate to Them?" *Nonprofit and Voluntary Sector Quarterly* 48 (5): 1023–44. 10.1177/0899764019843340.

Sharma, Rakesh. 2023. "What Is Decentralized Finance (DeFi) and How Does It Work?" *Investopedia*. 2023. https://www.investopedia.com/decentralized-finance-defi-5113835.

Simon, Nina. 2010. *The Participatory Museum*. Santa Cruz, California: Museumz.

Szabo, Nick. 1997. "The Idea of Smart Contracts." *Nick Szabo's Essays, Papers, and Concise Tutorials* (blog). 1997. https://www.fon.hum.uva.nl/rob/Courses/InformationInSpeech/CDROM/Literature/LOTwinterschool2006/szabo.best.vwh.net/idea.html.

Tanaka, Kohei, Murao Kazuya, Shojiro Nishio, Satoshi Tanaka, Kohei Kinoshita, Yasuhiko Minami, Tsutomu Terada, and Masahiko Tsukamoto. 2009. "IT-Enabled Donation Boxes to Promote Donation." In *Proceedings of the International Conference on Advances in Computer Entertainment Technology*, 400–3. ACE '09. New York, NY, USA: Association for Computing Machinery. 10.1145/1690388.1690471.

The Giving Block. 2022. "NFT Taxes: A Guide for NFT Artists and Collectors." *The Giving Block* (blog). 2022. https://thegivingblock.com/resources/nft-taxes-a-guide-for-nft-artists-and-collectors/.

Ticketmaster Business. 2022. "NFL Partners with Ticketmaster to Offer Limited Edition NFTs to Celebrate Super Bowl LVI – Ticketmaster." https://business.ticketmaster.com/business-solutions/nfl-partners-with-ticketmaster-to-offer-limited-edition-nfts-to-celebrate-super-bowl-lvi/.

Transfer Gallery. 2021. "Press Release – Pieces of Me." https://docs.google.com/document/u/1/d/e/2PACX-1vRGYgHWqCmqgiudOYMDjY6Obn4ZkwwGxXjo9ZXFaqLP5vE9sFlM49oUiNl6dIxweSymNvjuAHMCWMIr/pub.

UNESCO. 2021. "Museums Around the World: In the Face of COVID-19." *UNESCO*. https://unesdoc.unesco.org/in/documentViewer.xhtml?v=2.1.196&id=p::usmarcdef_0000376729_eng&file=/in/rest/annotationSVC/DownloadWatermarkedAttachment/attach_import_381488d9-2f4b-4e9f-af51-59f57eeb4a0e%3F_%3D376729eng.pdf&locale=en&multi=true&ark=/ark:/48223/pf0000376729_eng/PDF/376729eng.pdf#EN%20Rapport%20Musee%202021%20Version%2012%20avril%20OK%20MHM.indd%3A.7127%3A93.

Valeonti, Foteini. 2022. "Are NFTs a Real Solution for Museums?" 2022. https://www.rightclicksave.com/article/are-nfts-a-real-solution-for-museums.

Valeonti, Foteini, Antonis Bikakis, Melissa Terras, Chris Speed, Andrew Hudson-Smith, and Konstantinos Chalkias. 2021. "Crypto Collectibles, Museum Funding and OpenGLAM: Challenges, Opportunities and the Potential of Non-Fungible Tokens (NFTs)." *Applied Sciences* 11 (21): 9931. 10.3390/app11219931.

Vergo, Peter. 1989. *The New Museology*. London: Reaktion Books.

Walsh, Peter. 1997. "The Web and the Unassailable Voice." *Archives and Museum Informatics* 11 (2): 77–87.

Whitaker, Amy, Anne Bracegirdle, Susan de Menil, Michelle Ann Gitlitz, and Lena Saltos. 2020. "Art, Antiquities, and Blockchain: New Approaches to the Restitution of Cultural Heritage." *International Journal of Cultural Policy* 27 (3): 1–18. 10.1080/10286632.2020.1765163.

Whitaker, Amy and Roman Kräussl. 2020. "Fractional Equity, Blockchain, and the Future of Creative Work." *Management Science* 66 (10): 4594–611. 10.1287/mnsc.2020.3633.

Young, Martin. 2020. "Ethereum Gas Usage Tops All-Time High Amid DeFi and Stablecoin Tear." Be[in]Crypto. BeInCrypto. 2020. https://beincrypto.com/ethereum-gas-usage-tops-all-time-high-amid-defi-and-stablecoin-tear/.

22

ACCOUNTING FOR DIGITAL ASSETS IN MUSEUMS

A Brief Discussion on Why, What, and How

Ying Chong Wang

Introduction

Museums today are increasingly tasked with new responsibilities as their definitions expand from institutions primarily carrying out educational and esthetic purposes to institutions engaged in broader social services such as fostering diversity, inclusion, and empowerment (Dubuc 2011; Alexander et al. 2017; International Council of Museums 2022b). To accomplish their increasingly complex tasks, museums leverage a variety of tangible and intangible resources. Over the past two decades, digital technology has been widely embraced by museums as one of their essential resources for achieving their missions, improving the efficiency of their operations, and transforming the perception of museums from an old-fashioned institution to a more modern image (Henning 2006; Taormina and Baraldi 2022). From virtual and augmented reality to 3D printing and digital collections, museums are leveraging technology to create more innovative and memorable experiences for their visitors.

Via digital technology applications, museums can tailor customized offerings for visitors through data collection, provide content accessible to visitors beyond their physical locations, and reach a wider audience, thus revolutionizing the relationship between museums and the public (Waterton 2010; Cassidy et al. 2018). In addition, with the emergence of the "prosumer" trend from Web 2.0, the role of museum visitors has evolved from passive knowledge receivers to potential content creators (Pulh and Mencarelli 2014). This has enabled museums to create participatory spaces that encourage visitors to share their experiences and knowledge, thus contributing to a renewed concept of community and collaboration. The COVID-19 pandemic

DOI: 10.4324/9781003308003-27

that broke out in late 2019 further emphasized the importance of maintaining technology in museums as it almost became the only feasible method of providing museum services to the public during a lockdown or quarantine (Choi and Kim 2021). Research indicates that many major museums have developed a significant number of online cultural initiatives and content to maintain their online presence and engagement (Agostino et al. 2020). Digital resources application during the COVID-19 pandemic has become even more closely related to museums' daily operation and revenue generation, leading more practitioners and researchers to rethink digital asset investment and maintenance in museums.

Museums are adapting to their role in an information-based society where digital resources are expected to be exploited to meet the evolving and diverse needs of the public. It is recognized that the application of digital technology is gaining prominence through the creation of technology-related positions, the formulation of strategic plans, and, most importantly, the allocation of financial resources for technological programs and projects. It is crucial to examine the adaptation and transformation of museums in this trend in order to gain a deeper understanding of the dynamics between museums and technology investment. In general, this chapter will begin by discussing digital resources in museums, thereby providing an overview of the concept of digitized assets. There will then be a discussion regarding the issues and methods of evaluation of the financial management of digital resources. This chapter will conclude by proposing some recommendations for management based on an analysis of some relevant cases.

Defining Digital Assets

Digital transformation has recently become a major focus area for the museum sector. As described in the International Council of Museums (ICOM)'s Strategic Plan for the planning phase from 2022 to 2028, a digital future for the museum sector is delineated as follows: "a forward-thinking museum sector that can use digital to connect in new ways with their communities, better manage their collections, and provide unprecedented access to the publics they serve" (International Council of Museums 2022a). An expert advisory group has also been established to keep ICOM up-to-date on the latest developments in the digital field. Nowadays, it would be virtually impossible to imagine a museum not engaging in any form of technology on a daily basis. Digital technology has been adopted in a broad spectrum of domains, including web portals, e-commerce systems, database management systems, mobile applications, interactive and immersive installations, and social media tools for communication (Damala et al. 2019). The broad scope of digital technology applications raises a question for both researchers and practitioners: what constitutes a digital asset in the museum field?

Digital technologies are discussed in museum literature in a variety of terms, indicating the numerous ways in which digital technology is viewed and understood (Damala et al. 2019). Several discussions have been held regarding the concepts of digitization and digitalization as they pertain to improving museums' operational efficiency and impact (Liao et al. 2020). Museums investing in digital technologies can be seen as an expression of digitization and digitalization. During digitization, physical objects are converted into digital resources through the use of technology, and in the case of museums, a typical example could be archiving collections in digital format (Liao et al. 2020). Digitalization is the process of connecting digital resources to projects, activities, and visitors (Esposito et al. 2021). As digitalization and digitization can go beyond merely technological changes, they could lead to more radical changes in museum development and planning. However, there are currently few comprehensive reviews of digital assets in museum operations. In light of the rapid evolution of the technological landscape, a systematic description of related concepts in relation to museums is imperative in order for museum managers to be aware of the potential of the digital assets they have or will invest in. Taking into account the wide range of technologies available and their vastly varying investment costs, the following summarizes digital assets not in terms of their cost, but rather in terms of their intended use.

Digital Assets for Research and Preservation Purposes

Digital assets provide a means of preserving and protecting significant documents and objects that are integral to museums' collections. Digital assets in this category, such as digital imaging and database systems, are often described as digital archives or digital repositories. Among the examples could be Teylers Museum in Haarlem, Amsterdam, recognized as the best-preserved museum of 18th-century public knowledge in the world (Teylers Museum n.d.). A digital archival file format referred to as MrSID compression technology is used by the museum to preserve the visual integrity of its collection. This technology allowed Teylers Museum to compress the size of its high-resolution digital images to less than half without compromising image quality (Simon 2022). Because of high-fidelity image compression and smaller file sizes, storage costs are reduced, and sharing and finding files become significantly more user-friendly.

Digital Assets for Accessibility Purposes

A museum can invest in digital assets to increase accessibility for visitors, such as offering video, images, and descriptions of their collections online so that a wide range of visitors can explore them virtually. Digital assets in this category are capable of delivering open-access content to diverse audiences in order to reduce barriers imposed by physical limitations. Using digital technology for this purpose enables museums to provide a range of services, including but not limited to public education, outreach, community engagement, and empowering emerging scholars and researchers. Among the examples could be the UK's Victoria & Albert Museum, which launched a digital online platform during the UK's lockdown during COVID-19 (McGivern 2021). The open-access online platform invites online users worldwide to explore more than 1.2 million collections through immersive virtual experiences ("V&A · Explore the Collections" n.d.).

Digital Assets for Engaging Purposes

Museums invest in digital assets to provide visitors with quality experiences, which aim to increase responsiveness, immersion, and interaction during the visit. There are many types of digital assets that fall under this category, including virtual reality, augmented reality, audio and video guides, museum applications, touchscreens, etc. Tate Modern and Shanghai Museum, for example, have developed augmented-reality apps that allow users to interact with artworks in these museums in a creative and interactive manner. The user is able to take a virtual tour of the original painting as well as engage with the painting via a multi-sensory digital experience by tapping the cellphone screen (Tate n.d.). A second example would be the Los Angeles Museum of the Holocaust, which uses holographic technology and machine learning to enable visitors to converse with Holocaust survivors via holograms (Estrin 2021). Digital assets in this category are mainly used to create captivating and engaging experiences for visitors, allowing them to fully interact with the museum and its offerings.

Digital Assets for Operational Purposes

Museums can benefit from digital assets to facilitate smooth and efficient operations. Digital assets included in this category are often software applications or digital systems aimed at supporting administration functions such as ticketing, event planning, donor relations, fundraising, etc. For instance, the International Spy Museum uses Assesso ticketing software for its retail operations. Not only does the software automate the ticketing process and enable print-at-home ticketing, but it also assists museums in maintaining their membership relationships through online membership renewals and demographic and geographical data collection (accesso Technology Group 2022).

As can be seen from the examples above, although some digital technologies can serve the same purpose, their forms, uses, investments, and maintenance costs differ significantly. A museum can, for example, install software to manage memberships, but they can also utilize their websites or social media profiles to enhance their member relations. Aside from this, some digital assets, such as hologram devices, are more of a physical asset investment, whereas some other digital assets, especially software for administrative and operational purposes, require a more intangible investment, such as employees' skill training. Thus, it can be inferred that digital assets are diverse, multifaceted, and rapidly changing. Defining digital assets for museums in a comprehensive and summative manner would require not only that they be digital, but also that they help museums represent value, create value, and realize value.

Accounting for Digital Assets in Museums

Financial Management in Museums

Financial management has always been a major concern for museums, particularly those operating in a nonprofit format. Over the past decade, many museums have experienced a decline in conventional funding as economic and political fluctuations have adversely affected nonprofit cultural institutions (Lord and Lord 1997; Massey and Lewis 2003). Due to these fluctuations, institutions have had to find alternative sources of funding as well as improve their capabilities to manage their finances. Museums' financial well-being is therefore a crucial indicator of their performance.

As maintaining organizations' financial health becomes one of the major responsibilities of museum administrators, researchers have proposed various methods of financial control. Apart from the emphasis on budget planning, cost control, and risk management (Lord and Lord 1997), museums are expected to generate revenue through an activity-based, stakeholder-focused approach.

Income-generating activities are usually related to or support the primary role and function of the museum. Revenue streams are generated from both core activities and by-products of core activities, for example, by offering visitors additional services such as catering, expanding educational outreach, and taking advantage of specific assets (Massey and Lewis 2003). There are a variety of revenue sources that support museums' activities (Camarero and Garrido 2008), including earned income such as admissions, donor contributions, as well as public and private funding (Toepler and Dewees 2005). The diverse sources of income for museums demonstrate their dependence on a variety of stakeholders, who are identified as players with significant influence over the financial stability of organizations (Stieb 2008). To ensure the long-term financial viability of organizations, it's imperative for museums to acknowledge the significance of their dependence on these stakeholders. Museums are advised to communicate proactively with their identified stakeholders in order to ensure the legitimacy of their program and budget (Lindqvist 2012).

In order to ensure sound financial management of museums' activities, projects, and investment plans, a 3E principle in financial planning—economical, efficient, and effective—was proposed by Půček, Ochrana, and Plaček in 2021. A museum must utilize its resources in accordance with the 3E principle if it is to achieve its goals and missions. By being effective, museums can increase their planned productivity and decrease their costs, while still accomplishing their mission-related goals without impairing the performance of their programs. Economicality in museums' financial management means that a successful museum does not incur unnecessary waste and is capable of generating reasonable savings. Museum efficiency is its ability to achieve its stated goals in a more rational manner without accruing additional costs (Půček et al. 2021). In addition, museums should maintain transparent procedures for managing their resources throughout the process. Essentially, the 3Es are a combination of cost control, budget planning, risk management, and open, transparent communication with stakeholders. Together, these approaches to financial management require museums to minimize financial risks and threats while not limiting opportunities and creativity. Consequently, museums should also consider these principles when investing in digital assets. The next section will discuss the principles and approaches that need to be considered when managing digital assets.

Financing Digital/IT Assets in Museums

There is no doubt that museums can increase their revenue streams by investing in and leveraging digital assets. A museum may increase its revenue through admissions, museum store sales, space rentals, and other economic activities in order to become more economically self-sufficient. Digital assets, as described in the previous section, can be used to engage audiences, and provide smooth and efficient operation by enhancing interactivity, immersion, dialog, and technological skills. In fact, it has been noted in the previous sections that museums are increasingly featuring digital technology devices in their exhibitions, such as personal digital assistants and kiosks. However, it is unclear to what extent museums will achieve a return on their investment in digital resources. Conventionally, accounting methods and techniques evaluate whether such investments have increased revenue and visitor numbers, without considering the museum's agenda and mission (Lehn and Heath 2004). While these methods focus on the quantitative side of digital investments, they do not reflect well on the educational, cultural, or social effects that digital technology can have on a museum. In addition, a significant portion of the profits derived from digital asset investments may not be realized in the short term, such as the improved managerial environment resulting from the adoption of an information technology system, or the increased visitor attachment to the museums and visitor retention as a result of overall satisfaction with museum visits. Management of digital assets should therefore also address a variety of qualitative needs and impacts.

The 3E principle and the stakeholder perspective discussed in the previous section provide some guidance on how to measure the payoff of digital assets investments. In accordance with the 3E principle, museums should strategically plan their investments with discretion and rationality, to avoid reducing costs at the expense of lost opportunities, and vice versa. It is undeniable that digital assets present museums with the opportunity to generate additional revenues, but museums should consider their own financial situation, organization size, and expertise and knowledge pool when making such investments. Due to their limited staff, museum professionals at small-scale museums often serve as generalists, handling tasks ranging from curating to outreaching, and have little time to devote to learning specific technology (Duff et al. 2009). It is therefore often logical for these museums to invest in digital assets with a relatively low technology threshold. Alternatively, larger institutions, such as the Palace Museum in Beijing and the Metropolitan Museum of Art in New York, have specialized information technology departments with personnel with technological expertise, including the development of websites, multimedia applications, ticketing, and event planning systems maintenance. Due to their renowned reputations in the arts and cultural community, these institutions also outsource a portion of their technology needs to third-party vendors or utilize collaborative models for the development of digital assets (Duff et al. 2009). The Metropolitan Museum of Art, for example, has partnered with scientists from Microsoft and MIT to develop open-access digital assets using artificial intelligence (Choi 2019).

Furthermore, the 3E principle and the stakeholder perspective discussed earlier indicate that investment in digital assets is supported by relevant stakeholders. In other words, in addition to the question of whether the investment will pay off, implementing technology in museums requires the support of all museum stakeholders in order to secure investment and funding. A museum investor or sponsor can be likened to engaged visitors who are deeply connected to museum programs through their visits as well as professional technology partners (Suroto et al. 2020). Generally, modern technologies can be either welcomed for their potential to improve the existing system or distrusted as threats (Henning 2006). This is particularly true of digital assets. Advocates of digital technology argue that it can be used to enhance the appeal of museums. In the view of some skeptics, the use of digital technology may turn museums into commercial places only for entertainment. Thus, museums should prepare a narrative detailing the benefits of investing in their institution that can be presented both to their boards and to their loyal donors and visitors. A museum must consider, for instance, whether digital assets included in an exhibition will be supported by its visitors. A notable example of this is the World Museum in Liverpool, which implemented facial recognition technology to strengthen security during a high-profile exhibition of Terracotta Warriors loaned from China (Pes 2019). Although the museum stated that the technology had been installed after consulting with local police and counterterrorism advisers, and signage was visible throughout the venue, the use of the technology still raised privacy concerns (Sky 2019). The technology was eventually put to rest after the exhibition concluded.

However, these methods are insufficient to adequately examine the quality of museum experiences brought about by digital asset investments. Several methods of addressing this issue have been proposed in current research.

Firstly, it is argued that museums should include interactivity, entertainment, and engagement from the visitor's perspective when measuring the returns generated by digital asset investments. The results of a survey conducted by Suroto, Dewantara, and Wiradarmo in 2020 indicated that visitors can become bored because they are not captivated by the exhibitions or activities in the museum. Therefore, museums can experience declining interest from visitors in exploring collections and digging deeper due to lack of innovation. In this regard, investment and innovation in museum digital assets, on the one hand, helps museums to keep up with the trend of learning beyond the classroom (Thomas and Brown 2011) by promoting interactive and simulated learning experiences, while also providing visitors with more opportunities to engage and interact with museum programs (Hein 2006), allowing museums to compete with other leisure activities.

A second method of measuring digital asset investment is to incorporate qualitative methods of analysis into accounting. Research conducted by Lehn and Heath (2004) has found that ethnographic and video-based approaches have the potential to address the shortcomings of traditional accounting techniques and visitor studies. An ethnographic or video-based approach can shed light on the ways in which visitors organize their actions and interactions within an exhibition, thus increasing their understanding of its content and overall experience. A visitor's experience can be measured not only in terms of the amount of time they spend interacting with digital devices, but also in terms of the relationship between their visiting behavior and digital devices.

Thirdly, digital asset investments are evaluated according to their mission statements (Esposito et al. 2021). To maintain relationships with donors and maintain financial stability, it is critical that the activities of nonprofit organizations adhere to their mission. Consequently, whether the mission of digital asset investments is aligned with the overall mission and vision of the museum is an integral indicator of whether the investment will yield positive outcomes.

Fourthly, emotional factors should be included in the measurement process (Esposito et al. 2021). The museum industry is considered to be part of the "experience economy" in which the sale of memorable experiences to customers is the most essential part of business operation (Pine and Gilmore 1998): visitors are seeking connections between themselves and the environment they are experiencing in the museum. Depending on the context, these connections can be both intellectual and emotional (Bedigan 2016). Storytelling by museum visitors is included in the museum's metrics in order to measure its payoff as it is a vital component of the museum's digital experience (Esposito et al. 2021). Essentially, telling stories allows the user to participate in an experience that transcends geographical boundaries. Storytelling and emotional connection are also reflected in the extent to which stakeholders are actively involved. For instance, due to the application of some digital media technology such as social media engagement, the relationship with audiences may not start with a physical visit. As long as the engagement between museums and their visitors is maintained, the relationship can be sustained without being limited by space or time.

These proposed methods provide a more holistic understanding of assessing the return on investment of museum digital assets. Based on the methods mentioned above, the next section will provide recommendations for museums to invest in and manage digital assets from a financial management perspective.

Recommendations

The purpose of this section is to provide museums with recommendations they can refer to on investing in and managing digital assets. An evaluation framework is presented in this section, which includes three stages: pre-investment research and planning, post-investment evaluation, and reflection and adjustment. Based on the examples and literature discussed in previous sections, this section aims to discuss how museums can better tailor their digital asset investments and use digital technology to promote creativity and increase value creation.

Firstly, pre-investment research and planning. This is when museums need to take into consideration not only the 3E principles (economic, efficient, and effective), but also stakeholder perspectives. It is critical that museums understand their own financial situation, their own talent pool, and their stakeholders. A museum should recognize the purpose for investing in digital assets, which assets will satisfy that purpose, and which of those assets can create opportunities without burdening the museum with a huge financial commitment. In addition, when a museum hires an external IT professional to assist with their IT needs, the museum should integrate internal expertise with external knowledge. This is done so that the contractor or IT partner will understand why certain approaches may fail in the museum, as well as ensuring cost-effectiveness by not committing to a single digital asset solely to jump into the technology trend. Moreover, communication with stakeholders is of particular importance at this stage. Through communication, museums can clarify their requirements for acquiring digital assets as well as forecast the return on their investments.

Second, a post-investment evaluation. The museum must at this stage measure not only visitor growth, efficiency of digital assets, additional revenue, and funding growth, but also qualitative indicators such as visitor experiences and emotions, management environment, and alignment with the museum's mission. The museum first needs to assess whether the actual usage of digital assets aligns with the overall mission statement of the museum, thereby providing a clear message for stakeholders, donors, as well as potential sponsors. In addition, museum digital assets are likely to bring about changes to the museum management model and environment. The changes can affect not only the efficiency and effectiveness of the museum's operations, but also its personnel. The acquisition of technological expertise and a more sensitive attitude toward technological trends, as well as the creation of new jobs, are all possible results of investing in digital assets.

Third, reflection and adjustment. At this point, museums need to consider the creation of added value. As part of this process, museums should not only consider short-term returns, but also anticipate the long-term benefits of their digital assets, so that they can make more accurate decisions regarding their use and maintenance cycles. For example, investing in digital assets for outreach purposes, such as social media, can enable museums to reach out to their stakeholders across a broad range of geographical and temporal boundaries. The relationship between stakeholders and museums may begin before the actual physical visit and will continue after the physical visit ends. Thus, strategic social media usage may enhance engagement and attendance in a long-term manner beyond the fiscal year cycle. Additionally, investment in digital assets provides a means of dematerializing information sharing and exchanging, stimulating the establishment of partnerships, including but not limited to technology partnerships, physical economic collaborators, and co-organizers of fundraising events. Museums can use these reflections to continuously adjust their investment management policies for digital assets.

Overall, limited funds often make it difficult for museums to maintain, upgrade, and implement cutting-edge technology. The process of technology implementation can be an essential part of financial management. This three-stage framework can be applied to museums based on their specific needs.

Conclusion

The objective of this chapter is to discuss museum investment and management of digital assets from the perspective of financial management. The chapter starts by briefly describing the importance of digital technology applications to museum operations today. The chapter then classifies representative digital technologies with real-life examples into groups from the perspective of their purpose and gives a definition of museum digital assets. Additionally, the chapter discusses existing research and literature, explores how existing financial management principles can be applied to digital assets, and states that traditional accounting methods cannot adequately measure the returns generated by digital assets. Based on previous research, this chapter proposes a three-stage evaluation framework that seeks to assist museums in managing digital assets more effectively.

References

accesso Technology Group. 2022. "Cultural Institution Ticketing & POS." August 25, 2022. Accessed November 28, 2022. https://www.accesso.com/markets/cultural

Agostino, Deborah, Michela Arnaboldi, and Antonio Lampis. 2020. "Italian State Museums during the COVID-19 Crisis: From Onsite Closure to Online Openness." *Museum Management and Curatorship* 35 (4): 362–72. 10.1080/09647775.2020.1790029

Alexander, Edward, Mary Alexander, and Juilee Decker. 2017. *Museums in Motion: An Introduction to the History and Functions of Museums (American Association for State and Local History)*. 3rd ed. Lanham, Maryland, USA: Rowman & Littlefield Publishers.

Bedigan, Kirsten. 2016. "Developing Emotions: Perceptions of Emotional Responses in Museum Visitors." *Mediterranean Archaeology & Archaeometry* 16 (5). 10.5281/zenodo.204969

Camarero, Carmen and María-José Garrido. 2008. "Improving Museums' Performance through Custodial, Sales, and Customer Orientations." *Nonprofit and Voluntary Sector Quarterly* 38 (5): 846–68. 10.1177/0899764008319230

Cassidy, Catherine Anne, Adeola Fabola, Alan Miller, Karin Weil, Simón Urbina, Mario Antas, and Alissandra Cummins. 2018. "Digital Pathways in Community Museums." *Museum International* 70 (1–2): 126–39. 10.1111/muse.12198

Choi, Byungjin and Junic Kim. 2021. "Changes and Challenges in Museum Management after the COVID-19 Pandemic." *Journal of Open Innovation: Technology, Market, and Complexity* 7 (2): 148. 10.3390/joitmc7020148

Choi, Jennie. 2019. "Exploring Art with Open Access and AI: What's Next?" Metropolitan Museum of Art. June 11, 2019. Accessed November 29, 2022. https://www.metmuseum.org/blogs/now-at-the-met/2019/met-microsoft-mit-exploring-art-open-access-ai-whats-next

Damala, Areti, Ian Ruthven, and Eva Hornecker. 2019. "The MUSETECH Model." *Journal on Computing and Cultural Heritage* 12 (1): 1–22. 10.1145/3297717

Dubuc, Élise. 2011. "Museum and University Mutations: The Relationship between Museum Practices and Museum Studies in the Era of Interdisciplinarity, Professionalisation, Globalisation and New Technologies." *Museum Management and Curatorship* 26 (5): 497–508. 10.1080/09647775.2011.621734

Duff, Wendy, Jennifer Carter, Costis Dallas, Lynne Howarth, Seamus Ross, Rebecka Sheffield, and Cassandra Tilson. 2009. "Museum Knowledge Workers for the 21st Century." Government of Canada Report. Toronto: The University of Toronto. Accessed October 30, 2022. https://www.canada.ca/en/heritage-information-network/services/other-heritage-research-tools/museum-knowledge-workers-21st-century.html

Esposito, Paolo, Alessandro Braga, Alessandro Sancino, and Paolo Ricci. 2021. "The Strategic Governance of the Digital Accounting Environment: Insights from Virtual Museums." *Meditari Accountancy Research* October. 10.1108/medar-03-2020-0837

Estrin, Robin. 2021. "Holocaust Museum LA Reopens with New Virtual Installation Featuring Auschwitz Survivor." *Los Angeles Times*, August 1, 2021. Accessed December 30, 2022. https://www.latimes.com/california/story/2021-07-31/holocaust-survivor-hologram

Hein, Hilde. 2006. *Public Art: Thinking Museums Differently*. Lanham, Maryland, USA: AltaMira Press.

Henning, Michelle. 2006. "New Media." In *A Companion to Museum Studies*, 302–18. Oxford, UK: Blackwell Publishing Ltd. 10.1002/9780470996836.ch18

International Council of Museums. 2022a. "Strategic Plan 2022-2028." 2022. Accessed December 5, 2022. https://icom.museum/wp-content/uploads/2022/08/EN_OGA2022_StrategicPlan_Final_.pdf

International Council of Museums. 2022b. "Museum Definition." August 24, 2022. https://icom.museum/en/resources/standards-guidelines/museum-definition/

Lehn, Dirk Vom and Christian Heath. 2004. "Accounting for New Technology in Museum Exhibitions." *International Journal of Arts Management* 7 (3): 11–21.

Liao, Han-Teng, Man Zhao, and Si-Pan Sun. 2020. "A Literature Review of Museum and Heritage on Digitization, Digitalization, and Digital Transformation." *Proceedings of the 6th International Conference on Humanities and Social Science Research (ICHSSR2020)*. 10.2991/assehr.k.200428.101

Lindqvist, Katja. 2012. "Museum Finances: Challenges beyond Economic Crises." *Museum Management and Curatorship* 27 (1): 1–15. 10.1080/09647775.2012.644693

Lord, Barry and Gail Dexter Lord. 1997. *The Manual of Museum Management*. Amsterdam, Netherlands: Amsterdam University Press.

Massey, Claire and Kate Lewis. 2003. "Exhibiting Enterprise: How New Zealand Museums Generate Revenue." *International Journal of Heritage Studies* 9 (4): 325–39. 10.1080/1352725022000155063

McGivern, Hannah. 2021. "Immerse Yourself in V&A's New Digital Platform of 1.2 Million Objects." *The Art Newspaper – International Art News and Events*, February 9, 2021. Accessed December 30, 2022. https://www.theartnewspaper.com/2021/02/09/immerse-yourself-in-vandas-new-digital-platform-of-12-million-objects

Pes, Javier. 2019. "Privacy Advocates Slam a UK Museum for Using Facial-Recognition Surveillance at Its Terracotta Warriors Show." *Artnet News*, August 16, 2019. Accessed December 31, 2022. https://news.artnet.com/art-world/facial-recognition-1627780

Pine, B. J. and J. H. Gilmore. 1998. *Welcome to the Experience Economy*, Vol. 76, No. 4, 97–105. Brighton, Massachusetts, USA: Harvard Business Review Press.

Půček, Milan Jan, František Ochrana, and Michal Plaček. 2021. "Financial Management of the Museum." In *Museum Management (Arts, Research, Innovation and Society)*, 139–49. Cham: Springer. 10.1007/978-3-030-82028-2_6

Pulh, Mathilde and Rémi Mencarelli. 2014. "Web 2.0: Is the Museum-Visitor Relationship Being Redefined?" *International Journal of Arts Management* 18 (1): 43–51.

Simon. 2022. "What Can Museums Do with Technology – Museum of African American History and Culture." November 10, 2022. Accessed November 20, 2022. https://www.arnabontempsmuseum.com/what-can-museums-do-with-technology-2/

Sky. 2019. "Facial Recognition Technology 'an Epidemic in UK', Says Big Brother Watch." *Sky News*, August 16, 2019. Accessed December 31, 2022. https://news.sky.com/story/facial-recognition-technology-an-epidemic-in-uk-says-big-brother-wtach-11786567

Stieb, James A. 2008. "Assessing Freeman's Stakeholder Theory." *Journal of Business Ethics* 87 (3): 401–14. 10.1007/s10551-008-9928-4

Suroto, Peni Zulandari, Made Handijaya Dewantara, and Aulia Ardista Wiradarmo. 2020. "The Application of Technology in Museums." *International Journal of Applied Sciences in Tourism and Events* 4 (2): 170–81. 10.31940/ijaste.v4i2.1853

Taormina, Francesca and Sara Bonini Baraldi. 2022. "Museums and Digital Technology: A Literature Review on Organizational Issues." *European Planning Studies* 30 (9): 1676–94. 10.1080/09654313.2021.2023110

Tate. n.d. "Landscapes Reimagined App." Accessed December 30, 2022. https://www.tate.org.uk/about-us/projects/landscapes-reimagined-app

Teylers Museum. n.d. "A Place Worth Seeing." Accessed December 27, 2022. https://www.teylersmuseum.nl/en/visiting-the-museum/what-is-there-to-see-and-do/a-place-worth-seeing

Thomas, Douglas and John Seely Brown. 2011. *A New Culture of Learning: Cultivating the Imagination for a World of Constant Change*. 1st ed. Scotts Valley, California, USA: CreateSpace Independent Publishing Platform.

Toepler, Stefan and Sarah Dewees. 2005. "Are There Limits to Financing Culture through the Market? Evidence from the U.S. Museum Field." *International Journal of Public Administration* 28 (1–2): 131–46. 10.1081/pad-200044548

"V&A · Explore the Collections." n.d. Victoria and Albert Museum. Accessed December 30, 2022. https://www.vam.ac.uk/collections?type=featured

Waterton, Emma. 2010. "The Advent of Digital Technologies and the Idea of Community." *Museum Management and Curatorship* 25 (1): 5–11. 10.1080/09647770903529038

GLOSSARY

Accessioning The acquisition process of adding an item to a museum's collection, involving documentation, cataloging, and preservation.

Accounting The process of recording financial activities, reporting financial data, and keeping financial records.

Acquisition Policy Guidelines outlining criteria and processes for adding items to a museum's collection, often influencing decisions about deaccessioning.

Assets Resources with economic value that an organization owns and/or controls with the expectation that they will be useful or beneficial in the future. *Types of assets: See Current Assets, Fixed Assets, Restricted Assets, Unrestricted Assets.*

Balance Sheet A financial document providing a snapshot of an organization's financial position at a specific point in time. The document presents assets, liabilities, and shareholders' equity with the following formula: Assets = Liabilities + Shareholders' Equity.

Budget A financial blueprint allocating amounts of money received and spent over a defined period of time into designated income and expense categories. *See also Income, Expenses.*

Budget Cycle The period of developing, reviewing, approving, and executing a budget, typically following a specific timeline or fiscal year.

Budget Variance The difference between the budgeted amount and the actual amount spent or earned, used to analyze financial performance and identify areas for improvement.

Budgeting The process of creating a financial plan that outlines expected revenues and expenses for a specific period.

Capital Budget A budget specifically dedicated to funding long-term investments such as building renovations, major equipment purchases, or expansions.

Cash Budget A projection of the museum's cash inflows and outflows, allowing for better management of cash reserves and ensuring that expenses can be covered by available funds.

Cash Flow The movement of money in and out of an organization, indicating its liquidity and ability to meet financial obligations.

Cash Flow Statement A financial document detailing the changes to an organization's cash and cash equivalents throughout an accounting period, and divided among three categories: operating, investing, and financing. The statement outlines the organization's liquidity and ability to meet its financial obligations.

Collections Management The strategic planning and administration of a museum's collection, including acquisition, documentation, preservation, and deaccessioning.

Contingency Budget A reserve fund set aside to cover unexpected expenses or emergencies that were not accounted for in the original budget.

Contributed Revenue Money an organization receives without providing goods and/or services in exchange; examples include gifts, individual giving, corporate sponsorship, private and public grants, or in-kind donations.

Cost-Benefit Analysis Evaluating the potential benefits of an action against its costs to determine if the investment is worthwhile.

Current Assets Short-term assets that can be converted into cash within a year.

Current Liabilities Short-term liabilities that are payable within a year.

Deaccessioning The formal process of removing objects or artworks from a museum's collection, often through sale, exchange, transfer, or disposal.

Development The process of acquiring assets, especially money, to keep a nonprofit organization in operation.

Earned Revenue Money an organization earns for providing goods and/or services; examples include admission charges, store sales, tuition, and other fees.

Economic Value The worth of a good or service based on people's preferences and willingness to pay.

Endowment Funds permanently held as long-term investment in a nonprofit to support its operations or donor-designated programs.

Expenses The costs incurred and money spent to acquire something or procure services.

Financial Data Information that helps to determine an organization's health and financial performance.

Financial Management The management of finances, assets, and resources in order to understand and interpret financial activities in order to oversee financial control systems, gather financial data, scrutinize financial reports, and make informed financial decisions.

Financial Planning An ongoing process to review an organization's financial situation and create strategies to support financial management. *See also Financial Management.*

Financial Records Any documents reflecting an organization's financial activities.

Financial Statements Reports summarizing an organization's financial performance, including balance sheets, income statements, and cash flow statements.

Fixed Assets Long-term assets that cannot be easily converted and spent within a year.

Fixed Costs Expenses that remain constant regardless of an organization's level of activity, performance, or production; examples include rent, insurance, or salaries.

Fixed Liabilities Long-term liabilities where payment extends beyond a year; examples include mortgage balances or loans.

Fundraising Activities aimed at soliciting donations, grants, or sponsorships to support the museum's operations and projects.

Funds Pool of money and monetary resources allocated for specific organizational purposes.

Grants Financial aid provided by government agencies, foundations, or corporations to support specific projects or operations.

Income The gains and money received for providing something. *See also Revenue, Net Income.*

Income Statement (Profit and Loss Statement) Details an organization's revenues, expenses, gains, and losses over a specific period, typically quarterly or annually. It provides the net income or loss by subtracting expenses from revenues.

Incremental Budgeting A budgeting method where the current budget is based on the previous period's budget with incremental adjustments, rather than starting from scratch.

Liabilities The total value of debt, typically money, owed to external parties. *Types of liabilities: see Current Liabilities, Fixed Liabilities.*

Net Income The difference between revenue and expenses incurred by an organization's operations in a given accounting period. Also known as profit.

Nonprofit Organization A business that operates in public benefit activities rather than profit-making activities and is primarily funded by contributed revenue. *See also Contributed Revenue.*

Operating Budget A detailed projection of income and expenses necessary for the day-to-day operations of an organization within a given period of time, typically a year. *See also Budget.*

Provenance The place of origin of something, including its ownership history and chain of custody, often considered in the decision-making process for deaccessioning. *See also Deaccession.*

Restricted Assets Assets, especially money, earmarked for specifically stated purposes or periods; for example, *see Endowment.*

Revenue The total amount of money generated by an organization. *Types of revenue: see Earned Revenue, Contributed Revenue. See also Income.*

Revenue Streams Different sources of income for an organization; examples include ticket sales, memberships, merchandise, or donations.

Risk Management Identifying, assessing, and mitigating potential risks that may impact an organization's operations or finances.

Social Impact The effect an action or inaction has on people and communities in society.

Social Value The worth of improving people's lives and communities.

Statement of Activities A financial document summarizing the amount of income an organization has earned and the expenses associated with earning that revenue within a specific timeframe, typically a complete fiscal year.

Statement of Financial Position *See Balance Sheet.*

Statement of Shareholders' Equity Summarizes changes in shareholders' equity over a specific period, outlining share issuances, repurchases, dividends, and retained earnings.

Sustainability Managing finances and resources in a way that ensures an organization's long-term viability and minimizes negative impacts on the environment and society.

Tax-Exempt Freedom from certain taxations regulated by national, regional, and local government entities, such as sales tax and income tax.

Unrestricted Assets Assets available to use for any operational purpose or expenditure within an organization's mission.

Variable Costs Expenses that fluctuate in direct proportion to the level of an organization's activities, such as exhibit materials or event-related costs.

Zero-Based Budgeting A budgeting approach where each expense must be justified for each new budgeting period, starting from a zero base, rather than using previous budgets as a reference. *See also Incremental Budgeting.*

INDEX

Note: Italicized and bold page numbers refer to figures and tables. Page numbers followed by "n" refer to notes.

www.ingramcontent.com/pod-product-compliance
Ingram Content Group UK Ltd.
Pitfield, Milton Keynes, MK11 3LW, UK
UKHW020155200926
475702UK00016B/2718
9781032310916